COME SHOUTING TO ZION

SYLVIA R. FREY AND BETTY WOOD

AFRICAN AMERICAN PROTESTANTISMIN
THE AMERICAN SOUTH AND

BRITISH CARIBBEAN TO 1830

COME

SHOUTING

TO ZION

THE UNIVERSITY OF NORTH CAROLINA PRESS / CHAPEL HILL & LONDON

Library of Congress Cataloging-in-Publication Data

Frey, Sylvia R., 1935-

Come shouting to Zion : African American Protestantism

in the American South and British Caribbean to 1830 /

by Sylvia R. Frey and Betty Wood.

p. cm.

Includes bibliographical references.

ISBN 0-8078-2375-9 (cloth: alk. paper). —

ISBN 0-8078-4681-3 (pbk.: alk. paper)

1. Afro-Americans—Southern States—Religion.

2. Blacks—Caribbean Area—Religion.

I. Wood, Betty. II. Title.

BR563.N4F74   1998

277.5'07'08996073—dc21   97-21477

CIP

02 01 00 99 98   5 4 3 2 1

THIS BOOK WAS DIGITALLY PRINTED.

CONTENTS

MAPS

ACKNOWLEDGMENTS

The writing of *Come Shouting to Zion* was both a collaborative and a collegial process. We had a good deal of help and advice from a great number of people in the profession. Unfortunately we cannot mention everyone who aided our work, but we would like to recognize those to whom we owe a particular debt. Earlier work by historians, anthropologists, and historians of religion of Africa, the Caribbean, and the American South provided a compass for our work. The help of librarians and archivists was indispensable to our research. We are particularly grateful to the following for directing us to important collections: Michael Plunkett of the Manuscript Division of the Alderman Library of the University of Virginia, Reverend Edwin Schell and his assistant Betty Ammons of the United Methodist Historical Society at Lovely Lane, Phoebe Jacobsen of the Maryland State Archives, Darlene Slater of the Virginia Baptist Historical Society, Linda McCurdy of the Special Collections Department of the Perkins Library of Duke University, Ann Smith and the staff of the Georgia Historical Society, and Godfrey Waller, Superintendent of the Manuscripts Reading Room, University of Cambridge Library.

Colleagues in the profession generously shared notes and little-known sources with us. It is a great personal pleasure for us to acknowledge the generosity of Robert Calhoon, Blair Pogue, Constance Schulz, and especially John Thornton, who allowed us to use his translations of important African manuscript sources. Mary Turner, Ira Berlin, and John Thornton each read all or parts of the manuscript. Their critical readings prevented us from making grievous errors, and each of them has had a fundamental impact on the book. Cora Presley of Tulane University and Richard Simmons of the University of Birmingham offered valuable insights that decisively influenced our interpretations on several major points. Their generosity and collegiality does not make them liable for any of our errors or lapses in judgment.

We would also like to thank John Diem of Tulane Computing Services for making available to us the computing skills of Maryann Decoteau, a member of his staff. Peter Caron's own considerable computer skills and rich knowledge of West African history were of invaluable help in producing the maps and in introducing us to several important sources. Jennifer Gross helped us with special research tasks. Our friend and colleague Lewis Bateman, Executive Editor of The University of North Carolina Press, followed this project from its inception. His interest never flagged and his encouragement never waned. We thank him for his support, and we thank our editor, Mary Caviness, for the skill and care with which she prepared this manuscript for publication.

INTRODUCTION

Come Shouting to Zion is a study of a paradox. The conversion of African Americans to Protestant Christianity was a, perhaps *the*, defining moment in African American history, yet, as Peter Wood wrote in 1979, it is "a forgotten chapter in eighteenth-century southern intellectual history."[1] True, portions of the religious landscapes inhabited by the peoples of the early South and the British Caribbean had been mapped by historians writing prior to 1979, but usually they had adopted a decidedly and an unashamedly Eurocentric approach to the subject.[2] Moreover, despite the work of folklorists and African American scholars and churchmen dating back to the late nineteenth century,[3] and the pioneering anthropological studies of Melville J. Herskovits during the 1930s and 1940s,[4] the dominant impression that continued to be conveyed through the 1950s and 1960s by all but a handful of historians was that the religious history of African Americans and Afro-Caribbeans began only with the arrival of the slave ships in the ports of the New World, that virtually no West and West Central African religious beliefs and practices of any substance or significance survived either the Middle Passage or the subsequent experience of enslavement in the early South and British Caribbean.[5] Indeed, as recently as 1990 Jon Butler confidently asserted that West and West Central African religious systems were shattered beyond repair as a result of the Middle Passage, a process that he described as a *"holocaust."*[6] In this bleak scholarly scenario, Africans, African Americans, and Afro-Caribbeans have almost always been depicted as reactive rather than as proactive, as shaped by rather than having helped to shape the Protestant Christianity presented to them by white missionaries.

During the past few years, however, a new and immensely vibrant scholarship has emerged that, without necessarily being wholly and uncritically Afrocentric, places Africans, African Americans, and Afro-Caribbeans at center stage, recognizes the existence and the significance of their agency, and emphasizes both the continuance and the adaption of West and West Central African beliefs and rituals in the shaping of various New World religious cultures.[7]

Come Shouting to Zion builds upon this recent work to offer what we believe are new departures and an original contribution to scholarship on Southern and Caribbean religious history. It takes from Eugene D. Genovese's *Roll, Jordan, Roll* and Mechal Sobel's *The World They Made Together* the lesson that black and white Southerners inhabited the same world and shared many of the same experiences, each shaping the other individually and collectively in tangible and intangible ways.[8] Our initial understanding of West and West Central African religious systems has been greatly informed by the work of anthropologists and comparative religionists, whose analyses of contemporary religious systems offer useful insights into traditional practices.[9] From African historical studies by Robin Horton, T. O. Ranger, Ann Hilton, John Thornton, and others we developed an appreciation of the dynamic and reciprocal nature of cultural interaction and the necessity of differentiating the variable regional and cultural responses to missionary Christianity.[10] The vast recent literature on women's history made us acutely aware of the distinctive roles that women have always played as both guardians of traditional cultures and cultural innovators.[11]

Our starting premise is that religious change was everywhere the product of a reciprocal process rather than of conversion by confrontation. Among the distinguishing characteristics of this entire process were the active agency of Africans, African Americans, and Afro-Caribbeans in their own religious transformation; the simultaneous transformation of white religious cultures as part of the same reciprocal processes by which Africans, African Americans, and Afro-Caribbeans became Christians; and the critical role played by black women in the formation of revival culture, in the creation of affective ritual worship, in the establishment of institutional foundations of the early black church, and in the dissemination of religious values within and between generations. Our concluding proposition is that the spiritual and the material lives of enslaved people were inextricably linked. And we close with an analysis of the ways in which Protestant Christianity influenced the family lives and domestic economies of African American and Afro-Caribbean Christians.

Come Shouting to Zion does not claim to be the definitive work on the subject. Because of the scope of the project, important themes had to be ignored or treated incidentally rather than comprehensively. Topics that have been treated more extensively or in different contexts by other scholars, such as religiously inspired resistance, are given a secondary place here. Informal religion, or the "invisible institution," for which little or no evidence exists for the early period, remains all but invisible in our text. However, we investigate in some depth areas that have been hitherto ignored by other works. Two major developments of the post-Revolutionary period, geographic expansion and the institutional foundations of the black church, receive far greater attention here than in any previous work. African Americans are given a prominent role in both the internal and external migration of religious cultures. The contributions of women constitute a central theme of our analysis.

Whereas earlier studies of black Christianity have tended to take a narrow geographical focus, *Come Shouting to Zion* takes a broad spatial perspective, incorporating both the American South and three of the major islands of the British Caribbean, Jamaica, Barbados, and Antigua. The reasons for doing so are several: first, because of the metropolitan-based institutional links that characterized the Anglican and Moravian missionary activity prior to the American Revolution and the conversion techniques employed by the Moravian, Baptist, and Methodist churches both on the American mainland and in the Caribbean after the Revolution; second, because of the movement of Africans and Europeans in both directions between the British sugar islands and the Southern mainland during and after the colonial and Revolutionary periods; and third, because of the critical significance of African American missionaries in establishing the Baptist and Methodist faiths among the enslaved populations of the British Caribbean during the last two decades of the eighteenth century.

The time frame of our study is equally broad and sweeping. The periodization of black religious history developed by most older works begins around 1750, with the first evangelical efforts to convert slaves.[12] Led by the new scholarship on African conversion we take as our points of departure precolonial West and West Central Africa, the initial places of cultural interaction that comprise the central theme of our book. Our study concludes with 1830, which marks the beginning of the plantation missionary movement originally launched by the South Carolina Conference of the Methodist Episcopal Church. This movement, a massive organized effort at converting slaves at the same time that it seized control of the missionary effort, eventually sent hundreds of white missionaries onto plantations throughout the American South and the British Caribbean.[13]

In the British sugar islands, the Jamaican slave rebellion of 1831,[14] apprenticeship, and the eventual ending of slavery in 1838 would produce fundamental alterations and permit and demand the persistence of equally important continuities in the context and contours of religious life.[15] In the Southern mainland, the cumulative effects of Gabriel's Revolt in Virginia, the Vesey Revolt in South Carolina, and Nat Turner's Rebellion in Virginia in 1831, produced a vehement white backlash that manifested itself in stringent measures that severely curtailed the independence of the African churches and the rights of assembly of black Christians. The black preachers who had from the outset dominated the evangelical effort among blacks were virtually stripped of the preaching rights they had claimed and won for themselves.

Some of the South's autonomous African churches survived this purging as did certain ritual and worship practices. But the religious community that finally emerged was fundamentally different from what had gone before. It was largely dominated by white missionaries sent out to teach a more orthodox form of Christianity than had been created by the self-proclaimed black preachers. The institutional structure of the evangelical community took on a new configuration. In many if not most churches white ministers displaced the old black leaders without managing to destroy completely their authority in the slave quarters. The result was the "invisible" black church that Albert Raboteau has described and a visible, predominantly biracial religious community that persisted through Reconstruction. Though its messengers continued to proclaim the doctrine of spiritual brotherhood, the new religious community was structured on the basis of white authority and the fundamental inequality of black Christians.

COME
SHOUTING
TO ZION

1

AFRICA

THE INTRODUCTION OF CHRISTIANITY

The passage from traditional religions to Christianity was arguably the single most significant event in African American history. It created a community of faith and provided a body of values and a religious commitment that became in time the principal solvent of ethnic differences and the primary source of cultural identity. It provided Afro-Atlantic peoples with an ideology of resistance and the means to absorb the cultural norms that turned Africans into African Americans. The churches Afro-Christians founded formed the institutional bases for these developments and served as the main training ground for the men and women who were to lead the community out of slavery and into a new identity as free African American Christians. Religious evolution was not a single process but several processes operating at once.

Africa is the starting point for the historical trajectory of religious change. Unfortunately the historical study of precolonial African religious systems is severely hampered by a lack of data. Most of our knowledge of African religions in the past derives from biased European accounts or from inferences drawn from African religions in the present. Material evidence uncovered by archaeologists and systematic analyses of language evidence and oral traditions hold out some possibility for at least a partial reconstruction of early concepts and practices.[1] In the meantime, our understanding of African religious beliefs and practices consists, for the most part, of representations of African religions as European missionaries saw them. Religiously arrogant, some missionaries denied that Africans had any religion at all; others recognized African religiosity but assumed the superiority of the Christian God to African divinities and struggled relentlessly to convince African peoples of that "truth."[2]

The necessity of relying on missionary records has also contributed to an historical preoccupation with the first period of encounter and has created a false impression of what T. O. Ranger has called the "timeless" character of African religions. In fact, indigenous African religions had been undergoing changes for centuries, some of them precipitated by internal developments, some of them by external forces, such as war. The anthropological focus on the twentieth century also ignores change and development, and assumes the "quintessential identity" of Christianity and of indigenous religions.[3] Social and cultural anthropologists have been recently challenged by a new wave of scholars, many of whom are affiliated to such disciplines as theology and comparative religion and have created their own theoretical orthodoxy. Labeled "Africa worshippers," or the "Devout Opposition," by Robin Horton, they depict Africans as uniquely religious and, strongly influenced by their own Christian faith, claim universality for the conception of God in all systems of African religious thought.[4]

Robin Horton has posed a conceptual challenge to the growing popularity and influence of both the anthropological and the "Devout" approach. In a seminal article published almost a quarter of a century ago, Horton sketched the broad outlines of a general theory of conversion. It rested on the premise that all human societies develop and adjust cosmologies in response to changing social conditions. In the case of West and West Central Africa, traditional religions that had developed within the microcosm of the local community were rendered unsatisfactory by the massive development of commerce and communication and of nation-states, which weakened the boundaries of local communities and raised doubts and anxieties about the ability of traditional cosmologies to explain or control events in a changing world. African peoples responded by making cosmological adjustments and ritual changes. These developments were well underway, Horton theorizes, when Islam and Christianity were first introduced into Africa. Thus African acceptance of Islam and Christianity was "due as much to development of the traditional cosmology in response to other features of the modern situation as it [was] to the activities of the missionaries."[5]

In a more recent elaboration of this theory, Horton describes African Christianization as two mutually reinforcing processes wherein missionaries "extracted" basic religious ideas and terminology from the peoples they encountered and reinterpreted or translated them in terms of Christian discourse. Indigenous peoples, for their own reasons, responded by adopting in whole or in part that which they found useful in Christian theology.[6] The outcome of the dialectic between missionaries and "converts" was forms of Christianity that, in T. O. Ranger's formulation of the Horton thesis, were "shaped as much by the 'converts' from below as by the missionaries from above."[7] The dialectic was continuous, marking not only the first period of encounter in Africa but also extending to and including the process of interaction between Christian missionaries and Africans in New World societies.

Religious development in the New World was, as John Thornton has observed, an outgrowth of prior religious development in West and West Central Africa. Since much of it predated the Reformation, it was, for the most part, dominated by Catholic rather than Protestant efforts. The Portuguese were the first in the field, having made the initial contacts with Africans on the western coasts some fifty years before European voyagers departed for the New World.[8] There are only a few scattered references in European accounts to the first African converts, but they appear to have been captives who had been sold into slavery in Portugal, where they were taught to read and write and to speak Portuguese. Once they "adopted" the religion and language of their masters, many of them were purchased and freed to serve as interpreters aboard Portuguese trading vessels.[9] At least nominal adherents of Christianity, they served Portugal as the first cultural missionaries to West African peoples.

It took very little time for Catholic countries to realize that the best prospects for achieving their commercial and spiritual goals was contingent upon gaining the active support of the political leadership of the various African kingdoms. They became key religious targets. One of the earliest original accounts of European conversion efforts was left by Alvise da Ca'Mosto, or Cadamosto, a twenty-three-year-old Venetian sailor in Portuguese service. Cadamosto's first voyage took him past Arguim, the first factory, or *feitoria*, founded by Portugal in 1445. By the time Cadamosto arrived ten years later on his second voyage, the trade at Arguim amounted to roughly ten thousand slaves a year, an indication of the rapid growth of the slave trade to the Americas.

From Arguim, Cadamosto sailed southward to the mouth of the Senegal River, a fertile, low-lying region inhabited by the garrulous Jalof, or Wolof, people and ruled by a chief called Budomel. Here in the Kingdom of Senega, as he did at Arguim, Cadamosto reported the strong presence of Islam. Introduced into the region by Arab merchants who had been carrying on a lucrative trade between the Barbary ports and the important interior port of Timbuktu since the eleventh century, the faith was jealously guarded from Christian competition by the local Muslim clerics called *malams,* or *marabouts.* Their opposition proved to be a major impediment to Portuguese dreams of gathering a rich spiritual harvest in Upper Guinea.

Cadamosto's account of his debate with Budomel over the relative merits of Christianity and Islam is interesting for the light it throws on the process of conversion. With characteristic confidence in European cultural superiority, Cadamosto proclaimed to the chief "that his faith [was] false" and that the *malams* who instructed him in it were "ignorant of the truth." However, his easy optimism over "getting the better" of the *malams* in debate was soon tempered by Budomel's response: "The lord laughed at this, saying that our faith appeared to him to be good" because "God had bestowed so many good and rich gifts and so much skill and knowledge upon us [but that he had not given us good laws]." But "to the negroes, in comparison with us," God had given "almost nothing" except good laws. Although his traditional religion had no well-defined idea of heaven or a hereafter, Budomel's interpretation of Christian theology anticipates African American Christian notions of divine justice as well as a disconcerting sense of their own ethical superiority: "He considered it reasonable that they would be better able to gain salvation than we Christians, for God was a just lord, who had granted us in this world many benefits of various kinds. Since he had not given them paradise here, he would give it to them hereafter."[10]

Budomel's tendency to look on Christianity as a source of material rather than spiritual power was characteristic of the response of many African rulers during the early years of cultural encounters. It was in part generated by the fact that Europeans cultivated the friendship of the kings of Guinea by giving them gifts, in effect paying an annual tribute. For example, Diogo Gomes won the confidence of Battimansa, lord of the land around the estuary of the Gambia River, by giving him "many presents." The apparent connection between the pearls of heaven and earth was not lost on the shrewd Battimansa, who invited Gomes to debate a local *malam.* Gomes's proselytizing so impressed Battimansa that he ordered the *malam* expelled from his kingdom and proclaimed "that no one, on pain of death, should dare any more to utter the name of Muhammad." Battimansa professed a sincere belief in "the one God only" and pleaded for baptism, but Gomes declined on the grounds that as a layman he lacked the authority. Gomes's success in trafficking and communicating

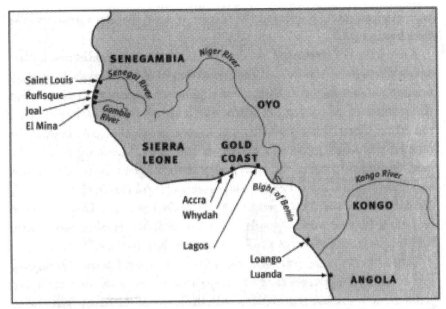

Map 1. West and West Central Africa in the Eighteenth Century

with African rulers convinced the infante to send the first mission to the Gambia in 1458.[11]

King João II entertained no doubts about the causal relationship between Portuguese tribute and the conversion of African kings. Indeed, it became a major factor in Portuguese diplomacy beginning in 1482, when the fortress of São Jorge Da Mina was built on the rocky headland of the Mina Coast. João gave classical expression to that policy when he ordered the construction of a church at São Jorge, "knowing that in the land through which ran the traffic of gold the negroes liked silk, woolen and linen clothes, and other domestic goods . . . and that in the trade with our men they showed they would be easily converted. . . . Thus, with the bait offered by the worldly goods which would always be obtainable there, they might receive those of the Faith through our doctrine."[12]

Between 1482 and 1637, when the Dutch captured the last Portuguese fort at Axim, the governors of São Jorge and the other minor forts in the area were in continual negotiations with the rulers of the coastal kingdoms, who controlled access to the trade routes into the interior gold-producing regions of Denkyira. Sporadic attempts were made to convert the Comani people, who inhabited the kingdom of Commenda, to the west of Mina, and the Fetu, who lived to the east of it. The conversion of Sasaxy, king of the Fetu, in 1503 exemplifies the symbiotic efforts of African rulers and Europeans to gain advantage from that kind of relationship. At the insistence of the Portuguese governor, Sasaxy sent his son and a member of the royal court to the castle as hostages as a sign of good faith. In exchange he demanded that the Portuguese build him a house and chapel and provide him with a mule or a horse and two leather trunks in which to store his gold. Once the chapel was complete Sasaxy and 300 members of the royal household and roughly 1,000 of his subjects "received with much devotion the water of baptism."[13]

In time, and very much on their own terms, other local rulers did accept Christian baptism, and small clusters of African Christianity slowly appeared on the western coasts near Portuguese settlements in Upper Guinea, Sierra Leone, and the Gold Coast. Eager to penetrate the interior and secure a larger and more constant supply of slaves, in 1481 the Portuguese established contacts with the highly organized city-state of Benin, which, until the eighteenth century, was a major center for European trade in the great delta of the Niger River. The idea that Benin was fertile ground to propagate the faith stemmed from early reports that the Oba, the temporal and spiritual ruler of the Edo people, was an adherent of some form of Christianity. But over the next 200 years intermittent efforts by Spanish and Italian Capuchins to convert the warrior obas and their people encountered considerable resistance. The imperviousness to Catholicism displayed by the Edo people and the rise of the delta villages of Bonny, New Calabar, Old Calabar, and Brass, led to the precipitous decline of Benin. At the same time, the counter-Reformation turned the attention of Catholic missionaries away from Africa and brought a temporary end to missionary activity in the Niger Delta.[14]

It was a different story south of the River Zaire in the old Kingdom of Kongo. John Thornton calls the conversion in 1491 of the *mani Kongo,* King Nzinga a Nkuwu, and his son Mvemba a Nzinga "the crowning achievement of nearly a half century of missionary efforts in western Africa."[15] Portuguese success in forging an alliance with the Kongolese monarchy was, in large measure, due to a compatibility of interests and needs, which until the seventeenth century involved the exchange of military assistance during the Kongolese wars of expansion for slaves acquired from peripheral areas of the kingdom. The "Christian Revolution" that accompanied the alliance involved the assimilation of those aspects of Christian cosmology that both harmonized with the Kongolese's own view of the universe and served their needs and interests.[16]

In the late fifteenth and early sixteenth centuries, the *mani Kongo* and the dominant Mwissikongo elite of the Kingdom of Kongo legitimated their political power by establishing a Christian cult under the direct control of the *mani Kongo.* When the first Portuguese arrived in 1483 the Kongo regarded them as water or earth spirits, in part because they came from the sea, which in Kongo cosmology was a barrier between the earthly and spirit worlds; the King of Portugal was called *nzambi mpungu,* or "highest spiritual authority." The *mani Kongo's* baptism was thus an initiation into the Christian cult. Not by coincidence, the *mani Kongo* chose as his Christian name João, the same name as the Portuguese king. Within a few years, João's wife and son, Afonso, and a majority of Mwissikongo office holders and their relatives were also baptized.

At João's death in 1506, Afonso seized the throne, apparently with the aid of some mounted Portuguese men dressed in white, who were presumed to be St. James and his horsemen. In the succeeding years Afonso established Christianity as a royal cult in Mbanza Kongo, the capital of Mbata province, and used it to claim a unique source of authority so as to distinguish his kingship from all others. In order to create a hierarchy of priests he sent thirty or forty of his sons and relatives to Europe to study for the priesthood. He had churches built in the provincial capitals of Mbanza Mbata, Mpangu, and Mbanza Sonyo and dispatched Christianized Mwissikongo to establish schools and teach Christian doctrines there. Afonso's Christian policies were continued by his grandson, Diogo I.[17]

For the ruling elite conversion was never solely a matter of politics, it was also one of gaining access to education and its consequent rewards. By the seventeenth century, missionary schools had been established in all the provincial capitals. For the sons and relatives of provincial leaders the religious schools provided access to the magic of the written word, which in an oral culture carried high prestige and occupational advantages. As purveyors of education the mission schools created links between Christianity and learning; acceptance of one usually led to acceptance of the other. Literacy also had a direct bearing on the effective control of Christian doctrine and the emerging church. Priests made annual visits to towns and villages to baptize and administer the sacraments, but for the most part they failed to exert effective control over the process of popular evangelization. The propagation of the faith was instead the work of literate lay teachers and catechists.

By means of their service as village catechists and interpreters for the occasional missionary tour and by means of the KiKongo catechismal literature produced by Kongo church staff, this corps of literate lay Christians interpreted, or reinterpreted, the fundamentals of the Christian faith. In the process they helped to create what John Thornton has called a "unique form of Christianity" in the Kingdom of Kongo. In this respect as well as in the voluntary aspects of conversion and the predominating presence of indigenous leadership, the process of African conversion formed a pattern for later interactions between Christian missionaries and Africans in the American South and the British Caribbean.[18]

Elsewhere in central Africa, Portugal's intermittent efforts to implant Christianity met with fierce opposition, nowhere more violently than in Ndongo. This kingdom, a small chiefdom formed in the mid-fifteenth century on the Kwanza River, had expanded north to the River Dande and in 1556 became independent from Kongo. Catholicism gained a brief foothold in Ndongo, or Angola, in 1622, when as part of a peace settlement with Portugal, the new Queen Nzinga converted and was baptized as Dona Ana de Souza. This promising beginning was interrupted in 1630, when Nzinga became an Imbangala and embraced the rites of Jaga, including ritualistic cannibalism. The formidable Nzinga continued war with Portugal until 1656, when she reconverted to Catholicism as part of the peace terms imposed by Portugal. Nzinga subsequently allowed Capuchin priests to enter Matamba, and she cooperated in their efforts to convert her subjects.

Among the most feared and powerful rulers in Africa, Queen Nzinga was apparently a sincere convert. As a condition for receiving the Catholic sacrament of communion, Nzinga gave up wearing traditional amulets dedicated to the ancestors or deities. At the age of seventy she reluctantly renounced polyandry and agreed to solemnize her union with a young man according to the rites of the Catholic Church, which united them in a permanent bond so that her subjects "should have no opportunity or excuse not to imitate her." In a pattern that would be replicated elsewhere in Africa where Christianity was state imposed, Nzinga exhorted her people to practice monogamy and have their children baptized on pain of exile and to abandon "diabolical relics" like horns and girdles and gourds dedicated to various deities in favor of Christian reliquaries. On Nzinga's orders Christian holy days such as Christmas and Easter were substituted for traditional festivals and the traditional paraphernalia of worship was either confiscated and burned or given to the missionaries for use in the Catholic liturgy. According to Father Giovanni Cavazzi, Nzinga "no longer honoured or revered the witch-doctors and sorcerers, but became their enemy and persecutor," executing some, exiling and banishing others.[19]

When the organized European slave trade began in the seventeenth century, a small minority of West and West Central Africans were Christians, a larger percentage professed Islam, and the great majority adhered to traditional religions. The second half of the seventeenth century brought wholesale changes in African culture. The spread of sugar cultivation into the French and English colonies of the Caribbean greatly increased the demand for slave labor and the competitiveness of the trade, both domestic and international. For most of the seventeenth century slave trade was concentrated in the kingdom of Allada and later in Whydah on the Slave Coast, the area between the mouth of the Volta River eastward to the Lagos channel.

The commercialization of the domestic economy that followed these developments was accompanied by a protracted period of disorder caused by frequent wars among the major African states over access to and control of the slave trade. Warfare and the increasing use of European firearms contributed to the decline of formerly great African states, such as Allada and Benin, and the absorption in the early eighteenth century of many of the old Slave Coast kingdoms, such as the Kingdom of Dahomey and the Yoruba kingdom of Oyo, by new military powers. In the course of their struggles to legitimate power and to consolidate empires, kings frequently embraced religious beliefs and practices of conquered peoples, creating in the process religious innovations. The seventeenth- and early-eighteenth-century encounters between European Christianity and indigenous religions thus involved several processes operating at once and working toward the creation of various unique African forms of Christianity.[20]

Like Cadamosto earlier, European missionaries and settlers went to Africa with the preconceived notion that all Africans were "pagan." In fact, Christian missionaries did not encounter a single society with a single set of beliefs and practices; they found wide variations in African religions, differences not only "between societies but also within societies."[21] There were as well broad variations in the approach of different denominational and national missions toward conversion. But as John Thornton has pointed out, the missionaries came not as conquerors but as guests of powerful kings, at whose pleasure they served. Until the advent of colonialism in the nineteenth century, most missionaries, regardless of denomination, of necessity adopted a tolerant approach to conversion. The African peoples they encountered accepted Christianity because they were able to adapt the new beliefs and practices to suit themselves.[22]

The determined evangelism of Christian missionaries during the initial period of encounter centered on the saliency of the Supreme Being. With some notable exceptions, most missionaries and settlers agreed that Africans believed in "one true God . . . though in a crude indigested manner." Robin Horton has suggested that during the period of initial contact with missionary Christianity, African religions were developing concepts of a supreme being. Thus the European belief that Africans could not "form a just idea of a Deity" derived in some instances from the fact that the African concept of a supreme being was still largely unelaborated. In the Kingdom of Kongo, which accounted for the majority of slaves shipped to the Americas before 1675 and a major share after that, *nzambi* seems to have referred to the highest or ultimate power. Its meaning derived from a particular context and might variously refer to a family member or the *mani Loango,* or village chief. When the Europeans asked the seventeenth-century Mwissikongo who created them, the term had little meaning and led the Europeans to erroneously conclude that the people "had no knowledge of God at all, nor his word, but only the bare name." Eventually Christian Mwissikongo resolved the problem by translating the concept into indigenous terms.[23] Although the Igbo speakers regarded Chukwu as one of a number of powerful spirits, Christian missionaries ascribed supreme status to Chukwu and eventually the Igbo accepted it as the name of a supreme being.[24]

Even in the societies with more elaborate concepts of the supreme being, the African concept differed dramatically in character and power from the Christian God. Among the Slave Coast (Bight of Benin) groups whose traditions are most prominent in African American religion, including the Yoruba of southwestern Nigeria and their neighbors, the Ewe, and especially the Fon of Dahomey, God was the ultimate power.[25] Whereas the Christians believed God was creator, the Yoruba and Fon thought the supreme god was the organizer and controller of the universe, not its creator. While the "monotheistic" concept of an ultimate power shared certain common characteristics, each society conceived of the supreme deity differently.

In Yorubaland, for example, *Oludumare*, the high god whose existence from the beginning of time was presumed, was male. He was the supreme power, but he remained remote, controlling the world through lesser divinities, upon whom religious devotion centered.[26] A subordinate deity, *Orishala*, or *Orisanla*, whose name was used by missionaries to translate the name Jesus, was the creator of humankind. For the Anlo-Ewe of eastern Ghana, *Mawu*, understood to be a male, was the careful guardian of his creations. *Mawu* among the eastern Ewe, especially the Fon, had a dual nature, referring to both a female deity associated with the moon, the west, and the earth, and *Lisa*, variously described as *Mawu's* twin brother, son, or husband and associated with the sky, the sun, and the east.[27] Among the Fon, whose cosmology was undergoing dynamic change as a result of the blending of the cosmologies of the different peoples who formed part of the eighteenth-century Dahomian Empire, the dual deity *Mawu-Lisa* was the offspring of an earlier deity, *Nana-Buluku. Da*, also a dual male/female being represented by a rainbow, was the creator of human beings.[28]

In precolonial and early colonial West and West Central Africa, lesser spirits were often more important than the supreme being. Slave Coast peoples recognized a pantheon of divinities who lived in the spiritual realm but who were also thought to inhabit particular places, such as rocks or trees. Europeans called these lesser divinities "idols," or "false gods," or "fetish";[29] among the Yoruba they were known as *orisha*, among the Fon as *vodun*. Possessed of supernatural powers, the lesser divinities were associated with forces in the natural environment or with heroic human figures. By contrast to the Catholic cult of the angels and saints, whose power depends directly upon God, African divinities were worshiped as autonomous powers, each with its own temples, shrines, priests and priestesses, and cult groups. The snake god in Whydah, called *Dangbe*, was responsible for regulating rainfall and for guaranteeing military success; other cults in Whydah developed around *Loko*, the African teak tree, and *Thunder* or *Hevioso*, who punished thieves with his bolts.[30]

Ancestral spirits also enjoyed a prominent place in traditional thought. As part of the community of the living and the dead, ancestors composed the apex of "a continuum of eldership" that extended from junior members of the lineage, to living elders, to ancestors and was known in the Kingdom of Kongo as *kanda*. The hierarchical *kanda* structure, which in the sixteenth and seventeenth centuries was often headed by a *kanda* female, was organized on a continuum of relative age, each level of which derived its authority from the preceding rank or grade. Ancestors, like living elders, were endowed with power and influence to curse or to bless the living, and in the Kingdom of Kongo, they were provided with power of *mbunba,* which was associated with fertility. Hence all members of the lineage visited their graves, performed rites to show respect, and paid them tribute to appease their anger or to implore their blessing.[31]

From the perspective of a concept of power, traditional cosmology had important implications for religious leadership roles. Like Western Christianity, traditional religion was profoundly ambiguous toward women. Unlike Western Christianity, traditional religion combined conventional attitudes with unconventional practices. Because of their specific biological functions, women were generally regarded as unclean, with a propensity toward evil. The fear of defilement of the sacred led to taboos and restrictions on women's activities and, in some cases, to their exclusion from important religious festivals. These attitudes found continuity and legitimization in Western Christianity's tendency to hold women primarily responsible for man's sinful state. Traditional religion also shared with Western Christianity and Islam the belief that the gift of prophecy was given to men and women alike but traditional religion accorded greater recognition to the mystical power of women.[32]

The commonly held belief that women had special inspiration qualified them for various leadership positions in traditional religion, although the major clerical and political positions were usually held by men. Although in most African societies men exercised political control, the participation of women in religious activities was built into the West African cosmological system. In contrast to Western Christianity, whose definition of the deity in wholly masculine terms provides a theological defense against active female spiritual leadership except as wives and spiritual consorts, traditional religions recognized the female as participating in the divine and thus allowed for the parallel and complementary development of male and female ritual leaders.[33] Because gender was not prohibitive among the qualifications for leadership, a number of sacred offices were open to women. In some societies, diviners, religious specialists whose functions are related to that of the medium, were women. Women were sometimes priestesses, working either independently of or with men.

One of the most powerful individuals in the eighteenth century kingdom of Dahomey was Hwanjile, *kpojito*, or member of the "palace" organization composed largely of women and eunuchs, probably created by King Agaja earlier in the century. An Aja priest, Hwanjile rose to the second most powerful position in the kingdom during the reign of Tegbesu (1740–74). When Tegbesu was engaged in a war of succession and conflict over the legitimacy of his dynasty, Hwanjile obtained the spiritual submission of the people by reordering the Fon pantheon of *vodon* and installing *Mawu-Lisa* to preside over them. As priest of *Mawu-Lisa*, Hwanjile was the head of religious life in Dahomey. During the reign of Agonglo (1789–97) the Christian deity was established in Dahomey by one of his wives, Sophie, a woman of African Dutch ancestry who married a French trader in Whydah. Thus, as Edna Bay has pointed out, "the god of Roman Catholic Christianity, despite its exclusively male priesthood, was established in Abomey under the direction of palace women."[34]

In traditional African religions each deity had a cult with its own priests, societies, and cultural centers.[35] Spirit mediumship was a central feature of cult religious activities. Attached to cult houses or temples, the mediums were highly trained in possession by spirits of the gods or the ancestors. In the patrilineal Yoruba society the cult of *Fa* and its associated system of divination, which spread into Dahomey and the other Slave Coast societies in the late seventeenth century, was exclusively male. Dahomian cult organizations typically included men and women and were led by a male and female priesthood.[36] The Dangbe cult assimilated by Dahomey in the conquest of Whydah in 1727 was predominantly female.[37]

Among the Yoruba and in traditional Dahomey the initiation period that brought devotees into the cult lasted several months. During his visits to Whydah between 1697 and 1699, the Dutch trader William Bosman observed that during the corn planting season female devotees "seize all the beautiful young women" and bring them to "a particular house built for that purpose, where they are obliged to stay several months." Secluded from the rest of society, the devotees learned about the personality of their deities and how best to serve them. What Bosman regarded as "a sort of Holy or Religious madness" was ceremonial possession by the deity, the ultimate act of religious expression when the deity entered the body of the devotee and displaced his or her personality.[38]

Devotees were highly trained to become ritually possessed by the gods. In traditional religion each deity had his or her own personal rhythm that manifested itself in stylized ceremonial behavior, such as drumming, singing, chanting, or dancing.[39] In Allada, female devotees spent from four to six months learning the religious dances and songs that were used to identify the possessing spirit.[40] Those women who were "promoted to the degree of Priestesses" were, according to Bosman, "yet as much respected as the Priests, or rather more, insomuch that they pride themselves with the distinguishing Name of God's Children." Whereas in most patrilineal societies women were "oblig'd to a slavish service to their husbands," priestesses "exert an absolute sway over them and their Effects."[41]

European Christians found the coexistence of a belief in a supreme being and the veneration of ancestors and spirits incompatible with the Christian notion of complete divine control. They equated Africans' use of ritual objects and ceremonies to supplicate or propitiate their ancestors and divinities with superstition or "idolatry" and uniformly condemned such practices as *fetich* or *grisgris*.[42] Convinced of their duty to convert Africans to Christianity, they sought to assimilate Africans to the assumptions, values, and beliefs of Christian Europe. African responses to their efforts varied according to what was deemed useful in Christian beliefs and rituals.

The progress of the Catholic missionaries who led the first wave of evangelization in West Central Africa and the spread of Islam in the Senegambia sheds some light on the dialectical process of conversion. While Protestant missionaries tried to obtain a personal acceptance of Christianity, Catholic missionaries assumed the right of rulers to command the religious faith of their subjects. The experiences of the Italian Capuchins in Kongo and Angola provide vivid documentation of the continuing dialectic of conversion.[43] Aware that the support of the provincial *mani* was essential to the success of their efforts to evangelize the provinces, the Capuchins initially concentrated not on any profound religious confrontation but on the provincial elite's desire for social, political, and economic advancement. According to Father Jerom Merolla Da Sorrento, as soon as a missionary arrived in the coastal province of Sonyo, the *mani*, or provincial governor, was expected to issue a call to all of the inhabitants to "appear before him to have their spiritual necessities relieved"; if the *mani* was uncooperative, "he will receive a deserved punishment, for we make it our business to get such person removed from his employment."[44] Such alliances probably provided the great bulk of the early converts. At Bamba, one of the five provinces of the Kingdom of Kongo, it was the authority and material help of the *macolonte*, who "sends a Black all about the *Libatte*

[town] to order the inhabitants to bring their children to be baptized," that first enabled the missionaries to make contact with rural villagers.[45]

It is more difficult to determine why the people themselves were drawn to Christianity in such numbers. One plausible explanation is that missionary Christianity coincided with massive and disruptive changes in West and West Central African societies. From the seventeenth century onward, profound changes were transforming the region. The rapid growth of the slave trade on the central African coast beginning in the first quarter of the seventeenth century affected a larger and larger geographic area, from Kongo and Luanda into the interior of the Zaire River basin. The intensification of political violence between the Imbangala, Kongo, and Portuguese warlords, the disintegration of Kongo, and the Kongo civil wars (1665–1718) created mounting social, economic, and political dislocations. When traditional cosmologies proved inadequate to explain or defend against the powers of destruction, some turned to the new Christian cosmology and to the missionaries who were its messengers.[46] The absorption of Christian magic was the first step in the process of conversion of the people of Kongo.

John Thornton's work on Roman Catholicism in Kongo stresses the willingness of Christianity to adapt itself to the national cosmology of its host.[47] This early approach to conversion is evident in the methods the Capuchins used to win converts, particularly in their assumption of the role of *nganga*, the local priests who specialized in healing, protection against evil and misfortune, the discovery of witches or evildoers, and other magical or religious functions.[48] Throughout much of rural Europe, sorcerers and healers were still respected and, even within Christianity, the notion of divine intervention enjoyed wide acceptance. Christian men and women patronized the practitioners of magic, astrology, and divination. Protestant churches formally denounced such practices, but in the Catholic Church magic and witches still played an integral part in its belief system and ministers and priests alike often resorted to charms and magic to confront and destroy evil.[49]

By contrast to Western theology, which is concerned with the origin of evil, traditional African religions were preoccupied with the causes and effects of evil. Traditional religions did distinguish between moral evil and natural evil, the latter referring to accidents, diseases, and misfortunes. Evil acts voluntarily committed by one human being against another, which damaged relationships, constituted a moral evil. The principal agents of moral evil were witches possessed involuntarily by the spirit of evil, who by their very nature "set to destroy relationships" and to visit disease, death, and misfortune upon the people. In order to neutralize the evil effects, Africans had frequent recourse to *nganga*.[50]

Every town and village had one or more ritual experts who, by virtue of their special sensitivity to the supernatural or of long years of training, had access to these mystical forces and through the power of ritual and the use of talismans and amulets were able to manipulate them for the benefit of individuals or communities. Among these sacred specialists were priests and mediums, diviners, herbalists, and rainmakers. Using closely guarded mystical rites or therapeutic remedies, they healed the sick, prevented disease, protected individuals and communities from unseen dangers, made or prevented rain, and carried out a host of other feats ordinary persons could not perform.[51] No clear distinction existed between the respected religious office of priest and of magician, nor were the functions of priest and sorcerer always differentiated.

Even while they deplored the exaggerated confidence that Africans placed in the occult, missionaries tried to present Christianity as a new, exotic source of power. For example, in order to persuade the BaKonga people to assist in the capture of persons reputed to be wizards, they were encouraged to wear medals "and other preservatives" so that "they were not afraid to touch" them.[52] Among the most important communal ceremonies performed in West and West Central Africa were the agricultural rites associated with the planting and harvesting of crops. At the beginning of cultivation farmers traditionally planted a "magic guard" or offering to the spirit of the earth and the ancestors to ensure the fertility of their fields and to preserve their corn.[53] In place of the symbolic offerings of grain or fowl, the Capuchin missionaries insisted that the farmers "make use of consecrated palm-branches, and here and there set the sign of the cross."[54]

In order to demonstrate the impotence of the local *nganga* as compared to their own mystical prowess, missionaries sometimes directly challenged one of the most important specialists in African society, the rainmaker. Experts in weather lore, rainmakers were especially prominent in the Kongo, where the agricultural cycle was dependent upon two annual rainy periods and two dry periods. The rainmaker, whose reputation was based on the possession of magical powers to control the weather, was employed to ensure the timely arrival of rain, or to stop prolonged rainfall at the times of sowing and harvest. In many parts of Africa the communal rites associated with rainmaking were, in the words of Geoffrey Parrinder, "one of the most important social religious activities."[55]

A failure to produce rain raised questions about the efficacy of the rainmakers' rites, and therefore required some explanation. Their source of livelihood and their status in the village at stake, rainmakers sometimes blamed their professional rivals, the Christian missionaries, for their lack of success. When a local *scinghili,* or rainmaker, of Sonyo attributed a drought to the Capuchin missionaries' construction of a two-story building "contrary to the custom of the country," a crowd of people came "in a great rage" to pull it down. One of the Capuchin fathers, "after representing their Folly, and the Imposture of their Schinghilli," suggested a more efficacious religious means of causing rainfall. The Christian God, he told them, was "the only disposer of all gifts, whether in heaven, earth, or sea," while the *scinghili* represented the forces of darkness, "who were only qualified to destroy men, both here and hereafter." If, he told the crowd, they would "make a devout procession to our Lady of Pinda," some twelve miles from the coast, then "I assure you God will relieve your wants." Fortunately for the missionary, "so it fell out, the earth being soaked with rain, the house remaining untouched, and the people satisfied."[56]

Because in parts of Africa it was customary for people to take gifts to the rainmaker in procession, the Catholic version was in substantial alignment with traditional custom. Moreover, although most African rainmakers were men, *nganga* of the *mbumba* type, who specialized in manipulating the natural world, included women.[57] Since success was always attributed to the rainmakers' magical means of controlling the elements, people logically concluded that the mysterious "rain-queen" of Pinda could be counted on to bring rain or to delay it. Thereafter they added the supplicatory procession to Pinda to their traditional religious corpus.[58]

The readiness of Christian missionaries to adapt themselves—and to some degree their beliefs and practices—to traditional religions extended to the incorporation of customary rituals into Catholic ones, starting with the rites of birth. For Africans procreation is, to borrow John Mbiti's phrase, "a religious obligation" through which the married couple perpetuate the community and guarantee the immortality of the ancestors who are, in some societies, "reborn" in their descendants.[59] The rituals surrounding childbirth marked and celebrated this symbolic unity of the living and the dead. Although the rituals took various forms according to the ethnic group and even family tradition, they all exhibited common characteristics.

The ritual of birth, which began with the pregnancy of the mother and culminated in a naming ceremony, generally included a sacrifice of thanksgiving to the ancestral spirits and to the divinities associated with fertility. In parts of the Kongo calabashes full of wine of the palm tree were poured out as libation before the sacred mirrone tree "for [the spirits] to drink when they are thirsty," and thus to ensure that the pregnancy would be successfully brought to term. At the same time protective amulets and necklaces were given to the expectant mother as a guarantee of safe delivery and as protection against evil spirits. Expectant mothers in the Kongo sometimes wore garments woven from the bark of the mirrone tree, "receiving them from the hands of the wizards, who tell them they ease the burden of the great belly, and cause them to be easily delivered." Missionaries tried to replace these traditional *nkisi* with suitably Christian ones. Pregnant women were enjoined "to wear religious relicks instead of the wizard mats," and mothers were urged to substitute blessed palm leaves for "superstitious" cords made by the wizards.[60]

Among the rites of passage, one of the most important was the ritual initiation of the infant into the human community. As soon as the child was born, the family send for a priest, "who binds a parcel of ropes and coral and other trash about the head, body, arms and legs of the infant; after which he exorcises, according to their accustomed manner, by which they believe it is armed against all sickness and ill accidents."[61] The naming ceremony, which in many societies took place on the eighth day following birth, symbolically represented the acceptance of the infant as a human person and as a member of the family and of the community.[62] On the Guinea coast the infant was given three names: one for the day of the week on which it was born; one for an ancestor, usually a grandmother or grandfather, depending on the sex of the child; and a third for a relative.[63]

Ignorant of their sociological function, the missionaries dismissed these ceremonies as "superstitious practices."[64] In the Kingdom of Kongo the Capuchins worked to displace the village priest and to substitute the Christian initiatory rite of baptism for the traditional rite of incorporation. Their remarkable success was due to African willingness to incorporate new ideas into the traditional belief structure and to the readiness of the missionaries to accommodate traditional beliefs. For example, in addition to the ceremonial application of water, the Capuchins placed salt—a traditional protection against sorcerers and witches—in the mouths of the initiates. Later, however, when the Capuchins attempted to reestablish customary ceremonial practice, the people refused to accept the rite without salt, an indication that they had developed their own definitions and concepts in indigenous terms.[65]

Although the people of Bamba submitted to Christian instruction and for thirty years had professed to be Christians, they apparently received baptism as a purification rite similar to certain tribal rites. For example, when a young woman was brought "stark naked to be baptized," Friar Denis Carli first covered her with "some leaves," instructed her in the principles of Christianity, and then baptized her Anne. Following the Christian ritual, however, a traditional ceremony was performed with music and dancing. Converts did not perceive any contradiction in the retention of traditional practices alongside recently acquired Christian ones. For instance, summoned by the *macolonte,* a large crowd of villagers piously attended mass, the climax of Catholic worship, and listened attentively to religious instructions afterward; that done, "they fell a playing on several instruments, a dancing and shouting so loud, that they might be heard half a league off."[66]

The Capuchins were regarded as exceptionally powerful because they could protect against *kindoki* witchcraft, a term that may have applied to all malevolent action.[67] The special power attributed to Capuchin missionaries was at least in part a result of the reciprocity between them and the *mani Kongo,* who accepted and perpetuated the missionaries' implicit claim to be supreme *nganga.* Their ideological influence also derived from the protective powers of Christian *nkisi,* or *fetich,* which they offered as suitable replacements for traditional *nkisi.* People eagerly accepted and wore medals and crosses and carried rosaries and relics and protected themselves from evildoers by repeating the sign of the cross.[68]

Throughout West and West Central Africa the cross was interpreted as the most powerful of the Christian *nkisi.*[69] The ubiquity of this distinctly Christian icon underlines an essential characteristic of the early development of Christianity in the region, namely the missionaries' lack of control over the new spiritual identity Africans were beginning to construct for themselves. An incident recorded by an exasperated Capuchin missionary shows how in the Kongo form of Christianity Christian icons were often simply incorporated into the repertory of indigenous graphic signs for use in magico-religious rituals that were condemned by the missionaries as *fetich.*

Invited by a *mani* to visit a local church in Noki on the south bank of the Zaire River, Friar Merolla was pleased to find a "pretty large one" with "a great wooden cross standing before it." Finding the door locked, Merolla instructed the *mani* to open it. Instead the *mani* and a curious crowd of onlookers fled in obvious panic, whereupon the friar broke open the door with his foot and then stood transfixed: "instead of an altar there was a great heap of sand, wherein was stuck a straight horn about five spans long, and on one side another of lesser size." On one part of the wall hung two coarse shirts. An enraged Merolla later recalled his reaction: "My hair stood an [sic] end, my tongue cleaved to the roof of my mouth, and I began to cry out aloud, . . . Are these the effects of the instructions ye have learned from our missioners? Is this the fruit of so much toil and anguish as has been undergone in your conversion?" Frustrated and disgusted that they had "rejected the worship of the true God, for that of an abominable idol" called *Cariabemba*, Merolla refused to administer baptism for some time.[70]

Aware of the need to develop new religious concepts to deal with the massive political, economic, and military changes that were transforming central African societies, some religious leaders eagerly accepted Christian concepts and biblical figures and transmuted them to Kongo. This practice was strikingly apparent in the celebrated case of the early-eighteenth-century Antonine movement founded by the prophetess Dona Beatrice Kimpa Vita. As she lay near death, Dona Beatrice, a former medium, was possessed by St. Anthony. "Resurrected" as St. Anthony, Beatrice began preaching to the people of central Kongo, urging them to reestablish the political and social structures that had been destroyed by warfare and slavery and to eradicate witchcraft. Her message attracted adherents from all ranks of society.

Dona Beatrice's movement derived much of its power from her conceptual innovation. Her rendering of the Christian concept of resurrection was at once a Christianization of the Kongo belief that at death the soul, or *moyo*, was "resurrected" and took a new form, and an Africanization of the Christian tradition of revelations by saints. She enlisted the powers of Christian saints, including St. Francis, St. Isabelle, St. Ursulla, and St. Anne, to perform miracles and to explain and control the evils attendant upon change. Her translation of the Christian concept of resurrection into indigenous terms and her appropriation of biblical figures enabled Dona Beatrice to seize from the missionaries the role of founder of a new moral order. For five years Beatrice and her followers, "little Antonines," traveled about the kingdom, performing the priestly functions of baptism and the sacrament of penance that they had appropriated from the missionaries. Her efforts to reunite the kingdom failed, at least partly because of the opposition of rival lords and the Capuchin missionaries, whose religious authority she challenged. Beatrice's execution in 1706 brought an end to the movement.[71]

Although missionaries and priests were necessarily tolerant of the indigenous worldview, they had no sufferance for the power of African *nganga*, who were the principal bearers of that view. In Kongo the Capuchins relied on traditional chiefs and rulers to destroy the power of the religious specialists, first by seizing and burning the cottages of "sorcerers and enchanters." At the beginning of the reign of Afonso I all of "the idols, deviltries, masks, and all the objects that were worshipped and regarded as gods were brought to the court," where they were thrown into a great pile. After all "these abominable images" were burned, the king "called together all the people and, in place of the idols, he distributed crosses and images brought by the Portuguese."[72]

When the wizards "still persisted to exercise their damable callings in their huts," local rulers themselves, with the encouragement of missionaries, attacked the practitioners of magic and healing. Persons who were suspected of being witches were seized and confined until a slave vessel arrived, whereupon they were transported to the Americas as slaves, by that means continuing and preserving many traditional beliefs and practices in Afro-Atlantic cultures. Unable still to break their power, Christian kings, with the full approval of the missionaries, resorted to more drastic measures. One Kongo prince put out a proclamation "to have all the wizards that should be found within his dominions burnt."[73] For example, after having "extirpated these wicked wizards almost totally out of his dominions," Count Stephen commanded his governors "that whenever they were found at any time to have returned, they should immediately be seized, and have their heads lopt off without any further ceremony."[74]

Missionaries also waged an all-out assault on "sinful" activities, most notably polygyny, which in several ways anticipated the "civilizing" Christian missionary attacks on "heathenism" in the nineteenth century. In many African societies polygyny served a variety of social as well as economic functions, among them the forging of alliances between lineages and the consolidation of political relationships. In some societies a harem of wives was valued as a labor force, especially for the processing of farm products and in the production of cloth.[75] Polygyny also played a key role in guaranteeing the immortality of ancestors through the process of rebirth in their descendants.[76]

The missionaries did not understand the place of polygyny in the social structure. They insisted that the practice was not consistent with membership in the church, and they tried by coercive means to enforce acceptance of canon law marriage. Their first efforts were aimed at the ruling elite over whom they had developed a measure of political influence. All of the *manis,* or governors of provinces or cities, were required to be married in the church or be "forthwith deprived of their governments, to the end that they may not by their ill examples withhold the common people from their duty." When the Count of Sonyo pleaded to have a ban of excommunication against him lifted, Father Merolla imposed as a penance "that he by his authority should oblige three hundred of those that lived in unlawful wedlock to marry." The reconciled count brought over 400 "to the holy state of matrimony," including one *mani,* two of his sons, and two of his daughters.[77]

Shortly after the first missions were established in the Kingdom of Awerri, east of Benin, two Capuchin friars, Angelo Maria d'Ajaccio and Bonaventura di Firenze, tried to persuade King Antonio Mingo to command his subjects "to embrace the holy state of matrimony." Antonio Mingo, the son of African King Mingo and his Portuguese wife, agreed on condition that he first be married to a Portuguese woman. Seizing this as a God-given opportunity to convert the entire kingdom, Father Angelo returned to St. Thomas and persuaded the uncle of a young Portuguese woman to permit his niece to marry the king. Once the couple was married "after the Christian manner," the people of the kingdom "submitted to be restrained by the rules of the gospel, that is, were all married according to the rites and ceremonies of the church."[78]

Although there was at least nominal acceptance of canon law marriage among the Christian elite, by the nineteenth century it had all but disappeared among the rulers' subjects and dependents.[79] The ravages of the slave trade and the bitter and bloody internecine warfare the trade encouraged, had made many Africans more willing to accept a new or different notion of being and power, but it did not prepare them for the complete assumption of Christian beliefs and practices, particularly when it involved the abandonment of their cultural inheritance. Rather than turn out their wives and children, or abandon the hope of attaining immortality through the multitude of their descendants, Africans rejected, almost wholesale, the Christian notion of monogamy. They also reasserted the importance of ancestral customs in a variety of other contexts, the most visible and dramatic demonstration being the rituals surrounding death.

Africans conceived of death as the climax of life, a transition, or journey, from the physical to the spiritual world. Not all peoples agreed on the nature of the afterworld. According to William Bosman, the chief Dutch factor in Elmina, Gold Coast peoples "take it for granted that the deceased are immediately conveyed to a famous river, situate[d] in the inland country, called Bosmanque," where "their god inquires what sort of life they have lived." If they had observed religious holidays and kept their oaths, the deceased "are gently wafted over the river, to a land abounding in all kinds of happiness"; if, however, the deceased had not lived a good life, "his god plunges him into the river, where he is drowned and buried in eternal oblivion."[80] In Kongo theology deceased ancestors became white creatures called *bakulu,* who resided in an underworld located under river-beds or lake bottoms.[81] The notion of the river as a boundary between the world of the living and of the spirits reemerged in African American cosmology, where it found expression in spirituals such as "Beulah Land," which take as their subject matter death as a crossing of the River Jordan.

The long and complex funeral ceremonies, the core of African religious behavior, were regarded as crucial to the successful completion of the soul's journey to the world of the spirits. A pious burial ensured the contentment of the spirit in the afterlife and the exercise of the ancestral power for the good of the surviving family and community. Without descendants to ensure a proper funeral, the dead became "ghosts," or in KiKongo, *Zumbi,* doomed to wander aimlessly, haunting the living as fearful apparitions "that to whomever it shall appear, that person will presently die."[82]

Funeral rituals varied widely from one ethnic group to another and according to the age, sex, and status of the deceased, but certain features were common to all. The concept of death as a journey was carried out in rich symbolism in virtually all funeral ceremonies. In anticipation of impending death it was customary among the Fanti peoples of the Gold Coast, for example, for each individual to collect appropriate burial clothing, "believing that their reception in the other World will be answerable to their dress."[83] As soon as death occurred the corpse was carefully washed and dressed in the best clothing the deceased had had in life. In the event that a person died at some distance from his or her place of birth, great pains were taken to return the body home for burial.[84] Funeral rites were divided into two phases. The first funeral, or actual interment, usually took place immediately, often at night.[85] The position of the body and the orientation of the grave varied considerably. The Fanti placed the corpse in a box resting in a fetal position. The BaKonga did not use a coffin but simply wrapped the body in a linen cloth or straw mat and buried it in a field under a mound of earth and a trestlelike structure. In Loango the corpse was mummified before burial.[86]

The ritual expression of death as a journey had another common element: the placement of grave goods of various types in the interior and on the exterior of the grave. The belief in the dead's continuing need for human essentials and the African belief in the permanence of life were symbolically represented in Senegal, for example, by two earthen pots, one filled with water, the other with couscous.[87] Among the Fanti a stool and an earthen pot, "the one for him to sit down, the other to cook his victuals," and a sprinkling of gold dust "for their use in the other World," were interred with the corpse, even of the poorest person.[88] In the Kongo in the seventeenth century it was still customary for a slave to be buried with the master "to the end that he may go and serve them in the other world."[89] In the Kongo and on parts of the Gold Coast a wooden structure was raised over the grave as a shrine through which surviving family and friends might communicate with the deceased. As a material symbol of the departed soul household goods and "such instruments as he used in his life," including platters, shovels, kettles, or armor, in the case of a man, were suspended from it.[90]

In most societies the conventions of burial were divided according to gender. Among most groups women wailed as an expression of grief. According to the French botanist Michel Adanson, in Senegal it was customary for the first "shriek" to be made by one of the female relatives of the deceased; at this signal "all the women in the village came out, and setting up a most terrible howl, they flocked about the place from whence the first noise had issued."[91] Along the Gold Coast all of the wives of a deceased man immediately shaved their heads and smeared their bodies with white paint. Like the "crying women of the Ancients," they made "a very dismal and lamentable noise, continually repeating the name of the dead, and reciting the great actions of his past life." This "confused tumultary noise of the women" continued until the corpse was buried.[92] In Benin the conventional high-pitched wailing of the women was accompanied by "the tunes of musical instruments."[93]

Contemporary European accounts suggest that emoting during African funeral rituals was not random but obligatory. According to Friar Merolla, mourners who were unable "to weep naturally" had "recourse to art" by holding Indian pepper to their noses, which "causes the tears to flow plentifully."[94] Undoubtedly the tears were often a genuine expression of grief or perhaps of fear of the possibility of witchcraft or vengeance of a "ghost." It is highly probable, however, that such conventions were culturally determined. In New World settings they probably contributed to the difference in the emotional tenor of black and white funerals frequently commented upon by travelers.

With the completion of the first funeral, the soul began its journey to the spirit world. The second phase of the funeral was essential to ensure that the deceased was secured a place in the company of the ancestors. The time at which it was held varied from a few days to as long as three years after interment. It consisted of a series of ritual events, including several animal sacrifices, through which family and friends provided ritual assistance in bringing to an end the spiritual transformation of the deceased from mortality to immortality. It culminated in feasting, singing, drumming, and dancing, the celebration of the soul's arrival at its destination, which lasted from several days to several weeks.

From the perspective of European observers, the "folgar," or dance, that concluded the second phase of the funeral defied description in conventional terms. Although each culture had its own distinctive movements, some groups emphasizing rapid footwork, others arm, leg, or body movements, Michel Adanson's description of a funeral dance he witnessed in Portudal in Senegal was typical of European reactions in general. According to Adanson, the spectators formed a square, in the center of which was lighted a great fire. The dancers were ranged at either end of the fire, men on one side, women on the other. The performers began with a song, whereby someone would give out a line that was then repeated by the spectators. At the same time, the dancers rushed toward one another, "striking their thighs against each other" to simulate sexual copulation, retreated, and then repeated the same movements. The dancers "do not dance a step, but every member of their body, every joint, even the head itself, expresseth a different motion, always keeping time, let it be never so quick." Although Adanson admired "the Negroes dexterity," he considered the movements and gestures made by the dancers "very immodest."[95]

In spite of appearances, European observers probably confused symbolic behavior with reality. Demonstrations of fecundity were a common feature of traditional dances, but actual promiscuity was not usually tolerated.[96] In most cultures the funeral dance was a physical formulation of African philosophy regarding death. Through a series of intricate steps the dancers related the ritual drama of the deceased person's life. Although their movements were generally not prescribed, the dancers used their bodies to express their beliefs and feelings: contortions showed their grief, shouting and twisting frightened away evil spirits, and spinning and leaping conveyed joy. Meant to honor the deceased, the funeral dance was at the same time a demonstration of sexual prowess, an assertion of life, a means of transcending death.

Blind to these clearly religious aspects of the dances, the missionaries tried to stamp them out. According to Friar Merolla, when the missionaries heard the rhythmic beat of drums, the traditional accompaniment of religious and recreational dances, they "immediately run to the place to disturb the hellish practice." In Loanda the Capuchin superior himself led a body of guards to break up an evening funeral; most of the mourners fled, leaving behind the wife of the deceased, who was afterward publicly whipped through the city on the orders of the governor. In Massangano, a garrison of the kingdom, a Capuchin friar was almost stoned to death by an angry crowd "for endeavouring to oppose these people in their wicked ceremonies."[97]

What was happening in public worship was antipathetic to Christian ideals, but in the end, as clients of the state, the missionaries had to adapt to what they could not change. The concessions they were obliged to make were strikingly apparent in the funeral rites commemorating the death of Queen Njinga in 1663. The first phase consisted of a series of rites known as "tambo," the main episode of which was a ritual reenactment of the long life and military triumphs of the queen through mourning dances and music used exclusively for funerals. At the conclusion of the "tambo" Queen Njinga's subjects attended a black, or mourning, mass said by Father Cavazzi on each of eight consecutive days.[98]

The pervasiveness of traditional rituals within the Catholic devotional structure was also apparent in the grafting on of an African liturgy to the Catholic festal calendar. Missionary efforts to install the Christian festal calendar rested upon the firm foundation of African seasonal observance. In Angola, the celebration of Christmas, the most important feast to Catholics, was a blending of standard Catholic liturgy and local communal and ritual practices that created a new ritual form that bore the unique character of Africa. According to Father Cavazzi, before and after the celebration of the mass, the principal act of Catholic worship, Angolans played "native instruments" and applauded "the newborn king . . . with shouts, clapping of hands . . . and all the firearms were discharged too." In the observance of Eastertide, Angolans continued to draw upon indigenous religious traditions even as they adapted to new Christian forms. On Good Friday new Christians demonstrated their penitence by "carrying Crosses, stones, pieces of wood" or by walking with their arms crossed, wearing chains around their necks. But on Easter Sunday they celebrated with traditional rituals of music, dancing, and the firing of weapons throughout the night.[99]

While they had not been able to impose strict Christian discipline anywhere, Catholic missionaries had succeeded in establishing a number of small congregations in coastal towns in Senegambia, along the Gold Coast, and in Dahomey. In the kingdoms of Kongo and Angola they were successful in establishing a close relationship with ruling elites and in achieving numerical growth on a scale unparalleled by missionaries of any other Christian denomination.[100]

The contrast of Catholic with Protestant missionary activity in West Africa could hardly have been greater. Despite general Protestant indifference toward the Christianization of Africa, the rise of Protestant powers following the Reformation ushered in a second phase of evangelization on Africa's west coast. Because the beginning of the Protestant missionary enterprise coincided with the expansion of the slave trade and the development of European competition over Africa, the Protestant mission movement quickly became identified with the political and economic ambitions of European powers. From the beginning the missionaries had a close association with the traders. Trading companies and missionary societies usually operated in the same area, often in conjunction. Occasionally a missionary society would take a stand against the slave trade, but usually they were silent; more often the missionaries gave their support to the economic war being waged by the traders over slaves and gold. Codependent, the two movements could never be wholly disentangled.

The growing fusion between economic and spiritual aspirations was reflected in the budding European competition for the bodies and souls of Africans that developed on the Gold Coast. The Dutch Republic was the first Protestant power to attempt the Christianization of the area it controlled through a partnership with Africans educated in Europe. According to William Bosman, chaplains were part of the regular establishment at all the Dutch posts on the Gold Coast. In 1737 the Church of the Brethren, which had already established the first Protestant missions in South Africa, sent Christian Protten, the son of a Danish father and an African mother, to Elmina, the Dutch headquarters on the Gold Coast. Protten worked briefly among the Fons in Accra before returning to Europe. Other missionaries followed, but they all died, and work was suspended there.[101]

In 1742 Dutch missionary activity was renewed through the agency of the Dutch West India Company, again with European-educated African clergy. The tendency to rely on an indigenous clergy for manpower was renewed with the training of a young slave boy, the property first of the captain of a trading ship and then of a Dutch merchant, Jacobus Van Goch. At the age of eleven the boy, now known as Jacobus Elisa Johannes Capitein, was taken to Holland for advanced study at the University of Leyden. The first African to receive Protestant ordination, at the request of the Dutch West India Company, Capitein was appointed chaplain and schoolmaster to Elmina beginning in October of 1742. Despite a promising start, the school Capitein established foundered when he died in 1747 at the age of thirty. It eventually closed for lack of company support.[102]

The close connections between the Protestant missions and the economic and political ambitions of the trading companies is also apparent in the evangelistic activities of the Church of England. In 1752 in conjunction with the Society for the Propagation of the Gospel the Company of Merchants Trading to Africa, which was responsible for managing England's fortified trading posts on the west coast, sent Thomas Thompson, the first missionary of the Church of England, to serve as chaplain to the Cape Coast Castle, the principal English settlement on the Gold Coast. After a brief stop in Sierra Leone, Thompson arrived there in May.[103]

Shortly after his arrival, Thompson preached the first Protestant sermon to an audience that included the governor, various company officers, and Cudjo Caboceer, the Fanti Chief of Cape Coast and the governor's liaison with neighboring peoples. Later at Cudjo's house Thompson preached for the first time to an African audience on the nature and attributes of God and on the Christian concept of the hereafter. Afterward he informed Cudjo of his intention to preach to Africans every Sunday. The chief's response reflected the growing tendency of Africans to identify all Europeans as Christians and to associate the manifold evils of the slave trade with the Christian presence. Although he "seemed to give assent to the Truth of our Religion," the chief "took occasion to remark [on] the immoral Lives of so many that profess Christianity."[104]

Acting on Cudjo's advice that "on Sunday [Africans] were about their Business, and he thought I should not get them to a meeting any other day but a Tuesday, that being a religious Day with them, on which they never go out a Fishing," Thompson began holding regular Tuesday classes for a small and listless audience of Africans. As a strategy of conversion he decided "not to insist much upon Points of Christian doctrine, but to strike at their false worship" by convincing them of "their absurd Notions" and exposing "the Folly of their Idolatrous and Superstitious Rites." A firm believer in the importance of personal conviction and decision, Thompson puzzled that the African catechists who "should have questions with me, proposed their Doubts and have raised Objections" instead sat passively and "never started any argument at all."[105]

Thompson ultimately concluded that their steadfast refusal to engage in theological debate meant "that they were the more resolved against Persuasion and Conviction." When attendance continued to fall off, the dispirited minister broke off the weekly classes, concluding that "I had no

Way to do but to apply myself to *Single* persons." But individual instruction was not very successful either. Three years after his arrival Thompson had baptized only two Africans; the following year two more. "They had no Principles to graft anything upon," he complained, and "I could not find by what Handle I might take them." Thoroughly confused by the contradictions between what the missionaries preached and the ungodly lives many of the Europeans lived, most Africans chose to adhere to ancient beliefs: "The Christian Religion they call white Man's Fashion, and white men, they say, know best, but black Man follow black Man's Fashion; as much as to tell me, they would not be put out of their own Way."[106]

Frustrated in his efforts to convert Africans, Thompson now spent most of his time serving as chaplain to the Cape Coast Castle, but he continued to search for a "handle" to win African converts. At the suggestion of Cudjo, he founded a missionary school for African children. Although the school was not notably successful, Thompson appealed to the Society for the Propagation of the Gospel to underwrite the cost of sending several of his better young African pupils to London to attend charity schools. Seeing in Thompson's proposal both a means of encouraging converts to read and understand the Bible for themselves, a way to promote new values, the SPG agreed to support the plan. Eager for the language and skills of the Europeans, if not for the Gospel, African chiefs readily surrendered their children for European education. Three boys were sent to London: two the sons of caboceers, the third, Philip Quaque, a relative of Cudjo.[107]

Philip Quaque, who was educated at the Parish Charity School in Islington, was baptized in the Parish Church of Islington in 1759. For seven years he lived in the home of Reverend John Moore, a member of the SPG, and was apparently educated in London. In 1765 he became the first African to be ordained in the Church of England. The following year he returned to the Gold Coast as "Missionary, School Master and Catechist to Negroes on the Gold Coast." Like his predecessor Thomas Thompson, Quaque extended his missionary activities from the fort to the town, preaching before the official establishment of the trading fort and the leading members of Fanti society. He encountered the same deep resistance: After divine services the Fanti elders "expressed a great thankfulness by obeisance," and then "immediately returned to what they term the liquor of life." Although they "expressed a great veneration" for Protestant psalm singing introduced by Quaque, they completely ignored his remonstrances on the "necessity and reasonableness of the sacrament of baptism in my own lingo," a reference to his lack of fluency in his native language after eleven years in England.[108]

Despite their rejection of Protestant Christianity, Africans accepted what was useful to them or could be adapted to African customs. For example, they incorporated the Christian celebration of Christmas into the annual yam festival, a traditional observance among Gold Coast peoples that celebrated the harvesting of new yams and commemorated ancestral spirits by music and dancing, the firing of muskets, and the flying of banners, "in short," as Thomas Thompson described it at midcentury, "with all the pompous Shews they can exhibit, and all the Gestures and Noise they can make." By the end of the century the celebration of the first fruits had merged with the European celebration of Christmas. "Black Christmas," as it came to be called, followed the annual yam custom and was a period marked by social activity and visiting. As their contribution to the festival, the inhabitants of the European forts presented gifts to the chiefs and elders of the towns, a custom that was apparently carried to the New World by African slaves and reinstituted on the plantation.[109]

Although Caboceer Cudjo had also turned a deaf ear to Quaque's pleas to accept baptism as an example to his people, he continued to promote the idea of European-style education for African children. At his urging Quaque established a school to replace the school founded by Reverend Thompson. It catered to mulatto children and the children of the rising African merchant class. The curriculum corresponded to that of English charity schools, with religion as its centerpiece. The school received little support from the Committee of Merchants and the Society for the Propagation of the Gospel, and by 1775 only two students were enrolled. The school struggled along until 1787, when the newly formed Torridzorian Society agreed to set aside funds for the purpose of "clothing, feeding and educating" twelve mulatto children. With support from the Society for the Propagation of the Gospel and the African Committee, the school prospered for a time before finally slipping into decline as a result of neglect. Although Quaque's ministry of fifty years left little permanent imprint on the Gold Coast, as a pioneering effort in educational development it prepared the way for Wesleyan Methodism in the 1830s.[110]

It is instructive to compare the growth of Islam with that of Christianity to further illuminate patterns of interaction between indigenous and world religions. Five hundred years before Portuguese caravels brought the first Christian missionaries to West Africa there were already several important centers of Islam in sub-Saharan Africa. The first Africans to accept Islam in significant numbers were the Takrurs, who lived on the banks of the Senegal River and converted around 1067. Around the same time, the Soninke peoples of the ancient kingdom of "Ghana" also adopted Islam, as did members of the royal court of Mali. Beginning in the fourteenth century waves of Fulbe Muslims, driven by a shortage of pasturage for their cattle, began drifting across the Upper Senegal and Gambia Rivers to Futa Toro and the Futa Jallon highlands, gradually Islamizing the area between the Senegal and Gambia Rivers. By the late eighteenth century the Senegambia was the principal continuing center of Islamic culture in sub-Saharan Africa.[111]

As trade routes lengthened, new Muslim centers were established by merchants and scholars, including a number of strong Muslim polities. Some of them, like Bondu, were founded by Fulbe Muslim clerics as asylums from the slave trade.[112] Through the influence of Mandingo merchants, whose commercial activities extended all along the coast and into the interior, Islam scattered inland and east as far as Nigeria. Often zealous Muslims, they were known as "both Merchants and Missionaries" for their efforts to "propagate the Mohammedan religion wherever they go."[113] Sierra Leone was one of their targets. When Mandingo traders first infiltrated Sierra Leone, they found the Susu peoples "in no disposition to change their own [religion]" for Islam.[114] By the mid-eighteenth century, however, European missionaries were describing the Susus as "a mixt People of Pagans and Mandingos, which are a sect of Mahometans," an indication that the Mandingos had created Muslim nuclei in Sierra Leone.[115]

Like their Christian rivals, Muslims were keenly conscious of the fact that they lived under the auspices of non-Muslim rulers, who often allowed Muslims to practice their faith without interference because literate Muslim traders had valuable commercial skills and the Qur'anic schools Muslims established contributed significantly to the spread of literacy throughout sub-Saharan Africa. As a minority religious group, Muslims adopted a compromising attitude in most areas of West Africa until the eighteenth-century *jihads* (holy wars). The consequence was that Islam was observed in varying degrees by different groups of peoples and that, as Nehemia Levtzion has put it, the "Islamization of Africa was paralleled by the Africanization of Islam."[116]

European travel accounts indicate that African Muslims observed at least three of the "Five Pillars" of Islam, but in Africanized form.[117] One of the more informative European sources, Richard Jobson, who traveled on the River Gambra in 1620/21, maintained that Muslims of the Upper Guinea Coast worshiped "the one true and only God," whom they called Allah.[118] Inasmuch as many Africans believed in a High God, acceptance of the concept of Allah was probably not difficult. As a matter of actual practice, however, even devout African Muslims continued the traditional practice of approaching God through the lesser deities. In certain rites the moon was called upon: According to Jobson, "the Mohammedans pay a great respect to the new planet, saluting it as soon as they see it, and opening their purses, and intreating it, that their riches may increase in Proportion as it increases."[119]

Among African Muslims, according to European accounts, Friday was widely observed as the Sabbath, as was regular ritual prayer, the second pillar of Islam.[120] Unaccustomed to regular daily prayer, except for specific purposes, African Muslims accepted ritual prayers but in so doing incorporated features of their traditional religion. Instead of making the Salah five times a day, "the Mohammedan Negroes are content with saying it thrice a Day, at Day-break, Noon, and Sun-set." The fast of Ramadan, the most widely observed of the five pillars, was strictly observed by African Muslims: "Their Devotees will not so much as swallow their spittle; and hang a cloth over their mouth for Fear a Fly should enter." However, while among the Moors Ramadan was a lunar, or movable, feast, it was always observed in September by the Africans.[121]

To paraphrase Newell Booth, if Africans incorporated traditional religion into Islam, they also incorporated Islam into traditional religion.[122] For example, the ceremony of circumcision performed by villagers from John Barre near the French Fort St. Louis in Senegal followed traditional customs, except that during the operation the candidate "must hold-up the right Thumb erected, and pronounce the Mohammedan confession: 'There is but one God and Mohammed is the Messenger of God.'" The reconciliation of Islam with traditional beliefs was most strikingly apparent in the great demand for Muslim amulets, even in areas where Muslim influence was slight, and in the Mandingo use of *grisgris*. Words or phrases from the Koran were inscribed on scrolls of paper in Arabic characters but with Mandingo vocabulary. Wrapped in linen or leather bags, they were worn as protection against injuries or accidents, for wealth or good health. Pregnant women wore them to ensure a safe delivery.[123]

The growing European presence on the coast of West Africa brought to an end the spread of Islam until the Muslim revolutions of the eighteenth and nineteenth centuries.[124] Beginning in the 1720s a series of *jihads* were launched by an alliance of Fulbe and Jallonke Muslims whose purpose was to purge Islam of its African features. They succeeded in establishing a number of religious polities, among them Jenneghe, Gonja, and Bondu, and were numerically dominant in many areas.[125] This movement of religious change in the direction of Islamic orthodoxy was paralleled by a similar movement among Christian denominations in Africa under colonialism in the nineteenth century.

The marginality of Christianity and Islam in West and West Central Africa had required a politics of accommodation of indigenous religions that lasted through the late eighteenth century. Everywhere, this policy had produced distinctive, yet authentic, expressions of Christianity and Islam, which were preserved and perpetuated by local catechists and interpreters and *malams* or *marabouts,* the local Muslim clerics. The advance of colonialism, developments in communications, cultural chauvinism, and pseudoscientific racism in the nineteenth century brought about a profound change in attitudes, from accommodation of local cultural forms to an uncompromising insistence on orthodoxy in theology and worship. Compared with earlier missions, the new missions were less dependent on local governing elites, catechists, and interpreters. Colonial occupation made it possible for missionaries, who were part of the apparatus of colonial rule, to establish control over church organizations and to ensure greater control over theological content and worship.[126]

Until then, neither Christianity nor Islam penetrated very deeply among the people anywhere in West or West Central Africa. To be sure, there were many ardent converts among the first African Christians and Muslims. But even communities of believers continued to live ambivalent spiritual lives, choosing what they wanted from the vast complexity of Christian and Islamic cultures without becoming fully committed to Christian or Islamic fundamentals. The mass of villagers were hardly affected at all but continued undisturbed in the practice of their ancient religions. Thus, when the first two phases of African evangelization ended, the missionaries discovered that they had Christianized individuals but not African society and culture.

Descendants in the diaspora represented a cross section of the African population. Far from being culturally deficient, they brought with them a variety of cultural forms: traditional religions, Africanized Christianity, and Africanized Islam. The transmission of religious beliefs and practices across continents and through time produced enormous differences between religious cultures that had been distinctively shaped by Africans and the forms eventually adopted by their descendants in the diaspora. There were also striking similarities that were ingrained in the historical experience of cultural interaction, most notably in the assimilative powers of indigenous religions and in traditions of patterned behavior, including resistance to spiritual indoctrination, the appropriation of Christian symbols and rituals to supplement traditional symbols and rituals, the reinterpretation of the Gospel message to meet the exigencies of time and condition, the prevalence of millenarian expectations that promised a defense against witchcraft to the first generations of African converts, and for their descendants in the diaspora an end to the evils and sufferings of slavery. Like the intrepid pioneer evangelists who gave African Christianity its special vitality and unique character, Africans in the diaspora were able to control the process of conversion and distinctively shape Protestant Christianity in Afro-Atlantic cultures in the New World.

2

THE AMERICAS

THE SURVIVAL OF AFRICAN RELIGIONS

Jon Butler has recently argued that the transatlantic slave trade shattered African systems of religion, describing it as "a holocaust that destroyed collective religious practice in colonial America."[1] It would not have been altogether surprising had those who experienced the trauma of separation and sale in West and West Central Africa, who were herded like cattle on to the slave ships, completely lost their faith in gods who seemed to have abandoned them and in deities who appeared unwilling or unable to protect them. Some, believing perhaps that their gods had indeed forsaken them or that the superior "magic" of their European oppressors had prevailed, might have lost their faith, either permanently or temporarily; the majority did not.

Enslaved Africans turned to their gods and deployed their religious convictions in ways that gave structure and meaning to the present and challenged the total authority over their persons being claimed by Europeans. By remembering and recreating the past, they produced hope for the future, whatever that future might hold. That those taken on board the slave ships had been torn from the institutional frameworks of their traditional religious cultures is patently obvious. However, those who survived the Middle Passage showed enormous courage, resilience, and ingenuity in devising new religious structures to cope with the demands that enslavement in the British plantation colonies made on them.

Millions of Africans were forcibly removed from cultural, social, economic, and political contexts that were not precisely identical and fed into the international slave trade. Indeed, the trade thrived on often violent antagonisms among different ethnic groups and African nations, which sometimes resurfaced in the New World. But there were also some highly significant similarities in the religious cultures and languages of many of those shipped to British America. Profits dictated that slave ships be filled and dispatched as quickly as possible, and this usually involved loading at a single port rather than "coasting." That did not necessarily mean that all those taken on board a particular vessel came from the immediate vicinity of the port, but they had probably been obtained "from a restricted and culturally quite homogeneous zone."[2] The "comparative cohesiveness" of the religious and linguistic traditions that crossed the Atlantic would be critically important in the reformulation of traditional West and West Central African religious cultures in the New World. Those cultures would retain some "explicitly West African . . . forms."[3]

Most Africans transported from their homeland before the closing of the slave trade in the early nineteenth century subscribed to traditional religious cultures, and they would encounter Christianity for the first time in the Americas. However, the slave ships also included a smattering of people who adhered to their own versions of Islam and Christianity. These religious convictions would also survive the Middle Passage and take their place alongside traditional beliefs and practices in the very different contexts of the New World.[4]

Capture and sale of slaves in Africa usually destroyed the ties of family and kinship that were of such significance to African peoples, and the personal and communal cost of that destruction to those who remained as well as to those who were taken should be neither forgotten nor underestimated. But the physical, psychological, and emotional brutality of the Middle Passage did not destroy memory, beliefs, experience, and expertise. Although stripped of much of their material culture, every African who survived the Middle Passage retained cultural attributes that could be put to creative use in the Americas.

The captains and crews of British slave ships felt no burning sense of mission to proselytize, but they were neither ignorant of nor indifferent to the often religiously inspired behavior of their human cargoes. Most were acutely conscious of the fact that those on board their vessels were not totally demoralized but at any moment might seek what was their common objective: their return to Africa. The arrangements on the slave ships made organized resistance difficult but not totally impossible once the vessels had left African waters.[5] There is no record of the number of uprisings that occurred on the Middle Passage, but during the eighteenth century they averaged two a year on British slavers.[6] Many involved women as well as men, and some depended upon traditional religious beliefs and practices for their inspiration and execution.

Throughout the duration of the slave trade most ships carried more men than women: somewhere between two-thirds and three-quarters of all the Africans transported to the Americas were men.[7] The consequences of this imbalance for shaping the contours and dynamics of slave culture in the New World were to be manifold. On slave ships, however, it is highly relevant that captains and crews mistakenly assumed that the women on board their vessels posed little danger to them. In fact, African women from a wide spectrum of ethnic backgrounds were deeply involved in many of the insurrections that occurred on the Middle Passage.[8] As Lucille Mathurin Mair has commented, whatever else it might have entailed, the Middle Passage involved "a crude levelling of sexual distinctions" that served to ensure that from the outset African women would "share every inch of the man's physical and spiritual odyssey."[9]

Whether or not they involved women, some shipboard rebellions were spontaneous; others were planned over hours, days, or even weeks. Some relied very heavily indeed upon the potency of various African beliefs, symbols, and rituals for the secrecy and solidarity deemed essential for their success. In 1751, for example, the crew of the *Duke of Argyll*, a slaver bound for Antigua, was "alarmed with a report that some of the men slaves had found means to poison the water in the scuttle casks upon deck." They were both relieved and amused when they discovered that the men concerned "had only conveyed some of their country fetishes . . . or talismans into one of them, which they had the credulity to suppose must inevitably kill all who drank it."[10] These African men, who might have included some experienced practitioners of witchcraft, were probably not trying to physically poison the white crew but had laid a form of curse or spell upon them.[11]

In 1789 James Arnold, who was employed as a surgeon on the *Ruby*, gave a graphic account of an uprising that also included a profoundly important West African component.[12] What is remarkable but not necessarily unique about this episode is that it involved the taking of a blood oath. West and West Central African oaths varied somewhat in their character and purpose, but all were taken immensely seriously.[13] Ritual oaths, such as the blood oath taken by the men on the *Ruby*, were highly significant instruments for the creation of moral solidarity. In this case, the oath served as a major "weapon" in the men's struggle to secure their freedom.[14]

The men on the *Ruby* failed in their bid for freedom, however. One of their leaders was shot and killed when he confronted the crew "with a Knife in each of his hands." Another, who held out for eight hours despite being "severely scalded with a Mixture of boiling Water and Fat, which was repeatedly thrown down upon him," was chained to the foremast, denied food or medical care, and after three days thrown overboard, possibly while still alive.[15] These men were killed for one purpose and one purpose only: to convince their compatriots of the futility of such defiance. These two men may not have wished to die, but they had sworn to each other in the most solemn African terms their eternal brotherhood and their willingness to die together as brothers. No doubt they were greatly fortified by the belief that even if they could not secure their bodily freedom, at least their death would ensure the return home of their souls to Africa.

Several men and women on board the slave ships made quite calculated decisions to die by their own hand. Some may have killed themselves, or tried to kill themselves, because of indescribable fear or deep clinical depression; many must have been comforted, if not prompted, by their unshakeable convictions concerning the hereafter.[16] West and West Central African peoples did not necessarily regard suicide as a negative act that placed the immortal soul in jeopardy. Among the Yoruba and Ashanti peoples, for example, suicide could be "acclaimed as praiseworthy." The Yoruba gave "great credit and honour" to those who killed themselves because they found "life burdensome, disgraceful and perilous."[17]

There is no record of the number who committed suicide en route to the Americas. However, much can be gleaned about their motives and methods from the observations of white crew members as well as from the few extant African accounts of the Middle Passage. The three most common ways women and men tried to kill themselves were by starvation, refusing "medicines when sick," and by throwing themselves overboard. For reasons that had everything to do with profits and nothing whatsoever with Christian beliefs, crew members used the most ruthless means to prevent suicides. Those who would not eat were likely to be whipped, force-fed, or both. On one ship two women who tried to starve themselves were flogged until they "fainted away with the pain," but still they would not take food. These women found the death they sought in another way: They "fold[ed] themselves in each others arms [and] plunged over the poop of the vessel into the sea, and were drowned." Other women who observed this scene "cried out in the most affecting manner [and] many of them were [prepared] to follow their compatriots."[18]

Thomas Phillips, captain of the *Hannibal,* which sailed from Whydah to Barbados in 1693/1694, remarked that on this particular voyage "about 12 Negroes did wilfully drown themselves, and others starved to death."[19] Phillips failed to mention whether those who threw themselves off the *Hannibal* did so at different times or, as was the case with "about an hundred Men Slaves" on another slave ship, *The Prince of Orange*, had committed mass suicide.[20] Europeans who witnessed these scenes may have been unfamiliar with African understandings of suicide, but they readily acknowledged that there were those on board their vessels who were totally unafraid of death, who "wished to die" and who, as they were dying, said "with pleasure" that they were "going home."[21]

The captains of slave ships sometimes tried to prevent suicides by employing a form of spiritual coercion. For example, it was not uncommon for Africans to be forced to watch the decapitation or dismembering of one of their number who had either mutinied or committed suicide. The rationale informing this threat to the living by mutilating the dead was perfectly simple. As Captain William Snelgrave explained, "Many blacks believe that if they are put to death and not dismembred [*sic*], they shall return again to their own Country."[22] By the mid-seventeenth century a similar form of coercion was being employed in the British plantation colonies.[23]

There are relatively few clues as to the hopes and fears that passed through the minds of those on board the slave ships as the New World coastline came into view. Many must have believed that their death, and the return of their soul to Africa, was imminent, for, as Job Ben-Solomon commented, Africans "entertained a Notion, that all who were sold for Slaves were either eaten, or murdered, [by Europeans] since none ever came back."[24] Probably the first reliable evidence that they would not be "eaten by these ugly [white] men" came some time after their arrival in the Americas.[25]

For captive Africans, in one sense the arrival of a slave ship in the New World marked the end of one stage in their journey and the beginning of another. On another level, however, surviving the Middle Passage proved to be but one point, albeit a critically significant one, in a continuum of religious beliefs and practices. Once they were in the New World, the convictions that had so fortified these men and women while they were en route to the Americas were neither casually forgotten nor discarded as unnecessary or irrelevant. The ritualistic expressions of these convictions would be broadly similar to West and West Central African ones, but the local circumstances in which enslaved Africans found themselves dictated that they could never be identical. Nowhere in the Americas would Africans be able to duplicate their traditional religious systems. What they were able to do, and often very successfully, was to piece together new systems from the remnants of the old.

There were significant variations in the plantation economies that evolved in British America through the middle years of the eighteenth century. Thousands upon thousands of Africans entered against their wills public worlds that increasingly they helped to shape and define and private worlds that they struggled to create for themselves. The precise ethnic mix on particular estates and in particular neighborhoods was of obvious importance, as was the size and proximity of those estates. Sex ratios and age structures played a critical role in the formation of sexual partnerships, in the definition of family and kinship networks, and in the reconstitution of spiritual community. Mortality rates, together with the attitude of slave owners toward the disposal of their human property, profoundly influenced the duration of partnerships, the integrity of family and kinship networks, and the precise composition of spiritual communities. All of these factors interacted in an infinitely complex, ever-changing fashion with traditional African beliefs and practices to shape the domestic and communal lives of bondpeople. The private worlds that evolved in the slave quarters of the British Caribbean and Southern mainland between the mid-seventeenth and mid-eighteenth centuries differed not so much in kind as in the degree to which it proved possible for enslaved people to draw upon their African pasts to deal with present realities and future possibilities.

Before the closing of the transatlantic slave trade, at least 500,000 Africans were shipped to British North America.[26] Between 1627 and 1775 approximately 1,500,000 Africans were landed in the British Caribbean, of whom around 80 percent remained there. The others were reexported to various destinations in the New World, including the mainland American colonies.[27] The volume of imports into the different plantation colonies varied over time, but everywhere they were comparatively high during the initial stages of plantation formation.

The conditions experienced by Africans imported into Barbados during the seventeenth century were so horrendous that their life expectancy was a mere seventeen years.[28] Avaricious sugar planters could easily afford to work their slaves to death and to purchase replacements as and when they needed them. Between 1670 and 1695 around 70,000 Africans were shipped to Barbados.[29] During the next three-quarters of a century annual imports ranged from a low of 1,027, between 1708 and 1710, to a high of 5,101, between 1766 and 1770.[30] Slave imports into Jamaica, whose plantation economy included the so-called 'minor staples' as well as sugar,

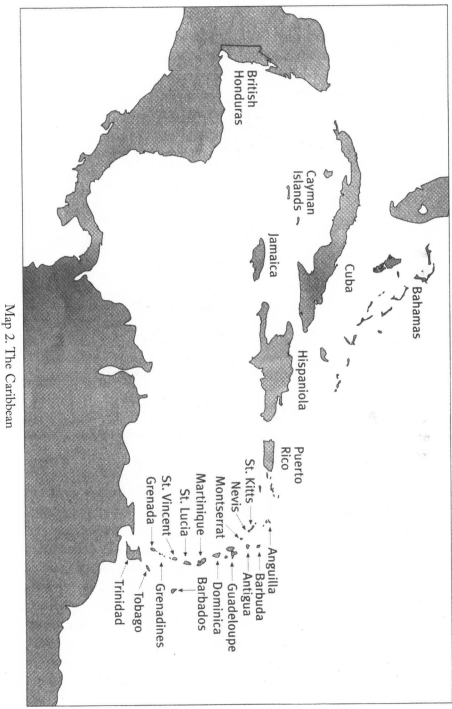

Map 2. The Caribbean

increased from around 2,000 per annum in 1700 to approximately 8,000 per annum in 1790. A surge in imports between 1792 and 1807, to 10,700 per year, was indicative of continuing high mortality rates as well as the impending closure of the British slave trade.[31]

Before the late seventeenth century Africans were demographically and economically insignificant in the Chesapeake. In 1650, for example, they accounted for only around 3 percent of the region's population, a proportion that increased to 15 percent in 1690 as the transition from indentured to involuntary servitude began to get under way. By 1710 the estimated 23,118 Africans in Virginia accounted for under 42 percent of the colony's population. Between 1700 and 1740 around 49,000 Africans were shipped to Virginia and Maryland, and by the latter date they accounted for approximately 28 percent of the total population of these two colonies.[32] Both in absolute and in relative terms this growth rate was of a very different order to that which characterized the British Caribbean.

As early as 1660 the black population of Barbados numbered around 20,000 and accounted for just over 47 percent of the island's inhabitants. Jamaica, taken from Spain five years earlier, had a total population of 3,500 and was around 17 percent black. The 2,000 Africans in the Leeward Islands of Antigua, St. Kitts, Nevis, and Montserrat accounted for one-fifth of the population. Within a few years each of these British islands had a black majority: by 1670 in Barbados, by 1680 in Jamaica, and by 1690 in the Leeward Islands. By 1713 Barbados was almost 74 percent black, Jamaica was roughly 89 percent black, and the Leeward Islands were around 77 percent black.[33] In the Southern mainland, only the Low Country of South Carolina and Georgia would come close to approximating these proportions.

Principally because of the Barbadian connection, chattel slavery was sanctioned from the outset in South Carolina.[34] Small numbers of Africans were brought to the Low Country, mainly from the British Caribbean, during the first three decades of settlement, but it was only with the development of rice culture that South Carolina planters began to rely heavily on the transatlantic slave trade. By 1708 South Carolina's population of 8,000 was half black. This trend intensified after 1720 as rice emerged as the Low Country's premier staple crop.[35] Between the mid-1720s and 1740 around 29,000 Africans were imported into South Carolina, with annual imports ranging from a low of 439 (in 1725) to a high of 3,097 (in 1736).[36] By 1740 South Carolina's black population was estimated at 39,155 and the colony was roughly two-thirds black.[37]

In the 1750s and 1760s South Carolina's slavery-based rice economy expanded into Low Country Georgia. In 1750 the Georgia trustees were forced to abandon their prohibition on slavery, and thereafter South Carolina planters and their slaves poured across the Savannah River. By the eve of the American Revolution Georgia's predominantly African-born enslaved population totaled around 16,000.[38]

Just as significant in the definition of slave culture as the total number of Africans imported and the ebb and flow of imports over time were the ethnic origins of those taken to the plantation colonies. Africans, wrote Richard Ligon in the mid-seventeenth century, were "fetched [to Barbados] from . . . Guinny and Binny, some from Cutchew, some from Angola, and some from the River of Gambia." They spoke "several languages, and by that means, one of them understands not another."[39] Toward the end of the century an anonymous British author explained that "the safety of the Plantations depends upon having Negroes from all parts of Guiny, who not understanding each others languages and Customs, do not, and cannot agree to Rebel, as they would do . . . when there are too many Negroes from one Country."[40] These two commentators were right about the diverse backgrounds of the Africans being shipped to Barbados, but they failed to record the often highly significant similarities between their "languages and Customs." These similarities reflected a combination of factors operating in West and West Central Africa together with evolving planter preferences for Africans from particular regions and ethnic groups.

The ethnic origins of the Africans shipped to the British plantation colonies varied regionally and over time. However, the ultimately reconcilable ethnic identities of many newly enslaved Africans are readily apparent. Before the mid-eighteenth century three regions of Africa, the Windward Coast, the Gold Coast, and the Bight of Benin, supplied roughly two-thirds of the Africans transported to the Americas by British slavers.[41] By 1807, however, "approximately two-thirds of the African-born populations" of the British Caribbean had been drawn from the Bight of Biafra and central Africa.[42] However, there were important variations in the African origins of the enslaved peoples of the British sugar islands. Thus, "the Bight of Biafra was the most important source of slaves [for] the southern Caribbean, but in the Leeward Islands Central Africa and Senegambia dominated."[43] Just under half of all the Africans landed in Jamaica before 1807 were Ibos from the Bight of Biafra or BaKongo people from Central Africa.[44]

In the Southern mainland, around 60 percent of the Africans imported into Virginia between 1718 and 1726 were from the Bight of Benin; during the 1730s roughly 85 percent came from the Bight of Biafra or Angola.[45] Under 70 percent of the 8,045 Africans shipped to Charleston during the late 1730s had been brought from Angola, and another 6 percent are known to have originated in the Gambia region.[46] Around 40 percent of the 2,500 Africans landed in Savannah between 1766 and 1771 came from Gambia, 16 percent came from Sierra Leone, and 10 percent came from Angola. Another 6 percent were said to be from "Gambia and Sierra Leone," while 3 percent had been brought from Senegal. Of the remainder, 14 percent were identified as having come from the "Rice Coast," 5 percent from the "Grain Coast," and the others simply from "Africa."[47]

The African regions that predominated in the slave trade to the British plantation colonies were not ethnically monolithic, but "a single ethnic group often accounted for a large proportion of the slaves from a particular region."[48] The extent to which particular groups were able to preserve their "cultural habits" once in the New World depended upon many factors, one of the most important of which was their concentration on any given estate or in any given neighborhood.

The precise local mix of ethnic origins in particular colonies varied, as did the size and the proximity of the estates upon which enslaved Africans found themselves. Slaveholdings in the Southern mainland were much smaller and far more dispersed than they were in the British Caribbean. Local ratios of Europeans to Africans also varied, but everywhere in the Southern mainland they were much higher than in any of the sugar islands. In the early eighteenth century, for example, the South Carolina parish of Goose Creek contained around 500 enslaved Africans but about twice that number of Europeans; in Barbados and Jamaica, on the other hand, a single sugar plantation was likely to be worked by two or three hundred slaves under the direction of one white overseer.[49] Colonial Georgia's largest slaveholder, Governor James Wright, held 523 bondpeople, thereby putting himself on a par with premier sugar planters. His slaves, however, were employed not on one but on eleven different plantations, indicative of the belief that the optimum number of workers per unit of rice production was between thirty and forty.[50] Eminent rice and sugar planters may have held similar numbers of slaves, but they organized their operations very differently and in ways that were to be highly significant in the definition of the private lives constructed by their workforces.

Sex ratios and age structures were important in shaping many aspects of life in the slave quarters. As we have seen, most slave ships carried at least two men for every woman, and this imbalance persisted for varying lengths of time in the New World. For instance, during the 1730s, a decade of particularly heavy slave imports in Prince George's County,

Virginia, the sex ratio was in the order of 187 men to every 100 women. On estates with more than ten slaves it soared to 249 to 100.[51] Between 1755 and 1775 the ratio of men to women on Georgia estates was around 146 to 100, but on plantations with more than forty slaves it rose to 152 to 100.[52] Depending upon the slaves' ethnic mix, the preservation of "cultural habits" might have been more viable on larger plantations, but it is also possible that their imbalanced sex ratios may have generated intense rivalries among men who were in search of sexual partners.[53]

Richard Ligon and the anonymous pamphleteer of 1694 believed that varied African "languages and customs" could be used by Europeans as a highly effective means of securing racial control. Their arrogant assumption was that Africans were intellectually incapable of transcending the linguistic and cultural differences that existed among them. In fact, these linguistic differences were not always as severe, or as insurmountable, as these contemporary commentators imagined them to be. Some Africans could find themselves in the unenviable position of Olaudah Equiano, who upon his arrival in Virginia discovered that he "had no person to speak to that I could understand,"[54] but many more, and perhaps the majority of those arriving in the plantation colonies through the middle years of the eighteenth century, did not.

The practice of loading slave ships at a single West African port meant that planters were often making their choices from among Africans who, if not "culturally homogeneous,"[55] were in all probability culturally compatible. These choices, especially in the case of eminent planters, usually involved the purchase of more than one person from any given shipment.[56] Such purchases often resulted in the separation of couples, families, and friends, but they could also mean that "on large estates . . . slaves would typically have no trouble finding members of their own nation with whom to communicate."[57] Subsequent purchases from slave ships that had set sail from a different African port could introduce to the plantation representatives from other ethnic groups. The resulting linguistic and cultural variations may have reflected a deliberate policy of ethnic mixing, but they could also have reflected nothing more than pragmatic decisions to satisfy labor requirements as and when the opportunities to do so arose.

The manner in which the transatlantic slave trade was organized and the purchasing habits of planters meant that enslaved Africans could be both united and divided by language. The reconciliation of linguistic differences was achieved in each of Britain's plantation colonies with a speed and a facility that often astounded Europeans.[58] The spread of Islam in West and West Central Africa was a particularly important part of this process, providing as it did the fragments of a common vocabulary, if not of a common language.[59] Within a comparatively short time, each of the plantation colonies had developed its own lingua franca.[60]

The resolution of linguistic differences went hand in hand with the recognition and interaction of often compatible African pasts. However, some European writers remarked on the persistence of clashes directly attributable to those pasts. In 1689, for example, Edward Littleton implied that in Barbados, encounters between different ethnic groups often resulted in physical violence.[61] Two later writers, Griffith Hughes and James Barclay, also remarked on the continuing significance of ethnic origins in the slave quarters. But neither of these commentators repeated Littleton's claim that ethnic antagonisms could be so bitter as to totally preclude any possibility of constructive cultural interaction.

Writing in 1750, Hughes, the Anglican rector of the Barbadian parish of St. Lucy, noted that the "Mirth and Diversions" of the island's enslaved population "differ according to the Customs of so many Nations intermixed." He added that "the Negroes in general are very tenaciously addicted to the Rites, Ceremonies and Superstitions of their *own Countries*," but he did not suggest that these strongly held religious convictions were a source of overt physical conflict.[62] Nor did he conclude, as have some recent scholars, that the communal performance of "Rites" and "Ceremonies," which he did not describe in detail, "may well have been occasions to recall national religions."[63] Instead, Hughes chose to emphasize a different aspect of these religious celebrations that surely must have been as obvious to those in the ethnically commingled slave quarters of Barbados as it was to him: the essential compatibility of many of these "Rites, Ceremonies and Superstitions."

It was, Hughes remarked, the "universal Custom" in Barbados for slaves, regardless of their ethnic origin, to adorn themselves with talismans and fetishes that usually took the form of "Strings of Beads of various Colours . . . in great Numbers twined around their Arms, Necks and Legs." In the case of "the richer sort of House Negroes" these "Beads" might be "interspersed . . . with Pieces of Money." Moreover, there was something else upon which the captive peoples of "so many Nations . . . all agree." According to Hughes, without exception they stood "in much Awe of such as pass for *Obeah* Negroes, they being a sort of Physicians and Conjurers, Who can, as they believe not only fascinate them, but cure them when they are bewitched by others."[64]

Twenty-five years later James Barclay, an Englishman who worked as an overseer on a rice plantation near Dorchester, South Carolina, remarked that he found it "diverting to hear" bondpeople "in their quarrels, reproaching one another with their respective countries." Like Littleton, Barclay attributed these "quarrels" to the "violent antipathy" that he thought existed between the peoples of different African "provinces." He believed that when "the people . . . are brought over here, the same antipathy subsists," and he claimed that this was particularly the case with "those of Gulli or Gully, and Iba." The latter, he reported, would goad the former with the taunt that "'You be Gully Niga, what be the use of you, you be good for nothing'" and receive the reply that "'You be Iba Niga; Iba Niga great rascal.'"[65]

These comments suggest that at a time when both Barbados and the Lower South still depended heavily upon the transatlantic slave trade, African-born people identified strongly with their ethnic origins and grouped themselves accordingly. Common African roots provided the most logical reference point for the understanding and organization of present realities and future possibilities. The broad similarity of many of the religious beliefs and the ritualistic expression of those beliefs that Hughes and Barclay alluded to ultimately made it possible for people from different African backgrounds to devise mutually acceptable ceremonies for marrying each other, naming their children, and burying their dead.

In the early 1680s Morgan Godwyn, a churchman who was instrumental in persuading the Anglican hierarchy in London of the necessity and the desirability of proselytizing enslaved Africans, had claimed that bondpeople in Barbados and Virginia clung tenaciously to their *"Heathen Rites,"* to their "barbarous . . . behaviour and practice in *Worship* and *Ceremonies* of *Religion* . . . their *Polygamy* . . . their *Idolatrous Dances,* and *Revels.*" They had "brought out of Africa," Godwyn continued, various *"Recreations* and *Customs"* that demonstrated beyond any shadow of a doubt their *"Impiety"* and their *"Barbarity."* Among the three *"Recreations* and *Customs"* specifically mentioned by Godwyn, probably because they were the best known to him, were the *"Idolatrous Dances,* and *Revels*; in which they usually spend their *Sunday* after the necessity of labour for their Provisions . . . has been complied with."[66]

Godwyn acknowledged that "the *Gentiles* anciently did esteem and practice *Dancing,* as a part of *Divine Worship*; and no less also did the *Jews,*" but he claimed that the dances performed by Africans in Barbados and Virginia were but one of the more obvious manifestations of their "Idolatry." He based his "Conjecture" on the fact "that they use their Dances as a *means to procure Rain,*"[67] presumably for their provision grounds rather than for their owners' cane and tobacco fields. Godwyn did not describe these ritual dances, but Ligon did. He emphasized that, in Barbados at any rate, there was "no mixt dancing" but that men and women performed their dances separately and "may dance a whole day [to] their Musick." As for "Their motions," Ligon recorded that "their hands [have] more of motion than their feet, and their heads more than their hands."[68]

Writing a quarter of a century after Godwyn, Sir Hans Sloane made no mention of men and women dancing separately, but he did comment that their ritual dances entailed "great activity and strength of Body, and keeping time if it can be." The dancers had "Rattles ty'd to their Legs and Wrists, and in their Hands, with which they make a noise, keeping in time with one who makes a sound answering it on the mouth of an empty Gourd or Jar with his hands." In addition, it was "very often" the case that "they . . . tie Cow Tails to their Rumps, and add such other things to their Bodies in several places, as to give them a very extraordinary appearance."[69] European commentators would continue to be both fascinated and repelled by what they regarded as the eroticism of the ritual dances performed by enslaved Africans. Unfortunately, their descriptions of these dances were usually so generalized as to preclude any possibility of linking them to specific African antecedents.

Just as distasteful to Morgan Godwyn as ritual dancing was the "confidence" placed by enslaved Africans "in certain Figures and ugly Representations, of none knows what besides themselves." In the absence of "more *Magnificent Temples*," these "Deities" were "usually enshrin[ed] in some *Earthern Potsherds*." Such was the power attributed to these "Deities," continued Godwyn, that "Fugitives and Runaways" were utterly convinced that they were "able to protect them in their Flight, and from Discovery." Godwyn failed to mention who had made and supplied these "Representations," but almost certainly they had been sanctified, if not made, by sacred specialists in the slave quarters.[70]

The third of the "Customs" that Godwyn correctly surmised had been "brought out of Africa" was what he mistakenly referred to as *"Polygamy."*[71] The main point at issue here was not the absence of sexual morality but the absence of a particular sexual morality: that predicated upon Anglican beliefs and assumptions concerning sexuality and marriage. In Barbados, Godwyn maintained, neither planters nor Anglican churchmen took much interest in the sexual partnerships formed by slaves. Bondpeople entered into such partnerships "by mutual agreement amongst themselves" and with a "frequent *repudiating* and changing of . . . Wives, usual amongst most *Heathens*."[72] Godwyn concluded that it was principally because of the "*Connivance* and Toleration" of their owners that enslaved Africans continued to practice "Polygamie." Most planters, he charged, "esteeming them but as Cattle, and desirous of their *Encrease,* are apter to encourage, than to restrain them from it."[73]

Godwyn erroneously believed that in Tidewater Virginia enslaved Africans had already chosen to abandon their traditional marriage patterns. There, he claimed, the "*Negro's* . . . tho imported from the same places [as those shipped to Barbados] are not (so far as I could learn) addicted to *Polygamies;* but rather of themselves choosing to follow the Custom of the *English.*" That this was not nearly true is suggested by an episode in 1712 or 1713 when a slave named Roger "hanged himself . . . not any reason he being hindred from keeping other negroes men wifes beside his owne."[74]

Reports from early-eighteenth-century South Carolina confirm the persistence, and universal occurrence, of polygyny in the British plantation colonies. Like Godwyn, Reverend Francis Le Jau talked in generalities and confused polygamy and polygyny. But he asserted that in his parish of Goose Creek "and elsewhere" in the Low Country there was "a constant and promiscuous cohabiting of slaves of different Sexes and Nations together: When a Man or Woman's fancy dos [*sic*] alter about this party they throw up one another and take others which they also change when they please." This, he added, was "a General Sin, for the exceptions are so few they are hardly worth mentioning." A year later he wrote that "One of the most Scandalous and common Crimes of our Slaves is their perpetual Changing of Wives and husbands."[75] This "Crime" was no more unique to South Carolina than it was to Barbados and Virginia. Enslaved Africans everywhere in British America continued to engage in polygynous relationships through the eighteenth century.[76]

Most European commentators, including the clergy, had little to say about the formation of family and kinship ties by slaves, including the patterns of courtship that preceded the taking of a marriage partner, whether the widespread African convention of dowries persisted, or the circumstances that might result in the voluntary dissolution of a marriage. However, from the few clues left by contemporary Europeans, it is clear that traditional African assumptions and practices were adapted to meet the requirements of the slave quarters. As John Woolman commented of the Chesapeake colonies in the 1740s, "Negroes marry after their own way."[77]

One of the earliest descriptions of a marriage ceremony devised by slaves in the Southern mainland dates from 1731. The ritual took place in North Carolina and, in its fundamentals, would have been instantly recognizable in many parts of West and West Central Africa. According to John

Brickell's account, "Their *Marriages* are generally performed amongst themselves, there being very little ceremony used upon that Head; for the Man makes the Woman a Present, such as a *Brass Ring* or some other Toy, which if she accepts of becomes his Wife; but if ever they part from each other, which frequently happens, upon any little Disgust, she returns his Present: These kind of Contracts no longer binding them, than the woman keeps the pledge give her."[78]

Writing of Low Country marriage practices on the eve of the American Revolution, James Barclay endorsed Brickell's observation that there appeared "to be no particular ceremony . . . but the married pair acknowledging themselves man and wife."[79] A private ritual not dissimilar to that described by Brickell persisted in the Low Country into the early nineteenth century. There, "the man would go to the cabin of the woman he desired, would roast peanuts in the ashes, place them on a stool between her and himself, and while eating propose marriage." If the woman accepted his proposal, "the couple repaired to his cabin immediately, and they were regarded as man and wife."[80]

These fragmentary reports suggest that everywhere in the Southern mainland the exchange of tokens, the taking of the marriage vow, was an essentially private matter. However, marriage was also a cause for public celebration, which affirmed and reaffirmed, at the same time it created, ties of family, kinship, and friendship that often extended beyond the boundaries of the plantation or plantations upon which the couple resided. In the 1740s, for example, Thomas Bacon wrote of the "small congregations . . . brought together" by slave marriages on Maryland's Eastern Shore.[81] Almost forty years later, James Barclay remarked of the custom in the Carolina Low Country that if the couple to be married were "well acquainted in the place, multitudes of men, women and children, to the amount of several hundreds," would "flock together from the neighbouring plantations" to participate in the festivities. He added that marriages were usually "kept in the night," not for any specifically religious reason but "because in the day-time [slaves] must work for their masters."[82]

The slaves who lived on the estate on which the marriage took place provided most of the hospitality and often spent several weeks beforehand making their preparations. They "commonly" fattened "a number of land tortoises" for the wedding feast and spent "what money they have got for their labour on Sundays on rum." Sometimes their owner would "allow them a hog or two to entertain the company." The assembled guests would spend "the whole night . . . in eating and drinking, singing, dancing and roaring, 'till all the victuals and drink are done, when each departs to his own home." Owners did not "interfere on these occasions, except they become riotous, and then the ringleaders are sure to pay for it."[83]

The rituals surrounding death attracted more, and more unfavorable, comments from Europeans than those involving marriage. Like their contemporaries who described burials in West and West Central Africa, Anglican clergy particularly were shocked at what they depicted as the depravity with which slaves buried their dead. They were especially scandalized by the feasting, drinking, music making and dancing that took place on these occasions. Unfortunately, even the commentators such as Thomas Bacon who claimed to "have attended several" slave burials provided few details about the funeral rites devised by Africans in the Southern mainland.[84]

Compared with the often lengthy descriptions of slave burials in the British Caribbean, only a few fragments of literary evidence survive from the colonial South. However, this limited documentation indicates that, as in the sugar islands, the rituals surrounding death, the joyous assertion and reassertion of the essential continuity between past, present, and future generations, drew heavily from what in their fundamentals was a common African heritage. Little is known about the ceremonials that might have occurred in the time between death and burial, but it may be safely inferred that the work demanded of the living by their owners precluded what Europeans depicted as the lengthy mourning that preceded burials everywhere in West and West Central Africa. Similarly, there is little detailed record from the colonial South of the way in which the corpse was prepared for burial, conveyed to the burial site, and subsequently interred.

As in Barbados, archaeological excavations of African burial sites in both the Chesapeake and the Lower South have revealed talismans, beads, and similar objects that probably had a profound religious significance.[85] Evidence from Jamaica and Barbados also documents the practice of providing food and drink to sustain the dead on their journey. In 1707, for example, Sir Hans Sloane remarked that in the British Caribbean "Rum and Victuals" might be buried "in gourds" with the corpse or "at other times" spilt "on the grave." In Jamaica, these "Victuals" included "casader bread . . . sugar, rum, tobacco, & pipes with fier [sic] to light his pipe." Sometimes, "After the Grave is filled up . . . a kind of Soup" was placed "at the Head, and a Bottle of Rum at the Feet."[86]

The ex-slave Charles Ball's graphic description of the burial of an infant that took place on a South Carolina plantation around the turn of the eighteenth century indicates that the practice was also observed in the Southern mainland. The child's father, who was African-born and claimed to have "been a priest in his own nation," conducted the burial ceremony. His wife, a country-born woman named Lydia, and Ball assisted him in preparing the body for interment. Ball did not say what this process entailed, but once the body had been made ready the father "buried" with his son

> a small bow and several arrows; a little bowl of parched meal; a miniature canoe, about a foot long, and a little paddle, (with which he said it would cross the ocean to his own country) a small stick with an iron nail, sharpened and fastened into one end of it; and a piece of white muslin, with several figures painted on it in blue and red, by which, he said, his relations and countrymen would know the infant to be his son, and would receive it accordingly on its arrival amongst them.

The "funeral service" ended with the father placing "a lock of hair from his head . . . upon the dead infant, and clos[ing] the grave with his own hands."[87] The burial of this child with various grave goods to ensure his safe return to Africa, was typical; the apparent privacy of his burial was not.

There is plentiful evidence from the British Caribbean and the American South that demonstrates that the three elements commonly associated with the interment of a slave—the procession with the body to the grave, the burial, and the subsequent festivities—usually involved everyone on the plantation and often attracted large numbers of bondpeople from the immediate neighborhood. In mid-eighteenth-century Antigua, for example, it was the usual practice for the corpse to be "carried to the grave attended by a numerous concourse." Some of those who processed to the burial site played "an instrument . . . resembling a Drum, called a 'Gumba'; others . . . what they call a 'Shake, Shake' . . . and all singing some heathenish account of the Life & Death of the deceased."[88] In 1740 Charles Leslie spoke of the "vast Multitude" of slaves who processed to burials in Jamaica. Singing "all the way," they carried the corpse, which if not in a coffin would be wrapped in cloth, "on their Shoulders" to the grave.[89] After the interment "the songs grow more animated, dancing and apparent merriment commence."[90]

Just as in European accounts of burials in Africa, reports of interments in the plantation colonies often emphasized the prominent part women played in the proceedings. For example, according to Leslie, throughout the burial "the Attendants scream out in a terrible Manner, which is not the Effect of grief but of Joy; they beat on their Wooden Drums, and the

Women with their rattles make a hideous Noise."[91] Sometimes one of the women would sing "a melancholy dirge, the chorus of which is performed by the whole of the other females, with admirable precision, and full-toned and not unmelodious voices." This "dirge" did not take "the strain of a hymn, or solemn requiem" but was "a loud and lively African air."[92]

The evidence that has survived from the colonial South strongly suggests the continuing significance of grave goods and points to four other similarities to the much more richly documented burial rites of West and West Central Africa and the Caribbean: the holding of a second burial ceremony, often some months after the interment of the corpse; the large numbers of slaves who attended both burials; the importance of instrumental and vocal music at graveside ceremonials; and the almost universal practice of holding both the first and the second burial after dark.[93]

Unfortunately, European reporters provided very few details about what actually happened at slave burials in the early South. However, what evidence is available indicates that graveside rituals were highly reminiscent of those known to have taken place in the British Caribbean. In 1766, for example, Georgia's Grand Jurors complained about the "rioting" that occurred at slave "funerals," by which no doubt they meant singing and dancing as well as feasting.[94] A decade later Janet Schaw, a Scottish traveler, attended the funeral of Jane Corbin, a white woman, at Point Pleasant Plantation in North Carolina. According to Schaw's account, "the Negroes assembled to perform their part of the funeral rites" for their mistress, "which they did by running, jumping, crying and [doing] various exercises."[95] Presumably, these "rites" were broadly similar, if not identical, to those they would have performed for one of their compatriots.

One of the earliest extant accounts of a second burial in the American South was penned by Henry Knight, who visited Virginia in 1816. Knight implied that when a planter's slave died it was usual for him to give "the rest a day, of their own choosing, to celebrate the funeral." This, he continued, was "perhaps a month after the corpse is interred." It was "a jovial day," on which those present "sing and dance and drink the dead to his new home, which some believe to be in old Guinea."[96]

Later reports suggest that, as in West and West Central Africa and the British Caribbean, there was no hard and fast rule in the American South as to the time allowed to elapse between first and second burials. An undated report from Gloucester, Virginia, intimated that the second burial might be "three days after death, or six months."[97] A similar variation was also mentioned by ex-slaves from Georgia.[98] Caroline Gilman was probably close to the truth of the matter when she commented that the precise timing of second burials, "where religious ceremonies are performed, and refreshments provided," depended upon the distance that family members and friends who were able to attend had to travel.[99]

In some instances deceased ancestors were commemorated annually. In mid-eighteenth-century Antigua, for example, they were venerated "on Christmas mornings."[100] The choice of Christmas day had no specifically Christian connotations. It was selected for the performance of this ritual simply because it was the custom in Antigua, as it was in all the plantation colonies, for slaves to be given Christmas day off. According to one report, "The Grave yards & burying places, both in Town & Country, would be crowded . . . with the friends and relatives of deceased persons strewing quarters of boiled, and roasted, meat; of fowls & yams & pouring bottles of Rum, upon the graves of their departed friends."[101] Very similar rituals, described by one contemporary as "the principal feasts . . . [the slaves] ever give," took place elsewhere in the British Caribbean.[102]

By the mid-eighteenth century another calendrical celebration associated with time off work at Christmas that some scholars believe was an adaptation of West and West Central African yam festivals was taking place: what became known variously in the New World plantation colonies as *John Canoe, John Cornu,* or *Jonkonnu.*[103] First described by Edward Long in the mid-1770s as taking place in Jamaica, the *Jonkonnu* festival was held "in the towns during the Christmas holidays." According to Long's description, *Jonkonnu* involved a parade consisting of "several tall robust fellows dressed up in grotesque habits, and a pair of ox-horns on their head, sprouting from the top of a horrid sort of vizor, or mask, which about the mouth is rendered very terrific with large boar-tusks." These men would go about the town, each of them "followed with a numerous crowd of drunken women, who refresh him frequently with a sup of aniseed water, whilst he dances at every door, bellowing out *John Connu!* with great vehemence." Perhaps because of what Long had gleaned from the participants, he concluded that the parade was "probably an honourable memorial of John Conny, a celebrated cabocero at *Tres Puntas,* in *Axim,* on the Guiny Coast."[104]

By the end of the eighteenth century *Jonkonnu* was well established in Jamaica and was celebrated elsewhere in the Caribbean in various forms. As Elizabeth Fenn has recently pointed out, *Jonkonnu* fulfilled similar functions to certain seasonal rituals performed by European underclasses. It entailed "sharp criticism of the privileged classes," and when the participants wore "white masks" or powdered their faces a "racial inversion" occurred that "turned plantation society into a world in which nothing was as it seemed—a world of uncertainty, confusion, and unlimited potential."[105]

For reasons that are not clear, *Jonkonnu,* in its elaborate Caribbean form, did not emerge as a major calendrical ritual in the Southern mainland. Music making and dancing were a part of the Christmastime festivities of slaves in the American South, but the costumes and parading associated with *Jonkonnu* seem to have been comparatively rare occurrences, and references to them date from the nineteenth century rather than the eighteenth. With one notable exception, the versions of *Jonkonnu* that were reported took place in North Carolina and Virginia rather than in the Lower South.[106] In 1843 Henry Benjamin Whipple, a visitor to St. Mary's, a town on the Georgia/Florida border, commented that December 27 was the "last day" of the slaves' Christmas holiday and that they referred to it as the "'great day.'" His description of what took place on that day closely resembles accounts of Caribbean *Jonkonnu* festivals. The slaves, Whipple wrote, "have paraded, with a corps of staff officers with red sashes, mock epaulettes & goose quill feathers, and a band of music composed of 3 fiddles, 1 tenor & 1 bass drum, 2 triangles & 2 tambourines and they are marching up & down the street in great style. They are followed by others, some dancing, some walking & some hopping, others singing, all as lively as can be." If any one refused to "join them they seize him & have a mock trial & sentence him to a flogging which is well laid on. Already they have had several such court martials." Any whites they encountered were expected to give them cash "& thus [they] find themselves in pocket money."[107] Whether this version of *Jonkonnu* was brought to this part of the Low Country directly from Africa or by slaves imported from the Caribbean and how long it had been performed there is not recorded. Nor is there any firm evidence that it was replicated elsewhere in the Low Country.

From the mid-seventeenth century in Barbados and by the late seventeenth century in the Chesapeake and South Carolina, the gathering together of "large numbers" of slaves for the celebration of religious rituals, especially after dark, was a matter for widespread white consternation. In 1687 nighttime burials were banned in Westmoreland County, Virginia, because the local authorities were convinced that they provided ideal cover for the planning and execution of rebellions.[108] Virginia planters may have known about the uprisings in Barbados in 1675, but had they not, Bacon's Rebellion, in which Africans participated, provided an alarming image of black militancy much closer to home.[109]

Whether for spiritual or secular reasons, or a mixture of both, slaves could and did evade legislation that sought to prevent them from associating with those on neighboring estates. They continued to congregate in significant numbers during the hours of darkness to celebrate the marriage of the living and the burial of their dead. If they so chose, planters and slave patrols could make life difficult for those who wished to attend such celebrations. However, in practice there was comparatively little they could do to prevent slaves from leaving their plantations after dark. As Charles Ball explained, all that had to be done was to wait until the owner or overseer was asleep and then slip off the plantation.[110]

Yet, as James Barclay's comments suggest, not all slaves had to resort to this kind of subterfuge in order to attend religious gatherings. Owners usually knew of the arrangements being made in the slave quarters for the celebration of a marriage; in fact, sometimes they contributed to the festivities. And they must have known, or suspected, that these festivities would not be confined to their own slaves. Similarly, they almost certainly knew of the arrangements that would be made for the interment of dead slaves. Their main concern was not to prevent these celebrations but to try to ensure that they did not get out of hand.[111]

Exactly the same was true of slave owners' dealings with those in the slave quarters whose influence rivaled, and arguably surpassed, their own: the sacred specialists who, by design or chance, had been placed on board the slave ships destined for the New World. The reputation of priests, prophets, herbalists, rainmakers, witch doctors, and witches and the reverence and fear in which they were held by African peoples survived the Middle Passage largely intact. In the Americas it was to these people, with their specialized and intimate knowledge of the spiritual "pasts" of Africa, that enslaved Africans turned, as they had always turned, for physical and spiritual curatives, for guidance and support, for protection, and for the mediation of their differences. The authority and prestige of sacred specialists varied both regionally and over time. However, for varying lengths of time in each of the plantation colonies they wielded a power that planters and the Anglican clergy alike could only envy.

By the mid-eighteenth century sacred specialists figured prominently in virtually every European account of Africans in the British Caribbean. Europeans frequently confused the activities and precise significance of different sacred specialists, more often than not employing the generic term Obeah, or Obi, abbreviated forms of the Ashanti word *Obaye*.[112] However, they were accurate on several points: It was generally held that "the Professors of *Obi* are, and always were, Natives of Africa, and none other" and that they had "brought the Science with them." This "Science," claimed Europeans, was "universally practiced" in the British Caribbean.[113]

In describing Obeah, Europeans wrongly applied the term to witchcraft or sorcery and often confused witches with Myalmen and women. In fact, Obeah was the result of a fusion of religious offices, several of which originally had overlapping powers and functions, and shared common beliefs and practices of different African peoples.[114] The fusion of functions is apparent in the powers that were ascribed to them by European observers. They included diagnosing and treating diseases—in Africa usually the work of a medicine man or a herbalist and sometimes a diviner; obtaining revenge for injuries or insults, or curing the bewitched—in Africa the responsibility of the witch doctor; the discovery and punishment of theft or adultery—in Africa the work of the diviner; and the prediction of future events—in Africa the work of highly trained mediums or diviners.[115]

The cultural traditions of the various religious specialists were preserved directly through the slave trade, the vehicle by which they were transported to the New World. Under the disintegrating effects of bondage, most of the regalia of the sacred specialists and the paraphernalia of their practices was lost. However, many, if not most, of the ancient remedies, magical potions and ornaments, rattling gourds, and feathers and animal parts used in the conduct of religious offices, survived. The sacred offices themselves also survived, but they too began to change. By the eighteenth century they reappeared in a different form known in all the plantation colonies as Obeah.

Most plantations in the British Caribbean were said to have at least one practitioner of Obeah, and Europeans generally agreed that those who inspired "the greatest Devotion and Confidence were the oldest and the most crafty."[116] It was also reported that there were a significant number of women among them. The "Devotion and Confidence" inspired by female sacred specialists was deeply rooted in African religious pasts and was unbroken by the Middle Passage. In their capacity as sacred specialists, as females, and as mothers, African women were to play a pivotal, and eventually a dual, role in the definition of the religious lives bondpeople carved out for themselves in the plantation colonies. They were "essential bearers of tradition" and among the "primary agents" in preserving and promoting "traditional (African-derived) culture [and] conventionally accepted modes of behaviour."[117] During the second half of the eighteenth century they would also become highly visible as agents of change and cultural redefinition.

Great secrecy surrounded the usually private practice of Obeah, but it seems clear that the conventional conceptions of male and female religious roles was reaffirmed in the New World. The majority of spiritual practitioners were probably men, but women continued to be prominent in the conduct of religious affairs. A "considerable part" of the African women sold into slavery in the Americas was reported to have been convicted of witchcraft. Many of them were found "distributing drugs; in particular such as occasion abortion."[118] Edward Long, a member of the Jamaican planter class and an early and powerful advocate of slavery, attributed the low birthrate among Jamaican slaves to various causes, among them a high ratio of men to women, the "unskillfulness and absurd management of the Negro midwifes," and the fact that many West African women— most of whom he thought were "common prostitutes"—"take specifics to cause abortions."[119]

Male and female sacred specialists used their knowledge of drugs and magic to attempt to heal the physical ailments suffered by their compatriots. In Jamaica, for example, it was said to be the usual practice on many plantations for slaves who suffered from "certain disorders—as yaws, ulcers, bone-ache, etc" to be cared for by "an elderly negro woman who professes a knowledge of this branch of physic."[120] That same knowledge of drugs and magic could also be used to manipulate and control relationships with owners or to intimidate fellow bondpeople. Quite exceptionally, given the secrecy surrounding Obeah, in Jamaica in 1775 an enslaved woman informed on "her Step-Mother (a woman of the *Popo* Country)" who "had put *Obi upon her.*" Convinced of her impending death, the younger woman "thought herself bound in Duty" to reveal to her owner "the true Cause of her Disorder." She also claimed that her "Step-Mother" had "put *Obi* . . . upon those who had lately died; and that the old Woman had practiced *Obi* for as many years past as she could remember."[121]

Some women continued to function as mediums, or oracles trained in possession by spirits of the gods or ancestors. The enslaved population of Surinam reportedly had "*locomen,* or pretended prophets," who were generally male, as well as "a kind of *Sibyls.*" A European account of "these sage matrons dancing and whirling round in the middle of an assembly, with amazing rapidity, until they foam at the mouth, and drop down as convulsed" is an apparent description of mediumistic possession.[122] In Africa the medium's power was benign, used to carry messages from the spirit world or to offer guidance to those who sought help. In the slave societies of the British Caribbean it was often used against the oppressors. According to one European account, "Whatever the prophetess orders to be done during this paroxysm, is most sacredly performed by the surrounding multitude; which renders these meetings extremely dangerous, as she frequently enjoins them to murder their masters, or desert to the woods."[123]

After witchcraft became pervasive during the rebellion of 1760, Myalism was introduced into Jamaica. The Myal society, a cult whose purpose was to identify and negate the influence of evil spirits that threatened danger or harm to the community as a whole and that sought to break the power of the witches, had its roots in the traditional West African religion, wherein the ceremony of public burial and resurrection culminated the long and complex training of witch doctors. In Edward Long's decidedly unsympathetic description of Myalism, "The lure hung out was, that every Negro, initiated into the Myal society, would be invulnerable by [sic] the white men; and, although they might in appearance be slain, the Obeah-man could, at his pleasure, restore the body to life." Long's account of the initiation rite of the Myal society sounds remarkably like the principal rite in the initiation of Azande witch doctors: "The method, by which this trick was carried on, was by a cold infusion of the herb *branched colalue*, which, after the agitation of dancing, threw the party into a profound sleep," or apparent death, which sometimes lasted for several hours.

A possession-inducing "Myal dance" formed part of the ceremony. One of the earliest descriptions of the dance as performed in Jamaica was written by Matthew Gregory Lewis, an absentee sugar planter who visited his estate in 1815/1816 and again in 1817. According to Lewis, the ministrations of the "chief Myal-man" were accompanied by "a great variety of grotesque actions, and chanting all the while something between a song and a howl, while the assistants, hand-in-hand, dance slowly round them in a circle, stamping the ground loudly with their feet to keep time with his chant." In time the initiate was restored to consciousness by the application of more medicine ("as yet unknown to whites"), and the Myal dance concluded. Armed with the secrets of magical potions and ointments, the newly initiated witch doctor was then prepared to fight against the malign activities of witches and heal those people who had been bewitched.[124] Myalism, and the frenzied possession-inducing Myal dance associated with it, later became the "Cumina" cult.[125]

Information on pre-Christian life in the Southern mainland is fragmentary. As with the communal rituals associated with marriage and death, what little survives suggests close similarities to that of the African peoples of the British Caribbean. Divination and healing were practiced; a rudimentary version of Obeah still functioned; and traditional male and female ritual leadership roles survived, particularly in the Low Country, which continued to receive African peoples until 1808. "Root doctors" played a prominent, if somewhat ambiguous, role in black and white life throughout the American South. Colonial governments sought both to repress and to exploit their skills; whites both feared and sought the herb-based skills of enslaved African "Doctors." The superiority of certain African cures over those prescribed by European doctors was tacitly conceded by the granting of cash payments, freedom from bondage, and sometimes both to slaves who revealed their knowledge of a remedy deemed to be in the public interest. In 1733, for example, an unnamed slave in Virginia was freed and granted a lifetime pension of £30 for discovering an "effectual Cure for all Distempers arising from an inveterate Scurvy, such as the Yawes, Lame Distemper, Pox, Dropsy etc." In the same year in South Carolina Caesar was freed by the General Assembly and awarded an annual allowance of £100 for life for his discovery of a "cure" for poison and "the bite of a rattlesnake."[126] Both men were probably African diviners or medicine men, perhaps former members of a religious cult whose purpose was to treat and cure specific diseases. Almost certainly their wide knowledge of the curative properties of herbs, plants, and roots had been handed down to them from other African medicine men, and they, in their turn, would pass on their knowledge to chosen members of the next generation. Like other sacred specialists, however, they were obliged to adapt their herbal expertise to the different ecosystems of British America.[127]

Traditional African healers, female as well as male, normally employed their extensive knowledge of medicinal herbs and poisonous substances for therapeutic relief, or as a defense against witchcraft and sorcery. But under conditions of New World bondage they also used their expertise to harm others. The skill, or art, of poisoning was one of the most powerful weapons available to enslaved Africans, and it was one that they were by no means reluctant to employ.[128]

Although there are many authenticated cases from both the British Caribbean and the American South of whites being poisoned by slaves, the actual number can never be known, if only because a growing white obsession with such a possibility meant that many unexpected deaths were mistakenly attributed to this cause. Court records offer a few clues but do not tell the whole story. In Virginia between 1740 and 1785, for example, a total of ninety slaves were accused of poisoning whites; thirty-five were convicted and sentenced to death. They comprised a microscopic proportion of Virginia's enslaved population.[129] Yet white fears of being poisoned by slaves were not entirely irrational. "Poisoning Offences" happened infrequently, but they happened often enough to intensify white anxieties.[130]

Slaves did not restrict the use of poison to their white "status enemies."[131] As in Africa, for those who had the knowledge, means, and opportunity poison was a convenient way of disposing of, or threatening, an adversary in the slave quarters. It is as difficult to determine how often slaves used poison against one another as it is to determine how often they used it against whites. Between 1745 and 1785 in Virginia, for example, forty-four, or under a quarter, of those tried for "Poisoning Offences" were charged with poisoning, or attempting to poison, another slave.[132] How many other undetected cases there might have been is a moot point. Similarly, there are few clues as to the precise nature of the jealousies and enmities that prompted the use, or the threatened use, of poison. Some of those who survived to tell the tale did so perhaps because they hoped to secure protection from their owners or to gain revenge on their assailants. In 1712, for example, a slave named George, who lived in King William County, Virginia, claimed that "his country men had poysened him for his wife."[133]

Although the details remain obscure, it is evident that the ability to administer poison and the herbal expertise that this often presupposed was a potent source of power within the slave quarters. As Matthew Gregory Lewis recorded, one of his slaves, a man named Adam, was "strongly suspected of having poisoned twelve negroes, men and women." Sometimes Adam administered the poison himself; sometimes he prevailed on others in the slave quarters to do it by threatening to take their lives. According to Lewis, "The terror thus produced was universal throughout the estate" and "several" bondpeople believed that "their lives were not safe while breathing the same air with Adam." Eventually Adam was put on trial, "but all the poisoning charges either went no further than strong suspicion, or . . . were not liable by the laws of Jamaica to be punished, except by flogging or temporary imprisonment." The situation was resolved, however, when a gun, some ammunition, and "a considerable quantity of materials for the practice of Obeah," were found in Adam's cabin. For these offenses Adam was sentenced to be transported from Jamaica and, according to Lewis, few, if any, of the enslaved people on the plantation were sorry to see him go.[134]

Herbal expertise employed for malevolent purposes was a source of power that directly threatened the lives and property interests of owners, and, for these most pragmatic of reasons, it was something that they and the colonial governments they dominated sought to destroy. No clear distinction was made, and by definition could not be made, by colonial legislators between benign and malevolent herbal practitioners; all were potentially suspect. The resultant legislation enacted by various colonial governments during the course of the eighteenth century differed only in detail. In addition to sanctioning the death penalty for slaves found guilty of "procuring, conveying or administering poison," colonial governments tried to prevent the spread of herbal expertise within and between generations by making it a capital offense for "any slave [to] teach or instruct another slave in the knowledge of any poisonous root, plant, herb, or other poison whatsoever." In an attempt to deny slaves easy access to deadly substances, whites were often forbidden to employ slaves "in the shops or places where they keep their medicines or drugs."[135] Despite these organized efforts to repress them, traditional African healers continued to ply their skills. Indeed, in the Southern mainland they succeeded in establishing a legacy for the black physicians trained through apprenticeships who began to appear during the Revolutionary War years and for the black medical profession that emerged in the mid- to late nineteenth century.[136]

It might have been expected that the Anglican clergy, who would have been incredulous at the proposition that Africans had been stripped bare of their religious cultures as a result of the Middle Passage, would sing the praises of planters and colonial governments for their attacks on the sacred specialists whose activities so appalled them. But, in fact, beginning with Morgan Godwyn, the clergy reserved some of their most vituperative language for the slave-owning members of their flocks. Anglican churchmen wanted something more than the suppression of sacred specialists and the total eradication of traditional African beliefs and practices. They insisted that these beliefs and practices be replaced in their entirety by Anglican beliefs and rituals. According to Godwyn, owners had to bear much of the responsibility for the fact that their slaves were not "being made *Christians*."[137] He would not be the last churchman to underestimate the strength of enslaved Africans' commitment to their traditional religious culture and sacred specialists or their antipathy to the Anglicanism deemed fit for their consumption.

Beginning in the last two decades of the seventeenth century saving the souls of enslaved Africans became an increasingly important imperative of the Church of England. The diametrically opposed agendas of the planters who the clergy sought to convince and of the slaves who they strove equally hard to convert combined to ensure that before the mid-eighteenth century Protestant Christianity would feature scarcely at all in the private lives of the enslaved populations of the British plantation colonies.

3

THE ANGLICANS

EARLY ATTEMPTS AT CONVERSION

From the mid-seventeenth century onward, many European visitors to the British plantation colonies were scandalized by what they saw there: the brutal physical treatment of enslaved Africans and the virtually universal refusal of Christian planters to tend to the assumed spiritual needs of men and women who continued to cling tenaciously to the *"Ceremonies of Religion"* and "Customs" they had "brought out of Africa."[1] Anglican churchmen, including Richard Baxter,[2] who never visited the Americas, and Morgan Godwyn, who did, sought to refute the reasons given by planters for refusing to proselytize their slaves and to stimulate metropolitan interest in securing that end.

The extensive lobbying carried out in England by Godwyn,[3] Francis Brokesby,[4] and Thomas Bray,[5] bore fruit in 1701 with the founding of the Society for the Propagation of the Gospel in Foreign Parts (SPG), an organization that had as one of its main goals the conversion of enslaved Africans.[6] In each of the plantation colonies, the missionary activities sponsored by the Society and, beginning in the 1720s, those initiated by another Anglican group based in London, the Associates of the Late Reverend Dr. Thomas Bray, would meet with a combination of fierce hostility and total indifference from planters and slaves alike. The Church of England would play only a modest part in the conversion of African Americans to Protestant Christianity, and this despite the fact that during the first half of the eighteenth century it enjoyed a virtual monopoly on missionary work in the plantation colonies.

In Barbados, the mid-seventeenth-century efforts of Quakers to instruct slaves did not long survive the repressive measures enacted by that island's planter-dominated government.[7] In South Carolina, the Huguenot exiles who settled in the Low Country during the 1680s and 1690s displayed little interest in trying to convert their slaves. In keeping with their Anglican neighbors, they feared that slaves might employ Christian doctrines as a means of securing either an amelioration of their conditions of servitude or—the most alarming prospect of all—their liberation from slavery.[8]

In South Carolina, as in the other plantation colonies, by the early eighteenth century there was some interaction between enslaved Africans and other Protestant sects and denominations, most notably Baptists and Presbyterians. But these groups did not embark upon concerted missionary activity among slaves until the middle of the century.[9] The Church of the Brethren, more commonly known as the Moravians, would in time attract significant numbers of black converts, particularly in the British Caribbean. The Moravians began their missionary work in the Americas in 1732, but in the Danish rather than in the British Caribbean. The plan they devised in the mid-1730s to establish a mission in South Carolina came to nothing, and it was not until 1754 that they installed a station in Jamaica, the first of any in the British plantation colonies.[10]

The Anglican clergy, who had the missionary field virtually to themselves, waxed lyrical about how *"fond and desirous"* enslaved Africans were "of being made *Christians.*"[11] From their perspective, the main obstacles to their missionary activities were Anglican planters who constantly denied them access to the slaves they sought to convert. Planters, they insisted, were largely to blame for the continuing attachment of enslaved Africans to their traditional religious cultures.[12] The clergy mistakenly assumed that if only they could secure the backing of elite Anglican planters they could be certain of reaping a rich harvest of African souls for the Church of England. Beginning, perhaps, with Morgan Godwyn, the clergy consistently underestimated the strength and vitality of the traditional African beliefs and practices they so abhorred and were so determined to totally eradicate. From first to last, Anglican churchmen retained a supreme, and largely misplaced, confidence in their own ability, if offered the opportunity, to completely transform the religious lives of enslaved Africans. They signally failed to appreciate that slaves found it difficult, if not impossible, to identify closely with either them or their version of Protestant Christianity.

Some of the early Anglican missionaries claimed to detect encouraging signs. In 1713, for instance, Reverend Taylor reported approvingly from St.

Andrew's Parish, in South Carolina, that two of his women parishioners had "taken extraordinary pain to instruct a considerable number of their Negroes, loose and wicked, in the principles of the Christian religion." Taylor was delighted by their ability "to rehearse the Apostles Creed, and the Ten Commandments, and the Lord's Prayer . . . very distinctly and perfectly." Fourteen of them were "so very desirous to be baptized" that he "thought it my duty to do it."[13]

Taylor's "two Gentlewomen" parishioners were great exceptions to the general rule of animosity or apathy displayed by South Carolina's Anglican planters toward the attempted conversion of their slaves. Reverend Francis Le Jau, who assumed the living of Goose Creek Parish in 1708, constantly complained about the obstinate refusal of his parishioners to send their slaves to him for instruction. In 1709 Le Jau set aside one day a week for the religious education of "Children, Servants and Slaves," but so few slaves attended his classes that within six months he decided that a new approach was needed. His next tactic was to organize a class for slaves who were permitted, or required, by their owners to attend Sunday services. By this means he was able to attract a weekly audience of around fifty people.[14]

One of the more familiar arguments employed by Le Jau's parishioners was that the religious instruction of their slaves would make them "proud and Undutiful."[15] A similar view had long prevailed in Barbados, and in Virginia it was also widely held that Christianity not only made bond-people "prouder" but also "infuses them with thoughts of freedom."[16] Anticipating what by the mid-eighteenth century would become a central theme in the effort to win over Anglican owners, Le Jau insisted that the reverse was true: Christian slaves, he claimed, could be depended upon as being docile, obedient, and productive workers. Moreover, he tried to reassure owners that, in his parish at any rate, baptism would be no formality. As required by the Church of England, baptism would be preceded by a period of instruction, and slaves would not be baptized unless and until they could display a satisfactory knowledge of "the Creed, the Lord's Prayer . . . the Commandments [and] the Catechism" based on teaching that Le Jau would tailor to their "Want and Capacity."[17] All baptismal candidates would be required to swear two oaths of Le Jau's devising "in the Presence of God and before this Congregation."[18] This plan was an indication, perhaps, that the missionary appreciated, and sought to exploit, the significance attached to sacred oaths by the African-born people who comprised the majority of his black parishioners.

The first oath required catechumens to swear that they were not seeking baptism in order to secure their freedom from slavery. This was designed to placate owners as well as to quash any hopes slaves might have entertained that baptism would automatically result in their liberation.[19] The second oath sought to replace "Polygamie" with Anglican standards of sexual morality. Baptismal candidates had to "promise truly to keep to the Wife you have now till Death dos [*sic*] part you."[20] This demand reflected the Anglican insistence that Africans who sought admission into the Church of England must instantly, and unconditionally, abandon their cultural and religious traditions as well as giving up all hope of securing their secular freedom.

As far as most of Goose Creek's Anglican planters were concerned, both oaths were meaningless. They did not regard the first as providing a cast-iron guarantee of docility; the second addressed an aspect of slave life that was of little interest to them. Far more worrisome to them than the sexual mores of their bondpeople was the truculent, if not the overtly rebellious, behavior that they expected from Christian slaves. An incident in 1709–10, which significantly involved the earliest extant record of the millennial theme in African American Protestant Christianity, seemed to lend credence to their concerns.

Early in 1710 Le Jau reported to his superiors in London that "thro his Learning . . . The best scholar of all the negroes" in Goose Creek, "a very sober and honest Liver," seemed "likely to Create some Confusion among all the Negroes in the County." Apparently this man had placed his own interpretation "upon some Words of the Holy Prophet's which he had read" concerning "the several judgmnts. that Chastise Men because of their Sins in these latter days." Whether he included slaveholding among these "Sins" is unclear. What is clear, however, is that this man had "told his Master abruptly that there wou'd be a dismal time and the Moon wou'd be turn'd into Blood, and there wou'd be dearth of darkness." His dire prophecies had been overheard by another slave, and soon "it was publickly blazed abroad that an Angel came and spake to the Man, he had seen a hand that gave him a Book, he had heard Voices, he had seen fires, etc."[21]

Le Jau tried to dispel both the possible expectations of Goose Creek's enslaved population and the anxieties of their owners by remonstrating with the man whose remarks had stirred up so much excitement and ordering him "not to speak so." Initially the man refused to recant, "ingeniously" insisting upon the truth of what he had read in the Scriptures— presumably in the Old Testament or in the Book of Revelations—but eventually "promised" Le Jau that he would not "speak so" in the future.[22] Le Jau may have extracted this "promise" not so much by the force of his arguments as by simply reminding the man, if he needed any reminder, of the brutal punishments meted out to slaves who offended in this way.

Over the next few weeks Le Jau reflected on the possible implications of this episode. His understandable concern was that black Christians were placing their own interpretation upon what he had taught them and upon what some of them were able to read for themselves in the Bible.[23] The spiritual authority and leadership being asserted by the man whose prophecies had caused such a furor directly challenged Le Jau's claim to be the sole and undisputed font of religious knowledge in Goose Creek. Le Jau believed that he had managed to silence this dangerous voice and reassert his own authority, but for how long? This was a question that sorely vexed the missionary in the spring of 1710.

As Le Jau saw it, the problem was not that Africans lacked the capacity to think for themselves but that they *were* thinking for themselves. He believed, however, that they were incapable of making "good use" of what they had been taught. Le Jau thought that he might have inadvertently encouraged the agitation in his parish by allowing catechumens "to ask Questions." He also pondered the wisdom of teaching slaves to read as part of their preparation for baptism. Access to the Scriptures, he concluded, ought to be closely controlled, and it would be most politic to let owners make the decision as to whether or not their catechumens be taught how to read.[24] Le Jau seemed oblivious to the fact that slaves would not conveniently discard the reading skills they had already acquired or desist from passing them on to their children and compatriots in the slave quarters.

Three years later Le Jau was greatly reassured by the apparent non-involvement of his black parishioners in what proved to be an abortive rebellion organized by a group of slaves "living upon the North side of the Cooper River." To Le Jau's immense relief, not a single slave in Goose Creek was charged with having known about, let alone having participated in, this projected uprising. It must have seemed to the missionary that his authority was secure when some of his black parishioners declared that, in future, if they heard that a rebellion was being planned they would immediately inform him of the fact. Le Jau was confident he could trust them, "knowing them to be exemplary Pious and Honest."[25]

No doubt for very different reasons, Le Jau's white parishioners were as relieved as their minister. However, they were not sufficiently persuaded by this turn of events to agree with him that the conversion of their slaves would be greatly to their secular advantage. As far as most of them were concerned, even if they did not always achieve the desired end result, the gallows, public burnings and whippings, shackles, and branding irons did at least have the merit of not lending themselves to any possibility of misinterpretation. Physical, rather than spiritual, coercion was, and for many years would remain, the method favored by South Carolina's Anglican planters in their continuing quest to secure placid and productive black workers.

Despite the alarms of 1709–10 and 1713, Le Jau was generally pleased by the conduct of Goose Creek's black Christians but frustrated by the fact that there were so few of them. At any given time he might be instructing forty or fifty bondpeople, but between 1708 and 1715, when his parish contained somewhere around 2,000 slaves, he managed to baptize only 19 of them.[26] By the end of his decade in Goose Creek Le Jau had little to show for his efforts. He believed that his intercessions might have prompted a few modest improvements in the physical treatment of the slaves in his parish, but the "profane & Inhumane practices" that so appalled him continued unabated.[27] There was little evidence that the Anglican message he championed had led to any fundamental reorientation of the religious beliefs and practices of more than a handful of slaves.

Le Jau's experiences, and those of the few slaves he instructed and baptized, were typical of the first twenty or so years of the Anglican missionary endeavor in the plantation colonies. Nowhere were the limited achievements of that endeavor more starkly revealed than in the replies received by Edmund Gibson, the bishop of London, to the questionnaire he sent to the colonial clergy in 1723 asking them to report on the progress they had made in converting the slaves in their parishes. Whether from the Southern mainland or the sugar islands, these replies were virtually interchangeable. A few clergymen openly admitted that they were encountering such opposition from local planters that they were not attempting to instruct slaves and had no plans to try to do so in the foreseeable future. Most continued to pin the blame for their failure on the owners rather than on the slaves in their parishes.[28]

Gibson was so appalled by these replies that in 1727 he fired off two abrasive pastoral letters that would have left the clergy and laity of the plantation colonies in no doubt as to what he expected and demanded of them.[29] The bishop conceded that there were two problems associated with the instruction of slaves, but he claimed that neither was insurmountable. The first, something that the colonial clergy were often reluctant to acknowledge, was that "grown persons" imported from Africa were "accustomed to the Pagan Rites and Idolatries of their own Country and prejudiced against all other Religions, particularly the Christian, as forbidding that licentiousness which is usually practis'd among the Heathen."[30]

Secondly, Gibson understood that in the case of newly imported slaves language could prove problematical, but he insisted that this did not apply to the children because, "like all other Children," they "may be easily trained up to any Language whatsoever." Moreover, and clearly underestimating the significance of parental and kin influences, the bishop argued that children would be less resistant to Christianity than their parents because they had "never been accustomed to the Pagan Rites and Superstitions" of Africa.[31] Although Gibson did not elaborate on this point, it is possible to detect here the beginnings of a strategy of focusing on slave children, a scheme that would become a central part of Anglican missionary activity during the quarter century or so before the American Revolution.

Gibson also hinted at an important change of direction that would become closely allied with the targeting of children: ending the virtual monopoly enjoyed by the clergy in the instruction of slaves. Gibson believed that "many Negroes" quickly learned enough English to enable them to cope with "the ordinary Business of life" and proposed that those who seemed "more capable and serious than the rest" might be persuaded to present the Anglican message to their compatriots in the slave quarters "in their own Language."[32] Bishop Gibson seems to have been the first to appreciate the influence that African preachers could exert on their own people.

The bishop's comments did not prompt a groundswell of support in any of the plantation colonies for proselytizing slaves, young or old. During the late 1720s and 1730s the colonial clergy continued to complain about the obstructive attitude of all but a few Anglican planters and the minuscule number of slaves they were instructing and baptizing.[33] Only for a brief time in Virginia did it seem that Bishop Gibson's tart comments might be having some effect.

Like their counterparts in the other plantation colonies, Virginia's Anglican planters were adamant that the proselytization of their slaves would not produce compliant Christian servants. Their fear that slaves would draw their own conclusions about the relationship between Christianity and bondage were fully realized in 1731 when one, and possibly two, slave uprisings were at least partially inspired by how enslaved people were interpreting Christian teaching. As in Goose Creek, by the late 1720s millennialism had emerged as a vitally significant ingredient of the Protestant Christianity of Virginia's enslaved population.

The Anglican clergy who worked in Virginia were not oblivious to the fact that, as one of them explained to Bishop Gibson in 1729, "although some of the Negroes are sincere converts," most of those who received instruction did so for two other reasons. First, they hoped that by so doing "they shall meet with so much the more respect" from their co-religionist owners.[34] In other words, Christian beliefs could help ameliorate slaves' conditions of servitude. Second, some slaves believed that "at some time or another Christianity will help them to their freedom."[35]

These words proved prophetic because in 1731 Virginia was swept with rumors of an impending slave rebellion. Several slaves were taken in for questioning and when "Examined" cited their conversion to Christianity as the justification for their intended uprising. Despite "all the precautions Ministers took to assure them that Baptism altered nothing as to their servitude or other temporal circumstances . . . they were willing to fool themselves with a . . . fancy that it did."[36] With or without the assistance of the clergy, some enslaved people in Virginia had reached the conclusion that Christianity and bondage were incompatible and that if freedom continued to be denied them, they had every right to resort to force in order to secure their liberation. Moreover, they were convinced that there were those in England who would support them in their armed struggle. The Virginia authorities never tracked down the source of the apparently widespread conviction that no less a person than the king of England had "ordered all those slaves free that were christians" but his instructions had been "Suppressed."[37] Almost certainly, it was this belief rather than any dramatic change of heart on the part of Virginia planters or their slaves that explained the sudden surge of slave enthusiasm for religious instruction in 1729 and 1730.[38]

The abortive rebellion of 1731 did not dispel the millennial hopes that had partially inspired it. And, predictably, this projected uprising, and another that was nipped in the bud a few weeks later,[39] further stiffened the resolve of Anglican planters not to permit the religious instruction of their slaves. Bishop Gibson's demands and his novel suggestion that the clergy focus their attention on enslaved children fell on deaf ears. It was not until 1740 that the bishop's proposal was taken up in what, at face value, was the most unpromising environment of South Carolina.

The architect of the plan to open a school for black children in Charleston, which was unveiled in 1740, was Reverend Alexander Garden, who, sixteen years earlier, had informed Bishop Gibson that "no means are used for the Conversion" of the roughly 2,000 slaves in his parish of St. Philip's.[40] The year the plan was put forth would not seem to have been the most auspicious one in which to propose to South Carolina's Anglican planters that they tend to the religious instruction of their slaves, young or old. Three years earlier, the pages of *The South Carolina Gazette* had crackled with the news of the failed Antiguan slave uprising of 1736.[41] The news could have only confirmed the fears of white Carolinians as to what they might expect from their own predominantly African-born enslaved population, a population that heavily outnumbered them.

In the Antigua uprising, "many hundred Slaves" had "by drinking a Health in Rum or some other Liquor mixt with Grave Dirt and some time cock-blood infused [sworn] an Oath of Secrecy and Fidelity." These oaths varied somewhat, "but the tenor was to stand and be true to each other, and to kill the Whites, Man, Woman and Child . . . and to suffer Death rather than discover." According to one commentator, there was a subplot involving Christian slaves who when "Swearing the Multitude to their Scheme swore them and administered the Sacrament to all such as professed themselves Christians, according to the rites of the Bishop's Church; the others they swore according to their several Country forms." This, the anonymous reporter concluded, was "a Specimen of what may be expected from Converting Negroes."[42]

Closer to home, in 1739, as the South Carolinians were still digesting the news from Antigua, the Low Country was rocked by the Stono Rebellion. White commentators ascribed this uprising to the machinations of the Spanish, but they also acknowledged the significance of the shared African past and religious beliefs of many of the black rebels. As John Thornton has recently pointed out, Christianity appears to have been a central theme in the Stono Rebellion, but it was a Christianity that had been shaped in Africa rather than in the New World. The Kongolese people imported into the Carolina Low Country during the 1720s and 1730s came from an African nation that, ever since the conversion of King Nzinga Nkuwu to Roman Catholicism in 1491, had been "proud of their Christian and Catholic heritage, which they believed made them a distinctive people." Hence, the black insurgents were bound by a common religious ideology and, moreover, one that enabled them to identify more closely with the offers of freedom being made to them by their Spanish co-religionists in Florida.[43]

The Stono Rebellion was important for many reasons, and not least of all because it provided additional ammunition for the planters who for many years had been adamant that by permitting the religious instruction of their slaves they were simply asking for trouble. Antigua and Stono provided ample evidence of what form that trouble might take. Under the circumstances, it might seem highly surprising that Alexander Garden's project secured any support at all in and around Charleston.

By 1740 many Low Country planters were beginning to worry about how their slaves might interpret the fiery evangelical message being preached by George Whitefield. Whitefield, an English preacher who had arrived in Georgia two years earlier, and Garden clashed violently on doctrinal matters. They also disagreed about what had and had not been done by Anglicans to proselytize South Carolina's bondpeople.[44] Early in 1740 Whitefield penned a scathing piece in which he accused Anglican planters of so grossly abusing both the bodies and the souls of their slaves that it was remarkable that "we have not more instances of self-murder . . . or that they have not frequently risen up in arms against their owners." Whitefield warned planters that if they continued to ignore their Christian responsibilities toward their slaves then they must expect divine retribution. Whitefield concluded that the Stono Rebellion and a recent epidemic of "smallpox and fever" in the Low Country were "judgments" that must surely convince them that unless they repented then they too "must in like manner expect to perish."[45]

Garden responded with a spirited, if not an entirely convincing, reply in which he conceded that Anglican owners took "little or no proper Care . . . of the Souls of their Slaves." In part, he claimed, this was because of the lack of "one certain uniform Method of Teaching" bondpeople.[46] The school that Garden proposed to open in Charleston would provide such a "certain uniform Method." Almost certainly, Garden hoped that his institution would appeal to planters as a way of nullifying the impact of the evangelical Protestantism already beginning to infiltrate the slave quarters of the Low Country through the preaching of Hugh and Jonathan Bryan, Whitefield's two most eminent converts in South Carolina.[47]

The familial transmission of Anglican beliefs was at the heart of Garden's scheme and, like Bishop Gibson, he appreciated the potential influence of black preachers. Within a few years, he claimed, a relatively small cadre of trained black missionaries would be able to disseminate Anglicanism on a scale out of all proportion to their number.[48] There was a traditional gender dimension to Garden's conception of missionary work that could not have been more different from the gender equality implicit in evangelical Protestantism. Without exception, the future missionaries to be trained in his school would be young men.

When Garden was unable to persuade elite Anglican planters to fund his scheme he turned to the SPG for help, and over the course of the next two decades that organization provided the bulk of the funding he required. It was with money provided by the Society for the Propagation of the Gospel that Garden purchased the two boys, "Harry of 14 and Andrew of 15," who would be the school's first pupils and, in time, its first teachers.

Both boys had been baptized and, although they could recite the catechism, both were illiterate. After eight months of intensive tuition, Harry was proving "an Excellent Genius," and Garden believed that in another six months he would be fully qualified to teach in his school. Andrew was less intellectually gifted, but Garden was confident that he too would soon qualify as a teacher.[49]

Garden's "Negroe School House" opened in September 1742 and by the following spring had an enrollment of around thirty pupils. Garden confidently predicted that within a couple of years the school would be turning out up to forty qualified missionaries a year.[50] He continued to send glowing reports to his backers in London but by the late 1740s was forced to concede that he had not managed to reach his annual target of graduates.[51] No one disputed the number of boys Garden claimed attended the school (who were taught mainly by Harry), but few would have claimed that those who passed through doors prior to its closure in 1768 made any significant difference to the religious lives of the vast majority of enslaved people who lived in Charleston and its environs. Visitors to the Low Country and many of the resident clergy continued to register their shock and despair at what they depicted as the irreligion of the region's enslaved people.[52]

It was not until 1760 that the Anglicans made an attempt to formally target slave children in Virginia and North Carolina. In the meantime, the SPG continued to support the religious instruction of slaves of all ages in these two colonies by supplying hymnals, prayer books, and other religious literature for use by the clergy. Despite their support for Garden's school and their agreement to fund that established by Thomas Thompson at Cape Coast Castle,[53] the SPG did not become involved in the founding of schools for slave children in the Chesapeake. Another Anglican organization, the Associates of the Late Reverend Dr. Bray, founded in the 1720s, took the initiative.[54] The Associates were already funding schools in the Northern colonies when, in the late 1750s, they turned their attention to Virginia and North Carolina.[55] The large, sprawling parishes of the Chesapeake and the continuing recalcitrance of Anglican planters and their slaves, virtually guaranteed that their efforts would meet with but minimal success.

Notwithstanding the string of gloomy responses from the local clergy to their initiative, the Associates pressed ahead with their plan, and in the early 1760s, schools for enslaved children were opened in Williamsburg, Norfolk, and Fredericksburg.[56] The best that could be said of the Williamsburg school before it closed in 1773 is that in terms of pupil enrollment it held its own. Numbers remained steady at around thirty, but it often proved difficult to fill the places on offer because many owners withdrew their slave children from school as soon as they were old enough to work or they sent them to school only when they could find no work for them.[57]

Yet, meager though the numbers were, more slave children received a formal, if irregular, education with a strong Anglican component in Williamsburg than did those anywhere else in Virginia. If anything, the reports sent to the Associates of Dr. Bray from Norfolk and Fredericksburg made for even bleaker reading than those from Williamsburg. But the story was essentially the same: the poor performance of the schools was due to the lack of local support and, in Norfolk, an Anglican minister who was at odds with some of his most influential parishioners.[58] The extensive literary evidence concerning Anglican attempts to establish schools for slave children should not be allowed to obscure the fact that those that were founded were of only marginal significance in relation to the ever-increasing enslaved populations of the Southern mainland. The children who attended them, often intermittently, comprised a modest proportion of those in their age group. Anglican planters remained unenthusiastic about the education of their slaves, whatever their age.

In 1771, in what proved to be the last significant metropolitan Anglican appeal to the consciences and pocketbooks of their co-religionists in the Southern colonies, the Associates of Dr. Bray sent forty copies of a tract entitled "A Letter to an American Planter from his Friend in London" to their supporters in Williamsburg.[59] The main significance of this piece, penned by the organization's secretary, Reverend John Waring, is not that it changed colonial Anglican attitudes but that it could have been written by Bishop Gibson in the 1720s, or even by Morgan Godwyn in the 1680s. Waring's "Letter" contained no fresh arguments or insights. On the eve of the American Revolution the gulf between metropolitan churchmen and Anglican planters was as deep and as unbridgeable as it had ever been.

The schools founded in the Southern mainland were innovative, but otherwise there was something of a static quality about the Anglican missionary endeavor during the first three quarters of the eighteenth century. Colonial churchmen continued to ascribe most of the difficulties they were encountering to the intransigence of Anglican slave owners rather than to the obstinacy of the slaves whose souls they were bent on saving for the Church of England. They never fully grasped the real reasons why they and the doctrines and rituals they sought to promote proved so unattractive and so unpalatable to the enslaved populations of the plantation colonies.

It may well be asked why enslaved Africans should have found the Anglicanism presented to them in any way appealing. The relevant question, perhaps, is not why so few slaves sought admission to the Church of England but why so many did. Anglican owners believed that it was because they saw Christianity as a viable means of ameliorating the conditions of their bondage or, more dangerously, as a sufficient justification for seeking an end to that bondage altogether. Both those assumptions were correct. That black Anglicans remained few and far between in each of the plantation colonies throughout the colonial period was not simply because owners sought to prevent their slaves from receiving instruction. The truth of the matter was that the vast majority of bondpeople found little in Anglicanism with which they could or wished to identify; they were offered no convincing, or compelling, reasons to abandon their traditional beliefs and rituals in favor of those espoused by the colonial clergy.

The colonial clergy themselves were scarcely prepared to spread Anglicanism in the slave quarters. None had received specific training as a missionary.[60] Moreover, many of those who served in the plantation colonies were British or had been educated in Britain, and their social attitudes and expectations both reflected and served to reinforce elite ideals of a strictly ordered and orderly society.[61] The relationship forged in the plantation colonies between the clergy and elite Anglican planters was mutually reinforcing: The spiritual authority of the one was used to bolster the secular authority of the other.[62]

It was also the case, however, that although they received their livings from the bishop of London and ultimately were answerable to him, the colonial clergy were in many ways dependent upon the eminent local planters who controlled the vestries. They could ill afford to offend these influential patrons, and few were prepared to do so, especially over the question of proselytizing slaves. It was one thing to criticize local planters in the privacy of their letters to London but another matter entirely to publicly voice those criticisms, let alone to go against the express wishes of owners and instruct their slaves. Planters could be easily "Disobliged" by ministers who displayed an "overactive zeal in Instructing and Baptizing Slaves." As Reverend Alexander Rhonnald of Norfolk, Virginia, discovered, to upset "the Great Ones" in this way was to be "branded . . . as a Negro Parson" and to be "vilified." Rhonnald, who nevertheless took pride in the fact that he taught and baptized "more Negroes than other brethren here" and who refused to be intimidated by "the Great Ones," was a great exception.⁶³

The attitude of the clergy toward the slaves who came voluntarily or were sent by their owners for instruction was, at best, patronizing. There were those, such as Le Jau, who empathized with their plight, but that empathy did nothing to lessen or to undermine the social, racial, and doctrinal deference they demanded from their enslaved catechumens. The finer points of Christian theology might be discussed over a glass of port with the local gentry, but they were not matters that the clergy expected to negotiate with underclass whites, let alone with enslaved Africans. Underclass whites and slaves were there to be instructed, to be talked down to, rather than to be talked with; they were there to listen rather than to be listened to. It was the exceptional Anglican minister who reported, as did Reverend Benjamin Dennis in 1711, *"discoursing with* one of the Negroes."⁶⁴

The clergy expected their enslaved catechumens to absorb uncritically doctrines that were predicated upon the generally assumed intellectual inferiority of Africans and designed to emphasize the meekness, humility, and obedience, the duties and the obligations, demanded of the Christian servant. Catechumens and Christian slaves were told constantly that their reward for a lifetime of blind, unthinking submission would be "plenty of all good things . . . in the other world, after they die." The earthly reward held out to them was not the prospect of eventual manumission but, provided they did "their work without knavery or murmuring," an amelioration of their servitude. The Christian God, they were promised, would "put it into their masters hearts to be kind" to obedient, hardworking slaves but could be depended upon to punish "all roguery, mischief, and lying, either before death or after it." Fractious black Christians must expect to be physically corrected by their owners, and "after death . . . God would give them to the Devil to burn in his place."⁶⁵ This was the uncompromising message Anglican clergy constantly sought to hammer home from their pulpits and in their catechismal classes.

The slaves who underwent instruction, were baptized, and became communicants of the Church of England were reminded of their lowly and inferior status every time they attended church. As in England, seating arrangements in colonial churches both reflected and reinforced differences in social rank. In the plantation colonies, they served also to emphasize racial distinctions. As Morgan Godwyn remarked of late-seventeenth-century Barbados, "the Negro's . . . were quartered in the most distant part of the Meeting-Place."⁶⁶

Exactly the same was true of Anglican churches in the Southern main-land, where blacks and whites, slave and free, were seated separately, often at the insistence of elite-dominated vestries. In the early 1770s, for ex-ample, "a number of Poor White People" petitioned the vestry of St. Michael's Church in Charleston for permission "to carry chairs to the church, to be placed in the Aile [sic] for seats." The "Gentlemen" of the vestry agreed to this request and arranged "to have Benches made, and fix'd in the Aile [sic] leading from the No. to the So. Door, and others near the Pulpit solely to be appropriated to the use of the Poor White People." The sexton was ordered to "remove the Benches the property of Negroes, now plac'd in these places, either into the Gallerys, or under the Belfry—and no Negroes should be permitted to sit on the Benches."[67] Farther north, in Portsmouth, Virginia, black Anglicans were "not allowed to sit with whites" but made to sit "next to the door, on both sides [on] two benches painted black."[68] In Alexandria's Christ Church, two pews "below the stairs" were set aside for black church members and another two were reserved for poor whites.[69]

The spatial distancing of free and enslaved church members at Sunday services was the visible statement of a spiritual distancing firmly grounded in white Anglicans' pervasive racism. White and black Anglicans might worship the same god and cohabit the same local church, but as far as white Anglicans were concerned, the racial boundaries that characterized the world outside the church must also be strictly maintained within it. Should black Anglicans ever be audacious enough to behave in a way that seemed to ignore or blur those lines, then there were those white church members who were only too eager to remind them of their place. An episode that occurred during a baptismal ceremony in the parish church of Fredericksville, in Virginia, at the end of the 1750s exemplified the rigid racial divisions that white Anglicans sought to enforce.

According to Reverend James Maury, who held the Fredericksville living between the mid-1750s and his death in 1770,[70] "when the white People presented their Children for Baptism at the Altar . . . some Negroes, as has constantly been the Custom I believe, all over the Colony, advanced at the same Time to present theirs also, As far as I observed, they behaved mod-estly & orderly, neither crowding nor jostling their Betters." At this point, "Mr. Thomas Johnson, a Warden of this Parish, thought proper to order them to withdraw. And, in obedience to him, tho' with some seeming Re-luctance, they . . . Return[ed] to their Seats." Maury, who seems to have been somewhat surprised at Johnson's intervention, "called to them, when they were near half way down the Isle [sic], to stop & return, telling them . . . that Mr. Johnson only intended to keep them at a due distance from, & to caution them against intermingling with, the white People." But what Johnson really meant was that "they should be entirely gone, that, as warden, it was his Duty to preserve the order in that Place, & that he would not allow Whites & Blacks to be baptized together."

Maury thought that the "solemnity of the Place" and the occasion "rendered altercation improper & indecent" and he continued baptizing the white children. When he had finished he inquired of his congregation, or more specifically of its black members, whether there were any more children to be baptized. There were not. Maury "conjectured" that "the Blacks" had been "intimidated . . . by the warden's peremtory [*sic*] repeated orders, [and] adventured not to present any of their Children, &. . . carried them away all unbaptized."[71]

Maury, one of those exceptional Anglican clergymen who empathized with his black parishioners, was incensed by Johnson's behavior and took up the matter of what he described as an "outrage against Christianity" with Commissary Dawson. He pondered on the reasons why Johnson, and other of his white parishioners, took such great exception to biracial baptismal services. He ruled out the possibility that it might be the "unsavoury Effluvia from those African constitutions" that prompted their objections because, after all, they tolerated it for hours at a time from their domestic servants. So on what grounds could they possibly object "to submitting to the same for a few Minutes once a Month"?[72] In Maury's opinion, Johnson's action had been prompted by something else, by something rather more sinister but no less racist. His intent, Maury suggested, had been to "drive" slaves from the church by denying them and their children the right of baptism.

Somewhat dramatically, Maury then went on to claim that if Johnson and his supporters were not stopped it would not be very long before "many white People [will] be excluded from that Sacrament, under the pretence of [having] fetid Feet, or strong Breath, a nauseous Distemper, or some other Pretence, as plausible for debarring these, as what is urged for excluding Blacks." The time might come, Maury concluded, when "Poverty, Sordid & tattered Apparel, or even a dirty Face [is] deemed by the haughty & over delicate a sufficient Bar against admission into the christian church."[73]

Clearly, Maury empathized as much with underclass whites as he did with slaves, but he was appalled by the revelation of such deep-seated racism on the part of one of his church wardens and among the white members of his congregation. Johnson and his supporters had made no secret of their wish to segregate the ceremony of baptism, if not to totally deny enslaved people entry into the Church of England. This blatant racism was not lost on the slaves who were already communicant members of the church, and it can scarcely have encouraged those in the slave quarters who might have been contemplating the possibility of joining them. In practice, and contrary to what some bondpeople might have hoped and expected, baptism offered little guarantee of respect from their white coreligionists and absolutely no prospect of advancement within the church. It was inconceivable to the clergy and elite-dominated vestries, as it was to their white parishioners, that underclass white men, let alone enslaved black Anglicans, should be appointed as church wardens. At best, admission to the Church of England offered black Anglicans the most grudging acceptance by their white co-religionists.

By 1740 the virtual monopoly on religious belief and practice sought by the Church of England in the plantation colonies was still being confronted by the compelling power of traditional West and West Central African religious convictions and rituals as well as by the authority claimed by African sacred specialists. Thereafter, however, an increasingly potent challenge to Anglicanism and to traditional African religious cultures began to present itself in the shape of alternative versions of Protestant Christianity.

Anglican doctrines and rituals held little intrinsic appeal for the enslaved populations of the Southern mainland and British Caribbean. Yet, as Alexander Garden, for one, appreciated, this would not necessarily be the case with the fervent evangelicalism of George Whitefield, John Wesley, and their followers in the Southern mainland, nor with the pietistic imperatives of the Moravians in the sugar islands. Anglican churchmen were simply unwilling, or unable, to adapt themselves, their teaching, and their rituals to meet these new challenges. The seeds of evangelical Protestant Christianity that began to sprout during the 1740s and 1750s would yield a rich harvest during the second half of the eighteenth century and, in the process, effect a profound transformation in the religious cultures of the American South and British Caribbean.

4

THE FIRST AWAKENING

PATTERNS OF FOUNDING

The Anglican ministers sponsored by the Society for the Propagation of the Gospel (SPG) were, in a sense, the advance guard of Protestant Christianity in the plantation colonies of British America. Their efforts to Christianize enslaved Africans did not take root because their version of Christianity found no confirmation in the reality of daily life in the quarters. There were, to begin with, important institutional barriers, not the least of which was planter opposition to the proselytization of their slaves. The initial encounters between deeply alienated bondpeople and Anglican churchmen were characterized by strong suspicions and extreme caution on the part of the former. Moreover, the colonial clergy confronted potential African converts from a distinctively superior position, effectively precluding mutual understanding. Linguistic barriers, which for varying lengths of time in each of the plantation colonies prevented communication on all but the most rudimentary level, probably enhanced the ethos of an English ethnocentricity, a racial superiority that was mirrored in the use of words such as "pagans," "heathens," and "barbarians" in reference to non-Christian slaves. Thus, despite the interest and concern of some Anglican churchmen and a minuscule number of planters conversions were rare, sporadic, and probably superficial. There is no evidence that African "Christians" "understood" the Scriptures or that SPG missionaries saw their conversion in any other terms than a total, and unconditional, acceptance of Anglican teaching.

During the second quarter of the eighteenth century, however, cumulative demographic and social developments were beginning to change the face of plantation society, creating in the process a different dynamic of cultural and religious evolution. The transformation occurred at different times in different places. Among the most important social factors affecting the spread of Protestant Christianity were the demographic composition of the enslaved populations of Southern and Caribbean societies, their geographic distribution, and their African origins. By 1750 over half the enslaved population of the mainland colonies lived in Virginia and Maryland. A sharp drop in the immigration of Africans to tidewater areas in the quarter century before the American Revolution produced dramatic changes in demographic conditions. By 1755 Virginia's roughly 165,000 bondpeople constituted around 37 percent of the colony's total population.[1] Around 85 percent had arrived in Virginia before 1740 and were English speaking.[2]

In South Carolina, by contrast, positive natural increase among the colony's 110,000 bondpeople did not begin to occur until the early 1750s. Thus the growth of the enslaved population continued to depend upon importations,[3] which ended briefly in 1775 but resumed with vigor in 1782, when the direct trade with Africa was reopened. The same was true in Georgia, whose predominantly West African-born slave population increased from an estimated 420 in 1751, when chattel slavery became legal, to around 1,000 in 1755, to 16,000 out of a total population of 33,000 by 1773.[4] The great majority of slaves imported into both colonies/states came from the Gambian and Gold Coasts, where the influence of Islam was strong, and from Angola, Sierra Leone, and Senegal, parts of which had experienced at least a minimal Christian presence.[5] In both Low Country colonies linguistic barriers remained pronounced and the persistence of African cultures strong. The largest slave concentrations in North Carolina were in the Cape Fear region, which received most of its black population from South Carolina and consequently shared many of its ethnic and cultural characteristics. By midcentury the interior regions of Albemarle and Neuse-Pamlico contained slightly over half of the colony's total black and white population, the majority of whom had arrived from Virginia.[6]

The spatial distribution of Southern society also played a highly significant part in shaping patterns of religious transformation. For most of the eighteenth century the Southern population, black and white, was scattered across the region. There were only a few towns, and they were small. Both in the Upper and in the Lower South slaves were the most geographically concentrated group. In 1755 they were in a majority in fourteen of the sixty-three Chesapeake counties, all of them in Virginia.[7] In Virginia more than half the enslaved population lived in the counties between the Rappahannock and the James Rivers, another 40 to 50 percent lived on the Northern Neck. Newcomers were concentrated in the Piedmont counties. Approximately 46 percent of Maryland's slave population lived on the lower Western Shore.[8] The area around Upper Marlboro in Prince George's County, Maryland, was over three-fifths black; Elk Ridge, near Baltimore, was about half black.[9] In the Low Country South Carolina districts of Beaufort, Colleton, Charleston and Georgetown, and Charleston County, blacks increasingly outnumbered whites.[10] Across the Savannah River by the end of the century blacks outnumbered whites by nearly four to one in Liberty and Chatham Counties in Georgia.[11] Everywhere on the mainland the sex ratio was decreasing, and on almost all plantations, regardless of size or location, African mothers reared their children.[12]

The volume of slave imports from Africa to the Caribbean varied significantly between the different colonies, the largest proportion of Africans being found in Jamaica and the Windward Islands, the smallest in St. Lucia. Jamaica's slave population continued to grow rapidly until the abolition of the slave trade, while that of Barbados and the Leeward Islands started to taper off around 1710. Although the majority of Afro-Jamaican bondpeople still labored on sugar and coffee plantations and livestock pens, the rapid growth in the late eighteenth century of major towns such as Kingston and Georgetown generated an increase in the urban concentration of slaves and a general tendency toward a low sex ratio in urban areas. The vast majority of Antigua's slave population worked on sugar estates; the rest were employed in the production of other crops and livestock.[13]

The growth of the enslaved African population and its geographic concentration coupled with a general lowering of linguistic barriers, especially in the older plantation societies, created conditions uniquely favorable to the evangelical missionaries who made their first appearance in the late 1730s. Of even greater significance, and what more than anything else differentiated evangelical Protestantism from the Anglicanism that fell on such stony ground in the slave quarters, was a powerful integrating ideology and an ethos whose emphasis on spiritual equality had the potential for creating the first distinctive changes in African values in relation to Protestant Christianity. The fact that evangelical groups depended upon oral means of communication with the supernatural gave them unique access to peoples who were accustomed to the use of graphic signs for magico-religious purposes. "Literate" religions, such as the Anglican and

Presbyterian faiths, were in important ways less accessible to the preliterate slave populations of colonial British America. The fact that religious ideas were not communicated by literary means also allowed the African peoples who received them to reinterpret and transmit them.

It would take time for the missionaries to work out precisely how enslaved Africans fitted into the paradigmatic structure of emerging evangelical religion. Their ability to convert bondpeople and the willingness of the latter to accept one version or another of Protestant Christianity varied significantly from place to place. The inevitable result was that Christianity spread at different rates—sometime in the 1740s in Virginia and South Carolina, in the 1750s and 1760s in the Caribbean, and in the 1770s in Georgia—and in a variety of forms. The patterns of interaction between Europeans and Africans set in West and West Central Africa in general continued to prescribe those between the two groups in the development of American Christianity. The principal motif was the substantial and enduring role of black men and women in the spread of the new faiths.

The Moravians, a pietistic offshoot of the Lutheran Church, marked out the path already half traveled over by the Capuchins and the first African Christians in West Central Africa for other evangelical groups to follow. The inspiration for the first Moravian mission came from Anna, a slave woman on the island of St. Thomas, through her brother Anton, a servant in the retinue of a Danish count. At the behest of the Moravian leader Count Nicholaus Ludwig von Zinzendorf, Anton made a passionate appeal on behalf of Anna to the brethren in Herrnhut in Saxony to send missionaries to the enslaved population of St. Thomas. The "terrible idea" Anton advanced that "the teacher of the slaves himself had to become a slave" in order to gain access to the slaves quarters was apparently intended for the white missionaries, but it nevertheless anticipated the actual involvement of black men and women in the enterprise. Moved by Anton's story, two single brethren, Johann Leonhard Dober and David Nitschmann, volunteered for the work that began in 1732 on the island of St. Thomas.[14] Although the Danish islands are outside the geographical scope of this study, the mission techniques pioneered there by the Brethren are crucial for understanding the pedagogy of conversion employed with particular success by the Methodists, who adopted almost all of the Moravian innovations.[15]

Many slaves in New World plantation societies had had some acquaintance with Christianity before the first Moravian missionaries arrived, either through contact in Africa or through Anglican missionaries. But the Moravians presented a different view of the world, one that carried an implicit promise of a new social order. While Moravians accepted slavery as part of God's structured universe, they also welcomed slaves into the multiracial communities they created in the Caribbean and on the mainland.[16] One of the most open and inclusive Protestant churches, the Moravians drew heavily upon early Christian models of worship, such as the kiss of peace, laying on of hands, and the ritual washing of feet, to powerfully symbolize their belief in mutual support and Christian communion. They affirmed their belief in a total religion that shaped all aspects of life by visiting slaves in their cabins and sharing their food and clothing, by greeting them with a warm handshake "in the manner of good friends," and by sitting and talking with them "as if they were . . . equals." To further "God's work among the Negroes" on St. Thomas they experimented with interracial marriage between Matthaus Freundlich and a mulatto woman named Rebekka.[17] The message of universal fellowship communicated by these means had a compelling power to undermine established notions of racial inferiority, a fact that was not lost on either masters, who sought to suppress it, or slaves, who sought to appropriate it.

Conversion to Christianity was a means by which some Africans came to terms with their disrupted lives. For others it was a way to express defiance of the authority of the master and opposition to slavery. One missionary noticed that "those slaves who enjoyed the greatest freedom and had to face the fewest obstacles were also the least likely to become converts."[18] For slave women "who no longer wished to allow themselves to be abused for sinful purposes," conversion was a desperate act of defense against the lust of white masters. For slave families, Christian marriage was the only guard against family separation.[19] For peoples from oral-aural cultures the evangelical Protestant emphasis on the spoken word and on oral performance had a special attraction. Life experiences and cultural heritage had taught Africans the violence the spoken word in the form of a curse could inflict. Experience had also ingrained in them the importance of the word as sound, especially in its ability to create unity and to constitute culture.[20]

From the first contacts with European missionaries, Africans showed a determination not simply to receive but also to share in the production and dissemination of the knowledge of God. The first missionaries, unable to communicate in the creole spoken by most Africans, had to rely on translators, usually free black men who understood Dutch and in some cases could read the Dutch Bible. White missionaries quickly found that their "helpers" were "particularly useful and important, insofar as his message to the Negroes could be confirmed by a believer from their own nation." Accordingly, on February 5, 1738, Moravians installed the first five "national helpers," so designated because they represented different ethnic groups then coexisting on the island. These four men and one woman were entrusted with the religious instruction of small groups of five to ten persons organized by gender, an innovation the Methodists later adopted as the class system.

The success of these efforts led to the elevation of slave converts to several church offices, among them that of plantation exhorter and elder, which were open to both women and men. Inevitably pious and strong-minded lay elders took up preaching, the focal point of evangelical worship. Abraham was one example. His right to exercise public authority was based on the recognition that he possessed qualities of leadership previously unnoticed by the white community. Through his "extraordinary gifts as a preacher" Abraham found "a ready access to the hearts of his listeners," binding them to him and to one another. His command of creole, which as late as 1744 white Brethren still struggled with, and his personal knowledge of "the superstitions, customs, and practices of his fellow Blacks," allowed him to produce his own rendition of church teaching and at the same time create a shared awareness of a common language and a common cultural heritage, the bedrock of community.[21]

The strength of the evangelical appeal to Africans also lay in the magic of the written word, a reflection of a pattern that had been established in Islamic Africa and in areas touched by Christianity. Despite the central importance of the spoken word for evangelical Protestants, God's inspired word was centered in Scripture. Shortly after their arrival on St. Thomas, missionaries began teaching the rudiments of reading as an inducement to slaves to attend the religious instruction that followed. The program generated widespread enthusiasm: "Everyone wanted to have a textbook. Whoever was lucky enough to have one carried it with him everywhere and devoted every free moment to studying it." The attraction of literacy, aside from its pragmatic value, was that it was a means of acquiring the knowledge stored in books. "The book will make me wise," one African said of the Bible. In rare cases, the written word provided protection against masters and overseers. For example, a slave woman who was being assaulted by an angry overseer "took her Bible in hand and started to read him several passages from the text. The episode caused him to relent." Because of its association with priests and *iman*, literacy was also believed to provide unique access to the supernatural.

Although acceptance of literacy often led to acceptance of the religion associated with it, it soon became apparent that "many Negroes merely took advantage of that opportunity as an end in itself, considering them-

selves sufficiently good and wise when they were able to read a little."
Consequently in 1741 instruction in reading was restricted to those who
were "intent on their own conversion." The Moravian Brethren continued
to extend to Africans a prominent place in their communal social order,
but behind the decision to restrict literacy to "sincere" catechumens was the
clear assumption that the price of direct access to the divine through the
Scriptures was spiritual submission. This development can be seen as the
beginning of a long-term effort on the part of clergy and slave owners to
discipline slave society and make it culturally dependent—in some cases
through the generous use of the whip and the rod or in others through the
confiscation and burning of religious literature belonging to bondpeople.
This one symbolically powerful act of burning religious books carried out
by slave masters on St. Thomas serves as a paradigm of the experience of
African Americans in the process of conversion over control of the word,
and hence over the spiritual and moral lives of black men and women.[22]

The essential features of the pedagogy of conversion developed by the
Moravians in the Danish islands were extended to the infant missions
they established in Jamaica in 1754, Antigua in 1756, and Barbados in
1765.[23] The West Indian mission stations were usually based on estates,
and the destitute missionaries who operated them were totally dependent
on slave owners, their own labor, or the modest voluntary contributions of
their catechumens for their support. Missionary reliance on planter patronage created a state of dependency that necessitated a large measure of
cooperation with slave owners. Nowhere was this more true than in Jamaica, where Moravian missionaries came to be regarded as "attaches" of
the plantation.[24] The Brethren continued to challenge the very system
that provided them with the means of subsistence by introducing radical
social values into the existing social order. Partly through conviction, partly
through necessity, estate missionaries also served the interests of propri-
etors by acting as "spiritual police," as one missionary later described the
Brethren's use of church discipline to enforce the plantation work regimen
and their insistence on the Christian duty of slaves to submit to their
masters.[25] These dichotomous themes of racial equality and racial submission became the hallmarks of the Christian message.[26] The possibility of
equality attracted slaves; the promise of submission appealed to their masters.

The missionary alliance with particular estates also determined patterns
of denominational growth and development. In Jamaica, for example,
Moravian influence tended to be concentrated in the southwest region of
the island, where the first estate churches were established. Baptists and

Methodists, who were excluded from the estates where Moravians enjoyed a virtual monopoly, began missionary work in the 1780s and gained their first footholds in urban centers in the southeastern third of the island.[27] Later, local planters created a licensing system that permitted accredited missionaries to take up residence on their estates. They also subsidized mission buildings, but on terms that placed severe restrictions on missionaries' religious activities among slaves and obliged them to conform to the social conventions of the ruling elite.[28]

The determined evangelism of the Moravian Brethren had mixed results, depending upon a number of factors, including the density and distribution of the slave population and the rapprochement between missionaries and planters. The greatest success of the Brethren was in Antigua. By the end of the eighteenth century over 11,000 communicants and catechumens belonged to one of three flourishing mission stations there. In Jamaica and Barbados the Moravians established footholds, but their missions languished until the end of the eighteenth century. This was due in large measure to the universal fear and distrust of the evangelical message on the part of planters and to the failure of the missionaries to identify themselves with the Africans they sought to convert, which was the key to their success in the Danish islands.[29] Although Zinzendorf dispatched missionaries to Carolina in 1737 with express instructions to evangelize slaves, the Brethren had little impact on the mainland before 1822, when regular preaching to slaves was inaugurated. This was due in part to the location of Moravian settlements in the remote western Piedmont, where there were few slaves, and in part to their preoccupation with the conversion of Native Americans.[30]

The missionary organization and discipline pioneered by the Moravian Brethren to evangelize the dense, heavily concentrated slave populations of the Leeward Islands were adopted in whole or in part by other Protestant groups. John Wesley, who in the mid-1730s was still operating under the auspices of the Church of England, developed the most effective organization for propagating the gospel among the widely dispersed population of mainland North America. "About eight in the morning I first set my foot on American ground," Wesley reported. At this exact moment on February 6, 1736, when John Wesley's feet first touched the sands of tiny Peepers Island, now known as Cockspur, there began in Georgia a second, and in the longer term an infinitely more successful, period of European proselytization of enslaved West Africans. At the head of a party of English immigrants, the thirty-three-year-old Wesley and his brother Charles walked through marshy land to a clearing of myrtle and cedar trees, where they knelt and gave thanks to God for a safe landing.[31] It was a moment of the utmost significance, for, though none could have possibly imagined it then, it led to the first effective implantation of what later became Methodism. The Wesleys laid the foundation for the religious transformation of the Southern mainland and of the African peoples who comprised such a high proportion of its population.

Invited to Georgia to minister to Native Americans, the Oxford-educated John Wesley quickly found himself in charge of a small pastorate in Savannah, a mixed community of 518 British, Spanish, French, Hebrews, and Germans, about 180 of whom were members of the Church of England.[32] The well-laid-out town of regular streets consisted of wooden houses and three rather substantial buildings, a courthouse, a storehouse, and a parsonage. Wesley, robed in surplice and master's hood, settled into a wearisome routine of morning and evening services in a hut that served as a church, in addition to house-to-house visitations, daily catechism classes, and private prayer, meditation, and reading in the little garden adjoining the parsonage.

Sometime in April 1736 Wesley gathered together some twenty or thirty of his more "serious" parishioners into "a sort of little society" to meet once or twice a week "to reprove, instruct and exhort one another." Smaller sectional meetings, presided over by laymen and laywomen, were scheduled to meet for "more intimate union." A special feature of these meetings was psalm singing. "Our little companies," as Wesley called the Savannah society and the one he organized in Frederica two months later, constituted what might fairly be called the first Methodist societies in British America. Wesley still identified himself as a High Churchman, but later he singled out the establishment of this kind of meeting as one of the three "beginnings of Methodism."[33]

One other development was pointing in the same direction. To his dismay, as he traveled to the isolated villages and hamlets that made up his parish, Wesley discovered "above 500 sheep that are (almost) without a shepherd." Here, he anguished, are "children of all ages and dispositions. . . . Here are adults, from the farthest parts of Europe and Asia and the inmost kingdoms of Africa." In his concern for their souls, Wesley began a schedule of regular visits to the small settlements of Frederica, Thunderbolt, Skidaway, Irene, Yamacraw (or Cowpen), New Ebenezer, and Darien, thus anticipating itinerating evangelism and the circuit system that eventually became hallmarks of Methodism.[34]

Since chattel slavery was still prohibited in Georgia, Wesley had few, and perhaps no, opportunities for conversing with the African population.

His visit to Charleston in July 1736 gave him his first direct encounter with colonial slavery and his first personal contacts with enslaved Africans. At the invitation of Alexander Garden, Wesley preached a sermon in Charleston on the first Sunday of August. "I was glad to see several negroes at church," he wrote afterward. Following the service, and apparently on Wesley's initiative, he had what was probably his first extended conversation with an African, a woman who claimed to have received religious instruction from her mistress. Wesley's distress at her inability to answer the most fundamental questions about Christian teachings and his pain at the neglect of her soul is palpable: "When shall the Sun of Righteousness arise on these outcasts of men, with healing in His Wings," he wondered?[35] The effect of the encounter is all the more resonant when it is coupled with his deep disappointment two days later when his weary horse was unable to carry him the distance to Alexander Skene's plantation, where he had hoped to meet with about fifty Christian slaves, probably converts made by missionaries of the SPG.

Wesley's encounter with the woman in Charleston marked the beginning of the evangelical Protestant mission to enslaved Africans. In April 1737 he made a second visit to South Carolina to attend a meeting of Anglican clergymen. Afterward Wesley attempted to return to Savannah by water, but high winds and rough seas forced him to borrow a horse and travel overland. As he made his way south through the rich rice country, he stopped at the homes of some of the most prominent planters of Low Country Carolina: Colonel Stephen Bull, Hugh Bryan, John(?) or William(?) Palmer, and William Bellinger, among others. Hugh Bryan, whose interest in educating and converting bondpeople apparently began in 1734, when he first received Bibles and Psalters from the Associates of Dr. Bray for the express purpose of "Converting his Negroes," and several other planters gave Wesley a warm welcome and permission to speak to their slaves.[36] The origins of evangelical Protestant efforts to proselytize bondpeople began here, some three years before George Whitefield's more celebrated crusade to reform the institution of slavery.[37]

At the Reverend Thompson's plantation at St. Bartholomew's, near Ponpon, Wesley had one of the most important conversations of his American ministry with Nanny, a young bondwoman from Barbados. His probing questions—which he recorded in detail in his journal—revealed that although Nanny regularly accompanied her mistress's children to church services, she herself knew nothing of such basic principles of Christian faith as the existence of a soul and an afterlife. The deep ethnocentric insensibility that led missionaries of the SPG to characterize enslaved West and West Central Africans as "pagans" or "heathens" is absent from Wesley's account, although it appears in a somewhat more benign form in his distress over the fact that Christianity was denied to a woman who lived under a clergyman's care and in his implicit assumption that Africans had no religion.

As we have seen, nowhere in the Southern mainland were enslaved Africans bereft of a spiritual life. Nevertheless, the psychological dislocations they suffered in bondage left many feeling spiritually isolated. For them the overriding question was how to survive the misery, suffering, and violence, the bewilderment and despair of life in slavery. Anglicanism provided no convincing answers to that question. Wesley's assurances to Nanny were of a different order and unquestionably persuasive. In the Christian heaven, he promised her, she would "want nothing, and have whatever you can desire. No one will beat or hurt you there. You will never be sick. You will never be sorry any more, nor afraid of anything."[38]

The effect this conversation had on John Wesley's development was profound. In the last months of his American ministry, and in his vehement denunciation of chattel slavery thereafter, giving the gospel to slaves was a constant, recurrent goal he seemed scarcely able to get out of his mind. At Bellinger's he "conversed with negroes on the plantation, who were seriously affected." One elderly African, "who was tolerably well instructed in the principles of Christianity," told him that "When I lived at Ashley Ferry, I could go to church every Sunday, but here we are buried in the woods." And in a moving testament to what must have been the great strength and power of traditional beliefs, the old man avowed that "if there was any church within five or six miles, I am so lame I cannot walk, but I would crawl thither." The subject preoccupied Wesley as he rode in the company of "a negro lad" provided by Bellinger to guide him to Purrysburg, which was said to be the birthplace of chattel slavery in Georgia. As they traveled through the night, Wesley began to teach the boy to sing and pray and afterward pronounced him "very desirous and capable of instruction."[39]

By the time he boarded the boat for his seventeen-mile trip downriver to Savannah, Wesley had conceived the outlines of the policy that Methodism would adopt in the years to come. "Perhaps one of the easiest and shortest ways to instruct the American negroes in Christianity would be first, to inquire after and find out some of the most serious of the planters. Then, having inquired of them which of their bondpeople were best inclined and understood English, to go from plantation to plantation, staying as long as appeared necessary at each." Doubtless referring to Bryan,

Bull, and Bellinger, he continued, "Three or four gentlemen at Carolina I have been with that would be sincerely glad of such an assistant, who might pursue his work with no more hindrances than must everywhere attend the preaching of the gospel."[40]

Sometime in December, as he prepared to leave Georgia in the midst of a growing controversy over his ministerial discipline, Wesley wrote to his friend George Whitefield in England, "Only Mr. Delamotte is with me, till God shall stir up the hearts of some of His servants, who, putting their lives in His hands, shall come over and help us, where the harvest is so great and the labourers so few. What if thou art the man, Mr. Whitefield?" Upon reading this, Whitefield recalled, "My heart leaped within me, and, as it were, echoed to the call."[41] On January 31, 1738, the twenty-three-year-old Whitefield sailed from Deal for Georgia; Wesley arrived in Deal at four o'clock the next morning, neither aware of the others presence.[42]

Events in the closing months of his Georgia ministry had left Wesley deeply disappointed, and he could make only a modest assessment of his accomplishments there: "A few steps have been taken towards publishing the glad tidings both to the African and American heathen."[43] A month after his arrival in Georgia, Whitefield had a very different view: "The good Mr. Wesley has done in America is inexpressible. . . . He has laid such a foundation, that I hope neither men nor devils will ever be able to shake."[44] Whitefield was referring to the process Wesley had begun that was to firmly implant evangelical Protestant Christianity in the Southern mainland. In less than two years he had made considerable progress toward the development of the Methodist system—the circuit, the society, the itinerant ministry, and lay leadership—that was destined to play a crucial part in the journey of African Americans to a new faith and, in general, in the making of Methodism. His special relationship with a handful of African women and men had established the fitful beginnings of the evangelical ministry to bondpeople, and it prefigured a tradition in Methodist evangelicalism exemplified in the careers of George Whitefield, Francis Asbury, Thomas Coke, Thomas Rankin, Freeborn Garrettson, and other British and Northern itinerants.

Whitefield lacked Wesley's organizing genius, but in his seven tours of the American mainland between 1738 and 1770, still under the auspices of the Church of England, the great evangelist's rare oratorical power helped launch the nascent Wesleyan revival that ultimately changed the religious configuration of the South. If Whitefield did not share Wesley's enduring antipathy to chattel slavery, he came to share Wesley's vision of Africans as professing Christians. Significantly, Whitefield's evangelical style did not initially excite interest among the Southern gentry. In Maryland and Virginia he found religion at "a very low ebb"; in North Carolina not "so much as the Form of religion;" and in South Carolina "no stirring among the dry Bones." Whitefield's comments about the "polite Auditories" he preached to in Annapolis, Williamsburg, and Charleston must be set in sharp contrast with the deep fellow feeling he experienced among captive West Africans, who in the beginning formed his most eager audiences.[45]

As he crisscrossed the American continent, Whitefield discovered that Africans could be "effectually wrought upon, and in an uncommon manner," which he unabashedly attributed to his own "most winning way of addressing them."[46] Just as likely it was Whitefield's new brand of ecumenism that had deep resonance among bondpeople: the promise of the millennium and spiritual regeneration. The developing relationship between Whitefield and his catechumens can be traced through Whitefield's own accounts of his Southern plantation tours. At the end of each long day's journey down the numerous waterways that cut the Low Country terrain, Whitefield formed the practice of praying together with the enslaved boatmen who were his daily companions.[47] Aware that "I was their friend," several John's Island bondpeople did their work in less time "that they might come to hear me." When Whitefield fell ill at Huspah Chapel, thirty miles from Hugh Bryan's Port Royal plantation, "the poor Negroes crowded around the windows, and . . . express'd a great concern for me."[48]

The mutually supportive relationship that one can sense developing between Whitefield and a small number of African men and women appears to have played a crucial part in his decision to educate them. By the time he reached North Carolina, Whitefield was convinced that "if early brought up in the Nurture and Admonition of the Lord," African children "would make as great a proficiency as any white People's Children whatsoever." Before he reached South Carolina he was projecting an ambitious plan to educate bondchildren: "I do not despair, if God spares my life," he wrote, "of seeing a school of young negroes singing the praises of Him who made them in a psalm of thanksgiving."[49] At a meeting in Charleston in August 1740 he persuaded one of the wealthy Bryan brothers, Jonathan, to build "a negro school." One of Whitefield's New York converts, a young English actor named William Hutson, "providentially came to Georgia" and agreed to be the first schoolmaster.[50]

Whitefield's implicit recognition of the natural intellectual equality of Africans signifies a marked change in the cultural ethos of the evangelicals in relation to the older Anglican approach, which mentally separated Africans' souls from their bodies and accorded them little, if any, intellectual capacity. Whitefield's attitude resonates through his "Letter to the Inhabitants of Maryland, Virginia, North and South Carolina," published in Charleston in 1740. If the slaveholders' argument that Christianity made slaves rebellious and proud were true, why, he wondered, "are you generally desirous of having your children taught?" Both black and white children are born in sin, Whitefield insisted, and "are naturally capable of the same improvement."[51] Unfortunately, despite his public denunciation of chattel slavery in 1740, by the mid-1740s he was an unashamed advocate of the legalization of slavery in Georgia and by the 1750s was himself a slave owner.[52]

The general hostility toward Whitefield engendered by his scathing attack on slavery did not abate, although he did succeed in persuading a small group of prominent planters, who had been predisposed by the work of Wesley, to publicly advocate reforms of that institution long insisted upon by Anglican bishops. The work centered in Port Royal, the local designation for the series of islands loosely bound together by the Combahee River to the north, the Savannah River to the south, and the Atlantic Ocean to the east. It was carried out through a network of personal relationships, which included Hugh Bryan, who first heard the evangelical message of new birth in June 1740, his brother Jonathan, and Jonathan's brother-in-law, Stephen Bull. The web of connection extended to Georgia to include James Habersham, Hugh Bryan's friend and fellow evangelist with whom he routinely exchanged copies of Whitefield's sermons.[53] Habersham, who entered Georgia as a schoolmaster in 1738, went on to establish the 15,000-acre Silk Hope Plantation on the Little Ogechee River, and with Whitefield was later instrumental in the legalization of slavery in Georgia. These wealthy merchant-planters formed the nucleus of a small network of Christian planters who joined Whitefield's evangelical crusade to reform the institution of slavery and to save their bondpeople's immortal souls through Christian baptism.[54]

Hugh Bryan took the lead in the evangelization movement in St. Helena Parish, where the Anglican missionary Lewis Jones had labored for twenty years without notable success. Reconstructing events there is difficult, but there is evidence of revival-type activities. After having undergone a mystical experience of some sort while preparing to receive "the holy sacrament of the Lord's supper," Bryan began to proclaim "sundry enthusiastic Prophecies of the Destruction of Charles Town and Deliverance of the Negroes from servitude." Although he subsequently renounced his "delusion" and denied his intention of leading or inspiring a slave rebellion, Bryan was severely punished by the South Carolina Assembly.[55]

Some bondpeople of St. Helena Parish, however, eagerly seized upon the millennial theme, which had made its first recorded appearance in Afro-Christian theology in the parish of Goose Creek in 1709–10. The Reverend Jones dismissed what went on at Bryan's plantation as emotional enthusiasm rather than religion. The "great bodies of Negroes assembled together on Pretence of Religious Worship," Jones wrote disapprovingly to his SPG superiors, "are taught rather Enthusiasm, than religion" and pretend "to see visions, and receive Revelations from heaven and to be converted by an Instantaneous Impulse of the Spirit."[56] The mounting fear of disorder created by such reports of ecstatic release emanated from the high-pitched anxiety of an anonymous writer who complained to *The South Carolina Gazette* that white evangelicals were "filling their [slaves] Heads with a Parcel of Cant-Phrases, Trances, Dreams, Visions, and Revelations and something still worse, and which Prudence forbids me to name," a veiled reference to Hugh Bryan's alleged attempt to provoke a slave uprising.[57]

It is not clear how many actual converts there were among "Mr. Whitefield's followers," as Lewis Jones covetously called them, although a letter published in England and addressed to the converted slaves of Jonathan Bryan mentions that twelve bondpeople had been "brought home to Christ."[58] In 1741 Pastor Johann Martin Bolzius reported that some of his colleagues had "heard a Moorish slave woman on a plantation [probably the Bryans's] singing a spiritual at the water's edge." Later the woman's master told them that "this heathen woman attained a certain assurance of the forgiveness of sins and the mercy of God in Christ and that she, along with others who love Christ, was shouting and jubilating because of this treasure."[59] When Bolzius himself visited Jonathan Bryan's plantation in 1743, he found popular criticism that "[Bryan's] Negroes do nothing but pray and sing and thereby neglect their work," contradicted by "the most beautiful order in the housekeeping and among the Negroes, of whom several were honestly converted to God."[60]

When the Bryans and some of their dissenter neighbors broke from the Church of England in 1743 and formed the Stoney Creek Independent Congregational Church, later the Stoney Creek Independent Presbyterian Church, some of their bondpeople followed suit. The first to do so were George and his wife, Sarah, who signed the church covenant and were accordingly admitted in 1745. Over the next fourteen years, thirty-five more bondpeople were baptized, thirteen of them men, fourteen of them women, and eight of them children. A total of twenty-four of the thirty-two converts, whose owners' names are inscribed on the register, belonged to William Hutson, pastor of the church, and to members of the Bryan family. Two owners, Mary, Hugh Bryan's wife, and William Hutson, accounted for eighteen of the twenty-four. While these figures serve to spotlight the importance of patriarchal sanction, they also suggest that the role of female religiosity in the inauguration of religious revivalism and in the religious transformation of slave society was far more extensive than historians have acknowledged.

Even so, it would be erroneous to conclude that whites coerced or even brought evangelical Protestantism to their bondpeople, or that conversion had the same meaning to them. Despite their owners' active encouragement, bondmen and -women usually resisted conversion efforts, as Hugh Bryan's complaint that "my Servants were called to prayers but none came" reveals.[61] Fragmentary though it is, the Stoney Creek Church register offers a suggestive but incomplete notion about the African convert population and about early patterns of conversion. First, the roster suggests a family pattern of conversion. Among the thirty-five enslaved members were three couples, George and Sarah, David and Hannah, and Jacob and Lessey. Two of the three couples presented four of their children for baptism. The roster also suggests that women formed the fragile backbone of the congregation. Enslaved women made up a simple majority of those admitted to full communion, thus establishing a pattern of female numerical dominance. Two mothers, Priscilla and Molly, unaccompanied by partners, gave four children in baptism, thereby establishing a tradition of religious bonds between mothers and children. These trends instituted by the first generation of black evangelicals—the planting of familial roots in the church and the mother's assumption of moral and religious responsibility for the slave household—became the building blocks of black evangelicalism.

At about the same time that the Bryans and a few of their neighbors were seeking converts among the bondpeople on their Low Country rice plantations, a young New Light Presbyterian preacher named Samuel Davies arrived from Delaware to carry the message of the Great Awakening to the white planters and yeoman farmers of the Pamunkey Valley in Hanover County, Virginia, whose rough energies were often devoted to horse racing and gambling. Initially, the scholarly Davies was licensed to seven meeting houses in Hanover and neighboring counties by the General Court at Williamsburg, which had barred most dissenting preachers from Anglican Tidewater jurisdictions. Davies settled in Hanover County, about twelve miles from Richmond, and began his ministry among the upcountry folk in a plain wooden building on land owned by Samuel Morris, a bricklayer. However, elite anxiety over the spread of religious enthusiasm soon led to restrictions on his preaching activities, mainly by the revocation of his licenses for additional meeting houses.[62]

Presbyterians like Davies were not committed to missionary activity among the unchurched. Their ministers went to the frontier looking primarily for Presbyterians. The families Davies gathered together in small frame meetinghouses originally consisted of believers from the settled Scotch-Irish community. Almost from the start of his ministry, however, and like dissenting ministers before and after him, Davies discovered among the unconverted black majority of Hanover and surrounding counties "multitudes" who were "willing, and even eagerly desirous to be instructed, and to embrace every opportunity for that end."[63] At the Presbyterian church he established at Pole Green in 1749 and the three others he formed in the county shortly thereafter—Salem, Bethelem, and Beulah, and four in the neighboring counties of Henrico, Caroline, Goochland, and Louisa— Davies began building the first Christian fellowship of enslaved Africans in the Chesapeake. By 1755 he had baptized 100 bond-people. The next year he reported having baptized 150 adults, although he counted over 1,000 slaves attending services at various preaching places. Almost sixty-five years after Davies made his first African converts, their descendants still supported "a considerable congregation" at Pole Green.[64]

By the mid-1750s the tide of emigration to the Virginia frontier was running fast and strong, carrying thousands of land-hungry migrants, most of them driven from the old Tidewater areas by falling tobacco prices and shrinking economic opportunities. As they pushed their way down the Appomattox, Roanoke, and Nottoway Rivers toward Piedmont North Carolina, Davies, to avoid charges of itinerancy, sent out a plea for help from the New York Synod, which dispatched a new contingent of six ministers to form the Hanover Presbytery and to fill the vacancies south of the James River.[65] Three of the six, John Todd, Robert Henry, and John Wright, were influenced by Davies and continued and extended his work among the African population.[66]

John Todd, an Irish emigrant, became Davies's assistant and took over the services to the churches in Louisa and Hanover, which were all twelve to fifteen miles apart. In 1755 he took up residence in Louisa County, near Paynes Mill on the South Anna River, and became minister of the Providence Church, the oldest in the county. Following the example of Davies, Todd built up a following among Africans and, according to Davies, baptized at least 100 of them.[67] Simultaneously, New Light Presbyterianism among the enslaved population was developing in a different direction, the section of Virginia Piedmont known as Southside. In 1755 the Reverend John Wright, a Scot, was installed pastor of the church in Cumberland, one of the seven original places licensed for Davies. Wright built up a sizable congregation of 180, mostly English, Scotch-Irish, and Huguenots. But the Cumberland church also attracted "a great number of negroes, and not a few of them thoughtful and inquisitive about Christianity, and sundry of them hopeful converts." Davies wrote glowingly that Wright was "very laborious in his endeavors to instruct negroes, and has set up two or three schools among them, where they attend before and after sermon, for they have no other leisure time."[68]

Like most of the frontier Presbyterian churches, the congregation at Cub Run in Charlotte, then part of Lunenburg County, was made up principally of Scotch-Irish, who had arrived in the area around 1738. Robert Henry, another Scot, whose "besetting sin was in exciting levity in others by his humor and eccentricity," was made pastor of Cub Creek in 1755.[69] Henry's "vehement manner, and vein of humor," which often broke out in the sermons he delivered extemporaneously, "rendered him peculiarly acceptable to the African race, among whom he gathered many converts." During the spring, summer, and fall of 1756 a harbinger of things to come occurred in the form of "some remarkable revivings" in Davies's, Henry's, and Wright's congregations. According to Wright's account, the revival was "chiefly among the negroes" in Davies's congregation and among the very young in Henry's congregation. In his own church Wright reported "something of a stir among the negroes" and "among little children."[70] The Hanover Awakening marked the beginning of the Great Awakening, the long period extending to the American Revolution that was punctuated periodically by bursts of religious energy.

The details of Davies's dynamic ministry to the Africans of Hanover and neighboring counties are too well known to require description. However, several recurrent threads run through his evangelical correspondence that tends to bear out the idea that between the evangelicals and enslaved Africans there existed a unique, reciprocal relationship but one that was fraught with ambiguity and uncertainty.[71] Davies's letters to evangelical clergy in England are infused with paternal affection for "the poor neglected negroe [sic] slaves" who crowded his simple meeting houses: "Never have I been so much struck with the appearance of an assembly, as when I have glanced my eyes to one part of the Meeting-house adorned (so it has appeared to me) with so many black countenances, especially attentive to every word they heard, and some of them washed with tears."[72]

Enriched by the simple devoutness he saw in the faces of the converted,

Davies was totally disarmed by their "pious thirst after Christian knowledge": "There are multitudes of them in various parts, who are willing, and even eagerly desirous to be instructed, and to embrace every opportunity for that end."[73] Casting himself as "an advocate in their behalf," he pleaded with Wesley and other British evangelicals for Bibles, hymnals, and spelling books for his "poor Africans," who, he confessed, "are the principal objects of my compassion, and I think, the most proper subjects of your charity." As soon as the books arrived Davies distributed them among the bondpeople, but, he reported, "my house is still crouded [sic]" with "importunate Petitioners."[74] His appeal for more books fairly vibrates with admiration and respect for their zeal for learning: "Every new benefaction of Books sets hundreds upon attempting to read with fresh eagerness," he exclaimed. "In almost every house in my congregation, and in sundry other places, they spend every leisure hour in trying to learn, since they expect BOOKS as soon as they are capable of using them."[75]

But for Davies African piety was a volatile mixture of orthodox Christian submission and dangerous spiritual autonomy that he found both exciting and disturbing. Sensitized to the human qualities and spiritual needs of African converts, Davies keenly felt the urgency of their search for a means of reversing, or at least attenuating, the terrible psychic damage done by enslavement: "Many of them only seem to be, they know not what. They feel themselves uneasy in their *present* condition, and therefore desire *change*." He perceived in some of them an implicit millennialism of an entirely different order from that of white Christians. Salvation to them meant freedom from the pitiful subjection of slavery, a spiritual revolution that would turn the moral universe upside down. These slaves, he cautioned, believed that they "would be baptized in compliance with the Fashion, and that they may be upon an Equality with their Masters." Still other potential converts viewed Christianization as a means of empowerment through access to knowledge. Mindful of the fact that such radical desires undermined orthodox religion and posed a threat to the social and political order, Davies concluded that they were not ready for the gospel: "I am obliged to exclude [them] from that Ordinance."

While the Africans' joyful acceptance of the message of salvation thrilled and excited Davies, the power and intensity of their conversion disturbed and troubled him. "I find the hardest thing," he complained, "to convince their judgments, and make their minds properly sensible of the Reasonableness, the Glory, and the Necessity of a *Mediatorial Religion*," by which he meant meditation and reflection as the means to achieve practical piety. Although experimental, or emotional, religion was a part of Whitefield's revivalism, Davies implied that African experimental piety somehow differed from what was usual and customary in the 1740s: "They have very high notions of the necessity and efficacy of Baptism. Indeed, it seems to be their common opinion, when they first become a little thoughtful, and uneasy in a state of Heathenism, that if they were but baptized, they should become Christians instantaneously; and it is hard to convince them of the necessity of proper preparatory qualifications for it."[76]

Fragmentary as it is, Davies's account of his struggles to restrain black enthusiasm without discouraging black piety reveals the nature and the significance of the process of conversion. Like Anglican missionaries earlier, Davies's moderate evangelism stressed formal, if limited, knowledge of the faith as a prerequisite for baptism. His success in converting bondpeople depended to a large extent on his assurance to planters like William Byrd that the gospel message would provide security against social upheaval. Little wonder, then, that he was skeptical of African emotions undisciplined by instruction, even, perhaps, finding something vaguely threatening about the power inherent in conversion: the moral superiority of converted bondpeople over their spiritually indifferent masters and mistresses. For Africans in slavery, however, spontaneous conversion was a vehicle—one could say *the* vehicle—to a new spiritual world. With each successive generation the process of conversion continued to unfold, accelerating during the Great Revival until it formed the principal motif of their pilgrimage, the key to their religious transformation.

The Baptist revivals of the 1760s gave a new character to conversion and created new religious opportunities for the explosive spirituality that Samuel Davies had found so disquieting. Regular Baptists had been in Welsh Neck, on the Pee Dee, in Charleston, South Carolina, since 1683 and in the Northern Neck above Fredericksburg, Virginia, since the mid-1750s. But it was a small company of militant New England Separate, or New Light, Baptists who launched the revival that spread through Virginia, the Carolinas, and Georgia.[77] Led by Shubal Stearns, a small man with a penetrating gaze and a strong musical voice, the little group traveled south, stopping briefly at Opeckon, in Berkeley County, Virginia, where Stearns met his pious but unprepossessing brother-in-law, Daniel Marshall.[78] The two joined company and pushed on some 200 miles to Sandy Creek, in Guilford County, North Carolina, where they built a meetinghouse and formed a church composed of sixteen communicants.

From Sandy Creek, the mother of the new seed, the branches of the Baptist faith spread southward to Georgia, northward to the Potomac, and eastward to Chesapeake Bay. Scores of young prophets, raised up under the ministry of Stearns and Marshall, began holding nightly meetings in the tobacco barns and crude homes of simple folk, preaching the indispensable necessity of the new birth, of being born again. The preaching style of these poor, illiterate, unrefined, and unsophisticated young men, says Baptist historian Robert Semple, was "much more novel than their doctrines."[79] According to Morgan Edwards, a contemporary of Stearns, all the Separate Baptists "copied after [Stearns] in tones of voice and actions of body." Tidance Lane, who felt the visual and spiritual impact of Shubal Stearns's preaching, thought Stearns had "an evil eye, and ought to be shunned; but shunning him I could not more effect than a bird can shun the rattle-snake when it fixed its eyes upon it." His mesmerizing gaze fixed on his audience, Stearns used his sonorous voice "in such a manner, as . . . to make soft impressions on the heart, and fetch tears from the eyes in a mechanical way; and anon, to shake the very nerves; and throw the animal system into tumults and perturbations."[80]

John Leland, the eminent Regular Baptist minister, described Separate Baptist worship as "very noisy" compared to the "solemn and rational" services of the Regulars. "The people would cry out, 'fall down,' and, for a time, lose the use of their limbs; which exercise made the bystanders marvel."[81] Not all observers were as restrained as Leland in their reactions to the tears, tremblings, screams, and cries of dread and anxiety that reverberated through the Separate Baptist meetinghouses. Anglicans, whose worship consisted almost entirely of prescribed readings from the Book of Common Prayer,[82] were repelled by the Separates' emotionalism. One of the angriest critics was the Anglican minister Charles Woodmason, who after observing a Separate Baptist congregation singing, dancing, skipping, laughing, and rejoicing during worship service in the South Carolina backcountry, mockingly compared "our Solemn, Grave, and Serious Sett Forms" to the Separates' "Wild Extempore Jargon, nauseus [sic] to any Chaste or refin'd Ear."[83]

To many among the enslaved African population, however, Stearns's austere itinerants, with their closely cropped hair and homespun dress, their expressions grave even to severity, were messianic figures struggling to lead the gentry-dominated slaveholding society into a new spiritual and ideological era. In Separate theology and worship they discovered the promise of a millennium. As Mechal Sobel reminds us, there was much in Baptist theology that was compatible with traditional West and West Central African religions. Belief in salvation, or rebirth in Christ through personal salvation, was "the central focus of Baptist belief." In contrast to mainline denominations, which stressed instruction in and acceptance of a formal set of beliefs, evangelical groups such as the Methodists and Baptists emphasized the conversion experience as the chief means of entry into the Christian community. Central to most, if not all, evangelical doctrines of conversion was the claim to extraordinary communication and of witness of the spirit.

As Sobel's pioneering work demonstrates, traditional West and West Central African religions and evangelical Christianity shared to a considerable degree a common vocabulary and certain overlapping beliefs and practices, among the most important being that regeneration can occur instantaneously.[84] In many West and West Central African societies initiation rituals were associated with the symbolic death and rebirth of the initiates. Rebirth was further symbolized by the ritual bath that preceded the return of the initiates.[85] For enslaved Africans, conversion to Christianity obviously involved a reorientation of beliefs and practices, but the fact that they revolved around a constant cultural core provided continuity with the African past, making the transition to evangelical Protestant Christianity possible.

African belief in the imminence of the millennium, which entered African American Christian theology early in the eighteenth century, also found confirmation from the Separate Baptist acceptance of men and women, black and white, as spiritual equals. As Arminians, or General Baptists, the Separates preached redemption for all and welcomed Africans into their small religious communities made up mostly of poor and uneducated men and women.[86] In the beginning, Separate churches allowed women to pray in public, and women "also retained the offices of elderesses, and deaconesses," as the eminent Regular Baptist minister John Leland reported with scarcely concealed displeasure. They added new rites to the traditional Protestant sacraments of the Lord's Supper and baptism, including love feasts, laying on of hands, washing feet, anointing the sick, the right hand of fellowship, kiss of charity, and devoting children, or "dry-christening," as the ritual of laying hands on a newborn infant was derisively called.[87]

The intrusion of women into the male ritual sphere and the physical intimacy of the nine rites symbolically represented the Separates' universal moral outlook, which envisaged a moral community that transcended all social, economic, cultural, and racial divisions. The physical intimacy of touching and kissing confirmed the spiritual bond between worshipers, testified to their love and respect for one another, and thereby promoted the psychological and sociological integration of the group, including even socially and racially despised slaves.[88] The reversal, or suspension,

of the normal rules and structures of society symbolically abolished hierarchical class, gender, and racial distinctions. The strong antislavery state-
ments regularly adopted by the yearly associational meetings powerfully
reinforced the Separates' symbolic structure and further raised millennial
hopes about the abolition of the social and racial order.

In 1756 two young, illiterate, Separate preachers, Philip Mulkey and
William Murphy, rode into Bluestone Creek in the vast, thinly settled
frontier area known as Lunenburg County and introduced the new symbols of Christian unity and spiritual power to the enslaved population of
Virginia. Their first converts were drawn from the dispersed bondpeople
of the Byrd estate. According to the historians of the Virginia Baptist
Church, Mulkey and Murphy gathered together "several white members
besides a large number of blacks." The number of converts continued to
grow steadily, and within two years the predominantly African congregation began "to exercise the rights of a church."[89] This development marked
the beginning of a period of rapid growth that led to the creation of
thirty-four Separate Baptist churches in Virginia, with over 3,000 members, by 1773.[90]

In the meantime, Stearns's restless itinerants pushed their pious conquest south toward the Congaree Settlement of South Carolina, where
Philip Mulkey and a handful of migrants from the Deep River Church in
North Carolina established the first Separate church at Fairforest in 1762.
In 1771 a similar party, led by Daniel Marshall, settled on Kiokee Creek,
about twenty miles above Augusta, and established the first Baptist church
in Georgia.[91] From these focal points, Baptist missionaries moved in all
directions, their ritual behavior and powerful religious symbolism communicating the millennial message to the thousands of Low Country Africans struggling, not always silently, against their chains.

Nothing exemplifies the compelling force of the prophetic message
of divine deliverance—and the dynamics of conversion—more strikingly
than the success of the great Baptist evangelist Elhanan Winchester in
converting native West and West Central Africans to Christianity. Born
in Massachusetts, Winchester started out as a Particular Baptist but gradually moved away from Calvinist orthodoxy toward Universalism, which
accepted salvation for all. His evolving theology, which coincided with
his first contact with chattel slavery in Virginia, was reflected in the famous antislavery address he delivered in Fairfax County in which he
denounced the slave trade and warned slaveholders of divine retribution.[92] When in 1775 he accepted a call to serve as pastor of the all-white
Welsh Neck Regular Baptist Church in the Pee Dee area of South Caro-

lina, his millennial convictions became joined with African bondpeople's millennial expectations. When Winchester began his ministry, not a single bondperson, man, woman, or child, had been baptized in the entire area, a condition that Winchester attributed to the indifference of his predecessors and to the "prejudices which the slaves had against Christianity, both ministers and people."

But Winchester's condemnation of slavery and the slave trade "being pretty generally known, operated so upon the minds of these poor creatures that they shared a disposition to attend my ministry more than they had ever shewed to any other." On one occasion "a great number" of slaves, about thirty of them from the plantation of Colonel Alexander McIntosh, appeared at the door of the house where Winchester was preaching. Afterward he went to them and told them "that Jesus Christ loved them and died for them, as well as for us white people, and that they might come and believe in him and welcome." Their conversion, Winchester later recalled, was immediate. They went home, "settled every quarrel among themselves[,] and according to their form of marriage," married "every man to the woman with whom he lived." On June 27 Winchester baptized the first black Baptists in the Pee Dee area: Alingo, owned by Aaron David, and Plato, Stephen, Darien, and Susannah, who belonged to Alexander McIntosh.

The key to Winchester's success was that he offered a broader theology whose message of salvation was relevant to the religious and social needs of an oppressed people. His emphasis on the theme of general restoration imparted a dynamic to Christianity that previously had been missing. Its immediate effect was to accelerate the process of Christianization among bondpeople. Within three months, Winchester had baptized 100 slaves, 63 of them men, 37 of them women, all of whom had been born in Africa or who were immediate descendants of African parents. On August 24, 1779, the African Baptists "were constituted into a church by themselves." On the following Sunday, the African church received into fellowship twenty-six new converts. Before Winchester departed in September 1779, he led a revival, which on one occasion drew almost 1,000 persons.[93]

Regular Baptists, who held to the more rigid theological conviction that Christ died for an elect few, looked askance at Winchester's noisy revivals and the ecstasy of grace that brought swelling numbers of Africans into the Baptist communion. No sooner had Winchester left the province than the interim pastor, Joshua Lewis, excommunicated the majority of those baptized by Winchester, both black and white, on the grounds that they were "very ignorant of the nature of true religion." When Edmund Botsford, the son of a well-to-do English grocer and ironmonger, accepted a call to shepherd the Welsh Neck Baptist Church, he returned the congregation to Particular Baptist orthodoxy. Anxious to win Winchester's followers over to religious orthodoxy, Botsford invited the membership of the African church to join his Welsh Neck congregation. Being without a pastor, a number applied, were examined, and forty-six of them admitted. By the time the seat of the church was moved from Welsh Neck to Society Hill in 1789, the church had a black majority of sixty-four, compared to sixty-three white members.[94]

Another seminal moment in the development of African American Protestant Christianity occurred in the 1760s: the arrival of organized Methodism. Perhaps six years before an obscure Irish preacher named Robert Strawbridge began conducting prayer services in his two-story log house at Sam's Creek, Maryland, Methodism made its appearance in Antigua in the household of Nathaniel Gilbert, a large landowner and Speaker of the island's Assembly. In Antigua, as in all of the British sugar islands, the vast majority of the African population still clung steadfastly to traditional religious beliefs and practices. Reflecting on the spiritual demography of Antigua's enslaved population in 1760, Ann Gilbert, Nathaniel's wife, pronounced them to be "in a state of inconceivable darkness and diabolical superstition."[95] The transition to Christianity began with three bondpeople from the Gilbert household. During a visit home to England in 1758, Nathaniel Gilbert, who had been introduced to the writings of Wesley by his brother Francis, members of his family, and three of his house slaves, at least two of them women, heard Wesley preach at the family estate in Wandsworth. Wesley's journal entry for January 17, 1758, notes that "two negro servants of [Gilbert's, one of them possibly Sophia Campbell] and a mulatto [probably Mary Alley] appear[ed] to be much awakened." Eleven months later, Wesley joyfully recorded, "I rode to Wandsworth, baptized two negroes belonging to Mr. Gilbert . . . , one of these is deeply convinced of sin, the other rejoices in God her Saviour."[96] Upon their return to Antigua, Gilbert began to hold Sunday prayer services for members of his household. Then he became an evangelist. Before his untimely death in 1774, approximately 200 persons, mostly Africans, had been "joined in society."[97]

Most contemporary accounts credit Nathaniel Gilbert with introducing Methodism to the African population of Antigua. But in point of fact, the role of women was far more extensive than contemporary male historians were prepared to acknowledge, and white women Methodists were keenly aware of the contribution made by Mary Alley and Sophia

Campbell.[98] Given the language barrier that still existed in 1763,[99] it is reasonable to hypothesize that these two women were the real missionaries to the Africans outside of the Gilbert household. Free from the scrutiny of church authorities, they publicly assumed moral and religious responsibility for the "scattered flock . . . left in the wilderness without a shepherd" after Gilbert's death. As part of their self-designated evangelical mission, "Evening and Morning [they] would convene a little church in their humble habitation." As Elizabeth Montague asserted to the Methodist Missionary Society in London in 1814, the formative contributions of Alley and Campbell were critical: "But for their exertions the name of Methodist would have been extinct in this Country."[100]

In the meantime, however, the two self-appointed female evangelists had devised a sphere for women that had not been anticipated and was not acceptable to the venerable leadership of male ministers. When John Baxter, a shipwright and Methodist convert arrived in English Harbor, he took over the missionary society, relieving the two women of their evangelistic responsibilities. They subsequently designed for themselves an alternative role on the borders of the public sphere that in time became the peculiar province of religious women: providing financial and institutional support to the revival ministry. When Baxter finally decided to build a church he discovered that the expense involved would be greater than his poor, predominantly slave society could bear. Campbell and Alley responded by selling their earrings and bracelets to buy lumber and hire carpenters. They accepted a small plot of land for the church site in lieu of payment from the parents of children to whom they taught sewing and reading. They raised an army of women workers to clear the land of rubbish, to prepare food for the construction workers, and to haul the stone and marl to the building site.[101]

The St. John Methodist Society built by this small coterie of British men and black evangelical women became the center of Methodism in Antigua and the cradle of conversion in the archipelago. Methodist influence extended horizontally from it, through the enslaved community and vertically up and through the ranks of the island's white female society. Black women were the lynchpins in this religious transformation. Sketchy though it is, the evidence clearly disproves the notion that the Christianization of slaves was a weapon wielded by planter-slaveholders to make their bondpeople more pliant. Rather, it argues that female members were recruited on the basis of voluntary associations and that in the lineage of conversion black women, black men, and white women preceded white men into the evangelical fold. The society grew from 600 members in

1779, most of them bondpeople from plantations within a ten-mile radius of the town of St. John, to over 1,000 members by 1783. It was composed almost entirely of black women. Except for a few bondmen, men were conspicuously absent; John Baxter was the solitary white male member. When the English itinerant Thomas Coke made his last visit to Antigua in 1793 there were 2,420 Methodists, of whom only 36 were white. A decade later, 22 of the island's 3,516 Methodists were white, but that number included only 6 men. There were "many women . . . in Society" and "Some of the coloured women have good gifts in Prayer and hold prayer meetings."[102] It was from Antigua, "the favourite of heaven," as Coke called it, that Methodism radiated out in all directions after missions were launched beginning in the 1780s to St. Vincent, St. Kitts, and Dominica, leading in the end to the permanent establishment of Methodism in the British Caribbean.[103]

The first effective implantation of Methodism in Antigua began a period of Methodist evangelistic activity that in forty years also made it a major religious force in the North American mainland. Sometime in 1766 Robert Strawbridge built the first Methodist preaching house in the mainland colonies, a rough log cabin in a meadow near the tributaries of Sam's and Pipe's Creeks in Frederick County, Maryland.[104] From his home in Frederick, Strawbridge made hundreds of preaching tours, mapping out a wide circuit extending across Baltimore and Harford Counties, organizing preaching places in the unpretentious homes of his converts, in their barns, and in their tobacco houses. These then became preaching centers for the local preachers who had been under Strawbridge's tutelage. Among the first of these local preachers was Jacob Toogood, a slave of John Maynard, who was one of Strawbridge's first converts.[105]

The aggressive spirit of Methodism rapidly spread throughout the Chesapeake as itinerants, singly and in pairs, responded to John Wesley's question: "Who is willing to go" to the newly designated fiftieth circuit in America? Between 1772, when Robert Williams, the first Methodist itinerant, preached the first sermon to noisy and disorderly crowds in Norfolk and across the river in Portsmouth,[106] to the outbreak of hostilities in the American Revolution in 1775, Methodist missionaries, most of them from Britain, formed six circuits: three in Maryland, in Baltimore and Frederick on the Western Shore, and Kent, the first circuit on Maryland's Eastern Shore, and three in Virginia, in Fairfax, Norfolk, and Brunswick.[107]

Circuit riding brought Methodist preachers into the vast rural hinterland of the Southern mainland, where half a million enslaved Africans labored in sweltering tobacco fields and snake-infested swamps. These firsthand, face-to-face encounters probably took place in the conducive environment of the small private homes of new white converts, women and men of modest means whose notions of Christian civility extended to include the bondmen and -women with whom they closely shared the world. The discovery was mutual. The missionaries first impressed themselves upon the African imagination with a message of social justice, first delivered from the high steps of the courthouse in Norfolk, Virginia, by Robert Williams, a poor Irish preacher who sailed for America with nothing more than a pair of saddlebags, a loaf of bread, and a bottle of milk.[108] Williams's warm optimistic message of salvation and his promise of divine justice had a singular appeal for women and men whose lives often centered on the nauseous work of picking off and crushing worms and caterpillars from tobacco plants. It had the opposite effect on the mayor of Norfolk, whose muttered comment that "if we permit such fellows as these to come here we shall have an insurrection of the Negros [sic]" was overheard by a young, bound English servant named John Littlejohn.[109]

Pained and perplexed by the boorish behavior of some of the tobacco-smoking whites who brought their dogs to meetings and by the violent attacks by others, the predominantly British itinerancy achieved an almost charismatic rapport with enslaved Africans. It was from the outset a reciprocal relationship, but one that was initiated by the latter. Joseph Pilmore had only just set foot in the Norfolk-Portsmouth area when "two poor slaves came to me and beged [sic] I would instruct them in the way of salvation so I gave them a short and plain account of the Plan of the Gospel, and shewed them how sinners may come to God and be saved. We then joined in singing and prayer, and they expressed great thankfulness for what they had heard, and seemed determined to be Christians." Three days later, when Pilmore preached again, guards had to be posted at the doors of the meeting house "to keep the Negroes out till the white people were got in."[110] Their guileless piety and respectful behavior at meetings rapidly erased whatever negative inherited stereotypes of Africans the British missionaries might have brought with them and provided the catalyst for the assertive proselytizing of Francis Asbury, Thomas Rankin, John Littlejohn, and others who traveled the field vacated by Pilmore.

Methodism began to make inroads in Virginia with the arrival of English missionaries in the 1760s. Beginning in 1770–71 at White Oak in Dinwiddie County, they launched a biracial revival movement that transformed Methodism from a fledgling operation to a mass religious movement around which other movements coalesced. The movement was carried into Sussex and Brunswick Counties by Robert Williams. Fol-

lowing the familiar cycle of alternate awakenings and stagnation, the movement gained renewed energy from a Methodist quarterly meeting at
Boisseau's Chapel. From there it spread rapidly over a four- to five-hun-
dred-mile radius, affecting finally fourteen counties in southern Virginia
and two North Carolina counties flanking the Virginia border. Along
with white converts, revival meetings attracted hundreds of African Americans, many of whom attended in defiance of their masters.

Itinerating preachers sought black converts with enthusiasm, often sched-
uling religious meetings in the early morning hours to accommodate the
plantation work regimen and to mollify slave owners suspicious of evening
meetings. They encouraged new white converts to allow their slaves to
attend family prayer meetings, thus pioneering new forms of racial interaction. In contrast to the Anglican ideology of spatial and psychological
separation, evangelical meetings dared to bring together under the same
roof women and men, rich and poor, slave and free. Patterns for organizing black and white relationships were already established in many, if not
most, aspects of Southern life. But the ethos of racial superiority that was
deeply embedded in the consciousness of most white Southerners could
not operate in quite the same way in the religious context as it did in the
context of social and economic relationships. Attitudes had therefore to be
worked out, the African presence to be somehow accommodated, and adjustments to conflicting values to be made—from those of aggression and
domination that operated in most ordinary relationships, to those of community and mutual dependence that ideally prevailed in the meetinghouse.

Freeborn Garrettson's account of a prayer meeting in the home of Thomas Hill Airey in Dorset County, Maryland, dramatizes the cultural process taking place in dozens of small house meetings where interracial dynamics helped to temporarily redefine black and white relationships. "I
shall never forget the time," Garrettson wrote, "I suppose about twelve
whites and blacks were present. The power of the Lord came among us:
Mrs. Airey was so filled with the new wine of Christ's kingdom, that she
sunk to the floor, blessing and praising the Lord. And many of the blacks
were much wrought upon."[111] As this example suggests, blacks and whites
were converted together through a direct conversion experience, a requisite part of which involved being overwhelmed by the Holy Spirit. Like
their black counterparts, white evangelicals shared a tradition of enthusiastic behavior, the antecedents of which reached back to medieval Christianity.[112] As a consequence, there were similarities in worship patterns
between the two groups. However, the similarities should not obscure

their differences, especially in aesthetic content. Conditioned by centuries of training in ecstatic performance, African Americans often inspired and catalyzed revivalism through an intense emotionalism that reflected their belief in the immediate call, the central tenet of the African American understanding of conversion.

Both sexes of both races participated in the creation of the conversion experience, but women predominated. The household origins of revivalism guaranteed the presence and participation of women in the evangelical movement. It also brought black and white women together in a joint spiritual pursuit that frequently transcended racial divisions. Within this setting women became the principal creators of an affective style of worship and of revival culture more generally. The most fervent proponents of religious enthusiasm tended to be Methodist women, whose charismatic leadership was a major source of spiritual inspiration for the conversion experience. White women demonstrated religious zeal equal to that of black women, but reports of individual mystical experiences focus in particular on African American women, who had inherited and acknowledged spiritual skills through their experiences as mediums and, in some societies, as diviners. Deprived of their traditional supernatural means of dealing with recurrent life crises, they discovered in evangelical conversion requirements an opportunity to reassert personal authority based on their ability to communicate directly with God and to bring others to recognize the need for personal repentance and acceptance of Jesus. Their efforts to carve out a ritual corner of their own manifested themselves largely through the phenomena of ecstatic behavior—visions, ecstatic trances, and prophecies.[113]

The first recorded appearance of a pattern that was to recur with some frequency in the decades ahead occurred in May 1740 during George Whitefield's second tour of America and involved a "poor Negro woman" of Philadelphia, a recent convert of Whitefield's. According to Whitefield, during a sermon by a Baptist preacher "the word came with such power to her heart, that at last she was obliged to cry out, and a great concern fell heavily upon many in the congregation," an indication that this was an unfamiliar phenomenon. The astonished preacher immediately stopped preaching. Whitefield personally believed that in that hour "the Lord Jesus took a great possession of her soul," but "many since then," he conceded, "have called her mad, and said she was full of new wine."[114] Six months later, Whitefield witnessed a similar happening among the slaves on Hugh and Jonathan Bryan's St. Helena Parish plantation when an African woman "received Christ in a Glorious Manner."[115] The next year, a "Moorish" woman on Hugh Bryan's plantation was observed "singing a spiritual at the water's edge." Bryan explained to curious observers that a few days earlier "this heathen woman had attained a certain assurance of the forgiveness of sins and the mercy of God in Christ, and that she, along with others who love Christ, was shouting and jubilating because of this treasure."[116] The same kind of holy spontaneity emerged again during the Methodist phase of the first Great Awakening in the Chesapeake. While on a preaching tour of the Fairfax Circuit in 1776, Freeborn Garrettson noted that a bondwoman "clapped her hands in an ecstasy of joy."[117] The repetition of episodes like this one nurtured the biracial revival spirit, and Methodist quarterly meetings provided the means to fulfill it.

Although credit for launching revivalism is shared by Baptists, Methodists, and Presbyterians, it was the Methodist quarterly meeting that routinized biracial revivalism and gave Southern religion its peculiar quality.[118] The quarterly conferences, initially the governing body of local circuit churches, had important executive powers. For example, it could determine pastors' salaries, make decisions about church property, enforce the book of Discipline, and ordain and license men to preach. A variation of the British pattern, quarterly conferences were generally two-day affairs until 1773, when the meeting days were changed to Saturday and Sunday in large part because "slaves could not attend these meetings except on the Lord's day."[119] The meetings brought together bishops, elders, deacons, itinerants, local preachers, class leaders, exhorters, and anywhere from several hundred to two or three thousand black and white men and women from within a ten- to twenty-mile radius. Separate seating was quickly adopted, but the shared experiences of prayer, public testimony, and the love feast contributed to a sense of common humanity that cut across racial lines.

The experimental climate that prevailed at the quarterly meetings that took place in Virginia and Maryland between 1774 and 1776 introduced a new stage in revivalism, one in which Africans not only stirred awakenings but themselves became the focus of spreading enthusiasm as well. Reverend Thomas Rankin's account of the 1774 quarterly meetings for the Baltimore and Kent Circuits reveals the part that Africans played in the production of the revivalist ethos. Following the love feast, preachers and communicants alike sat silently, overcome "with the divine presence." Near the end of the meeting, Rankin stood up "and called upon the poor people to look toward that part of the chapel where all the blacks were." Rankin's directive to "See the number of the black Africans who have stretched out their hands and hearts to God" served as a reminder that black and white were part of the same cosmic universe with equal access to God. Such a dramatic reversal of normal social relations was taken as a sign of sacred presence: "It seemed as if the very house shook with the mighty power and glory of Sinai's God. Many of the people were so overcome, that they were ready to faint and die under his almighty hand."[120]

The reciprocal experience between preacher and the religiously aroused black people in the gallery was also a radical breakthrough for ministers of evangelical temperament. Their discovery that appeals to the emotions could become a shortcut to conviction of sin and conversion encouraged even moderates like Rankin to abandon the stylized performances of many preachers and congregations in favor of spontaneity and emotional display. Sometime later, during a meeting in Virginia, Rankin himself experienced "an uncommon struggle in my breast"; the sermon he delivered "while under this amazing influence" produced a mass physical reaction from the entire congregation. Rankin marveled at the sight of singing, weeping, and wailing converts. But it was the intense emotionalism of the Africans in the gallery that he found "peculiarly affecting . . . almost the whole of them upon their knees; some for themselves, and others for their distressed companions."[121] The almost charismatic rapport between Methodist itinerants like Rankin and their African audiences was destined to play a major role in the religious transformation of the South.

The initial encounters of Methodist itinerants with slavery in the Southern mainland offered a genuine test of ministerial courage and conviction. In his "Thoughts Upon Slavery," published in 1774, John Wesley had denounced the slave system as "the vilest that ever saw the sun," but as yet Methodism had adopted no official antislavery position.[122] In their private writings, missionaries like Joseph Pilmore and Francis Asbury repeatedly touched on the awesome questions their meetings with bondpeople inevitably raised: "How many of these poor slaves will rise up in judgment against their Masters, and, perhaps, enter into life, while they are shut out?"[123] "How will the sons of oppression answer for their conduct when the Great proprietor of all shall call them to account?"[124] As yet, few were willing to launch an all-out assault against slavery in its most protected sanctuary, but this sentiment was clearly present. During his remarkable ministry to bondpeople in Virginia, John Littlejohn held out the alluring prospect of a new moral—and by implication social—order when he "exhorted [slaves] to serve God and be faithful, till they go where the Servant is free from the Master."[125] Thomas Rankin was perhaps the first Methodist anywhere in British America to publicly oppose chattel slavery.[126] As the divided colonists girded for war, Rankin told a large congregation at Gunpowder Falls that "the sins of Great Britain and her colonies had long called aloud for vengeance; and in a peculiar manner, the dreadful sin of buying and selling the souls and bodies of the poor Africans, the sons and daughters of Ham."[127]

Farther South, also in 1775, David Margate, another missionary who had recently arrived from Britain, preached an even stronger message to the enslaved and free populations of Low Country Georgia and South Carolina. That message was given an even greater potency by the fact that Margate was black, and almost certainly the only black British missionary to work in the American colonies. Little is known of Margate's origins or when he enrolled as a student at Trevecca College, one of the establishments founded by Selina, the Countess of Huntingdon, to train young men for various kinds of missionary work in the Old World and in the New. For many years the countess had been a friend and patron of George Whitefield, and it was by the terms of his will that in 1770 she assumed the responsibility for administering the orphanage he had established thirty years earlier at Bethesda, twelve miles outside Savannah.[128] Her inheritance included the bondpeople owned by Whitefield who worked the lands attached to the Orphan House.

In 1774 the Reverend William Piercy, who had taken charge of the Orphan House two years earlier, reported to the countess that "The poor Slaves lie very much now upon my heart. There are thousands & thousands on every side of us in these Parts & no one cares for their Souls." Piercy, who had preached on several plantations, claimed he had "never spoken to any of them but they have shewed the greatest Attention." What he sought from the countess was help. It is not clear who determined that David Margate fitted the bill. Perhaps he volunteered because in September 1774 the Countess of Huntingdon was informed that "David Margate is planning to go out to America."[129] In January 1775 "David the African" arrived in Charleston, en route to Savannah, in the company of John Cosson, a white missionary, and Cosson's wife, Elizabeth, who was to be employed as the housekeeper at Bethesda.[130]

Piercy's initial impression of David Margate could not have been more favorable: "I love the appearance of David. He appears pious & devoted & I do hope the Lord will make him a great blessing to these poor heathen around us." But based upon what he had just heard "from my dear friend [John] Edwards of C. Town," where David had already preached, Piercy harbored some doubts: "I rather fear he should speak imprudently to the black people."[131] Within a matter of days, Piercy's worst fears were to be realized: David Margate was not prepared to pursue his work within the bounds of missionary orthodoxy.

David's sexual proclivities, his insistence that "the Lord had told him that he should take a Negro woman in [the] house to be his wife that was already wife to one of [the] slaves," greatly disturbed Piercy. But far more alarming to the white missionary was the claim David made within two weeks of his arrival at Bethesda that he was a second Moses "& should be called to deliver his people from slavery."[132] Piercy warned David "that if he did not conduct himself properly he would lose his life as well as ruin my usefulness," but David continued with his "discourses to the negroes." Soon Piercy became terrified by the possibility that David would not content himself with inflammatory rhetoric but might devise "some dreadful scheme . . . to poison all the white people."[133] Word of David's "Imprudent" and "alarming conduct" spread like wildfire in the Low Country, and many white Georgians were "under a continual apprehension" that he would place himself at the head of an "Insurrection among the slaves."[134] William Piercy speculated as to the reasons for David Margate's "wicked conduct" and concluded that "a great part . . . arises from his pride . . . his pride seems so great, that he can't bear to think of any of his colour being slaves." "There was," he concluded, "no making him sensible of the state of the blacks in this country."[135]

Piercy was at a loss as to what to do with David, but the decision was taken out of his hands by white South Carolinians who were irate over and "terrified" by the black missionary's exhortations in Charleston.[136] According to John Cosson, who had heard him preach, David "not only severely reflected against the Laws of the Province respect[ing] slaves but even against the thing itself: he also compared their state to that of the Israelites during their Egyptian Bondade [sic.]"[137] Word reached Piercy that the Carolinians were so outraged and frightened by David's utterances that they intended to avoid legal niceties and "send a party of men to Georgia & take David & should they lay hold of Him he will certainly be hanged for what he has designed, as all the laws are against him." Piercy may have had no sympathy for David Margate's preaching and may have been scandalized by his sexual morality, but he was determined that the black missionary should not be lynched. With the help of James Habersham, David was put "privately" on board a ship leaving Savannah for England, and he managed to "get off with his life." In his less than seven months in the Low Country the black British missionary had "render'd himself . . . odious, to the whites," but just as significantly he had presented to the enslaved population, in the most unequivocal terms, an unforgettable image, and promise, of their ultimate deliverance from bondage.[138]

The outbreak of the Revolutionary War brought a sharp reaction among white Southerners against Methodism for several reasons: in part because Methodists were increasingly conspicuous in Virginia and Maryland,[139] in part because of Wesley's "Calm Address to Our American Colonies," and in part because suspicions grew that the British itinerants, most of whom refused to sign state-mandated oaths of allegiance, were "tories sent by Wesley to preach passive obedience and non-resistance."[140] Most were forced to withdraw from the itinerancy. Several prominent preachers, including Martin Rodda, Thomas Rankin, and George Shadford, returned to Britain.[141] Grand Jury indictments were brought against John Littlejohn and Francis Asbury, who was fined five pounds "for preaching the gospel."[142] Many native preachers were jailed, among them Freeborn Garrettson. After preaching to a large society near Bladensburg, Maryland, Philip Gatch was tarred and feathered and nearly blinded by an angry mob.[143]

Before the disruptions of the Revolutionary War brought an abrupt end to the religious awakenings, however, New Light frontier ministers had successfully created several small, stable, clearly defined African Christian communities from which the new seed of Christianity would spread. Wartime disturbances slowed down the momentum of the evangelical movement among whites but accelerated it among blacks. Quite independently of white missionaries, a number of self-proclaimed black preachers began missionary activity among their own people. Advertisements for runaway Christian slaves attest to this phenomenon. Throughout the war years Chesapeake slaveholders complained of new slave converts who were "fond of talking about religion," who "pretend to have a call to preach the gospel," or who were "fond of singing hymns, and exhorting [their] brethren of the Ethiopian tribe." The conspicuous presence of women like Hannah, who "pretends much to the religion the Negroes of late have practised," or Moll, who "speaks very good English, and has a most artful knack of framing and delivering a story, insomuch that she may be easily mistaken for a strictly religious and very upright person," bears quiet witness to the efforts of enslaved women who persistently raise questions about their place in the movement.[144]

Along the way, a core of able, articulate leaders arose from the ranks to give emerging Afro-Christianity a more indigenous character. Very early on these leaders, most of whom were unlike David Margate and willing to negotiate with whites, attempted to assert their independence by forming churches of their own. One of the most well known of these African messiahs, a man known only as Moses, began to seek and gain converts from among the enslaved population of Williamsburg in defiance of missionary efforts from outside. His work created such a sensation that the colonial government tried to stamp it out by having Moses whipped repeatedly for holding meetings. But the movement he initiated grew with renewed vigor under the leadership of Gowan Pamphlet, who began his preaching in Middlesex County. The Dover Association, one of four Separate Baptist associations in Virginia, tried to silence Pamphlet and his devoted followers through excommunication. But Pamphlet continued to preach and to perform the rituals of the faith. Soon he had built up a substantial following, which he gathered into a church. Its distinguishing mark was its spiritual independence from white support and control. Shortly before he died, Pamphlet petitioned for admittance into the Dover Association. In 1791, mindful of the black evangelist's success, the Dover Association granted official recognition to the 500-member-strong African church.[145]

The direction and approach of the developing African independence movement, to the extent that they can be attributed to a single individual, were determined by the power and personality of George Liele. A man of unique leadership skills, Liele's importance lies in his role as a catalyst and in his ability to maneuver successfully for his own measure of power. A strategy of personal diplomacy with powerful planters, who protected him and his followers, was a key element in his ability to use evangelical religion as a vehicle for the expansion and redefinition of leadership roles. Little is known about the personal side of Liele's life, or about his conversion, the central event of his life. He was born a slave in Virginia, the geographic source of the emerging black leadership. As a young man he traveled to "several parts of America," probably with his master, Henry Sharp, a Baptist from whom he might have received religious instruction. However, it is more likely that Liele was first introduced to Christianity by his father, "the only black person who knew the Lord in a spiritual way in that country." Liele's confession that "I always had a natural fear of God from my youth, and was often checked in conscience with thoughts of death," hints strongly at parental anxiety about the souls of their progeny and at efforts to rear their children to Christian standards of behavior.

Sometime in the early 1770s, Liele was taken to Georgia by Henry Sharp. There his decisive call came on a Sabbath afternoon when he went out of curiosity to hear Matthew Moore, a Baptist minister in Burke County, preach. The entire process of transformation lasted five or six months and followed the usual pattern of conviction, acceptance of salvation, and regeneration, or new birth. Sometime around 1773 Moore baptized Liele. After his call to grace, Liele "began to discover his love to other negroes, on the same plantation with himself, by reading hymns among them, encouraging them to sing, and sometimes by explaining the most striking parts of them." On Moore's recommendation, Liele was called to "exercise his gift" before a quarterly meeting. In keeping with the democratic tendencies of the Baptist faith, which attracted so many Africans to it, Liele was licensed as a probationer. Thereafter he quickly took over the function of preaching to bondpeople on different plantations and attracted a large following. On May 20, 1775, at precisely the same time David Margate was causing such a furor in Savannah and Charleston, he was ordained. Whether Liele and Margate ever met is not recorded, but Liele could not have been totally unaware of the fiery message of deliverance being preached by the British missionary. Liele, who on August 17, 1777, was freed by his master, chose to follow a very different, and under the circumstances arguably a rather more realistic, course. Three months after his ordination, he constituted the First African Church of Savannah, thereby institutionalizing African evangelism.[146]

From the ranks of Liele's converts came the future leaders of Georgia's African Protestant Christian community. The history of the conversion of David George, a fellow bondperson on the Galphin plantation, underscores the aggressive involvement of African converts in the religious awakening and in the process of African religious transformation. Born of African parents in Essex County, some fifty or sixty miles from Williamsburg, David George occasionally attended the "English church" but, by his own admission, generally lived a dissolute life. He ran away from a cruel master only to become enslaved by Native Americans, and eventually he ended up a slave on the plantation of George Galphin of Silver Bluff on the Savannah River across from Augusta in Edgefield County, South Carolina.

Galphin, apparently a Christian, encouraged or at least allowed his bondpeople to receive religious instruction. Like growing numbers of his fellow Africans, George received his first formal instruction in Christian moral and religious values at the feet of local preachers like Cyrus, a bondman from Charleston. It was Cyrus who exhorted George to reform his life, admonishing him that "if I lived so, I should never see the face of God in Glory." At this point still illiterate, George began to recite the Lord's Prayer that had been taught to him by Cyrus. Then he heard George Liele preach from the text "Come unto me all ye that labour and are heavy laden, and I will give you rest." George afterward told Liele that "his whole discourse seemed for me . . . that I was weary and heavy laden, and that the grace of God had given me rest." George, his wife, his brother, slave Jesse (or Peter) Galphin, and four other bondpeople were later baptized by the Reverend Palmer in a mill stream on the Galphin estate. When on another occasion George heard Liele preach in a cornfield he too was seized with a desire to do likewise. On Liele's advice, George began to pray with his fellow slaves. In the meantime, the Reverend Palmer gathered eight bond-people together, including George, George's wife, and Jesse Galphin, and formed a church at Silver Bluff. This church, the first black Baptist church in the Low Country, provided the forum for George to exhort and, with Palmer's help, to learn how to preach.[147]

The transition to religious leadership—and the form of leadership—represented by Gowan Pamphlet, George Liele, David George, and Jesse Galphin was a crucial step in the cultural and religious transformation of African Americans. Over time, the leadership of the traditional chief and sacred specialist would be replaced by that of the preacher, thus contributing to a new structure of identity. The public worship the new African religious leaders initiated and the congregations they gathered together up and down the Savannah River from Augusta to Savannah and in various places in Virginia, would help Africans from disparate ethnic origins to redefine their ethnic polity in terms of a new, an evangelical Protestant, religious ideology. These small enclaves, the citadels of African evangelism, would become the focal points of black Christian life, and it was around them that a settled religious life quickly emerged in the postwar South. From them emanated the first generation of black missionaries. Emissaries of the new faith, their energetic missionary activities throughout the South and the British Caribbean helped to build up a network of evangelical churches that closely bound the histories of African peoples throughout the hemisphere.

5

THE GREAT REVIVAL

PATTERNS OF WORSHIP AND THE
FORMATION OF CULTURAL IDENTITY

For more than a century and a half the vast majority of Afro-Atlantic peoples had clung tenaciously to their ancient beliefs. Excluded from the ranks of human society by virtue of their status as chattel slaves, culturally isolated from society at large and from one another by multiple identities and disparate cultural practices, they had struggled against incredible odds to recreate the domestic and communal lives that were brutally shattered by slavery and to define a new cultural identity that would transcend ethnic and cultural differences. In the forty years preceding the American Revolution the number of Africans claiming a Christian identity had slowly increased. Yet, apart from a few small enclaves in Virginia and Georgia and scattered mission stations in the Caribbean, African Christians remained an insignificant minority in all of the British Atlantic plantation societies. Beginning in 1785, however, Christianity made rapid advances, becoming by 1815 a dominant religious influence among Afro-Atlantic peoples. By 1830 a new and highly visible Afro-cultural presence had emerged. It rested on the firm foundation of evangelical Christianity.[1]

Evangelical religion provided a framework for the unprecedented social and cultural changes that mark this period of Afro-Atlantic history. As the only form of organized communal life available to slaves, evangelical institutions came to constitute important loci wherein African peoples could develop a sense of belonging and assert a cultural presence in the larger society through the creation of their own moral and social communities. Instead of a single, coherent movement, the process of conversion was a stepped transition that varied according to the local environment and in terms of temporal progression. The most critical factors affecting the timing and character of these disparate developments were the demographic configurations and the cultural and political frameworks in which religious cultures evolved. Despite these variations, the process had a global quality that derived in part from the fact that the evangelical missionaries who initially led the movement viewed themselves as emissaries of a universal church with the world as their mission field[2] and in part from the movements of people within and between societies in the wake of the American Revolution. The migration of cultures thus forms an important and continuing link between increasingly different regions of the plantation world.

The American Revolution and political independence ushered in a series of changes that dramatically transformed the religious landscape of mainland North America. The demand for religious freedom that paralleled the movement for political freedom was especially strong in the South, where evangelical sects flourished. Beginning with Virginia, old denominations like the Anglicans were disestablished and new denominations like the Baptists and Methodists established themselves. Old and new congregations split over ostensibly inconsequential matters of religious practice and ritual, and entirely new sects arose out of the religious disorder. What issued from the chaos was a keen competition for souls between the bewildering array of denominations and sects. As English and American evangelists surveyed the moral landscape, they discovered African Americans, and African Americans discovered them. It was an enduring attraction. With their deeply rooted spirituality derived from Africa and their profound religious need for a sense of meaning in life, African Americans became a great prize in the evangelical contest for church membership and gathered souls.

In the newly formed Southern states there were two discrete phases of religious change: a brief but intense postwar phase from 1785 to 1790 that remained largely confined to the Chesapeake states of Virginia and Maryland, and a general post-1800 phase precipitated by the Great Revival and extending episodically to 1830. Each phase had certain distinctive characteristics, but as historical sequences they are connected by the migrant communities that furnished the personnel and the revival culture that fueled both phases. In the spring of 1780 Francis Asbury gave up the relative security of semiretirement in Delaware and set out on an arduous tour of Virginia and North Carolina that lasted five months and covered over 1,000 miles. The long rides on bad roads, through dense woods, over rocks, and across dangerous creeks and rivers, gave Asbury a discouraging view of the effects of war and confronted him with the enormous difficulties ahead for the itinerancy. Everywhere he found "broken" societies and the region in a state of decline. People, he complained, were "so distracted with the times" that they were afraid to leave their homes or ride their horses. White Southerners, he concluded, were "insensible," and preaching to them was "of little purpose."[3]

A decade after Asbury made that discouraging assessment, two-thirds of all Methodists in the United States were located in three Southern states, Maryland, Virginia, and North Carolina.[4] Over half of all Baptists resided in five Southern states.[5] The phenomenal advance of evangelical Protestantism was a product of several different but interrelated processes operating more or less simultaneously. The first was the great spiritual awakening that began on the banks of the James River in 1785, spread through the Chesapeake until the 1790s, and faltered and then reemerged with the spectacular rise of the camp meeting revivals after 1800. The second was the physical movement of people that began in the 1760s and culminated in the vast migrations of the post-Revolutionary era, which served as the vehicle for the transplantation of the evangelical movement into the expanding West and the Caribbean. The third was the organization of a national, independent Methodist church in the United States and the extension of the itinerant system throughout the South. Central to all of these developments was the embrace of evangelical Protestant Christianity by African Americans.

The postwar revivals serve as a kind of laboratory wherein one can observe how, step by step, the religious rituals associated with black and white evangelical worship developed and established themselves. By and large what they reveal is that in certain ways African American Christianity was derivative of European American Christianity, and that often European American Christianity unconsciously borrowed from African American patterns. The outcries, tears, and tremblings often associated with camp meeting behavior were common features of Separate Baptist worship during the 1760s and of Methodist quarterly meeting revivals during the 1770s. They continued to occupy a central place in the revivals of the 1780s as well. Until the advent of the carefully orchestrated camp meeting, no rigid format shaped revival services, although for the most part worship consisted of prayers, testimonies, exhortations, preaching, and singing. The open format allowed for innovation and highly participatory forms of worship. It was within this experimental environment that African Americans began to structure and organize their own ritual devotion and to construct a belief system of their own. These collectively shared beliefs and practices formed the cultural essence of a new identity.

With the outbreak of religious awakenings in Virginia in 1785, revivalism began to take on aspects of a mass movement. In the highly decentralized structure of the quarterly meeting, conversion was increasingly characterized by charismatic phenomena, such as shaking and trances. Accounts left by Methodist itinerants of the work of revival provide graphic evidence that early on enslaved women established a definite cultural presence in revival meetings. What this suggests is that the fervor of black women's conversion led scores of men and women, black and white, to the same deeply personal, highly emotional affirmation of the faith. When the revival spirit broke out in Leesburg, Virginia, in October 1789, the Reverend John Littlejohn noted uneasily "the diff[eren']t effects produced. . . . [I] fear more evil than good w[ould] grow out of it." But "one circumstance I cannot pass over," he wrote in his journal, "a colour[ed] Woman of Mr. [John] Binns, was powerfully wrought over. A Physician pronounced she would die; our friends declared she would not. She went proved that religious affections are but little know[n] even by Phys[icians] who are strangers to God. She died indeed to sin," Littlejohn concluded, "but was made alive to God."[6]

Such anecdotal examples could be multiplied many times over to demonstrate the extent to which revival culture drew upon the energies and enthusiasm of women. An account of a house revival left by Reverend John Hagerty, elder of the Methodist Episcopal Church, is but one more example of their defining role as charismatic leaders. According to Hagerty, the Annapolis revivals of 1789 "began in a way I little expected." As he conducted a class meeting in Annapolis, Maryland, Hagerty heard a "poor soul groaning and praying." Upon investigation, he discovered a black woman in a hallway "in great distress." He began to exhort her and then proceeded to sing and pray with her. A second black woman "was soon on her knees beside the former, and God was pleased to set both their souls at liberty." The noise attracted others—an old man, the owner of the household, class members, relatives. By 9 P.M. fifteen persons were converted, at least six of them white, one of them Hagerty's brother-in-law. The following night "we had one of the loudest shouts I ever remember to have heard," and thereafter "we won converts daily." The vivid image left by Hagerty dramatically highlights the fleeting reality of black women and white men performing as functional equals in the work of conversion.[7]

Evangelical Protestant Christianity initially tolerated women as religious intermediaries, in part because of the emotional nature ascribed to women, in part because ecstatic behavior functioned more as ritual presence than active leadership and therefore did not represent an open challenge to male authority.[8] Religious enthusiasm did, however, represent an attempt on the part of women to empower themselves through mystical experiences, perhaps to establish a symbolic domain of authority by emphasizing the equal access of women to the spirit world. As a result, they had the potential to inspire reflections on the capacities of women and thereby to challenge indirectly the notion of a divinely created order with strictly male leadership. But this power was ephemeral because it was individual and dependent upon charismatic power. Female leaders whose powers were based upon expressive leadership disappeared as rapidly as they emerged, not, however, before they had made their mark on revival culture and African American worship.

The incident described by Reverend Hagerty highlights another important feature of early revival culture—the intense dialogue between black and white participants that formed the basis for the creation of a sense of shared culture. Revival meetings provided the most important institutional framework for African Americans to gain exposure to white religious forms. Their participation in evangelical meetings of various kinds initiated them into aspects of white culture and therefore served as a crucial part of the assimilative process that integrated them into the community. This is not to say, however, that African Americans merely adopted white religious beliefs and ritual practices. Simultaneous with these developments African Americans were creating a religious culture of their own through the appropriation and transformation of the worship service. An entirely different sort of revival meeting witnessed by the Reverend Philip Bruce, elder of the Methodist Episcopal Church, illustrates the point.

During a night meeting in Isle of Wight County "there arose a cry among the poor slaves (of which there was a great number present)." The noise and drama helped to build emotional excitement and to create the religious experience. Then "a number was on the floor crying for mercy, but soon one and another arose praising God." Those who had accepted conversion then provided collective support and approval for others to attain the state of spiritual ecstasy: "Those who were happy, would surround those who were careless, with such alarming exhortations, as appeared sufficient to soften the hardest hearts. If they could get them to hang down their heads, they would begin to shout and praise God, and the others would soon begin to tremble and sink. I saw a number brought to the floor . . . and there lie crying till most of them got happy."[9]

In this scene described by Bruce, an incipient form of the style of expression known as "shouting" emerges uncertainly as part of the conversion ritual. Early accounts of the First Awakening contain frequent references to vocalizations of various types, ranging from quiet rapture to wild weeping, forms of ecstatic expression congruent with both African and Protestant patterns. During the early revivals a different sort of aural expression seems to have developed among African converts. John Littlejohn's account of a meeting in Richmond in 1777 suggests subtle differences in the shouting form practiced by Africans: "The house much crowded, and many Blacks, towards the close the poor Africans could forbear no longer but with strong cryes [sic] and tears called for mercy." The alarmed reaction of the whites present is an indication that what they witnessed was quite foreign to the religious experience of many of them: "Most of the whites frightened, left the house, in confusion and dismay as if the great deep was going to overwhelm them."[10]

What exactly was the difference that so frightened white observers? Perhaps it was the often extravagant and unrestrained nature of black worship, which implied a view of the world that was wholly different from that which whites were prepared to accept. Long after shouting had become institutionalized and ritualized as part of the structure of conversion, black shouting could still incite awe and fear in whites witnessing it for the first time, as when, for example, the local preacher at Hites Chapel, on the Berkeley Circuit, "got the blacks to shouting, and some of the whites run."[11] When a black woman shouted during an evening service in St. Augustine, Florida, as late as 1821, the Reverend John Glenn observed that, "it Seamed [sic] to frighten the people." "I supposed," Glenn speculated, "it was the first time any one Shouted heare [sic]."[12] Apparently derivative of African forms, the shouting ritual was neither what it had been, nor yet what it would become. It belonged neither to the old nor to the new, but to both.

Bruce's account is a vivid description of a sacred community bound together by shared beliefs and distinctive ritual practices. For African Americans, if not for all white evangelicals, conversion was often a ritual of collective catharsis and collective commitment that was performed collaboratively. The shout they had invented to help them reach the spiritual ecstasy of conversion also served to forge social relations. It produced such a highly evocative sound that it invited a response. The reciprocal nature of the shout united the black group as a unique and distinctive spiritual community, a part of but separate from the white religious community.[13] While the evidence is admittedly sparse, it suggests the possibility that through a relatively brief period of sustained contact, the sort of possession behavior exhibited by black evangelicals may have carried over to white evangelicals. For example, from Francis Asbury's 1801 account of the youthful conversion of a "thoughtless young lady" named Gough Hollady, the niece of the wealthy Henry Dorsey Gough of Perry Hall in Maryland, we can infer a process of transmission. According to Asbury, Hollady "found the Lord among the black people" one evening and the next morning "leaped and shouted in the family pew at morning prayer,"[14] behavior that defied both racial and gender conventions.

Though not yet fully developed, the incorporation of vocalizations into the conversion ritual was well under way when Thomas Coke visited Maryland in 1789. Coke's amazement when he first heard the predominantly black Methodist society in Annapolis begin to "pray and praise aloud in a most astonishing manner" and his reluctance to "enter into the business" underscore the fact that shouting was very much a "popular" ritual, one that people learned from one another, and ministers learned from the people. Many preachers, including Coke, looked askance at such noisy worship, but as Coke reluctantly conceded, even "the softest, most connected, and most sedate of our preachers" gradually came to accept it as an appropriate expression of spiritual regeneration.[15]

As the conversion experience became more widespread and acquired greater power, male participation became increasingly common. And, although Virginia was not the sole source for the black itinerancy, it nevertheless provided fertile ground for its development and played an important role in its subsequent proliferation elsewhere. The very first waves of religious enthusiasm engendered a penchant for moral experiments, and black and white preachers often worked together in spiritual companionship. Perhaps the most striking example of such a collaboration was the partnership between Francis Asbury and Harry Hosier, an illiterate but gifted speaker whose first appearance with Asbury created a sensation in Fairfax, Virginia. A regular companion of Asbury's, Hosier also itinerated with Thomas Coke and Freeborn Garrettson, attracting large crowds of blacks and whites, some of whom angrily objected to a black man preaching before white audiences.[16]

Beyond the privileged few like Hosier were dozens of black preachers who went out on their own, quite independent of white ministers. Although most of them never rose above the rank of exhorter, the success of pioneer itinerants like Hosier encouraged a number of black men to venture into the formerly closed world of the ministry, thereby challenging at every turn the limited vision of a white clerical monopoly. In Maryland circuits, where blacks often outnumbered whites, gifted young men like Sam, at age twenty-three "very talkative among persons whom he can make free with," or the "very artful" twenty-eight-year-old Jem simply took it upon themselves to exhort or preach without benefit of ordination.[17] Not infrequently they became the focus of revivalism. From at least as early as 1778 until his death in 1795, Lewis, a slave from Essex County, preached before biracial crowds on Virginia's lower Northern Neck. At one gathering of about 300 people held at Jonathan Coates's farm, Lewis preached from Jude "to the astonishment of the auditory," as Richard Dozier, an overseer on Councillor Robert Carter's Billingsgate plantation, put it. According to Dozier, "his gift exceeded many white preachers." On a 1789 visit to the Eastern Shore Dozier heard another black itinerant, Jacob, preach to a mixed audience.[18]

These self-proclaimed preachers, sincere Christians intent on striking out on their own spiritual paths, were quick to seize upon and absorb the teaching authority of the preacher, as the Reverend James Meacham learned when he itinerated on Virginia's Greenville Circuit in 1789. Meacham opened one particular meeting as usual with prayers followed by an exhortation. Moved by the emotion of the moment, he "strove to encourage the black people out at the window." Much to his chagrin, Meacham was made aware of the inadequacy of his own evangelical methods and the pronounced superiority of Africans in proselytizing their own people by "one poor slave beginning to move off a space and speak in Exhortation. The rest of the poor innocent delinquents immediately flocked around: while I myself could be suffered to preach and to pray in the church."[19]

The incident between Reverend Meacham and the unnamed slave centered around one of the most crucial issues raised by lay evangelism: the control of preaching. A sense of the power of the spoken word as the voice of God was well understood by all concerned, black and white, male and female. Bondmen and -women, the progeny of oral-aural cultures, associated vocal communication with power—the power to establish presence, to evoke responses, to unite groups, and to create community. White church leaders also appreciated the importance of controlling sound—to discipline backsliders, to express spiritual power, to establish domination. But by the time white church leaders awoke to the incipient challenge to their authority posed by these self-proclaimed black preachers, a separate black ministry had already emerged.

According to John Asplund's *Universal Annual Register of the Baptist Denomination, in North-America*, there were five black ordained ministers in 1795 and "a number of unordained Preachers, not inserted or numbered in this Register," who insistently asked to be invested with church power.[20] Forces of change in their own right, African Americans gradually widened the breaches in the white clerical fortifications, often by entering through the new portals of biracial churches. Congregations varied widely in their responses. The more common response of the biracial churches to the charismatic lay preachers and exhorters who dared to presume upon the prerogatives of white men to "extraordinary gifts" was to try to relegate them to a separate and restricted role, which carefully distinguished their church duties from the sacramental functions monopolized by the white clergy.

In 1790, for example, Virginia's Upper King and Queen Baptist Church expelled slaves Aaron and George for preaching without a license and admonished other black members "to be careful in exercising their Gifts at their meeting among themselves, and that none of them attempt to take a text to Preach from, unless they first obtain liberty from the Church."[21] The Buck Marsh Baptist Church repeatedly warned black members not to confuse preaching and exhorting by "tak[ing] it upon themselves to be teachers and preachers at funerals." In 1792 the church admonished Ned for speaking in public without church approval, and in 1799 it found Jesse guilty of preaching after being ordered by the church to desist. Subsequently Jesse was allowed the privilege of singing, praying, and exhorting, and in 1804 he was invited to give the church "a chance of hearing him exercise his gift."[22] In 1795 the Goshen Association recommended that each church minister examine the gifts of black members and "stop such as may not be in his judgment to the advancement of God's glory."[23] Individual churches complied with the recommendation by appointing committees to "examine into the Gifts of such Black brethren . . . as Exercise a Gift Publicly."[24]

White church leaders also had to deal with church women who sought to actively share with men the leadership of the emerging evangelical community. Enjoined to silence, both black and white women began to "speak" through their participation in ritual, particularly testimony and exhortation. Gradually, women's witnessing and exhorting became more sermonic in form and inevitably led to biblical exegesis, an assumption of a male ritual role that went well beyond symbolic power and profoundly challenged existing gender divisions. Although radical groups like Separate Baptists had a tradition of female exhorters, Margaret Meuse Clay of Chesterfield County, Virginia, appears to have been the only white Regular Baptist woman who attempted to preach. She was charged with unlicensed preaching and barely escaped a public whipping.[25]

The majority of known preaching women were Methodists, probably because the organizational structure of Methodism offered unsurpassed opportunities for women to challenge male dominance.[26] More black than white women attempted to take advantage of the situation.[27] Methodist churchmen dealt with this disruptive female presence in racially distinctive ways. When, for example, a white woman, Deborah Lynch Owings, became convinced that "God has called her to preach, and that he will not bless her till he [she] obeys the call," she sought the counsel of Reverend John Littlejohn. Littlejohn's advice, "to try, as the best way to get relief," was a psychological solution intended to actually reaffirm social norms by exposing her to the considerable psychological consequences of public preaching. It worked. Littlejohn noted with some satisfaction that twice Owings "made an attempt to address the people, and failed—this cured her enthusiasm."[28]

Littlejohn's characterization of Owings as "cured" carries with it an assumption of illness, or mental affliction. The behavior of self-proclaimed white preaching women like Deborah Owings was in fact often popularly depicted as pathological because it had the potential to subvert not simply clerical authority but power relations and the entire social order. Such women were said to be "mad," their claim to sacred power a delusion and therefore not really a form of power at all.[29] After the turn of the century literature directed specifically toward these women began to appear. An antirevival tract published in 1814, for example, explicitly condemned women's testimony and teaching as "inconsistent with the due subordination and modesty of their sex," thus linking for the first time questions of spiritual authority and gender.[30]

It is striking that the mental state of black women who challenged gender role definitions did not become an issue in the early revivals. Perhaps this was because expressive behavior was culturally viewed as inherent in black women's natures. The construction of separate spiritual identities for black and white women accomplished several things. It created dichotomous gender images by asymmetrically valuing male and female as rational/irrational, orderly/disorderly, thus reinforcing gender values and gender structures of society and at the same time providing reinforcement for a male monopoly of the ministry. It differentiated white women from black women, separating them from each other and establishing a racial boundary that ritually divided the religious community into two separate groups, thus foreshadowing the much greater divergence that appeared in the nineteenth-century revivals.

For all its power, by 1790 the revival movement seemed to be faltering, perhaps dying out. But the maturation of two separate processes, migration and the launching of missionary work, combined to give the movement new energy and power and contributed to its rapid diffusion after 1800. The story of Afro-Christianity is inextricably bound up with both of these processes. The local migration of black and white Virginians that began in the pre-Revolutionary years, expanded in the postwar period, lengthening westward across the mountainous wilderness into Kentucky and southward into the Caribbean. The migration carried the spirit and, in some cases, the personnel of revival religion. A good example is the movement of between 500 and 600 Virginia Baptists into Kentucky in 1781.

Led by the Reverend Lewis Craig, pastor of the Gilbert's Creek Church of Spotsylvania County, Captain William Ellis, from the Nottaway Baptist Church, and a dozen or so other preachers, the entourage of Virginia Baptists consisted of all or parts of several congregations.[31] Traveling with them was a large number of forced black migrants, among them a man known as "Uncle Peter," or "Old Captain," who had accompanied Captain Ellis on several earlier expeditions to Kentucky. Their story is exemplary of the experiences of frontier slave populations who struggled successfully to reconstruct the various types of communities that massive forced migrations inevitably disrupted or destroyed.[32]

The process of re-creating the spiritual community began on the long journey to the new country. To Peter belonged the task of binding separate spiritual communities to one another and to the Baptist faith and discipline: "At times . . . ," as the caravan made its toilsome way through the mountain passes, "there was a mighty lifting up of voices among the negroes for 'Uncle Peter' was with them and he set the example." Peter, a former member of the Boone's Creek Baptist Church, of which his master, the Reverend Joseph Craig, was pastor, was, in all probability, the first black nonordained preacher to deliver a sermon on Kentucky soil. In 1784, on John Maxwell's land near Maxwell Spring in Lexington, Peter founded the First African Baptist Church of Lexington and Kentucky. By the mid-nineteenth century it was the largest church in the Elkhorn Association.[33]

The march of Methodism into the Lower South was initially propelled by the movement of people that began in the 1760s and culminated in the vast post-Revolutionary migration of planters and enslaved people from Virginia and Maryland into South Carolina and Georgia.[34] Asbury's epic preaching tour of 1785 had led to the establishment of the first—and predominantly black—Methodist society in Charleston, but the annual conference remained doubtful "whether it would be for the glory of God to send even one Preacher" to the "barren soil" of South Carolina. However, as Asbury discovered, many of the migrants "that had no religion in Virginia, have found it in their removal into Georgia and South Carolina."[35] A petition of a group of migrants from Virginia persuaded the conference to send two "travelling preachers," Hope Hull and Jeremiah Maston, to the circuit then called Pee Dee, which included the coastal parishes and the region around the Great Pee Dee where enslaved people made up about 30 percent of the population.[36]

Thereafter Methodism in South Carolina "increased beyond any formed example," as South Carolina's first historian, David Ramsay, put it. Methodism grew at a faster rate than any other denomination precisely because its preachers went out to the advancing frontier. In keeping with the Methodist strategy for implanting Christianity, the state was divided into twelve circuits and stations through which twenty-six itinerants rode daily, except on Mondays. According to Ramsay's calculations, between them the itinerants preached 156 sermons weekly, 8,112 sermons yearly, exclusive of night and informal gatherings. In addition to the traveling preachers there were ninety-three local preachers who preached on the average two sermons each a week for a total of 9,672 a year. The total number of Methodist sermons annually preached in South Carolina amounted to 17,784.[37]

This highly organized missionary activity and the post-Revolutionary migration of peoples precipitated a different sort of cultural interaction and exchange on an international scale. Except for the Moravians, who in 1792 had 137 men and women at work in the West Indies and the trust estate operated by the Society for the Propagation of the Gospel on the Codrington estate in Barbados, there was no systematic attempt to convert slaves until the 1780s.[38] But beginning in the 1780s the British sugar islands experienced an influx of American emigrants and British missionaries. After the American Revolution a number of black émigrés, acting independently of white missionaries, began evangelizing in parts of the Caribbean that had never before heard the Christian message.

Whether they were émigrés from the mainland or missionaries sent from Britain, the sugar islands presented the missionaries of every Protestant sect and denomination with a cultural and political framework that was fundamentally different from that of the American South. For one thing, the population of the islands was overwhelmingly black. In 1790, for example, whites represented only 15 percent of the total population of Barbados and less than 5 percent of the total population of Jamaica.[39] In the same year Maryland was 65 percent white, Georgia was 64 percent white, and South Carolina was 56 percent white.[40] Moreover, compared to population of the American South, by the early nineteenth century the island population contained a significantly higher proportion of free black and free colored people, whose agendas did not always or necessarily conform to those of enslaved people. In 1800, for example, when the combined populations of Maryland, Georgia, and South Carolina included just under 23,800 free blacks, Jamaica alone was home to an estimated 10,000 free blacks and people of color.[41]

Unlike the scattered rural population of the American South, in most of the islands the creolized European population clustered together in towns or retreated to England, leaving the management of their estates in the hands of attorneys and overseers. Attorneys were an especially influential and powerful group who could admit or deny entrance to the estates they controlled, a power that would prove to be of critical and continuing importance in shaping the contours of formal missionary activity. However, although they might turn away white missionaries, neither attorneys nor overseers could totally prevent the transmission of religious ideas between and within estates.

Although the number of urban slaves was gradually increasing on some islands, the vast majority of enslaved people were plantation workers, most of whom worked on units of over fifty, a contrast to the relatively small units that characterized the American South.[42] Creolized Africans predominated among the slave populations in all of the islands, but they retained stronger elements of African culture than did their counterparts in almost any place on the mainland, with the possible exception of Low Country South Carolina and Georgia and the Sea Islands.[43]

By contrast to the political independence of the mainland, the islands continued to endure a colonial status that would directly influence the course of all missionary activity. Until the second decade of the nineteenth century relations between evangelical missionaries and planters varied from short-tempered toleration to active persecution. However, the planter elite's economic, military, and political dependence on the imperial government meant that local policies and interests were subject to the constant influence of the home government. As a result of all of these factors the dynamics of religious change in the Caribbean would be significantly different from those taking place on the mainland.

The activities of black American émigrés contributed decisively to the shaping of an Afro-cultural world that embraced the American South and a number of Caribbean islands. Individual case histories are sketchy, but several taken together illustrate both the transatlantic and the inter-American dimensions of the religious transformation of the British sugar islands in the aftermath of the American Revolution.

The First African Church of Savannah, Georgia, was the center from which the black Baptist movement spread. George Liele was instrumental in establishing the first evangelical foothold in Jamaica, where even the erstwhile Moravians had found little success. Another highly significant nexus in the religious history of the mainland and the islands was formed by Brother Amos, a black preacher who apparently left Georgia at the same time as Liele and established a church at Providence in the Bahamas. According to Asplund's *Universal Register*, the New Providence Church was established in 1788 with forty members.[44]

George Liele left Savannah with the British when it was evacuated not as an accredited missionary but as a refugee, and he and "four brethren from America" formed the first Baptist church in Kingston in September of 1784. Liele's church consisted mostly of slaves and poor, free blacks and people of color, with a sprinkling of equally poor whites, whom he baptized in the sea. By 1791 the Kingston church had 225 members in full communion and 350 adherents. The spread of the Afro-Baptist movement among the slaves on the sugar estates and mountain plantations in the interior was the work of other émigrés from Georgia, two of them former slaves, Moses Baker and George Vineyard, and a free black man from America, John Gilbert.[45]

Although British Baptists were divided over the efficacy of missionary activity, the example of the Moravians and the Methodists played an important part in inspiring the creation of the Baptist Missionary Society in 1792. The Society began its work two years later, but in India rather than in the West Indies. In fact it was to be another twenty years, and then at the suggestion of George Liele and other black Baptists, before the Society turned its attention to the Caribbean. In 1803 the Society considered sending a missionary to Jamaica, but it was not until 1814 that the first Baptist mission was established on the island, at Montego Bay.[46] It was to be highly significant that for almost thirty years the Baptist faith in Jamaica was allowed to develop without experiencing the interference or the particular orthodoxy of British missionaries. When British missionaries finally began their work on the island they would encounter not only the hostility of the planter class but also the deeply entrenched beliefs and rituals of independent Baptist congregations who had splintered from the black Baptist church founded by George Liele.

At least one of these independent congregations, one of the many sects that proliferated in Jamaica, was led by yet another American émigré, George Lewis. Converted to Christianity during the Virginia revivals, Lewis became a member of Liele's orthodox Baptist congregation in Kingston. During the early 1790s that congregation was rocked by a "dispute respecting speaking with tongues, a gift to which several pretended." Lewis was prominent among those who "separated from the church" to form their own "distinct congregations." Lewis and the other leaders of these splinter groups, who referred to themselves as "Independent Baptists" but who eventually became known collectively as "Native Baptists," offered a theology that "not a few, in different parts of the country," found highly attractive. And the reasons for its appeal are not difficult to fathom.[47] What Liele, and then British missionaries, lambasted as "visionary and absurd" interpretations of Baptist beliefs that were riddled with "many errors," "abounding in superstition," and infused with "false notions"[48] appealed to so many enslaved people precisely because they laid such a heavy emphasis on "all the ecstatic and experimental elements in religion."[49]

Despite the strenuous efforts of the more orthodox black Baptists and, during the late 1810s and 1820s, of British missionaries to quash a religious ideology they found both abhorrent and threatening, and to discredit influential black and free colored leaders whom with some justification they termed "Christianized obeahs," the "Native Baptists" not only survived but also assumed a critical religious and political role in "The Baptist War," the momentous Jamaican slave revolt of 1831.[50]

All evangelical missions in the Caribbean, and not merely the Baptists, sought to follow the example of the pioneering Moravians, whose flourishing missions in Antigua reported a membership of 7,400 slaves and free people of color in 1791.[51] Among other things, the Moravian experience had convinced white missionaries that a reliably trained and disciplined black missionary force could be put to productive advantage in instilling moral discipline and subordination in the large and potentially dangerous enslaved populations of the Caribbean. Nowhere perhaps was this more true than in Jamaica, whose 30,000 or so free white inhabitants were greatly outnumbered by enslaved people. The belief held by some that conversion would make hostile slaves more tractable and the sincere conviction held by others that Christians had a moral and religious obligation to convert slaves persuaded even reluctant Anglicans to enter the mission field.[52]

Among the first to do so was the Anglican cleric James Ramsay, who in 1784 recommended the appointment of a chaplain to begin mission work among the slaves on the large sugar plantations, "where they compose communities of themselves, and where the discipline necessary for humanizing them can be carried on." Ramsay's plan, which was closely influenced by the remarkable success of the Moravian slave missions in Antigua, called for the training of a number of "sensible and teachable slaves" to assist the chaplain because they "could talk more familiarly and feelingly to their fellows than the minister."[53] Although Ramsay's plan had the enthusiastic support of Beilby Porteus, bishop of London and diocesan of the Established Church in the West Indies, the Society for the Propagation of the Gospel managed to send only one missionary to the Leeward Islands before the end of the eighteenth century.[54]

Ramsay's fellow missionaries in Jamaica had no illusions about the nature and purpose of missionary efforts to the island's slave population. Reverend W. Stanford argued forcefully, if unnecessarily, for Christianization as a means to achieve thoroughgoing religious and behavioral change. In making his case Stanford recalled his experience as an army chaplain of the Mosquito Coast. Confronted by rebellious slaves, Stanford hastily instructed a small group of slaves "in the first principles of Christianity," then quickly baptized and exhorted them "to shew themselves worthy of the religion into which they were admitted" by helping to suppress the revolt. The sincerity of their conversion is at best questionable; nevertheless, the success of the operation "pointed to me the advantages that might be derived to Jamaica by a religious instruction of our Negroes."

Among the advantages Stanford counted was the shedding of all vestiges of traditional religion. Christianization, he promised, would end the "drunken nocturnal funerals" where "intestine dangers" to the white population were plotted and would break the "most powerful influence of Obea or witchcraft," which was viewed by white Jamaicans as a malevolent spiritual force and the source of the "dreadful rebellions" that periodically rocked the island. Stanford made little headway among white Jamaicans, who dismissed his proselytizing efforts as a self-interested attempt to collect the three dollar baptismal fee. Nor did he win many disciples among black Jamaicans, who initially saw little relevance in the Christian notion of an all-powerful God. Ironically, the hapless Stanford's decision to abandon the baptismal fee fostered the impression that "Christian obea [baptism] can be [of] little worth, since obtained at no expense."[55] Through the first decade of the nineteenth century black converts to Anglicanism would remain, as they had always been, comparatively few and far between. The Baptist faith, together with the Methodism that was also brought to the sugar islands by African émigrés from the North American mainland, would prove infinitely more alluring.

When Thomas Coke visited St. Eustasius in 1787 he found that a small Methodist society had already been organized by Harry and a black woman, "who came from America."[56] The Methodist society in Nevis was also built by "a few American slaves." Former members of an American society, they were purchased on the continent and brought to the island, where they assisted the work of the missionaries.[57] Five years after the first crusading black evangelists implanted evangelical Protestantism in the Caribbean, Thomas Coke launched the first organized effort to extend the Methodist mission system to the West Indies. Within three years Methodist stations had been established in Jamaica, Barbados, Dominica, St. Vincent, Grenada, Nevis, St. Kitts, and Tortola.[58]

It was the Wesley Methodists who, despite the intense and often violent opposition they encountered from the planter class because of their reputation as opponents of chattel slavery, made the most effective use of the pedagogy of conversion pioneered by the Moravians. However, a planter hostility that often prevented their own licensing as preachers and decreed that of black and free colored people to be strictly illegal, meant that in a purely formal sense white Methodist missionaries had little choice but to make covert use of their black and colored converts. And this they did with a remarkable degree of success. Through the symbiotic efforts of white missionaries and local black and free colored converts Methodism's reach was extended from the towns, where small societies were originally formed, to the rural areas, where black slaves so heavily outnumbered whites.

Although Thomas Coke had visited Jamaica and preached in Kingston during his third tour of America, no white Methodist missionary regularly served Jamaica until William Hammett took a post in Kingston in 1791. When Hammett arrived in Kingston he located eight Methodists whom he organized into his first class. Three of the eight were white; the other five were free colored and black people, all of whom had moved to Jamaica from the North American mainland during the 1780s. Included in their number was Anne Able Smith, a white refugee who had resolutely defended Coke against a white mob during his first visit to Jamaica.[59] Within a year Hammett and his group had gathered 234 converts in and around Kingston and had formally organized the Methodist mission into classes composed of twelve to twenty members, each of them headed by a black or colored class leader or exhorter.[60] The formation of cadres of devout, resilient disciples able and willing to withstand verbal abuse and physical assaults by stone-throwing gangs of white youths thus created a missionary alternative to the white ministry.

The new Christian converts delivered the Methodist message to enslaved peoples in towns and villages and on the mountain plantations surrounding Kingston with all the conversion zeal of early Christians. As in Antigua and the American South, enslaved, free black, and free colored women, as well as white women, assumed a prominent role in this process. Sometimes they were solely responsible for forming and, for varying lengths of time, pastoring and exhorting congregations. In the early 1790s, for example, a free colored woman named Burnett, who lived in the vicinity of Manchioneal Bay, in St. Thomas-in-the-East, was converted to Methodism, but by whom it is not known. However, she had "been informed of two principal duties which had been taught, namely that people ought to meet together to pray to God, and, that instead of living as they were doing, they ought to get decently married." The first of these "duties" she carried out by organizing meetings of "a few of her neighbours." The implementation of the second duty also involved the assumption of traditional male clerical authority. "Negro marriages . . . had never been heard of" in her part of St. Thomas, and she "saw no way but to perform the duties of a clergyman herself, and she actually married several couples." Precisely what form these marriage ceremonies took is not recorded, but Miss Burnett's "humble efforts" so antagonized the local planter class that she was forced to flee to Kingston "for her life."[61]

Despite the activities of Miss Burnett and others, the number of converts was small until 1795, when a religious revival centered in Kingston and Port Royal inaugurated a revival cycle that spread to large sugar plantations like Henry Shirley's Spring Garden, whose 600–700 slaves "were willing to hear." That they were able "to hear" owed much to John H. Constant, who had been born a free black in Antigua and worked as a servant in the Gilbert household. Constant was subsequently employed by a naval officer, and it was through this connection that he arrived in Jamaica, where he was converted to Methodism by William Hammett. How and when Constant first encountered Henry Shirley is unclear, but he managed to persuade this influential planter and custos of St. George Parish to allow him to preach at Spring Garden and Petersfield. Quite by chance another eminent planter, John Scott, heard Constant exhort to Shirley's slaves and was so impressed by what he heard that he gave his permission for Methodist preachers to visit his estate in St. Thomas-in-the-East.[62] The efforts of free black and free colored women and men like Barnett and

Constant were to be instrumental in the spread of Methodism and in the formation of new societies, each with a full complement of local leaders.

Members were divided into men's and women's classes, each with its own leader, a man or woman responsible for leading prayers and hymns and catechizing newcomers. Each society also had its own local exhorters "who [were] constantly employed on Sundays in the ministry of the word." So central to the Methodist mission were these black and colored leaders that they, rather than English missionaries, were the chief spokesmen for Christianity. Enfeebled by the baleful Jamaican climate and persecuted by wrathful whites, the handful of English missionaries who followed one another at irregular intervals looked to a local supply of missionaries, the chief source of which was the large black society at Kingston. At the turn of the century a single white missionary and nine black and colored local preachers or exhorters, "who spoke in public for God," ministered to the nearly 600 Methodists on the island.[63] The rapid growth of predominantly black mission churches and the proliferation of local preachers offering their own interpretation of a potentially dangerous gospel in Jamaican creole eventually induced in the white island inhabitants feelings of widespread insecurity that rapidly degenerated into pandemonium as a consequence of the French Revolution and the Haitian Revolution, the latter a mere ninety miles away.

Beleaguered by enemies within and without, the Jamaican Assembly launched a concerted effort to silence the missionaries and local preachers who were deemed the most serious threats to the island's security. Legislation of 1802, which prohibited the "preaching of ill-disposed, illiterate, or ignorant enthusiasts," precipitated a reign of terror that Coke said "far, very far exceeds all the persecutions we have met with in the other islands, unitedly considered."[64] Methodist missionaries were denied licenses to preach and were subjected to constant harassment. Hammett's life was threatened, and at one point he was so ill he was unable to preach for a month.[65] The law took particular aim at the emerging black ministry. George Liele and Moses Baker were charged with sedition and held in irons.[66] They were eventually allowed to resume preaching, but Liele dropped out of public work sometime around 1807.[67] His old congregation in Kingston "ceased to assemble to worship God" because Thomas Nicholas Swigle, who had replaced Liele as pastor, "was a man of color."[68] A few black Baptist congregations on plantation estates survived, but most were broken up, their membership scattered.[69]

Under pressure from the imperial government, the Jamaican authorities allowed Methodists and Baptists to resume work until 1807, when a consolidated slave code was enacted by the Assembly. The "persecution law," as it was commonly called, imposed fines and imprisonment for preaching to or teaching slaves. The Corporation of Kingston passed a similar ordinance making it illegal even to sing psalms or hymns. Henry Williams, the local preacher who led the Methodist society in the parish capital of Morant Bay, was sentenced to one month at hard labor for "singing and praying,"[70] a clear indication that singing was regarded as a form of religious instruction. Rigid enforcement of the laws effectively ended public worship and closed down the Methodist chapels in Kingston and Morant Bay. When black Jamaicans tried to enter the chapel in defiance of the order, the missionaries posted "leaders" at the doors to keep them out. Still they came and "frequently stood weeping in crowds about the chapel gate." Except for brief intervals when the corporation agreed to allow individual missionaries to preach, the chapels in Kingston and Morant Bay remained closed for ten years.[71] In Barbados, where threats of corporal punishment had kept slave membership in Methodist societies small, white mobs broke up the meetings and eventually succeeded in closing the Bridgetown chapel.[72]

Methodist missionaries continued to be special targets of repressive action because their social relations with slaves represented a dangerous undermining of the very foundation of inequality and subordination upon which the entire social structure rested. The charges brought by the Common Council and Assembly in Morant Bay in 1811 illustrate dramatically why missionaries were widely regarded as "enemies to Caesar." Charges were leveled for a variety of reasons, including "advancing improper persons to the office of the Ministry," which involved over twenty black and colored local preachers, some of them "very forward and bad"; "making people of colour equal or higher than White People" by seating colored women in the gallery on the east end of the chapel and placing white people between them and black men; "dreadful familiarity with slaves," including shaking hands in public and addressing one another as "brothers"; an "unchristian familiarity with Coloured and Black Women"; and "a dreadful contempt of slavery" in declaring from the pulpit that slaves were not obligated to work on Sundays.[73]

Ironically, the more violent the persecution the more attractive Christianity became to bondmen and -women, giving credence to the argument that conversion was for many enslaved people a form of resistance. The year before the "persecuting laws" were passed there were 622 black and colored members and 22 white members in the Kingston Methodist society, another 95 at Morant Bay, and somewhere under 100 in four other small societies elsewhere on the island. A year after the laws went into effect, membership in the Kingston society dropped to 560, only to soar up to 2,000 by 1814. By 1815 the Kingston society reported 2,700 members, thus approaching in size John Baxter's society in Antigua, which had a long-established tradition of planter patronage and by 1815 a well-developed institutional base of flourishing schools in English Harbour and Parham and two more in rural areas.[74] Only in Barbados, which reported fewer than twenty black and colored members in society in 1811, were repressive measures successful, probably due to the effectiveness of the well-armed and well-trained local militia in preventing and breaking up meetings.[75]

It was not until the second decade of the nineteenth century that the climate for mission work began to improve.[76] Two separate factors determined the central framework of religious development: the colonial status of the islands and mounting evidence that religion could be a stabilizing rather than a radicalizing force. International events beginning in the late eighteenth century reinforced the economic and military dependence of the colonies on the imperial government. Except for Barbados, the islands were heavily reliant on regular British troops for the internal protection of their white populations—a fact that was forcefully brought home by the Second Maroon War in Jamaica in 1795 and the Barbados Revolt of 1816. At the same time the Napoleonic Wars emphasized the dependence of the islands on imperial military protection for external defense. Under these circumstances, pressure from the imperial government to permit the religious instruction of slaves finally began to yield results. In 1816 the Jamaica Assembly agreed to allow missionaries to preach without legal restrictions but explicitly denied the same right to black preachers.[77]

The mild thaw in relations between planters and missionaries was aided by a decided weakening of missionary zeal for the early experiment with social equality that had drawn the wrath of slave owners. Under the pressures of persecution missionaries demonstrated a willingness to do whatever was necessary to convince the ruling order that they were not "enemies to Caesar." For example, during the French wars Moravian and Methodist missionaries in Antigua had helped raise several corps of armed black volunteers from the membership of their respective societies.[78] At the height of the panic surrounding the Barbados Revolt of 1816, Reverend S. P. Woolley went to the Antiguan authorities to offer his services to help contain the contagion of rebellion. Woolley's own investigation persuaded him that black Antiguan Methodists had "no disposition even to murmur at their situation; much less to rebel." As final proof of the stabilizing effects of Christianity, Woolley quoted a church leader who "took up and book and said 'Sir, with this book in your hand, you will do more to prevent rebellion, than all the King's men.'"[79]

Woolley's appraisal of religion as "the bulwark of our colony, the guardian of our peace, the author of our tranquillity [sic,] and the grand cause of our safety," signaled the beginning of the end of the evangelicals' grand experiment with social equality.[80] John Wiggins's report to the Missionary Society in London written a year later acknowledged the necessity of compromising certain religious values as the price of propagation of the gospel: "I imagine that our Missionaries will meet with great encouragement in future in this island if they will decline employing Brown or Black people as Leaders or other officers in the Society." As evidence that conciliation paid off, Wiggins claimed that although prayer meetings were still prohibited by law, estate overseers and attorneys were "generally very indulgent to our people and not only wink at their preaching in that way but in numerous cases encourage and assist in the building of Plantation chapels and otherwise assist in promoting the moral instruction of Negroes."[81] But Wiggins was guilty of exaggeration: most overseers and attorneys were not as "indulgent" as he intimated.

Although relations between planters and missionaries gradually improved during the 1820s, the Jamaica Assembly continued to search for ways to control the remarkable sect of popular preachers and exhorters, whose work had been vital to the survival of evangelical Protestantism during the decade of intense persecution. The 1823 and 1826 revisions of the slave code prohibited "ignorant, superstitious, or designing slaves" from preaching, as did the disallowed slave code of 1816.[82] Moreover, prospective white missionaries were still required to apply to local magistrates for licenses authorizing them to preach, and there was no guarantee that their applications would be approved. Much depended upon the disposition of the planters who dominated these boards.[83] Both despite and because of these constraints and because no missionary society had as yet the means to field a large missionary force, a far greater number of Afro-Jamaicans were exposed to Christianity through self-proclaimed black and colored preachers, exhorters, and male and female class leaders than by white missionaries. Nonetheless, no black preacher was licensed in Jamaica before emancipation in 1833. In the meantime, an institutionalized black clergy was rapidly emerging in the American South.

There were striking similarities and fundamental differences in patterns of religious growth and development in the British Caribbean and the American South. In the British Caribbean most whites, who were not particularly renowned for their religiosity, shunned evangelical Protestantism in favor of the established Anglican Church. As a consequence the overwhelmingly black evangelical churches formed the primary context for growth. In the American South, the Second Awakening, the dramatic resurgence of revivalism whose explosive spirit was unleashed by the Great Kentucky Revival of 1801, was the principle vehicle for growth.[84] The biracial character of Southern revivalism decisively shaped black and white religious culture.

After 1800 a decisive shift occurred in the character of Southern revivalism. The partnership between English missionaries and African itinerants had developed in a fashion that mirrored the ebullient freedom of early itinerant revivalism. In the more complicated geography of the Second Awakening, the white evangelical establishment sought to shore up the jagged boundaries of race, class, and gender by isolating African men and women behind the walls of cultural segregation. While there were significant continuities between the First and Second Awakenings, the latter had certain novel features that both reflect and recapitulate key changes in race and gender relations that reverberated through Southern society in the late eighteenth and early nineteenth centuries, namely the accommodation reached by evangelical leadership and slaveholding society on the question of slavery; the formation of a proslavery version of Christianity and the acceleration of the movement toward evangelical Protestantism by the upper ranks of Southern society that accompanied it; and the emergence of a coherent patriarchal ideology based on the subordination of women and the enslavement of Africans. The special sense of racial and class superiority and the gender roles associated with the rapidly developing patriarchy were dramatically reproduced in the spatial arrangements of the camp meeting and of the biracial churches that proliferated after 1800.

Camp meetings were to a large extent but extensions of the Virginia revivals. Most of the inhabitants of Kentucky were migrants from Virginia, and many of the personnel of the revival movement had received their training in Virginia. However, camp meetings differed significantly from the Virginia revivals in size and duration and, most importantly, in certain aspects of the ritual setting. The meeting site was usually situated near a stream or other source of water to accommodate the needs of the 8,000 to 12,000 people who commonly attended. Horses and carriages and rows of closely lined tents formed an oblong or semicircular, theaterlike enclosure, at one end of which were ranged rows of preaching stands or stages from which several preachers officiated day and night without interruption. Facing the preaching stand were rows of plank seats that were divided by a central aisle into two sections, one for white men and one for white women. Near the foot of the preaching stands stood a large post-and-rail mourners pen, admission to which was monitored by guards. Behind the preachers stands and at some distance from the white assembly were rows of tents occupied by black participants.[85]

The physical arrangement of seating represents the general direction of the Second Awakening: It destroyed the perception of a revolution in spiritual authority that had been perpetuated by spatially open meetings; and it delineated the fault lines of race, class, and gender and physically structured the idea that for men and women, and for blacks and whites, spiritual equality operated on different terms. Thus, while evangelical ideology continued to pronounce the doctrine of egalitarianism, the spatial arrangements of the meeting argued differently, reproducing as they did the race and gender hierarchies that had been temporarily suspended during the First Awakening. Beyond these new social and psychological walls, divergent forms of ritual behavior and a different constellation of worship patterns began to emerge.

From the beginning black and white evangelicals had drawn upon distinctive spiritual traditions, which in the intimacy of church and house revivals mutually reinforced one another. The separate spaces of the camp meeting encouraged the development of differences in the style and substance of the conversion ritual. Professional revivalists, who made their first appearance in the Great Revival, introduced a repertory of behaviors that took the white conversion ritual to remarkable and bizarre levels of expression known as "bodily exercises." The first appearance of a pattern that quickly became a recurring phenomenon was at a meeting of the Red River congregation in Logan County, Kentucky, in 1799. The meeting was presided over by a group of Presbyterian preachers locally known as the "Sons of Thunder," and John McGee, a Methodist preacher.[86] Nothing unusual occurred until McGee rose to speak. Concluding that "it was his duty to disregard the usual orderly habits of the denomination," McGee "went through the house shouting, and exhorting with all possible ecstasy and energy, and the floor was soon covered with the slain; their screams for mercy pierced the heavens."[87]

The paroxysms of ecstasy deliberately provoked by McGee became commonly known as the "falling exercise." The dancing exercise was added to the repertory at a meeting at Turtle Creek when John Thompson, a seceding Presbyterian preacher, danced around the preaching stand for over an hour, all the while chanting in a low voice, "This is the Holy Ghost—Glory!" Thereafter New Light Presbyterians began "to encourage one another to praise God in the dance, and unite in that exercise."[88] The most complete description of the procedures used to choreograph a ritual performance was recorded by Benjamin Latrobe, an eyewitness to a marathon effort by the blacksmith-preacher Seely Bunn that took place at a Methodist camp meeting near Georgetown in 1809.

Bunn used a formulaic composition to catapult the group into a kind of ecstatic trance: "Oh poor sinful damned souls, poor sinful souls all of ye, will ye be damned, will ye, will ye, will ye be damned, no, no, no, no, don't be damned, now ye pray and groan and strive with the spirit," he admonished. The general groaning and shrieking commanded by Bunn spread contagiously through the assembly, increasing in volume and tempo. Taking Acts 24–25 as a text, Bunn then used practiced gestures to put bodies in motion: "And so it was with Festus, he trembled, he trembled, he trembled." As he said the words, Bunn extended his arms sideways and then shook violently, giving literal expression to the popular phrase "shaking the dry bones."

Bunn's orchestration of the ceremony of conversion carried the meeting to a new emotional threshold by adding auditory and sensory stimulation to excite several senses simultaneously. First, he singled out one woman and directed the group "to see how her bosom heaves and throbs, how her whole frame is agitated, how the tears start into her eyes, how they burst forth . . . how she trembles, how she trembles, how she trembles. How she trembles, and now comes the stroke of grace, the stroke." With each utterance of the word "stroke" Bunn struck one hand into the other with a loud clap, an action he repeated some twenty times, each time crying out, "the stroke again, and another stroke, another stroke." Finally, the roaring Bunn triggered in the woman the supreme act of religious expression, the signal moment of the entire production: "and now it works, it works, it works, Oh God for Power, power, power, power, power, power, power, power, power . . . there it is, now she has it, she has it, glory, glory, glory, glory."[89]

These learned bodily techniques produced, or perhaps induced, a distinctive kind of motor behavior reminiscent of the patterned behavior exhibited during the Methodist revivals of 1758 at Cambuslang and Kilsyth in Scotland, and Everton and Bristol in England. In the American revivals of the Second Awakening, as in the earlier Scottish and English revivals, more men and a high percentage of children and youth were affected. In its most extreme forms the conversion ritual was characterized by the same eccentric repertory of motor behaviors seen in the Scottish and English revivals: violent contortions of the body and spasmodic jerkings, rolling and spinning, running and leaping. Sinners under conviction emitted deep groans and piercing shrieks, howled and growled, snapped and barked, their darkened and distorted faces revealing the horror and anguish of convicted sinners.[90]

Although the Scottish and English revivals furnished the prototype for white ecstatic behavior, white evangelical Christians had neither a persistent cultural tradition nor a religious framework to accommodate ecstatic performance regularly. By contrast, emotional ecstasy formed the central core of the black Christian ethos. Black men and women in the throes of conversion did, on occasion, exhibit the same motor behavior as whites. Among African Americans, however, behavioral expectations were different and different performance rules prevailed with distinctive ritual results. Their relative isolation at camp meetings afforded black worshipers an opportunity to gradually embellish the ritual forms they had begun to create during the First Awakening. Far from abandoning ancestral structures and forms, they fused characteristically African aesthetic elements with Christian forms to create their own distinctive religious rituals, which were at once Christian and African.

The stimulus for the emotional ecstasy that marked the climax of the black conversion experience was more often than not rhythmic, accompanied by music or sermon. Whether or not African Americans forged original music forms from an essentially African musical heritage and transmitted them to white co-religionists or whether they adapted and perpetuated basically white liturgical forms to suit their own cultural and social needs has been the subject of extended debate among scholars. Most scholarship now recognizes that there were elements held in common by both cultures: for example, the Protestant tradition of lining-out songs and the analogous antiphonal structure, or the call and response characteristic of traditional West African music.[91] Neither the ultimate origins nor the degree of musical interchange can be documented from the few shreds of evidence surviving from the eighteenth century.[92] What is certain is that an Africanized spiritual was fashioned by early black Christians.

Anglican missionaries were the first to give religious instruction to Africans and to teach them to sing psalms. During the 1740s Isaac Watts hymns were reprinted in the colonies and were probably introduced to black Christians by the Reverend Samuel Davies during the First Great Awakening. Although musical styles probably varied according to denomination and geographic location, a white liturgical tradition was thus implanted among a very small proportion of the African population. Simultaneously with this development, African slaves began shaping their own unique music forms in the isolated slave quarters where they lived and in the fields where they worked. The work songs they created preserved many of the characteristics of West African music: offbeat phrasing, staggered accents, musical interpolations, repetition, and call and response.

During the Virginia revivals black and white Christians began to compose their own religious songs. "Some of [them]," the Reverend John Leland wryly observed, "have more divinity in them than poetry or grammar," some of them "have little of either."[93] Contemporary sources have very little to say about the creative process or musical interchange, but in his history of early Methodism Jesse Lee affirms at the least the possibility of reciprocal influences. "It was often the case," Lee wrote, "that the people in their corn fields, white people, or black, and sometimes both together would begin to sing, and being affected would begin to pray, and others would join with them."[94]

Camp meetings were, however, the primary environment for the creation of new religious music. Within a decade, the new music, and emotional worship in general, had become synonymous with black worship in the minds of some white evangelicals. Perhaps as a way of disparaging the popular repertoire of religious songs they found so distasteful, the increasingly vocal critics of revival culture associated the early gospel forms with the African part of the revival community. Among the Methodist "errors" the Reverend John E. Watson protested were the religious songs that were extemporaneously composed by black revivalists: "In the blacks' quarter the coloured people get together, and sing for hours together, short scraps of disjointed affirmations, pledges, or prayers, lengthened out with long repetition choruses." The "idle expletives" Watson scorned frequently were word or line fragments isolated from hymns or from Scriptures, a sample of which he preserved: "'Go shouting all your days,' in connection with 'glory, glory, glory,' in which go shouting is repeated six times in succession."[95]

Watson was even more bothered by the unorthodox practice of fusing sacred songs with secular ones, a legacy of West Africa in which they "are all sung in the merry chorus manner of the southern harvest field, or husking-frolic method, of the slave blacks." Watson apparently recognized that the musical traditions of West African and European cultures shared certain features in common, among them the use of repetitive phrases, which he attributed to Welsh influence. Still, he implied that whites absorbed, perhaps unwittingly, the improvised religious music composed by black revivalists. "Merry airs, adapted from old songs, to hymns of our composing: often miserable as poetry, and senseless as matter" were, he wrote, "first sung by illiterate blacks of the society."[96]

The power and exuberance of extemporaneously composed religious music provided the stimulation for a new expressive mode, a unique ritual known as the holy dance, or the ring shout. Given the poverty of sources, precise reconstruction of the development of ritual trance dancing is next to impossible. However, the first motions of the holy dance were apparently hand clapping, foot stamping, and leaping, which first appeared during the Virginia revivals. None of these acts was unique to West Africans, but because they were not a regular part of the white aesthetic experience they were greatly altered or they disappeared from the white repertoires of religious expression once acceptability of such behaviors declined.[97]

Because they were intrinsic to African religious expression, these forms of musical behavior survived and heightened the rhythmic patterning of black worship. By the end of the first decade of the nineteenth century they had evolved into a choreography of sound and movement known as the ring shout, the ultimate refinement of the religious ceremony of shouting.[98] Scholars disagree as to the precise origins and form of the ring shout, but one thing is very clear: African-derived religious dances were, as Mechal Sobel has observed, "widespread if not ubiquitous," confined neither to a particular denomination nor to a specific locale.[99] There were, to be sure, varieties of reinterpretation of religious dance. African retentions were stronger and more obvious in areas of the Caribbean and South America, where a multitude of different dances developed,[100] and in those parts of the United States where the African slave trade continued for the longest period of time and concentrations of African peoples were heaviest.

Contemporary accounts suggest that the primary environment for the development of the ring shout was the camp meeting, although clandestine gatherings almost certainly nurtured ring dancing. The earliest written reports reveal that an elemental dance ritual had developed as part of black Methodist worship in the Upper South as early as 1809.[101] One such account came from Benjamin Henry Latrobe, in which he reported that after witnessing what he considered the excesses of a revival meeting near Georgetown in August, he left in disgust. His son Henry remained at the camp until midnight and later reported that "the negroes after the Camp was illuminated sung and danced the methodist turnabout in the most indefatigable and entertaining manner."[102]

John Watson's description of black Methodist dancing written ten years later reveals more ritualized behavior and disciplined movement patterns: "With every song so sung, they have a sinking of one or other leg of the body alternately; producing an audible sound of the feet at every step, and as manifest as the steps of actual negro dancing in Virginia, etc. If some, in the meantime sit, they strike the sounds alternately on each thigh."[103] While some things African, such as drums, which were so important to West African and West Indian religious dance, had already disappeared, the thrusting, sliding motion of the feet, the thigh slapping, the fact that singing and dancing formed a single cohesive whole, were all characteristic of African and Caribbean rhythmic patterns.

The ritual dance observed by Benjamin Henry Latrobe on Congo Square in New Orleans the same year was similar in many respects, although the circular movement of the dancers, the accompaniment of drums and other musical instruments, the interplay between dancers and drummers, and the dialect and quality of the singing he reported were more indicative of traditional African behaviors. "Most of the circles contained the same sort of dancers. One was larger, in which a ring of a dozen women walked, by way of dancing, round the music in the Center." According to Latrobe's account, the songs accompanying the dance were presented in African style: "A man sung an uncouth song to the dancing which I suppose was in some African language, for it was not french, and the Women screamed a detestable burthen on one single note."[104]

As these examples demonstrate, the process of acculturation and radical religious change ultimately diminished though never completely destroyed African dance characteristics. As a result of increasing cultural contact, Africans apparently took over certain European dance traditions and developed new dances with European motifs predominating. The most colorful evidence of this kind of cultural fusion was left by John Pierpoint, a Yale graduate who was hired as a tutor for the children of William Alston. Soon after Pierpoint arrived on Alston's Monjetta plantation on the Waccamaw River in the Georgetown District of South Carolina, he observed slave Christmas festivities. Pierpoint was unable to differentiate between secular and religious dancing, but his account demonstrates how cultural contact produced an infiltration of European dance concepts, while at the same time it explains why African dance was one of the few arts that survived slavery. According to Pierpoint, a group of acculturated slaves danced a European-type social dance on the portico to European-style music played on fiddles and drums. Off to themselves "were native Africans [who] did not join the dance with the others but, by themselves, gave us a specimen of the sports and amusements with which the be-nighted and uncivilized children of nature divert themselves before they become acquainted with the more refined and civilized amusements of life—clapping their hands was their music and distorting their frames into the most unnatural figures and emitting the most hideous noises in their dancing."[105]

The degree to which traditional African dance survived varied through-out the Americas. Dance rituals like the santeria, candomble, cumina, and the petro are only a few of the countless forms of religious musical expres-sion that proliferated in the Caribbean and throughout South America.[106] In North America, the ring shout became highly ritualized and remained an integral part of African American worship throughout the antebellum period. For example, the Swedish traveler Frederika Bremer saw the "holy dance" performed by black women at a camp meeting near Charleston in 1850. A year later she witnessed a similar performance at a Methodist class meeting in New Orleans. And in his recollections of his childhood in South Carolina, Samuel Gourdin Gaillard described a black worship ser-vice that he witnessed in a plantation chapel. The ceremony, which Gaillard speculated "must have come with the slaves from Africa," began with a low, moaning hymn sung by a woman. As the congregation joined in, the singing gradually increased in volume and intensity and the movements became more hectic. "One by one of the congregation slipped out into the center of the floor and began to 'shout'—(that is whirl around and sing and clap hands, and so round and round in circles). After a time as this went on, the enthusiasm became a frenzy and only the able bodied men and women remained—the weak dropping out one by one, returning to the 'side lines' to clap and urge the 'shouters' on."[107]

The liturgical traditions that emerged out of revival religious culture formed an important nexus in race relations within the biracial evangeli-cal community. For black Christians the creation of specific and distinctive rituals like the ring shout was part of the process by which they established a definite presence in the religious community. Their attempt to claim a cultural space disturbed white Christians like John Watson, who publicly demeaned such behavior as noisy, crude, impious, and, simply, dissolute. Despite its mixed origins, emotional worship was increasingly character-ized as "black" and, therefore, culturally inferior. Such an identification worked to reinforce the growing consciousness of racial distinction devel-oping behind the rising wall of spiritual separation. White Christians re-jected rituals that had an apparent African style or feeling and were associated with supposed racial inferiority in favor of the more carefully controlled European cadences with which they were familiar. For black Christians ritual music and dance became important cultural foci, symbols of their cultural independence and of their identity as a black group.

6

RELIGIOUS TRANSFORMATION

GROWTH AND SEPARATION

During the first quarter of the nineteenth century the American South and the islands of the British Caribbean underwent a religious transformation of unprecedented proportions. No movement before or since has done more to transform the religious landscape. In the first thirty years after American independence Baptist membership in the newly formed United States increased ten times. Methodism grew even faster, reaching a quarter million by 1820 and a half million by 1830.[1] Revivalism and the development of the itinerant and circuit systems and expanding migration carried evangelical Protestantism westward into Kentucky and Tennessee, across eastern and southern Ohio, Indiana, and Illinois, into the South and Southwest to Alabama, Mississippi, and Louisiana.

The most impressive cultural development in this period was the dramatic increase in the size and structure of the black evangelical community. Between 1800 and 1815, the number of black Methodists more than doubled—from 20,000 to over 40,000, which represented almost a third of the American Methodist population. Statistics for Baptists are less reliable, but estimates suggest an equal number of black Baptists during the same time period.[2] The scale of growth in the Caribbean was equally impressive. In 1815 West Indian stations reported 15,220 Methodists, the vast majority of whom were black.[3] In Jamaica alone mission membership totaled 27,000 by 1834.[4] In twenty-five years of missionary activity in the Leeward Islands missionaries had converted roughly one-quarter of the total black population.[5]

But the change was not merely a question of numbers. The long-term cumulative impact of these developments was that Protestantism became one of the central frameworks of African American society. The encounter between Christianity and Afro-Atlantic peoples encompassed a massive and continuous process of cultural interaction that involved on the one hand adaption and integration into the dominant white religious culture and on the other the assertion of separate Afro-cultural identities. These changes took place against a background of intensive social and political class and racial tensions that were reflected in the oscillations between tolerance and persecution that marked the entire period. The end result was that by 1830 new and racially distinctive parameters for membership in the Christian community had been established, and racial, class, and gender boundaries were marked in clear and explicit racial discourse that strictly separated Christians along racial lines.

By 1800 clear geographical patterns of religion could be discerned for both the black and white populations of the South. Denominational growth followed different patterns, with major regional and racial variations. Growth was the result of two related processes: spreading revivalism after 1802 and the vast movement of people from the Chesapeake between 1810 and 1820. It is difficult to chart a chronological progression because religious conditions were different everywhere and because the movement of revival and people produced marked advances in some areas and definite reverses in others. Generally speaking, Virginia was the spring from which growth ebbed and flowed.

It is impossible to determine exact church numbers, particularly for Baptists, for which estimates are based on scattered and often unreliable church records. A recent study suggests that in 1800 Baptists were probably more numerous than any other denomination in America.[6] The spread of revivalism and the highly organized itinerant and circuit system enabled Methodism to rapidly close the gap and easily surpass the Baptists, probably within no more than a decade. According to David Benedict's calculations published in 1813, there were approximately 90,000 Baptist communicants in the states of Virginia, North and South Carolina, Georgia, Kentucky, and Tennessee, 40,000 of whom were black, compared with 114,849 Methodists, 30,161 of whom were black.[7] By 1830 Methodist denominations led all churches in total membership. Presbyterians represented a significant presence among the Scotch-Irish population of the backcountry South but had only a small following among black Southerners.

Such statistics as are available indicate that religious preferences varied

Map 3. Major Centers of Black Baptist Churches, 1800

according to region and race. Although every state had a denominational mix, Baptists remained dominant in Virginia and Georgia, with sizable clusters in the South Carolina Low Country and Pee Dee regions, while Methodism captured the larger share of churchgoers in South Carolina, Maryland, and North Carolina. Methodist growth tended to follow the spreading ligaments of the itinerant system, which first took root along the coast and in towns before thrusting out into the interior, through the mountain districts and eventually into the developing Southwest. The result was a more dispersed Methodist population. Baptist numerical and geographical development was largely a result of the multiplication and division of churches, which produced more dense areas of concentration, particularly among black Baptists. Presbyterian expansion tended to follow the Scotch-Irish and centered in the Piedmont of North and South Carolina and in the great valley of Virginia, with significant clusters in central Virginia.

By 1800 there were clearly established centers of denominational strength. There were few Baptists in Maryland, the result perhaps of early and intensive Methodist missionary activity there. Although black and white Methodists were widely distributed throughout the state, and later in the Baltimore Conference, black Methodism was concentrated in urban areas and in heavily black counties, such as Calvert and Prince George's on the Western Shore, and Kent, Dorchester, Queen Anne, and Talbot on the Eastern Shore. By 1810 black Methodists outnumbered white Methodists in Annapolis and made up roughly 50 percent of the Methodist population of Baltimore City; almost 40 percent of Calvert County's total black population were members of Methodist societies.[8] Between 1810 and 1820, the number and proportion of white Methodists in Maryland increased significantly while there was a net loss of over 1,000 black members, owing to the exodus of the Baltimore and Snow Hill societies to join the African Methodist Episcopal (AME) Church formed in Philadelphia in 1816 under Richard Allen's leadership.[9] The AME Church continued to drain away black members from the Methodist Episcopal Church in Maryland, a loss that is reflected in membership totals of the Baltimore Conference. By 1830, black Methodists accounted for barely a third of all Methodists in the Conference.[10]

In 1800 populous Virginia was the strongest center of Methodism in America. But it was white Virginians who made up over two-thirds of the roughly 13,000 members in society. Despite a doubling of membership totals in the Virginia Conference during the next decade, the region lost its preeminence as the stronghold of Methodism due in large measure to the outmigration of black and white Virginians between 1810 and 1820 and direct competition from the Baptists. Comparison of the distribution of white and black Methodism in the Virginia Conference shows strikingly different racial patterns. White Methodism spread across Southside from Petersburg to North Carolina. It was heavily concentrated in the old Brunswick Circuit, which originally embraced Brunswick, Dinwiddie, and Chesterfield Counties, and extended across the southeastern Piedmont into Sussex, Amelia, and Mecklenburg Counties.[11]

The distribution of black Methodism varied markedly from this pattern. A tier of counties that stretched along the southeastern border of Virginia from Greensville east to Portsmouth and south into Camden County, North Carolina, formed the base of black Methodist strength. In the years since Joseph Pilmore had first traveled the "waste places of the wilderness," Methodism had hesitantly crept up the rivers of North Carolina, gathering strength all along the route where Pilmore had first sowed Methodist seeds, but with two chief focal centers: the port of New Bern, whose black Methodist population doubled every decade, reaching 900 by 1830, and Camden, whose 1,107 black Methodists constituted the largest black society in the Conference. The total proportion of blacks who were church members reached 39 percent of the total black population of Camden County by 1830.[12] Over the next two decades these general patterns remained fairly constant.

The denominational preference of black Virginians was the Baptist Church. By contrast to Methodist patterns of growth and development, the black Baptist community grew out of all-black churches located in enduring centers of Baptist strength under indigenous leadership. Virginia was the vital center of the Afro-Baptist faith and the breeding ground for its diffusion.[13] In 1812, 35,000 Baptists, over a third of all Southern Baptists, lived in the state. Between 1800 and 1830 the vast majority of Baptists were located in the eastern district of Virginia, particularly in its populous southeastern corner drained by the James, York, and Rappahannock Rivers. Roughly half of them belonged to independent congregations loosely affiliated with three associations: Ketocton, which extended up the northern reaches of the Potomac River to the base of the Blue Ridge Mountains; Dover, extending along the north side of the James River from the city of Richmond south and northeast to Chesapeake Bay; and Portsmouth, stretching out from Portsmouth and Norfolk along the coast northand west to Petersburg along the south side of the James River. In

1809 the three associations claimed a combined membership of 14,676, an estimated 9,000 of whom were black, almost twice the number of black Methodists in the Virginia Conference in the same year.[14]

Almost two-thirds of eastern district Baptists, and perhaps a third of all Baptists in the state, belonged to the Dover Association, which by 1830 contained fifty independent, self-governing congregations and 14,377 communicants.[15] No membership totals are available for the Portsmouth Association, which occupied the oldest Baptist ground in Virginia, but association minutes list thirty-two churches in 1830.[16] No Virginia Baptist association listed members by race until the Dover Association began the practice in 1838. It is therefore impossible to determine either the exact numbers or the precise geographical distribution of black and white Baptists. It is clear, however, that the region of the state encompassed in the Dover and Portsmouth Associations contained a disproportionately large share of the black Baptist population.[17]

Both associations were numerically dominated by a few large autonomous black churches. In the Dover Association the chief expansion after 1800 took place in old stable churches under the auspices of local leaders. One such church was the Williamsburg African, whose membership was 619 in 1830; another was the predominantly black First Baptist Church, the cradle of the faith in Richmond, whose membership surged from 360 in 1809 to 1,830 in 1831. Although the black membership was roughly quadruple that of whites, the First Baptist continued to be biracial until 1841, when it was organized as a separate church known as the African Baptist Church.[18] In the roughly sixty miles between the falls of Richmond and the flats surrounding Williamsburg black Baptists of Virginia created a number of rural churches, including a short-lived independent congregation and the all-black Elam Church formed by a group of free blacks in 1810, both in Charles City County.[19] Other predominantly black churches in the association included Pocorone, in lower King and Queen County, and Zoar, in the lower part of Middlesex County between the Rappahannock and Piankatank Rivers, which in 1818 had only one white male member. Virtually all other churches in the association were biracial. Isolated figures from extant church minute books, including Boar Swamp in Henrico County, Upper King and Queen on the Rappahannock River, Morattico on the Northern Neck, Wicomico in Northumberland County, and Nomini in Westmoreland County, the largest church in the association, reveal significant numbers of black members.[20]

The Portsmouth Association was also dominated by its black membership. From its founding, Davenport's (later Gillfield's) in Prince George

Map 4. Major Centers of Black Baptist Churches, 1830

County was the largest church in the association. Its membership increased from 165 in 1800, to 441 in 1821, to 715 in 1830. The black First Baptist of Norfolk had 477 members in 1830, while the Portsmouth church, which probably included all of the black Baptists in the Portsmouth area, had over 2,000 in 1809.[21] Following the Petersburg revivals of 1821–22, the number of black Baptists skyrocketed, and in 1826 the African Baptist Church was admitted to the Portsmouth Association. The congregation drew its 521 members from Prince George, Surrey, and Charles City Counties.[22] A number of biracial churches were also predominantly black. In 1800 South Quay in Southampton County listed 126 white and 226 black members. In 1813 Mill Swamp in Isle of Wight County had 60 white and 127 black members. If these isolated figures can be taken as representative, then David Benedict's conclusion that by 1845 blacks represented nearly two-thirds of the Portsmouth Association is probably accurate.[23]

In the more newly settled areas of the west and north of Virginia, where the slave population was rapidly expanding, white Baptists almost always outnumbered black.[24] There were, to be sure, several all-black or predominantly black congregations clustered around native prophets, charismatic figures whose roles were separate from but, significantly, not in competition with those of the white clergy. "Uncle" Jack was one of these figures. Kidnapped from Africa at age seven, Jack grew up a slave in Nottaway County. His first contact with Christianity was through two Presbyterian missionaries from nearby Prince Edward County. Jack, however, chose to become a Baptist. Eventually becoming a powerful preacher who favored orthodox forms of worship and doctrine, Jack enjoyed "the entire confidence of the whole neighborhood." He was licensed to preach, and he recruited a large following. His Nottaway County church was known simply as "Uncle Jack's."[25]

The redistribution of the Southern population contributed to a corresponding shift in the geographical distribution of evangelical Protestantism. Between 1810 and 1820 Methodism expanded significantly in the Lower South. The populous coastal areas of the Conference formed the demographic base for the Methodist Church. According to John Scott Strickland's calculations, in 1800 Methodists in the Low Country and Pee Dee/Savannah River regions outnumbered their counterparts in the Piedmont and mountains by a ratio of two to one, a pattern that persisted over the next three decades. Once again, however, these general patterns obscure striking differences in the rates of growth for blacks and whites and in the racial composition of the church. In the Low Country black Methodism increasingly preponderated, growing at an accelerating rate in both membership totals and the percentage of the total church population, from 37.6 percent in 1800 to 56.7 percent in 1830. The number of white Methodists continued to rise in absolute terms but fell as a percentage of the total church population, from 62.4 percent in 1800 to 43.9 percent in 1830. The reverse was true in the backcountry, where white Methodists represented never less than 68 percent of the total Methodist population.[26]

Charleston and its environs was the locus of development for black Methodism in the South Carolina Conference. Following the appointment in 1811 of William Capers to the Saluda District, the society grew at an astonishing rate, more than tripling in size to 5,699 in 1817, making it the largest society—black or white—in North America.[27] Generally speaking, black Methodism in the South Carolina Conference was an urban phenomenon. The predominantly black societies in the coastal community of Georgetown, South Carolina, and the urban port of Wilmington, both originally established by William Meredith as Primitive Methodist churches, were important centers of concentration. A significant center of black Methodism also developed in Fayetteville, located at the head of navigation on the Cape Fear River. Founded in 1809 by Henry Evans, a black preacher from Virginia, the Fayetteville society represents a direct connection between migration and religious experience.

These statistical differences in black and white church membership provide incontrovertible evidence of religious self-determination. They also demonstrate that by 1830 the transition to Protestant Christianity had already made significant progress among the African American population, particularly in urban areas. The exact proportions are, of course, determined by the size of the catchment area. In the case of Charleston, if the 1808 black Methodists reported in Conference records for 1800 was drawn entirely from the Charleston District, whose total black population was 32,000, then black Methodists composed II percent of the total black population. If, however, the number was drawn only from Charleston City, then they represented 20 percent of Charleston's black population of 11,000. Before the schism of 1817, which led to the withdrawal of virtually the entire membership of the Bethel MEC, the 5,699 black Methodists would have represented close to 45 percent of the city's black population.[28]

A highly organized itinerancy and a well-deserved antislavery reputation among blacks as well as whites gave Methodists a competitive edge in South Carolina, even though Baptists had organized a church in Charleston in 1683 and another in 1737 in Welsh Neck on the Pee Dee River. Estimates of the numbers of South Carolina Baptists depend on incomplete and often inconsistent reports from individual churches, thus making accurate measurements of growth over time problematic. Racially distinct figures are not available for the years prior to 1827, when three associations of the seven then in existence began to list black and white members separately. The statistics that survive suggest a surge in the number of both black and white conversions after 1802, when revivalism began to sweep the state. Estimates based on church admissions indicate that black conversions occurred at roughly the same rate as white conversions, but statistics provided by the various associations reveal distinct patterns of growth.[29]

Roughly half of all the Baptists in the state belonged to one of two Low Country associations, Charleston and Savannah River.[30] There were two flourishing centers of growth among black Baptists, the Low Country and Pee Dee River regions, both then contained in the sprawling Charleston Association formed in 1751. From a total membership of 1,970 in 1800, the Charleston Association increased to 4,159 members in 1827, 2,005, or roughly half of whom, were black.[31] Although no racial differentiation was made in the records, the Savannah River Association, which until 1818 included the populous African churches of Savannah, probably had a substantial number of black members since it took in heavily black areas such as Beaufort and Euhaw. It reported 1,982 members in 1804 and 6,807 in 1833. Although spreading waves of evangelical revivalism caused white membership to swell in backcountry associations, black membership remained comparatively small. The combined membership of Bethel and Edgefield Associations in 1829 was 3,536, only 810 of whom were black.[32]

These patterns cannot be explained in terms of the distribution of South Carolina's slave population because by 1810 almost one-half lived in the backcountry, an outgrowth of the massive up-country migrations of the post-Revolutionary years.[33] The denominational choices made by black Carolinians appear to have been tied to indigenous leadership and established institutional roots. Established clusters of the faith such as Charleston's First Church and Welsh Neck Church served as institutional bases for the recruitment of new members into the faith each year. Old congregations such as First Church trained and certified gifted individuals for evangelical work within their own neighborhoods and in the Charleston District, whose slave population fell within the range and influence of the black itinerancy.

By 1827, Charleston's First Church had 862 members, 697 (almost 81 percent) of whom were black. Although there were no independent black churches in the Charleston Association, several other churches were overwhelmingly black. The previously independent black Welsh Neck Church formed by Elhanan Winchester rejoined Edmund Botsford's white church in 1782. But the Botsford-led revival of the 1790s created several hundred black converts, who in turn became the executive arm of the Baptist mission to the black population of the Pee Dee region. In 1827 Welsh Neck Church reported a black majority of 102 out of 187 members. Two churches, High Hills and Congaree, had black memberships in excess of 90 percent. Beulah and Columbia had over 80 percent; Mechanicsville and Muddy Creek had over 75 percent. Blacks accounted for 59.34 percent of the membership in all South Carolina churches reporting black members.[34]

In Georgia and Jamaica, where sizable urban centers developed very early, the Afro-Baptist missionary movement was tied to urban churches, which owed their survival to the astuteness and courage of their leaders, men who conformed themselves as much as possible to orthodox forms of doctrine and polity and who exhibited an uncommon degree of tact in dealing with white churchmen. The all-black churches over which they presided served as focal points for the remarkable expansions of the Baptist faith among the black population in the surrounding countryside. Savannah was the seminal point for the growth of the black Baptist movement, and the Bryan Street African Church was the spiritual center of black Baptist life. Its pastor, Andrew Bryan, more than any other, typified the new wave of African leadership that was beginning to emerge from the separate black congregations that were springing up in the South around the turn of the century.

Bryan, with the support of some of Chatham County's most influential citizens, led a tenacious struggle to secure the right of black Georgians to worship in their own independent churches. Bryan's success in recruiting new members led to a division of the congregation, and in 1787 the First African of Savannah was created, with an initial membership of under 300. Within fifteen years the First African of Savannah spawned two more independent black churches. The Second African, pastored by Henry Cunningham, served the black community living on the east side of Savannah. The congregation that organized itself at Ogechee, fourteen miles to the south of the city, served plantation slaves in the rice belt along the Ogechee River. Together these three churches gathered in an ever-growing proportion of the local slave and free population of Chatham County.[35] In 1819 churches were formed in neighboring Abercorn and White Bluff, but in terms of membership the Savannah churches remained preeminent. Between 1803 and 1829 their combined membership increased from 600 to

3,397, and together they accounted for between 70 and 80 percent of the total membership of the five black churches affiliated with the Sunbury Association.[36]

By 1820, most of Chatham County's black population was within reach of an independent Afro-Baptist church, and, in all probability, Chatham County accounted for virtually the entire membership of the Low Country's five independent black churches. If this was the case, the proportion of the county's enslaved population, which between 1790 and 1830 increased from 8,201 to 9,052, who chose to become affiliated to these churches increased from around 9 percent in 1800, to roughly 35 percent by 1820, to somewhere in the order of 47 percent by 1830.[37]

In addition to these urban centers there were several biracial churches in coastal Georgia and in the Lower Piedmont. In 1822 the Sunbury Association created a church for whites at Darien in McIntosh County, but the predominantly black membership took it over as the First African Baptist Church.[38] The expansion of short staple cotton growing in middle Georgia and the interstate movement of slaves that accompanied it led in 1818 to the establishment of the First Baptist Church in the rural town of Augusta, some 200 miles upriver from Savannah. Although a Methodist society had been organized in Augusta by Stith Mead in 1798, the arrival of black migrants from Virginia, most of whom were Baptists, guaranteed the dominance of the Baptists.[39]

Although a number of bondmen and -women joined racially mixed Methodist congregations in Savannah, and a smaller number worshiped in the city's Presbyterian, Episcopalian, Lutheran, and Roman Catholic Churches, the black population of Savannah and its environs found the Baptist Church far more attractive than the Methodist. In 1831, for instance, there were only 6,187 black Methodists in the Georgia Conference, compared to 19,349 white Georgians.[40] William Capers attributed the failure of the Methodists to attract large numbers of African Americans to their preference for "the economy and doctrines of the Baptist church" and to the presence of two independent African churches in Savannah, with their own "pastors and deacons, and sacraments, and discipline all of their own."[41] Capers was undoubtedly right in his assessment, although other considerations entered into the exercise of choice. According to Moses Roper, the North Carolina-born slave who was transported to a plantation in Georgia, his fellow slaves emphatically rejected the Baptist faith of their master, "thinking him a very bad sample of what a professing Christian ought to be, [and] would not join the connexion he belonged to, thinking they must be a very bad set of people." Instead, under the pros-elytizing of a slave named Allen, many of them became Methodists.[42]

The massive outmigration of blacks and whites from Virginia and North Carolina between 1810 and 1820 cost Virginia perhaps a quarter of all Baptists in the state and its primacy as the principal seat of Methodism.[43] This great domestic migration was thus also a religious movement. In the early period Kentucky and Tennessee were the destinations of many of the emigrants, whose faith was as much a part of their possessions as the goods they loaded on pack animals and in wagons.[44] The Baptists were the first—and for a time the most numerous—in Kentucky, while Methodism was the largest denomination in Tennessee.[45] Following the closing of the international slave trade in 1808 the direction of the domestic slave trade and the tide of migrants shifted away from Kentucky and Tennessee to Alabama.[46] Methodism entered Alabama as early as 1808, but as late as 1832 it had enrolled only about 3,000 black and white members. Mobile had not a single church until 1823.[47]

Denominational statistics indicate that African Americans populated a distinct minority of evangelical churches of the frontier. Every church in the rapidly developing Southwest had black members, but black represen-tation in evangelical churches never equaled the proportions they held in the general population. In Kentucky and Tennessee they never exceeded 11 percent of church membership. In Mississippi they represented 27 per-cent of the church population in 1810, 12 percent of which was in the Nashville District.[48] But these figures obscure somewhat the dramatic growth in church membership after 1800, when revivalism and migration had a significant impact. Between 1805 and 1816, for example, white Methodist congregations in Mississippi increased by an astonishing 1,075 percent, and black membership increased by 469 percent.[49] Baptist mem-bership is more difficult to calculate, but growth can be roughly suggested by the increase in the number of churches in the Mississippi Baptist Asso-ciation: from five in 1807 to forty by 1818. By 1835 there were 5,000 Baptists in Mississippi.[50]

Denominational statistics convey only part of the story, however. What is left out is the part played by black migrants in shaping the sacred land-scape of the West. An account left by James Williams, the black driver responsible for leading a contingent of 214 men, women, and children from the Powhatan County, Virginia, plantation of George Larrimore, to wild land in Greene County, Alabama, is typical of the westward expan-sion of evangelical Protestantism. According to Williams, at least a third of the contingent were members of Baptist and Methodist churches of Virginia who, in Williams's words, had been "torn away from the care and discipline of their respective churches, and from the means of instruction, but they retained their love for the exercises of religion." Williams's recollection of meetings conducted by three black preachers and exhorters, the nightly air reverberating with the familiar slave lament, "How long, O Lord, how long?," is reminiscent of earlier accounts of "Uncle" Peter leading his disparate band in song while en route to Kentucky.[51]

Despite the social dislocation and the religious disarray caused by forced migration, black migrants stamped their own religious identity on the landscape of the developing West. So rapid was the westward movement of the frontier, so fluid the population, that little concrete evidence about the original planters of Methodist or Baptist societies survive. Initially, it is supposed, both blacks and whites joined whatever congregations were available. In the absence of permanent structures, biracial meetings were held in groves of trees or in bark wigwams until more suitable meetinghouses could be built.[52] It was not long, however, before black Christians were organizing separate churches and sending out lay preachers and prophesiers to the proliferating settlements.

Realizing that the supply of missionaries could never meet the needs of the numerous and scattered frontier settlements, Methodists looked to a native supply. Men like Josiah Henson, who was converted at a camp meeting in Kentucky, were able to secure preaching licenses at quarterly meetings, and they entered the traveling ministry.[53] They also participated in itinerant missions to Native Americans. A black preacher named Stewart reportedly made sixty-one converts among the Wyandots in the Ohio country.[54] Their evangelizing labors brought new congregations into being in longer-settled towns and cities. In 1822 a former Virginia slave organized the only autonomous black church in Lexington, Kentucky, and in 1833 established a school that enrolled thirty-two children.[55] Alabama's Flint River Association had at least two all-black churches, the African Huntsville Baptist Church, whose pastor was William Harris, and the African Cottonfort Baptist Church of Lancaster County, whose pastor was Lewis.[56] The Robertson family of free blacks, who migrated from North Hampton County, North Carolina, to Indiana, settled one of the first black communities in Indiana in Hamilton County and built there the first African Methodist Episcopal church in the state.[57]

In addition to the formally constituted, often urban-centered churches, there were numerous small, unorganized churches in rural areas throughout the South that formed voluntarily around local leaders from among neighboring plantations. There is no satisfactory way of determining membership numbers, and there is very little information on the ministers serving them, but scattered evidence about these churches provides part of their story. For example, for years Thomas Mann, presiding elder of the Salisbury District, regularly visited a black Methodist congregation in central North Carolina presided over by Jeremiah, probably a free black man. "Jeremiah's Society," as it was locally known, was the only Methodist society in Chatham County and was attended by several whites, including two white women of "note and of piety."[58] And a man identified as "Punch" had between 200 and 300 slaves from the Waccamaw Neck area of South Carolina under his spiritual direction.[59] Adam Hodgson reported that while he was traveling in the Georgia backcountry, "near the Indian nation," he came upon a black congregation of about 200 slaves "sitting on little planks under a large elm tree" as their preacher conducted a funeral service.[60] Venture Galphin's congregation met in a walnut grove near Waynesboro, Georgia.[61] And as he traveled the Green River circuit in Kentucky, James Gwin discovered a large Methodist congregation led by a slave named Jacob.[62]

These isolated congregations and the thousands of faithful adherents gathered in them and in established churches throughout the South reflect the successful ministry of evangelical denominations to African Americans, and in particular to African American women. No other movement in British America contained such a large proportion of women.[63] Fragmented and incomplete though membership data are, they do provide empirical evidence that black women represented a clear majority in most evangelical churches—biracial as well as all-black. A few examples will illustrate the general pattern. During the revival cycles that made up the Second Awakening, African American women increased in absolute and proportionate representation, making of the Southern black Christian community, to a very considerable extent, a women's organization. From 1780 to 1790 in all Baptist churches in Virginia, females outnumbered males by a least 4 to 5 percent.[64] Although the statistics are very incomplete, membership lists from biracial churches reveal that the female-male ratio increased significantly among black Baptists between 1790 and 1830. In Virginia, out of seventeen biracial Baptist churches for which data are available for the period before 1830, thirteen had a female majority.[65]

Women also composed a majority of black congregations in South Carolina. Between 1781 and 1830 women made up over 60 percent of the membership of the Welsh Neck Church, the only Baptist congregation in the Pee Dee/Savannah River region for which data survives. Females were also disproportionately represented in Low Country Baptist churches. In the Beaufort Baptist Church, which had almost 4,000 members, for example, female membership averaged over 66 percent between 1804 and 1830.[66] The pattern is much the same for Methodist churches across the South. In 1806 the First Methodist Episcopal Church, later called the Trinity United Methodist Church, of Alexandria, Virginia, enrolled 140 women and 74 men, or a ratio of slightly better than two to one (65.42 percent female). The most complete and continuous records were kept by the Sharp Street (Baltimore City Station) Methodist Episcopal Church of Baltimore. Those records reveal a continuous female majority, ranging from 55.9 percent in 1800 to roughly 65 percent in 1818.[67] In the early 1820s Charleston's Trinity Methodist Episcopal Church included 2,788 black class members, of whom almost exactly two-thirds were women. In no class did men outnumber women.[68] The baptismal records for St. Philip's Church of Charleston show that between 1811 and 1822, 419 African Americans were baptized, 52.5 percent of whom were children. Of known adult baptisms women represented 56.3 percent.[69] Between 1815 and 1830 women made up an average of 64 percent of the black Methodist society of Georgetown, South Carolina, the second major center of Methodism in the Lower South.

There is little direct evidence of motivations behind female conversion, but several explanations are suggested by the sources available. One apparent reason was maternal preoccupation with the protection of their offspring from witches or avenging spirits unleashed by whites, or against diseases or accidents of various sorts. In traditional society birth rituals protected newborn infants from dangerous forces. The environment of slavery demanded a new form of protection, which many anxious mothers believed, or hoped, might be provided by Christian baptism. For example, although Afra, an Ibo woman enslaved in Jamaica, declined to be christened herself, "she very earnestly begged" Reverend Matthew Gregory Lewis to "make a christian" of her infant son and of her young daughter.[70] In North Carolina Reverend James Meacham had a similar encounter with a black woman, who brought her three children to be baptized. When Meacham inquired about the state of her own soul, the woman frankly admitted that "she was careless and expected to remain so" and that "she did not fear nor serve God herself." Convinced that the woman "only mocked God in offering her children," Meacham refused to baptize them until the white owner assumed responsibility for their upbringing.[71] As Newell Booth observes of modern urbanized Zulus, these examples reflect a search for new securities, not by a return to old patterns, nor yet by a wholesale acceptance of new forms, but of a necessary adaption to a dangerous and difficult environment.[72]

The tendency to use religion as protection against the social order is also apparent in some African women's use of the spiritual legitimization conferred on them by baptism to resist the sexual exploitation that was so much a part of their daily existence. They used religion to considerable advantage to resist unwelcome sexual advances made by men in the slave quarters. For example, in response to a complaint by Molly, the Sandy Creek Baptist Church expelled Tom for acting "wantonly and unseemly" toward her; Ned was dismissed for the same offense against Nancy.[73] Clarke's Station Baptist Church of Wilkes County, Georgia, expelled Isham for making "unclean proposals or attacks" on Deluce.[74] The all-black Gillfield Baptist Church of Petersburg expelled David "for adultery and casting a Slander upon every Sister in the Church."[75]

Although slave women were understandably more reluctant to bring charges against slave owners, church records reveal that on occasion they did use religion to manipulate and control relationships with their white owners. For example, a free black mother appealed directly to Reverend James Meacham to shield her child from harm at the hands of her former master who, she said, "did not treat her children well," that he had "striped her Child and she could not bear it, . . . that he had striped one of his black Men and Whiped [him] severely." Meacham, who was opposed to slavery, advised the anguished mother that "her children needed correction some times in reason" and counseled her to be patient. He also "conversed" with the owner, demanding to know "how he could of conscience whip a man, that was a man as well as he was." Reminding the owner that he had "received conviction," Meacham "begged him to give himself to God" and concluded with the wistful hope that the owner might be sufficiently "ashamed" of his conduct to repent.[76]

One of the most remarkable examples of black women bringing charges of sexual misconduct against a white man appears in the Quarterly Conference Records of the Baltimore Circuit. In 1812 a meeting of local preachers was called to hear charges of sexual misconduct brought against a local preacher, John Chalmers, by two African women from Annapolis, Charity and Forty. The preachers' meeting found that despite "the liberty taken with [Charity]," Chalmers had no "criminal intention," yet "his conduct was highly imprudent and derogatory to the character of a Christian and minister." With respect to Chalmers's advances to Forty, the preachers decided "that such conduct, *with a woman professing religion*, was calculated to excite her to sin, and was very reprehensible in him, both as a preacher and a man professing religion, was criminal or sinful." Chalmers was suspended from all official service in the Methodist Church.[77]

The growth in size and the geographical expansion of Afro-Atlantic Protestantism coincided with a rising demand by black women and men for full integration into the Christian fellowship through the right to proclaim the gospel and to exercise authority among their own people without the mediating influence of white authorities and institutions. The local democracy of Baptist churches made it possible for black men to participate in church affairs, although the nature and degree of their participation varied considerably from one church and one region to another. Generally speaking, Baptist congregations ordained more black preachers than any other denomination.[78] In Virginia's Baptist churches men who professed a call or who demonstrated "gifts" for preaching frequently won the right to preach or to exhort. The Berryville church, for example, licensed three slaves, Phill, Mingo, and Jack, to preach among their black brethren.[79] In 1826, Richmond's predominantly black First Baptist Church licensed five black preachers and seven exhorters.[80] Even churches that refused to license black preachers often appointed men to serve as leaders or "overlookers" of black members and charged them with responsibility for maintaining order.[81]

Despite the acceptance, however grudging, of black men into the leadership structure in the Upper South, black preachers remained a relatively insignificant phenomenon in the Lower South. Aside from the black churches of Savannah and Augusta, which in 1790 contained 48 percent of all black Baptists in Georgia and 22 percent of the total Baptist population, Phillips Mill is the only biracial church known to have had a licensed black preacher.[82] Nearly 78 percent of South Carolina's comparatively small black Baptist population were members of biracial churches, but few of them were able to overcome white determination to maintain clerical control. Some black men were authorized to exhort, not a licensed church office among Baptists,[83] and others were appointed "as a guard for the Black members."[84] Ceasor was an exception to the general rule. In 1821 the Big Creek Baptist Church authorized Ceasor to "exercise his gift, provided he preaches sound Doctrin." Apparently pleased with the results, in 1824 church authorities allowed Ceasor to "travel into the state of Georgia and exercise his Gift," and in 1826 he was granted permission to "go wherever he is called," with the stipulation that his master approve.[85]

The Methodist establishment readily used black men as exhorters and eagerly sent them out on itinerant missions, but it was reluctant to trust them with church ordinances, baptism, and communion. The decision to ordain black men was made partly in response to intense pressure from black men, most of whom simply took it upon themselves to exhort or preach without benefit of ordination, partly because the Methodist establishment was incapable of committing sufficient numbers of white missionaries to the field, and partly out of the white establishment's genuine respect for their deep spirituality and for the credit and authority they so clearly commanded.[86] The first black man to receive ordination from the Methodist Episcopal Church was a former slave named Richard Allen, who was ordained a deacon by Francis Asbury on June 1, 1799. Allen preached in Delaware and New Jersey before establishing Bethel Methodist Episcopal Church in Philadelphia.[87]

In 1800 the General Conference of the Methodist Episcopal Church agreed "to ordain local deacons of our African brethren, in places where they have built a house or houses for the worship of God." Each candidate for orders was required to obtain a two-thirds vote of the male members of the society and the recommendation of the white minister who had the charge, as the local church was called in Methodism. Even then the Conference decided not to print the authorization in the Discipline, for fear of inciting opposition from slave owners, but instead they agreed "to enter it on the journals only."[88] The most common pattern seems to have been for black men to start out as licensed exhorters, the lowest category in the leadership hierarchy. The first step toward entering the ministry was to become licensed as a local preacher, either by an individual station, a church, or a quarterly conference. Although local preachers were authorized to preach the gospel, they were not entitled to church support, and most local preachers engaged in business or trade and preached in their own neighborhoods.

Quarterly conference records reveal that access to the "called ministry" was often a long and painful process for black men. Sharp Street Methodist Episcopal Church of Baltimore, from whose creolized membership the earliest institutionalized black Methodist clergy derived, suggests a typical trajectory of black men through the itinerancy." In 1800 the Sharp Street Church approved three free black men (James Cole, James Carlbin, and Thomas Dublin) as local preachers and five (James Bryan, Joseph Clean, Thomas Hall, Edward Rogers, and Peter Hill) as exhorters, and they permitted three more (James Joliffe, Aaron Hogan, and Andrew Crawford) "only to pray.[89] Apparently no more black preachers were licensed until 1815, when the church declared fit for church office five more local preachers (Jacob Fortie, John Whye, Vincent Blake, John Mingo, and Solomon

Welsh) and seven exhorters.[90] A similar pattern emerged elsewhere in the Baltimore Conference. Between 1827 and 1830 Annapolis Station, which maintained a black majority from its inception, licensed nine black exhorters and three local preachers.[91] During the same period Calvert Circuit, where black Methodists outnumbered whites by more than two to one, licensed nine black exhorters.[92]

A small minority of local preachers achieved special status through ordination to one or both of the two orders of the Methodist ministry—the order of deacons and the order of elders. Between 1818 and 1830 eleven local preachers were recommended by their churches for ordination by the Baltimore Conference, the main business meeting where deacons and elders were ordained. Six were from Baltimore's Sharp Street Church. The first black man to receive deacons orders was John Mingo, who was recommended by the Sharp Street African Church in 1818. Between 1824 and 1831 the Conference elected ten black men for deacons orders, the lowest of Methodism's two orders. In 1826 Joseph Cartwright of the Georgetown Station became the first black preacher elected to the order of elders, the highest ministerial order in Methodism; and in 1830 James Harper of Frederick Circuit was also elected elder.[93]

The Virginia Conference licensed some black men as exhorters,[94] and a few more were licensed as local preachers. David Payne of Richmond, a free black man, is believed to have been the first man elected to orders by the Virginia Conference. Ordained to the office of deacon in 1824, Payne was later sent to Liberia as a missionary, where he died soon after his arrival.[95] Thereafter the number of black men in the ministry began to increase rapidly in the Virginia Conference, especially in the heavily black Neuse District. During the 1820s the New River, Tar River, and Trent River Circuits in the Neuse District licensed thirty-six black men as exhorters and fourteen as preachers, the majority of whom, judging by the absence of surnames, were slaves. At least six of the exhorters became licensed preachers. Thus, in a ten-year period a cadre of officially recognized black male leaders had emerged in the Neuse District.[96]

Although black Methodists were sufficiently numerous to maintain a large and coherent Methodist society in Charleston and Georgetown, South Carolina, discrimination against Methodism and powerful white opposition to an ordained African ministry delayed the development of an established black ministry. Nevertheless, a cadre of trained leaders began to emerge in urban churches with predominantly black memberships. Trinity Methodist Church organized its large black membership, 93 percent of whom were slaves, into classes and appointed class leaders to direct their weekly meetings. Eighty-three percent of all class leaders were slaves.[97] Between 1815 and 1830 Georgetown Methodist Church listed 115 class leaders, all of whom were apparently slaves, and all of whom were men.[98]

The insistence of Presbyterians on an educated clergy limited the number of black preachers. The best known example was John Chavis, about whose early life little is known. Probably born in Granville County, North Carolina, Chavis was educated at Washington Academy (later Washington and Lee) in Virginia. He was licensed by the Presbytery of Lexington in 1801 and was appointed a missionary to the black populations of Virginia and North Carolina, work he pursued with rather limited success until the scare over the Nat Turner insurrection in Southampton County made it illegal for slaves or free blacks to preach or exhort in public.[99]

By insisting on recognition of their "gifts" in preaching and teaching, black men had effectively imposed their own definition of the priesthood of all believers on the established churches. Black women tried unsuccessfully to extend its meaning further. The gradual institutionalization of an indigenous black male leadership beginning late in the eighteenth century coincided with the categorical denial of ministerial privileges to black women. The leadership structure of all evangelical churches, whether black, white, or biracial, was shaped by the fact of fundamental domination: of blacks by whites, of women by men. From the beginning, Christian denominations had appealed directly to men. The early Sunday schools admitted female children, but the teachers trained to teach in them were male. The ministry of black women on a charismatic basis was accepted, but all claims to female religious authority were vehemently denied on biblical and doctrinal grounds. But a number of assertive black women, eager to test the boundaries of the evangelical belief in the spiritual equality of women and men, as well as black and white, mounted significant challenges to the doctrine and practices of established churches.

Women who aspired to public religious leadership roles met with unremitting hostility from both the black and the white religious establishment. Women countered with a radical attack on male clerical domination based on a doctrinal claim of spiritual ordination. For example, Elizabeth, born a slave in Maryland in 1766, experienced a vision at age twelve. When she was in her early forties she received a direct call to preach: "It was revealed to me that the message which had been given to me I had not yet delivered, and the time had come." She "went from one religious professor to another" and was told by all that "there was nothing in Scripture that would sanction such exercises." When public officials demanded to know if she were ordained, Elizabeth replied "not by the commission of men's hands: if the Lord has ordained me, I need nothing better."

Zilpha Elaw received her commission for the work of the ministry "not from mortal man, but from the voice of an invisible and heavenly personage sent from God."[100] And Clarinda, a self-appointed preaching woman from Beaufort, South Carolina, endured years of "cruelty and persecution" because she believed she had a divine commission to preach the gospel.[101] Clarinda's preaching earned her "a host of enemies, both white and colored," but nothing she endured "could make her relinquish the office of a Minister of the Gospel." When she was a hundred years old and so feeble she could scarcely leave her bed, Clarinda, referred to by Henry Holcombe as "one of the greatest prodigies in the Christian world," continued to hold weekly meetings "at her own little habitation" regularly on the first day of every week. Eventually the meetings were broken up, but "Clarinda's People," as her followers were called, continued to meet "sometimes elsewhere." Although widely acclaimed for her piety and preaching skills, Clarinda was never accorded formal recognition by her church.[102]

When Jarena Lee told Richard Allen that "the Lord had revealed it to me, that [I] must preach," he responded that "our Discipline knew nothing at all about it—that it did not call for women preachers," and he advised Lee to content herself with prayer and exhortation.[103] Refused ordination, most preaching women began their evangelical work within a female network. Elizabeth started holding women's meetings at a poor widow's house "in one of the lowest and worst streets in Baltimore." The meetings "gave great offense" and were disturbed by a city watchman. After the church elders ordered the meetings stopped and "that woman quieted," some of the women were afraid to open their houses "lest they should be turned out of the church." Elizabeth temporarily obliged, but still she felt she "must exercise in the ministry." Consequently she was "rejected by the elders and rulers [and] hunted down in every place where I appointed a meeting . . . for my holding meetings contrary to discipline being a woman." Eventually Elizabeth left Baltimore for an itinerant preaching career in Virginia, Canada, and "many remote places." She founded a school for "colored orphans" in Michigan, and in 1853, at age eighty-seven, she retired to Philadelphia.[104]

Black church leaders did approve some preaching women, if only after the women met with evangelical success and only when persuaded that they had an extraordinary call.[105] Even though they were not ordained, preaching women often became itinerant evangelists, holding prayer meetings in barns and groves, preaching in meetinghouses and courthouses to black and white audiences throughout the Upper South.[106] In each of the plantation colonies/states, African American women, bond and free, played a highly significant role in nourishing and sustaining the growth and development of Protestant Christianity, but ordination, and even licensing, guaranteed male clerical domination of the black community, which was rapidly taking shape around church structures.

Evelyn Brooks Higginbotham and Cheryl Towsend Gilkes have pointed out that the exaggerated emphasis on the male office of preacher obscures the multiple leadership roles played by black women.[107] In areas that retained more of the distinctive features of African culture—most notably a cultural and psychological inheritance that viewed female religious participation favorably—black women had prominent leadership roles. In the Caribbean a select group of black women enjoyed an equal, or at least parallel status, to black men. In the predominantly black Methodist society of Antigua the tradition of female leadership established by Mary Alley and Sophia Campbell continued into the nineteenth century. In 1803, Reverend Thomas Richardson reported the presence of six or eight local preachers, "besides several coloured women who are very useful, and possess considerable abilities for prayer and exhortation." On one occasion, Richardson observed unnoticed their weekly meeting and was "astonished at their eloquence and motion. Their abilities," he marveled, "far exceed those of most of the women I have heard speak or pray in England."[108]

In Jamaica, the rules governing the internal regulation of Methodist societies divided classes by gender but allowed most of the female classes to have female leaders.[109] There is some indication that in Jamaica black women instructed mixed classes that met outside the churches. In 1817, for example, the Reverends Marsden and Watson received a letter telling them that "fifty or sixty negroes" who lived on an estate about nine miles out of Kingston "are regularly met in class by a pious black women, who lives near them, and who was made the chief means of bringing them first to hear the word of salvation." The unknown author of this letter also mentioned that on Unity Plantation "a Society has been lately raised, about 80 in number." The group met regularly in the house of a free black woman, "an excellent member of our Society and a Class Leader." This unnamed woman had "freely given up her house for a chapel, and intends building another to live in at a small distance."[110] At least one male missionary in Jamaica freely acknowledged that "women when judicious and pious are capable of doing much good."[111]

In the American South women had no formal authority in the church, but they exercised considerable influence. In describing black leadership of the early Methodist church of Charleston, Reverend F. A. Mood singled out Mary Ann Berry, Rachel Wells, and Nanny Coates. Wells, the slave of Edgar Wells, the first native Methodist of Charleston, was the first black member of a Methodist society. At her death in 1849 she was the oldest member, black or white, of the Charleston Methodist Church.[112] While hardly a ringing affirmation of the equal standing of women in the church, the assessment of William Capers, who later became bishop of the Methodist Episcopal Church, South, of Berry's service to the church and the poor implies a complementary function for women: "I never knew a female in any circumstances in life who better deserved the appellation of 'deaconess,'" Capers wrote.[113] A European traveler who visited the predominantly black Methodist church in Georgetown in 1819 found "a mighty assemblage of priests and priestesses, for all preached, prayed and sung together." Yet the records of the Georgetown church between 1817 and 1830 do not reveal a single African American woman, bond or free, who served as a class leader.[114] In all-black churches the African tradition of female spiritual leadership apparently persisted. Although the office of deaconess in the Methodist Episcopal Church was not established until the General Conference of 1888,[115] the minutes of the all-black Gillfield Baptist Church of Petersburg show that women were elected as deaconesses and were given responsibility for several functions normally reserved for men, including citing wayward members to meeting, visiting excommunicants to "inquire into their lives and conduct" and reporting back to the meeting, and "attend[ing] to candidates at the water" during baptismal ceremonies.[116]

The struggles of black women and men to redefine the meaning of the "priesthood of all believers" was part of a larger struggle over values and beliefs, the context for which varied: in the American South, the black evangelical community was organized in all-black, predominantly black, and biracial churches, and in the Caribbean, in predominantly black churches led by white ministers.[117] This had important implications for the development of black religious cultures in North America and the Caribbean. Membership in the Christian community produced the same tendencies among Afro-Caribbeans but with one important difference: the almost complete separation of the black and white spiritual communities made it possible for Afro-Caribbeans to create a spiritual universe whose primary cultural essence derived from African antecedents. By contrast, African American Christians created semi-autonomous spheres of life based in part on cultural assimilation and in part on cultural resistance and autonomy.

As a result of their incorporation into the whole Christian community black church members were exposed to white cultural forms, which inevitably produced both cultural assimilation and cultural resistance. The tendency toward assimilation is manifest in a shift in naming patterns after 1800 and later in the notion that Sabbath work was sinful. Studies of naming priorities are important as an index of acculturation,[118] and analyses of church and plantation records in North and South Carolina reveal an evolution in naming patterns that coincides with conversion. Classical names were the most prevalent among those assigned by owners to later generations. Beginning around 1800 the percentage of classical, or assigned, names declined from 20 percent to 10 percent, while the percentage of self-selected biblical names doubled from 10 percent to 20 percent. The correspondence between this trend and conversion strongly suggests African Americans' religious conviction and identification with the values of the Christian community. The choice of Old Testament names such as Isaac and Abraham for men, Sarah and Hagar for women, and the rejection of biblical names such as Delilah because of the insinuation of inappropriate moral behavior was indicative of African American understanding of biblical history. And slave parents tended to pass these names on to their children.[119]

The assimilative process also involved the absorption of fundamental Christian beliefs in the Supreme Being and in the nature of the afterlife and the concept of heaven and hell. The description of the differences between the cosmologies of "native Africans" and "the American negro" written by the slave Charles Ball illustrates the developmental process. Whereas "native Africans" still expected "that after death they shall return to their own country, and rejoin their former companions, and friends, in some happy region," the "American negro" "pants for no heaven beyond the waves of the ocean . . . on the banks of the Niger, or the Gambia." Instead, "his ideas, of present and future happiness" are borrowed from "the opinions and intercourse of white people, and of christians."[120] Ball certainly overstated the case since, in fact, the African American cosmological construction of basic Christian beliefs was fundamentally divergent from European American interpretations.

Among the "sublime doctrines taught by the white preachers" none had more compelling power than the idea of divine justice. Instead of seeking justice from the immanent and transcendent being through lesser divinities, as their African forbears might have done, African American Christians believed themselves to be under the immediate care and protection of a divine being whose universal benevolence guaranteed them justice in the hereafter. In the Afro-Christian rendition the Kingdom of Heaven was a place where "all distinctions of colour, and of condition, will be abolished, and they shall sit down in the same paradise, with their masters, mistresses, and even with the overseer."[121]

Ball noted that African American Christians "are ready enough to receive the faith, which conducts them to heaven, and eternal rest, on account of their present sufferings," but a different set of "fundamental rules" defined their creed. Although they adopted the concept of hell, they elaborated a view aberrant from that held by their owners. For one thing, "they by no means so willingly admit the master and mistress to an equal participation in their enjoyments, this would only be partial justice and a half way retribution." According to Ball, who claimed to have learned the "fundamental rules" in the slaves' religious meetings, "Heaven will be no heaven" unless "those who have tormented them here, will most surely be tormented in their turn hereafter."[122]

Ball's analysis suggests how far concepts of evil had evolved as a result of Africans' interaction with Christianity. African cosmologies defined evil as that which destroyed health, life, or fortune. The sources of evil were supernatural or mystical forces or the malevolent powers of sorcerers and witches.[123] Afro-Christians of the Atlantic world absorbed a different theory of evil, one that encompassed ethical transgressions denounced by the missionaries as "sin." But they added to it their own diverse understanding in order to make sense of the appalling system of slavery and to identify slave owners as the personification of evil.[124]

Something of the same cosmological progression can be seen in Matthew Gregory Lewis's description of Afro-Jamaican religious beliefs. "There is no phrase so common on their lips as 'God bless you!,' 'God preserve you,' and 'God A'Mighty!,'" which Lewis believed confirmed Afro-Jamaican faith in a supreme being. In language that echoes Ball's, Lewis continued, "They have even got a step further: for they allow the existence of an evil principle. From their language they appear to believe that hell is a place of torment." A slaveholding Christian himself, Lewis apparently failed to grasp the precise implications of the Afro-Jamaican notion of divine justice for slave owners.[125]

Conversion to Christianity also introduced to Afro-Atlantic peoples a store of potent Christian symbols, among the most powerful being the Bible. Although the commitment varied from one denomination to another, Protestant missionaries in North America and the Caribbean shared with their brethren in Africa the aim of bringing the Bible to all Christians, including enslaved people.[126] Because of laws prohibiting the instruction of slaves, Christian teaching and literacy were severely limited to a very small number, mostly male. Peoples of the Afro-Atlantic world remained deeply committed to spoken words and song, which were available to everyone, but they also grasped the central importance of access to Scripture—the Christian God's own word and ultimately the maximal symbol of white power and control.[127]

The word was indeed sometimes seen as yet another source of magical power. According to Matthew Gregory Lewis, many Afro-Jamaican Christians counted two important advantages to be gained by converting to Christianity. First, "it being a superior species of magic itself, it preserved them from black Obeah." And second, having observed the importance attached by whites to oath taking on the Bible, they believed that "to buss the book" would "give them the power of humbugging the white people with perfect ease and convenience."[128] For instance, until well into the nineteenth century slaves on the Singleton plantation in South Carolina continued to employ the Bible as a divination instrument to drive away witches and to discover the identity of thieves within the slave community.[129]

Their own interpretation of the word led Afro-Christians to question and reject much of what most whites believed to be central to Christian faith. They way they transformed the missionaries' message took a particularly subversive and dangerous form in Barbados, which had the most oppressive slave society. Acting upon his understanding of the authority of Scripture and its meaning for the everyday experiences of life, a Christian slave publicly extended his hand to a white missionary. This extraordinary act more or less explicitly denied the social distinctions between black and white Christians that most Protestant missionaries in slave societies had come to accept as the price of rapprochement with owners. Since the power of the clergy lay partly in its ability to interpret the word and apply it to social practices and behavior, it also challenged clerical authority. However, in this case the missionary reasserted his authority as interpreter of the word and of appropriate social relations in a sermon that warned his congregation that "there is a distinction between a White person and a Black that when the Black and Coloured people comes into the Chapel they should bury their Heads." To make the point emphatic, after the incident two new pews were added between the white and colored sections "to hinder the coloured people from approaching the whites." Their sense of themselves as spiritual equals deeply offended, black congregants "very much without exception, they have got so hurt many will not attend."[130]

This pattern was repeated in the American South, where it took the form of a separation movement that was at once a protest against racial prejudice and an assertion of a distinctive theology. Pious and strong-minded black women and men enjoyed a certain amount of leverage in mixed churches, and they used it boldly in an effort to gain religious equality and to establish cultural identities of their own. The movement of the revival indoors to churches reinforced the strict racial boundaries drawn during the Second Awakening and widened the cultural divide between black and white ritual practices. The distinctive forms of interpersonal conduct that had prevailed at church and house revivals and at early Methodist quarterly meetings temporarily found reinforcement in Bishop Asbury's directive that elderly and infirm black Christians be permitted to sit on the ground floors of Methodist churches.[131] The complaint of a Rhode Island lawyer that Virginia Methodists not only welcomed black members into their congregations but "place [them] among the most select part of their white brethren," points up the radical, if temporary, upsetting of patterns of worship and social behavior that distinguished the early phases of the first Great Awakening when revivalist fervor burned hot.[132]

The relative equality of treatment accorded black members was, however, short-lived and produced no permanent alteration in racial or gender relations. Instead, the waning of evangelical zeal and radical enthusiasm in the 1790s combined with growing white unease with integrated worship brought about a marked change in the seating arrangements in houses of worship. A clear tendency not only to separate the races but also to increase the physical distance between them reflects the actual difference in black and white social relations and the need to actively create distinctions in order to justify and maintain the social order. Virtually all of the churches constructed after 1800 had specially built galleries or balconies for black members, with separate seating for men and women and separate entrances designated specifically for black members of the congregation. By 1820, segregated seating was fully institutionalized in all denominations and regions.[133] It signaled a desire on the part of white Christians to bound and limit black rights within the religious community. The continual renegotiation of those boundaries provided one of the most critical dynamics in the history of slavery.

Within the biracial churches white and black church members often found it necessary to negotiate their behavior pragmatically in dynamic relationships with one another, each resorting to the values of its own cultural systems as barometers. White churchmen may have believed that they were merely communicating a message of Christian piety and submission to their African converts, but they were in fact converting them to a belief in their equality as Christians. Frustrated by their failure to achieve actual equality, some black Christians chose to deal with their disparate understanding of Protestant beliefs and practices by asserting their own spatial claims, and thus their rights, within biracial churches.

The decision of the Coan Baptist Church of Fairfields, Virginia, to build a partition "to divide the white's and blacks" caused intense controversy and disruption. For almost a year the building of the partition separating the races was the subject of debate between the white male leadership and the representatives of the black membership, Brother Spencer Thomas, a free black, and Ned and George, two slaves. Ned and George eventually agreed that they "would be satisfied if there was a pass way cut through" the partition, but Thomas "still refused to come into that part of the meeting house assigned to Blacks." After months of negotiation Thomas was expelled "as a disorderly member." His refusal to comply with the "terms of conciliation" is a recurring theme that typifies relations in many biracial churches.[134]

Forced to accept discrimination in most other areas of Southern life, African American Christians insisted upon the realization of the Christian message of spiritual equality by directly challenging the white understanding of it. Some of them, like Sam, who was enslaved by Charles Gosnell of Soldiers Delight in Baltimore County, Maryland, declared their spiritual independence from the white religious establishment. Raised by a family of Methodists, Sam "lived with some of them for years past, on terms of perfect equality." When for some reason the family refused "to continue him on those terms," Sam took offense and ran away. Soon he began "instructing and exhorting his fellow creatures of all colors in matters of religious duty."[135]

Winney, a member of the Forks of Elkhorn Baptist Church in Kentucky, offered her own radical rendition of the evangelical message of spiritual equality. She was expelled for saying that "she once thought it her duty to serve her Master and Mistress but since the Lord had converted her, she had never believed that any Christian kept slaves." Lest anyone miss her point, Winney announced that "she believed there was Thousands of white people Wallowing in Hell for their treatment to Negroes—and she did not care if there was as many more."[136]

The most thoroughgoing critique of white religious culture was written by an unnamed black person, probably a slave, to Reverend John Fort. In it the author challenged Fort to explain whether "the reson you allwaze preach to the white folks and keep your back to us is because we sit upon the hill." The virtual exclusion of black men and women from the preaching area, the writer pointed out, contravened the egalitarian Protestant message and barred black men and women from its realization: "We have no chance a mong them we must be forgotten because we cant get near enoughf without getting in the edge of the swamp behind you we have no other chance because your stand is the edge of the swamp." How, the author wanted to know, could slaves become moral agents when they were thus denied access to religious instruction and even to the Scriptures, the moral foundation of the Christian community? "If I should ask you what must I do to be saved perhaps you would tel me pray let the bible be your gide this would be very well if we could read I do not think there is one in fifty that can read."

The writer was not inclined to let the contradiction between preaching and practice pass without notice, either: "If God sent you to preach to sinners did he direct you to keep your face to the white folks constantly or is it because these give you money but it is handed to you by our master if this is the case we are the very persons that labor for this money." The covetousness that compromised the moral purity of clergymen was linked with the great moral curse of slavery: "Money appears to be the object weare carid to market and sold a heathon or christian[.] if the question was put, did you not sel a christian, what would be the answer[?] I cant tell you what he was gave me my price thats all was interested in."

Prosperity based on the suffering of Africans violated divine law, ruptured communal bonds, destroyed ecumenical spirit, and, the writer warned, would inevitably incur divine wrath. Like Winney, the writer's spiritual understanding of divine justice and of appropriate rewards and punishments deviated sharply from the traditional version adhered to by most white Christians. "Is this the way to heavin if it is there will be a good miny to go there if not there chance will be bad for there can be many witnesses against them If I understand the white peole they are praying for more religion in the world of may our case not be forgoten in the prairs of the sincear." Confident in the correctness of this unique understanding of God's moral government, the writer called on Fort to "read it to their church if you think it proper."[137]

In a number of cases, black members of mixed congregations chose to deal with their disparate understanding of Christian beliefs and practices by withdrawing into their own already established religious culture. Until the Vesey Revolt put a stop to it, there was a distinct and partially successful movement toward church separations, especially in cities where black membership was large. The first secession involved the walkout of black members of the Lovely Lane and Strawberry Alley Methodist meeting-houses of Baltimore. The division that surfaced in 1787 had been developing since 1784, when the General Conference declined to ordain black preachers. The complete break came when blacks were denied the right to take communion with whites and were restricted to seating in the gallery.

The secessionists formed their own independent prayer group and consulted Asbury "about building a House and forming a distinct African, yet Methodist church."[138] Asbury's complaint five months later that "the Africans of this town desire a church, which in temporals, shall be altogether under their own direction, and ask greater privileges than the white stewards and trustees ever had a right to claim," reveals African American Christians' powerful desire for self-government as well as religious self-determination. Eventually the secessionists, led by Daniel Coker, established two separate churches in Baltimore: Sharp Street and Bethel.[139] In 1816 Coker and members of the Bethel society helped form the African Methodist Episcopal Church. The Sharp Street congregation continued its affiliation with the white-controlled Methodist Episcopal Church until 1864.[140]

The same scenario repeated itself. In 1805, after black members of Asbury Methodist Episcopal Church in Wilmington, Delaware, were restricted to the gallery during worship and class meetings, even when the church was empty, they split from the parent congregation and formed Ezion Church, the first all-black Methodist Episcopal Church on the Delmarva Peninsula.[141] And although black members continued to worship for some time in Alexandria's biracial Baptist church after they were confined to "that part of the meeting house below the North door of the house," they eventually formed a separate church, the Alfred Street Baptist Church, and built their own brick meetinghouse.[142] In 1825 the black membership of Ebenezer Methodist Church in Washington, D.C., left the church "due in part to dissatisfaction with white pastors['] refusal to take black children in their arms when administering rites of baptism." In 1820 it affiliated with the African Methodist Episcopal Church.[143]

The most dramatic of these episodes involved the withdrawal in 1817 of most of the black members of Charleston's Bethel Methodist Episcopal Church. Vastly superior in number, Bethel's black majority had over the years developed autonomous traditions, including independent control of their own church finances and the freedom to hold separate quarterly Conferences. The split occurred when Anthony Senter, a white minister, attempted to strengthen clerical authority by taking direct control over the church and all financial matters. The black membership and their leaders rightly saw these restrictions as an effort to rob them of financial autonomy and of ownership of the church building, which they insisted had been built largely with their contributions. The disgruntled parishioners, 4,376 in number, and virtually every class leader walked out in protest. They subsequently built their own church on the corner of Hudson and Calhoun Streets and pointedly named it the African Church. Its separate existence was cut short by the Vesey Revolt of 1822, and eventually the black membership returned to the biracial society. In 1834, however, the forcible eviction of free black members from the seats they occupied along the walls to make room for white congregants, split the church apart once again and led to the formation of the Protestant Methodist Church in Charleston.[144]

A similar pattern among predominantly black biracial Baptist churches in Virginia points up the complex dialectic between the Christian message of spiritual community on the one hand and black and white interpretations of that message on the other. In 1816 jealousy over the English pastor's perceived partiality toward the 250 black members of the First Baptist Church of Norfolk led to the withdrawal of all 25 white members. The Norfolk First Baptist Church continued to function as an independent black church until 1838.[145] The biracial Davenport's Baptist Church near Petersburg disbanded around 1800, apparently over the desire of the white membership to escape black dominance. The white membership scattered to rural churches, while the black members organized themselves as the Sandy Beach Church on the Appomattox River in Pocahontas. In 1818 they abandoned that site and moved to Petersburg, purchased land at Gill's Field, built a meetinghouse, and organized themselves as the Gillfield Baptist Church. In the meantime, a group of free blacks led by Abraham Brown broke from Gillfield and formed the Elam Baptist Church in Charles City. In 1813 Elam was admitted to the Dover Association.[146] Shortly before the Vesey Revolt brought the movement to a halt, the predominantly black membership of the First Baptist Church of Richmond asked permission of the Dover Association to form "an African Church." Although the cause "found some zealous advocates," permission was denied. In 1823, 700 slaves and free blacks petitioned the legislature to build an African Baptist church and were again rejected.[147]

The remarkable number of independent black churches that appeared after 1790 arose out of black Christians' need to claim a cultural space of their own, where they could define morality, ritual, and social behavior on their own terms. If the black churches were never totally independent of white religious and social culture, neither were they totally dominated by the white establishment. Instead they developed a spiritual identity both similar to and different from their African pasts and from evolving white religious culture. Their new identity was characterized first and foremost by a distinct moral universe. In contrast to the individualistic and egocentric message of the Great Awakening favored by white evangelicals,[148] black evangelical Christians preferred a more integrating theology, one that incorporated blacks as well as whites and that extended to both women and men. Although women were not permitted to serve as ordained ministers in all-black churches, they were allowed a more active role in the administration of church affairs than women were allowed in all-white or biracial churches.

All-black churches also favored a different ethos characterized by a tolerance for expressive ritual behavior and more participatory worship. At the same time, many of the urban churches (led by a black elite represented by men such as Andrew Bryan and Henry Evans) rejected the religious style of worship associated with revivalism and, increasingly, with "black" worship in favor of decorum and orthodoxy.[149] Even so, all of the evidence points to significant differences in black and white worship forms, particularly in rural churches, where spontaneous worship patterns were retained.[150] As in white churches, the sermon dominated but involved active lay participation, usually in the form of fervent expressions that functioned as a dialectical response.[151] Music continued to be a vital part of worship in both urban and rural churches, often culminating in ecstatic behavior, which, more than perhaps anything else, best expressed the distinctly different millennial expectations of Afro-Christians.[152]

7

THE RELIGIOUS COMMUNITY

RELIGIOUS VALUES AND FAMILY NEEDS

As in all other religious communities, members of the evangelical Protestant churches of the American South and British Caribbean were provided with a range of benefits. The comfort and the fortitude that derived from the promise of assured salvation and of ultimate and eternal freedom, the sense of dignity and self-worth conferred by their religious convictions, and the bonds of comradeship forged in the context of their churches were of inestimable significance for successive generations of enslaved Baptists, Methodists, and Moravians.

The benefits that flowed from their religious faith did not, and could not, totally eradicate the pain and brutality of enslavement for black Christians, but arguably they made those facts of life somewhat more bearable. In return for these benefits the evangelical churches made the most stringent demands of their members in respect to doctrine, religious practice, and personal morality. These demands, and the often difficult decisions and choices they entailed, fundamentally reshaped many aspects of the individual and communal lives of black Christians. However, they were to have their most consequential impact on the sexual relationships, the family lives, and the domestic economies of enslaved church members.

In many respects black Christians' individual interpretation and collective practice of their religious beliefs was a matter for negotiation with their white co-religionists. Increasing white attempts to channel patterns of black belief and expression into acceptable European forms proved largely unsuccessful. Bondpeople had never been passive, undiscriminating receptors of the evangelical message preached to them by their white co-religionists but had always critically appropriated that message to meet their own specific requirements. Moreover, they brought to their public worship an exuberance that many white churchmen came to condemn as unseemly but that they could never completely tame. From the outset black Christians had staked their own claim to Protestant Christianity in their patterns of religious belief and behavior; they attached their own meanings to Christian teaching.

The practice of black Christianity within the evangelical Protestant churches was in large measure reflective of continual negotiation with white church members. The latter never succeeded in shaping black Christianity to their own requirements, and neither did they remain totally untouched by the religious ideology and conduct of their enslaved co-religionists. To a considerable extent, religious dogma and patterns of church worship were negotiable because black Christians made them so. By the 1770s and 1780s, however, there was one subject that most white, and for that matter most black, church leaders regarded as entirely non-negotiable: the sexual manners and mores of the enslaved members of their congregations. Leaders of both groups were determined to recast those manners and mores along traditional Christian lines, establishing clearly defined limits on black sexuality. This endeavor met with comparatively little resistance from black Christians, but it might well have deterred many other bondpeople from joining the evangelical Protestant churches.

The demand made of all Baptists and Methodists, upon pain of public censure and possible excommunication, was that they rigidly adhere to the fundamental tenets of Christian sexual morality. They were expected to either live lives of strict chastity or engage in sexually faithful monogamous marriages. These requirements were not racially specific, but they were clearly targeted toward black church members. In effect, their white co-religionists were determined to eradicate what they regarded as the sexual licentiousness of enslaved West Africans. The polygynous relationships (which, in their often deliberate ignorance of West African traditions, many whites mistook for polygamy or the total absence of sexual morality) that persisted in the American South and British Caribbean into the nineteenth century would be rooted out and replaced by Christian marriage, by the Christian family.

By the 1770s and 1780s evangelical church leaders were insisting that the enslaved members of their congregations be spiritually eligible to enter into what John Asplund described as the "sacred relationship" of Christian marriage, and that, if necessary, they must be compelled into entering that "relationship."[1] However, these same church leaders acknowledged the secular authority of slave owners. They declared that masters' permission had to be obtained by bondpeople wishing to marry, and they formalized this requirement in their rules of procedure.[2] It was also not unheard of for the evangelical churches to veto the marriage partners chosen by their members, particularly if those partners were unawakened.[3]

Although white churchmen agreed that their black co-religionists had "as great a right to marry, as to the Ordinances of God's House" (provided they had their owners' permission), there was no consensus as to precisely what form their marriage ceremony should take. In 1780, for example, the Charleston Baptist Association held that because bondpeople were not "entitled to the privileges of freemen by the laws of the land; and the ceremony of marriage being circumstantial, we do not think the customary mode with us essential." However, the association insisted upon the formalization of partnerships, even if this entailed the couple concerned "entering into obligations to each other, according to the usual mode among Negroes." Moreover, they should be "admitted or debarred communion" according to their willingness to make those "obligations."[4]

In practice in Southern states such as South Carolina and Virginia the marriage ceremonies devised by church leaders for their black members varied somewhat, but all required the couple to make "vows of mutual constancy." These "vows" did not necessarily have to be taken before the entire congregation. The Wicomico Baptist Church in Virginia, for example, required the presence of only two church members as witnesses.[5] But, regardless of the circumstances under which they were given and received, two questions remained: Were these "vows of mutual constancy" expected to remain valid for a lifetime in societies where, however entered into, slave marriages enjoyed no legal recognition or protection? And precisely what was the marital status of enslaved church members who had been forcibly separated by their owners?

Compared with most Baptist and Methodist congregations, the Moravians took an exceptionally indulgent view of the prior marital status of their black members and of the standing of black partners who had been separated by their owners. They were as committed as the other evangelical Protestant churches to the sanctity of Christian marriage, but, unlike the Methodists and Baptists, they also acknowledged the sanctity of relationships entered into prior to the admission of one or both of the partners into the church. Thus, they held that it would be inappropriate for them to "compel a man, who had, before his conversion, taken more than one wife, to put away one or more of them, without her or their consent." The hope was that the wives concerned would agree to what amounted to a divorce. If either the husband or his wives refused to part, then, although the former would not be expelled from the congregation, he could not expect to be promoted to the post of "a helper or servant in the church." In the case of church members who were forcibly and permanently parted by their owners, "the Brethren cannot advise, yet they cannot hinder a regular marriage with another person." Their reasoning was that "a family of young children, or other circumstances [might] make a help-meet necessary."[6]

Most Baptist and Methodist congregations took the uncompromising position that the marriage vow entailed a lifetime commitment that was unaffected by enforced separation. A few churches adopted a more flexible approach. In 1807, for example, the Wicomico Baptist Church declared that the marriage vow remained inviolate "until death or removal." In the latter event there would be no formal impediment to the remarriage of the remaining partner.[7] Some Baptist associations simply equivocated and advised their constituent churches to "act discretionally."[8] The Georgia Association insisted that cases of "hopeless and distant separation" should be "diligently investigated and all the circumstances duly weighed." Only if the separation appeared to "preclude a reasonable probability of a re-union" and "the persons themselves have been no way instrumental" should "the allowance of a re-marriage . . . be granted."[9]

The vast majority of Baptist and Methodist churches were far less sympathetic to those of their black members whose spouses had deserted them or whose marriages had irretrievably broken down for other reasons. There were, however, some exceptions. In 1818, for example, the Charleston Baptist Association considered a "Query" from the congregation at Three Creeks asking if a bondman whose wife had left him "without just cause or offence, and take[n] another man for her husband" could be "justified by the word of God in taking another wife." The church emphasized that the man concerned had made "earnest endeavours to reclaim" his wife and had expressed his "willingness to forgive her offence." The association believed that in this case "the injured person has a right to take another wife." Two reasons were given in support of that decision. First, the association held that "the law of Christ. . . admits of a divorce in the fullest sense, in cases of adultery and obstinate desertion." Second, slave marriage was not recognized by civil law, "so that they are left, in this respect, in a state of nature, to be governed by the laws of God directly and alone." But the association warned its constituent churches to be "cautious" in the determination of such cases because of the "temptations to violate the marriage contract, to which persons placed in these circumstances are ex-

posed." The association believed that "numerous arts and misrepresenta-
tions . . . are too often employed by persons professing innocence to justify
forming new connections." Member churches could sanction divorce and
remarriage but only "on clear evidence that the alledged [sic] criminality
exists, and the complainant has acted his or her part well."[10]

More often than not, though, a deserted or otherwise aggrieved spouse
was seldom, if ever, granted permission to remarry. In 1804, for example,
Giles, a member of the Berryville Baptist Church, "complained" that his
wife had "left him." The church responded with an unequivocal "No" when
he asked whether he could "take another wife."[11] In another instance,
Lynches Creek Baptist Church in South Carolina appointed a fiveman
committee to look into Sam's request to remarry. It reported back that its
"Council is, that the sd. cleave to the Wife he has last taken."[12]

Whether Giles and Sam complied with these decisions is not clear
from the records of their churches. But Kitty, an enslaved member of the
biracial Baptist congregation at Society Hill (formerly Welsh Neck) in
South Carolina did not heed the instructions of those who sat in judgment
on her. In 1820 she informed the church that her husband had abandoned
her some time ago and that she now wished to remarry. Kitty "was so far
regarded by the church" that a committee was appointed "to inquire into
the cause of their separation & her conduct." The committee was satisfied
that Kitty was blameless and "regarded her released from the man as husband." Kitty had secured the divorce she sought, but there was a sting in
the tail of the committee's recommendations: It "could not view her at
liberty, to take another husband, whilst the former was living." Kitty was
forced to choose between her church and the man she loved. She chose the
latter— to commit adultery, in the eyes of her church—and in due course
this highly "regarded" member of the congregation was excommunicated.[13]

All Afro-Baptists, -Methodists, and -Moravians were confronted with
the possibility that at some point in their lives they might be forcibly and
permanently separated from their spouse. Either or both of the separated
partners might eventually wish to remarry, but they could not always be
sure that their churches would allow them to do so. Giles, Sam, and Kitty
were also innocent parties whose marriages had broken down for other
reasons, but they too were denied the possibility of the remarriage they so
evidently sought. The decisions that faced all those black Christians who
found themselves in similar situations could be stark and agonizingly difficult to make.

By the turn of the eighteenth century the sexual behavior and familial
relationships of black Baptists and Methodists were coming under the

increasingly intense scrutiny of their white co-religionists. Any church member, black or white, male or female, could report the improprieties and misdemeanors of others, but class leaders and deacons were accorded a special responsibility for "the oversight of our black members." If they thought it appropriate, they were authorized "to admonish" offenders.[14] Those who refused to change their ways or who were alleged or known to have committed a particularly serious transgression would be summoned before their church's disciplinary body to answer for their behavior. By the early nineteenth century this usually meant that their fate, like the fates of those who sought divorce and remarriage, would be determined by the white male members of their church. In some Baptist and Methodist churches, however, this had not always been so.

In 1802 the Dover Baptist Association of Virginia expressed its concern and dismay at the fact that some of its member churches "admitted to their church meetings, even for discipline and government, all the members of the church, male and female, bond and free, young and old. Others admitted all male members, whether slave or free." But what really worried the white delegates was that in some churches enslaved members sat in judgment on their white co-religionists. "The degraded state of the minds of slaves," the association asserted, "rendered them totally incompetent to the task of judging correctly respecting the business of the church, and in many churches there was a majority of slaves; in consequence of which great confusion often arose." After "some debate," the delegates agreed "by a large majority" to recommend to the association's constituent churches "that although all members were entitled to privileges, yet that none but free male members should exercise any authority in the church."[15] Elsewhere in the South other congregations had already reached a similar decision.[16] After 1800, however, it rapidly became the standard practice for white churchmen to deny bondpeople and free white women a formal voice in disciplinary proceedings, or at least in those proceedings that would require them to assess the morality and behavior of white men.

Some churches acknowledged that white women could be "very useful in certain stages of discussion" and agreed that "they may admonish, reprove or rebuke, either singly or united to others, others, meaning a right to cite refractory members to appear before the church & may act as witnesses for or against them." A few congregations thought it appropriate for disciplinary committees to be composed of "the most considerable & experienced" of those whose sex was "similar to that of the offender."[17] Women might sometimes be permitted to arbitrate in cases involving other women, but, as Virginia's Black Creek Baptist Church asserted in 1803, "under no circumstances" could they "use authority over the man."[18]

In most disciplinary matters in the majority of biracial Methodist and Baptist congregations what was true of white men and women was equally true of free and enslaved African Americans. More often than not black church members who were charged with particularly serious breaches of church discipline could expect to be tried not by a panel of their peers but by a panel of white men. And some churches refused to "hold the testimony of a black member valid as [that of] a white member."[19]

The zeal with which the white men who dominated the disciplinary proceedings of the biracial Baptist churches pursued their goal of recasting the sexual behavior of their black co-religionists, and the difficulties they encountered along the way, is readily apparent from the detailed records kept by most congregations. These records reveal that most of what the traditional Christian canon deemed to be unacceptable sexual practices, but most notably adultery, bigamy, and fornication, comfortably topped the list of charges brought against enslaved church members.

The importance white churchmen attached to chastity and monogamy, to eradicating traditional West African sexual and familial relationships, is evident from an analysis of the charges made against 262 Afro-Baptists (89 women and 173 men) belonging to twenty-eight different Southern congregations between the mid-1770s and 1830.[20] In all, 98, or 37.4 percent, of these cases involved adultery, abandoning a spouse in favor of another, and, in two instances, women having "Two Husbands." There was not a significant discrepancy between the proportion of women (over 39 percent) and men (just under 36.5 percent) who were charged with these marital offenses.

Although the absolute numbers involved were small, a highly significant fact in itself, unmarried bondwomen appear to have been rather more likely than unmarried bondmen to be faced with charges of fornication and promiscuity.[21] Not surprisingly, perhaps, women were far more likely than men to be held responsible for what their churches defined as illegitimate births. Among bondwomen, occurrences of this disciplinary offense ranked second only to adultery. Eleven women, or 12.3 percent of those surveyed, fell into this category. The records suggest that the enslaved fathers of illegitimate children got off rather more lightly. Only two men, roughly 1 percent of the male sample, were excommunicated for this reason.

The disciplinary records of the biracial Methodist churches tell a very similar story. During the 1820s, for example, 34.4 percent of the 112 bondwomen compared with 24.7 percent of the 85 bondmen who were expelled from Charleston's Trinity Methodist Episcopal Church had been found guilty of adultery or of having more than one spouse.[22] Cyrus Peters, a black class leader, was among those excommunicated for adultery.[23] Five bondmen (roughly 6 percent of those who were expelled), but no bondwomen, were thrown out of the church for abandoning their spouse. One difference between the expulsions from the Charleston congregation and those from the Baptist churches surveyed is that only one enslaved Methodist (a woman) is recorded as having been excommunicated for fornication.[24]

The divergence between the disciplinary charges brought against white and black church members in biracial congregations is also readily apparent from the records. A survey of 106 white Baptists (85 men and 21 women) drawn from seven biracial churches between the late 1780s and 1830 shows that exactly half of them were summoned to answer charges not of sexual impropriety but of drunkenness.[25] However, there was a significant but perhaps not an entirely surprising gender difference: 57.6 percent of the male sample compared to 19 percent of the women surveyed were charged with this offense. But the racial difference was equally remarkable. Compared with their white co-religionists, a sample of 262 Afro-Baptists who were disciplined reveals that only 6.3 percent of the men and 2.2 percent of the women faced charges of intoxication.

Just as noteworthy is the way in which the white men who pronounced on questions of sexual morality in these seven biracial Baptist churches dealt with the white women in their congregations. Over 33 percent of the white women members who appeared before them, but barely 1 percent of the white men, were charged with sexual improprieties of one sort or another.[26] The only white man to be summoned to answer for his sexual behavior was charged with attempted seduction. The sexuality of white women, as well as that of bondpeople, was of pressing concern to the white men who dominated the disciplinary proceedings of the biracial evangelical Protestant churches.

That the disciplinary procedures instituted by the evangelical Protestant churches were profoundly important in regulating the sexual conduct and family lives of enslaved church members is indisputable. That there were those who could not, or would not, comply with the demands being made of them and who forfeited their church membership as a result is equally incontrovertible. However, it is also evident from the church records that these women and men comprised a minuscule proportion of what, by the late eighteenth century, was an ever increasing number of black Christians. The fact is that the vast majority of enslaved church members freely chose and, often in the most harrowing of personal circumstances, did their best to order their sexual morality according to the Christian ideal espoused by their white co-religionists.

Their religious faith, together with the importance they attached to church membership, required black Christians to make often agonizing decisions about their sexual conduct, their personal relationships, and their family lives. But church membership also held other, more material, implications for bondpeople that required decision making of a rather different kind. By the 1770s and 1780s those enslaved people who sought it had secured for themselves the unwritten right to hold Christian beliefs and to exercise those beliefs publicly, either alongside their white co-religionists or in churches of their own. The struggle to retain this right was to be fraught with consequences for the exercise of two other rights universally claimed by bondpeople, regardless of their religious persuasion.

By the mid-eighteenth century slave owners everywhere in British America had been forced to concede two critically important customary rights to bondpeople: the right to their own time and the right to any produce or income they generated by working in their own time. The exercise of these economic rights was necessary and significant to enslaved people for many reasons, but mainly because this was the only way open to them to raise their material standard of living above the bare subsistence deemed appropriate for them by their owners.[27] Evangelical Protestant churches did not threaten to deprive their enslaved members of these customary rights. Rather, they sought to redefine the meaning of these rights and to redirect the manner in which they were exercised. Church membership began to make far-reaching changes in the ways that bondpeople elected to spend both their time and their money. Nowhere was the agency of black Christians more evident than in the time and resources they chose to devote to what they considered to be their churches.

One of Reverend Abraham Marshall's most enduring memories of Andrew Bryan's "ordination" in Savannah on January 20, 1788, was that those who attended this momentous event "made up eight dollars for him [Marshall] in six and a quarter, twenty-five and fifty cent pieces, [and] gave him two loaves of bread and a bottle of wine."[28] Marshall was deeply moved by a gesture that, he seemed to imply, not only involved a significant financial sacrifice but also was a somewhat unusual occurrence. In fact, bondpeople had long been accustomed to paying for various religious services that were supplied by their own sacred specialists.

The traditional communal rites associated with marriage and death in the plantation colonies of British America had always entailed an outlay of material resources, either in cash or in kind, as had the dealings between individual slaves and their sacred specialists.[29] Indeed, as Ann Gilbert commented of mid-eighteenth-century Antigua, the practice of sacred specialisms could prove highly lucrative.[30] Not all practitioners were as opulent as Gilbert intimated, but calls upon their skills usually entailed a financial transaction. Conversion to Christianity did not involve any expenditure, but church membership most certainly did. The willingness of black Christians to support their churches may have reflected, in part, the persistence of the belief that their spiritual health was directly related to the size and frequency of their monetary contributions.

The duty to financially support their churches did not mark a radically new departure for bondpeople, but church membership did necessitate a fundamental reappraisal of individual and family budgets. It also entailed a dramatic change in the way in which black Christians elected to employ one of their most precious customary rights: the right to their own time. For most enslaved church members the expenditure of time and money on their churches became top priorities. Initially this expenditure found its most visible, and meaningful, expression in the construction of meetinghouses.

During the early stages of the evangelical Protestant impulse, when existing churches were often closed to them, the faithful gathered periodically in various locations: in the open air, in private houses, in barns and sheds, and in slave cabins. As communities of believers formed and grew in number, so did their desire for meetinghouses of their own. These buildings would not only serve the obvious function of providing meeting places on consecrated soil but would also stand as permanent physical symbols of commonly held beliefs and values, of a shared purpose and commitment. Sometimes existing churches were there to be made use of by converts; in most parts of the American South, and everywhere in the British Caribbean, they were not. Baptist, Methodist, and Moravian congregations usually had little alternative but to build their meetinghouses. In biracial congregations the aspiration and the drive to do this was seldom, if ever, the sole prerogative of white or of male church members. Recall that the main responsibility for building the first Methodist chapel in Antigua was assumed by two black women, Mary Alley and Sophia Campbell.[31]

The Moravian missions in the Caribbean always received important financial assistance from their co-religionists in the Old World, as did the Methodist and Baptist churches established in the British sugar islands after the American Revolution. Between 1787 and 1793, for instance,

British Methodists subscribed "over £6,000 . . . for the support of the Methodist missions in the West Indies." Another £2,000 was provided by Dr. Thomas Coke. This money was used for various purposes, including the building of chapels.[32] Very occasionally, or so the records suggest, important financial assistance might also be forthcoming from non-church members. Writing from Jamaica in 1791, for example, George Liele remarked that "several gentlemen, members of the house of assembly, and other gentlemen" had "subscribed" toward the cost of the "meetinghouse" that he and his congregation of around 350 people intended to build on the three acres of land "at the east end of Kingston" they had acquired for this purpose. Liele did not identify these "gentlemen" or mention the size of their donations and reasons for wishing to support his church. Instead, he emphasized the financial contributions that had been made by his congregation, "the chief part of [whom] are SLAVES, [whose] masters allow them in common, but three or four bits per week for allowance, to feed themselves." It was unrealistic, Liele continued, "out of so small a sum [to] expect any thing that can be of service from them." Moreover, "the FREE PEOPLE" in his flock were also "poor." But even so, "they are willing, both free and slaves, to do what they can." It was crucially important to Liele's congregation that they contribute "what they can" to the cost of acquiring the land for their church and to raising the four to five hundred pounds needed for building materials.[33]

In the aftermath of the American Revolution, Baptist and Methodist congregations in the South could not expect any financial support from their British co-religionists. Regardless of their size and their racial, gender, and age mix, most congregations were dependent on their own resources when it came to the construction of their meetinghouses. Before 1800, during the first phase of church building few Baptist and Methodist congregations had wealthy members or outside patrons to whom they could turn for financial help. It is true that some congregations included in their number comparatively affluent women and men who donated the land for churches and sums of money with which to build them,[34] but most did not.

The cost of building a meetinghouse varied over time as well as from place to place, but it usually included both the cost of land and building materials. On rare occasions, as in 1789 when Thomas Gibbons donated a lot in Savannah upon which Andrew Bryan and his black congregation built their first church "with little or no outside financial help,"[35] congregations were given the land they needed for their meetinghouses. In fact, Gibbons's generosity was not repeated four years later when Bryan wanted to build a larger church to accommodate his growing congregation. Through the good offices of William Bryan and James Whitefield, who acted in the legally necessary capacity of his white guardians, the recently manumitted Bryan secured the property he sought, Lot 7 in Oglethorpe Ward.[36] The asking price for the land, which had a frontage of 95 feet and was 132.5 feet "deep," was "thirty pounds, equal to $150."[37] The entire sum was raised by Bryan and his congregation.

Most congregations also had to make some provision for the purchase of building materials. As a matter of preference, and indicative of financial constraints, the Baptist and Methodist meetinghouses built before the early nineteenth century were small, architecturally straightforward affairs. As David Ramsay commented in 1808, the 200 or so Methodist "churches or stations for preaching" in South Carolina were "constructed in so plain a style as to cost on average about one hundred and thirty-five dollars each, or $27,000 for the whole."[38] Wood, rather than brick, was the building material favored by most congregations, but there were some exceptions. In Richmond, Virginia, for example, "although . . . not the most flourishing sect," the Baptists "built, by public subscription, a large brick meeting-house."[39] Farther South, in Georgetown, South Carolina, the Baptists erected "a handsome and commodious meeting-house about sixty feet long." As Francis Asbury wryly observed, the Baptists *take the rich; and the commonality and the slaves fall to us.*[40]

Far more typical of eighteenth-century meetinghouses was the Baptist church built at Little Briar Creek in Georgia during the late 1770s, which was made of "unhewn logs, worth about fifty dollars."[41] The first Methodist chapel in Fayetteville, North Carolina, built by "a small society of colored people, under the care of a colored man named Evans," measured "twenty by thirty feet" and was fabricated "out of rough-edged" materials. Evans and his congregation had leased the land upon which they built their chapel "for seven years" and "met the expenses themselves, except five dollars, which was given to them by a white man."[42] In 1789 the biracial Baptist congregation at Black Creek, South Carolina, "Concluded to build a meeting house . . . 20 feet Square with hewed Logs & shingled roof, [and] a Shelter on each side 8 feet wide."[43] The first Baptist church built in Bruington, Virginia, in 1791 was "a wooden structure, unplastered, without stoves or heating appliances of any kind, without glass lights except a single narrow window in the rear of the pulpit."[44]

In Savannah, the "big meeting house" built by Bryan's black congregation in Oglethorpe Ward was wooden, "very plain, [and] without any attempt at architectural beauty." The seating consisted of "straight-backed pews without doors; and the only pretension to neatness was in the smoothing of the backs and seats and rounding and beading the edges and tops." No money was spent on painting the interior of the church.[45] To be sure, there was some architectural variety in Baptist and Methodist meetinghouses, but these were variations around a common theme of simplicity. Most were little more than "rough frame or log structures of square or oblong single rooms."[46]

Some congregations considered comparative labor costs and hired workers to build their churches;[47] many others determined that the cheaper option would be to utilize their own skills. In 1789, for example, the Baptist congregation at Black Creek, South Carolina, agreed that two of its members would "undertake the work" of building its meetinghouse and that "the other members to assist them, and that a Subscription be Drawn to see what help may be had either in work or produce."[48] In every sense, the building of meetinghouses reflected and reinforced a sense of community, of attachment, and of personal worth. However materially impoverished, every church member could contribute something of value to the venture.

The engendering of occupations determined the kind, but not the amount, of work that could be volunteered by black Christians toward the construction of their meetinghouses. The requisite artisanal skills were almost exclusively a male preserve, but this did not mean that women church members stood idly by and watched as their menfolk worked.[49] On the contrary, they pitched in to help with an enthusiasm and an effort that greatly impressed their male co-religionists.[50] In Savannah, for example, the "Men at work" on the city's first African Baptist church were "greatly encouraged by sisters, who would at times even assist in the work, holding up the ends of the boards while workmen scribed, cut, and nailed."[51] In every way, the building of meetinghouses was a cooperative effort. Black Christians had every reason to believe that in a physical as well as a spiritual sense "the chapel they attended . . . was partly their own creation."[52]

Many congregations may have found it difficult to raise the often modest sums they needed to build their churches, but the question of individual monetary contributions seems not to have been high on the agenda for debate, let alone controversial. What was to prove problematical, though, was the financial support of the churches once they had been completed. Provisions had to be made for cleaning the meetinghouse,[53] for physical wear and tear,[54] and occasionally for constructing extensions, or even an entirely new building, to house a growing membership.[55]

Baptist, Methodist, and Moravian congregations faced another ongoing financial liability over and above the cost of maintaining the physical fabric of their churches: the support of their ministers. Congregations in the Caribbean made substantial contributions toward the running costs of their churches, but by the late eighteenth century British-based missionary societies were assuming the main burden of supporting the ministers they sent to the sugar islands.[56] Often impoverished black Christians gave what they could to the upkeep of their churches and ministers. Among the Baptists and Moravians, contributions were voluntary, and "the average contribution" of each black Baptist worked out at "about a half-penny a week."[57] Black Methodists, on the other hand, were required to pay a quarterly fee for their admission ticket and a monthly fee for their class meetings and to contribute to a weekly collection taken on Sundays. The sums involved varied somewhat. In the Leeward Islands, for example, they totaled somewhere in the order of thirty shillings (currency) per person per annum.[58]

For some years the funding of Baptist ministers in the American South was a highly controversial subject. Initially, many Baptists were opposed to the Anglican practice of paying their ministers, and they gave little, if any, financial assistance to their pastors.[59] By the mid-eighteenth century, however, most pastors were receiving some support from their congregations, but there was no uniform policy. Payments varied from church to church in the same association and from year to year in the same church. In South Carolina during the 1760s and early 1770s, for example, annual stipends ranged from £350 to £800 Carolina currency per annum. Elhanan Winchester, the pastor of the biracial church at Welsh Neck, was paid at the rate of £400 Carolina currency per annum, and his congregation agreed that he could preach in the nearby church at Cheraw Hills every third Sunday, provided that the members there "do their part toward his support." In the 1790s Alexander McDougal, the pastor of the impecunious Cedar Spring Church, also in South Carolina, received part of his annual salary in the form of "salt [and] iron." In 1800 he was paid a total of $28.50 by his congregation, while Reverend Williams, who was attached to the same church, received $15.25.[60]

There were some Baptist ministers who were not financially dependent upon their congregations. In South Carolina, for instance, 40 percent of the white pastors in office between 1780 and 1800 who were recorded in the Federal Census of 1790 owned at least one slave and could be said to have "belonged to the more prosperous group of Baptists."[61] Much the same was true of a handful of free African American ministers, and perhaps most famously of Andrew Bryan. He was able to fully support himself and his family through his highly successful wagoners business, so he did not have to make any financial demands of his congregation. When he died in 1812 Bryan was worth at least $3,000.[62] Bryan's nephew, Andrew Marshall, who also served as pastor of the First African Church in Savannah, engaged in the same business as his uncle. Evan Great (or Grate), an assistant minister in Bryan's church and subsequently a deacon in Savannah's Second African Church, gave his occupation variously as pastor and wagoner.[63]

Men such as Bryan and Marshall could well afford to devote a good deal of time to their pastoral duties, but many others were not in this fortunate financial position. When they "ought to be out and working in God's vineyard behold they are forced to leave the flock to hunger for food, while they provide real necessaries for their families."[64] By the early 1790s the Baptist associations of the American South generally agreed that this was a highly unsatisfactory situation and that pastors and their families ought to receive "sufficient support" from their congregations."[65] Church members were being urged to fund full-time ministers, but they were not compelled to do so by their associations.

Methodist leaders also were emphasizing the need for congregations to maintain not only their resident ministers but also circuit riders. As John Asplund insisted in 1791, "practical religion" demanded "the support of the gospel, that God's servants may be wholly given up to their great calling, . . . and our poor brethren supported."[66] Congregations would be expected to maintain their own ministers and, through their Conferences, to establish a "common fund" for the support of circuit riders. As David Ramsay explained in 1808, these "travelling . . . preachers," of whom there were twenty-six in South Carolina, "generally preach on six days of each week to six different congregations." "For this extraordinary labor," Ramsay continued, they were paid only eighty dollars a year in addition to their travelling expenses.[67]

Like the Baptist associations, Methodist Conferences did not usually prescribe the salary of resident ministers. As Ramsay noted in his detailed description of the financial arrangements made by his own state's Methodists, South Carolina's ninety-three or so "local preachers" were "generally married men, who labor all the week" for "no salary or compensation." However, their "wives and children . . . draw a salary from a common fund equal to that of a travelling preacher." According to Ramsay, a similar "salary" was also paid to "worn-out, superannuated and supernumary ministers."[68] Like their Baptist counterparts, most resident Methodist ministers in the South lived on what they could earn and supplemented their income by collections taken at Sunday services and weeknight classes. As William Capers recollected of his time in Wilmington, "For support, as far as any was to be had, I was dependent mainly on my colored charge, whose class collections, added to the collection which was made in the congregation weekly, may have produced six or seven dollars a week>*for all purposes.* I had not expected such a deficiency, and was not provided against it." Joseph Cartwright, a local black Methodist preacher, received even less than Capers did. In 1824 he was hired to preach for the black congregation at Washington, D.C.'s Ebenezer Church at the rate of twenty-five dollars a year.[69]

By 1800 most Southern Baptist and Methodist congregations accepted that it was their "duty . . . to maintain their Ministers . . . and use every means in their power to rid [them] of worldly care."[70] But what was less clear and a highly contentious issue for some Baptists was the basis upon which individual contributions would be called for and made. Should those who were unwilling or unable to subscribe be permitted to retain their church membership? Would any allowance be made for disparities of wealth? Most associations concluded that church members should "pay according to their several abilities," but their constituent churches were left to determine how that recommendation would be implemented. As the Dover Association explained in 1799, it was "the duty of every member to contribute to the church he belongs to, as God hath prospered him[, but] it is the prerogative of the church to judge of it, and that contribution be made in that way, a church may judge best adapted to."[71]

Some churches had already reached the same conclusion. In 1781, for example, Virginia's Morattico Church had observed that "Societies of every Denomination require that collections be made Among the members thereof to satisfy certain necessary expenses" but that "there never has yet been any regular order fallen on among us to facilitate that business." The church agreed that "to avoid if possible any further complaints," the congregation would "be classed into three separate Districts . . . [and] that each of the three Deacons make out a list of the names of the church members residing in their Districts, and after each Person's name set down his property . . . according to the last publick [*sic*] assessment."[72] This information would be used to determine the appropriate annual contribution of each church member. Enslaved members, who were legally denied the right to hold property, would not appear on the tax lists, but they too would be required to contribute.

Unfortunately there is no record of the sums of money contributed by the enslaved members of the Morattico Church. Records from the Baptist church in Upper King and Queen County, also in Virginia, indicate that in 1785 it too decided to "levy tithes" on its members. They would be imposed "equally on whites . . . on each 100 acres of land" they owned. Recognizing the customary right of bondpeople to the income they generated in their own time, the church declared that "all the Black tithes" would be based on what "the members possess of their own property."[73]

By 1800 Southern Baptists generally accepted that the contributions of church members, enslaved and free, should be linked to their ability to pay. But there was still some disagreement as to whether or not churches had the right to compel their members to contribute and to discipline those who did not. Virginia's Ketocton Association held that those who refused to subscribe "according to their property . . . deserved to be excluded from the privileges of the church." This recommendation met with "violent opposition" in some churches.[74] In 1802 the Goshen Association in Virginia wrestled with this problem. Bethel Church had agreed "by a large majority" to compel "each person, under the penalty of the displeasure of the Church, to contribute towards her expenses according to what he was worth." A "minority" of the members had been deeply offended by a requirement that also "gave great umbrage" to several other churches in the association. After lengthy deliberation, the association somewhat pragmatically concluded that although assessments based on the ability to pay were "lawful . . . all things that are lawful are not expedient."[75] In practice, each church would be left to its own devices.

During the first third of the nineteenth century some congregations followed the Morattico and Upper King and Queen County example and imposed "tithes" on their members, which varied according to race and gender. The Baptist church at Nomini, Virginia, for example, required different sums from free and enslaved women and men. White male church members were asked for a minimum of fifty cents a year, "or more as [they] think fit," and white women were expected to give at least twenty-five cents per annum. An annual levy of twelve and a half cents was imposed on each bondman in the congregation and six and a quarter cents on each bondwoman.[76] In other congregations members were expected to contribute whatever they could afford on a weekly basis, and all the church's expenses would be met from these variable sums. This was the procedure followed in Richmond's predominantly black First Baptist Church during Elder Courtney's long term of office between 1788 and his death in 1824. Every Sunday after "the morning service . . . a hat collection was taken by the Deacons at each door of the church. The money thus collected was emptied into the handkerchief of the senior Deacon, wrapped up, carried to the Pastor's house, and put into a bowl in the cupboard. This same, much or little, was his salary." That these weekly collections were often insufficient for Courtney's most basic needs is suggested by the fact that "the sisters of the Church, by presents, from time to time, kept him in clothing."[77]

Biracial Baptist and Methodist congregations usually assumed that white women of every social rank and bondpeople would make regular financial contributions to their church. Moreover, they might also be made responsible for soliciting and collecting subscriptions from among their number. Following Pastor Courtney's death in the late 1820s, for example, this became the practice at Richmond's First Baptist Church. When in 1825 the church was seeking a new pastor "a committee . . . of the colored brethren" was appointed "to collect subscriptions." Two years later, when some members of the congregation, which "numbered about a thousand, more than two-thirds of whom were probably" black,[78] had "refused or failed" to pay their "subscribed sums," it was agreed that committees consisting of "ten white male members, five white female members, and [four] coloured male members be appointed . . . to take collections from the members . . . for the salary of our pastor." The committees were instructed to report "delinquent" members to "the deacons to admonish them." There is no record of the reactions of bondwomen, who had done so much to support the late Pastor Courtney, to their exclusion from these formally constituted groups.

These committees proved highly inefficient because a year later the church was once again reviewing its financial procedures. The outcome was a formal levy not on individual members per se but on three groups within the church: white men, the white "sisters," and the "coloured members." It was agreed that seventy-two of the ninety-two white men in the congregation were financially able to contribute, and that between them they should subscribe $800 of the $1,500 needed annually to run the church. "Many" of the white "sisters" were said to be "able and willing if called upon to lend their aid," and they were asked to contribute a total of $70. The "coloured members" were also reported to be "willing and able to contribute their mites" and, given their "number . . . and the privileges they enjoy . . . they ought to raise the sum of $300 between them." The shortfall of $330 would be raised by "monthly collections" and "from our friends."[79] Their methods varied, but by 1800 every Baptist congregation in the American South, regardless of its racial composition, paid something toward the maintenance of its pastor.

The formation of associations and Conferences of the evangelical Protestant churches also entailed expenditure for congregations. Most volunteered money for printing the proceedings of association and Conference meetings and usually purchased at least one copy for their own use. Sometimes they also helped to fund the publication of sermons and other religious tracts and occasionally bought "a few useful pamphlets, to bestow gratuitously to those who have it not in their power to purchase them."[80] Predictably, these expenses varied, but usually they amounted to no more than about five dollars per church per annum.[81]

By the early nineteenth century some Baptist associations were beginning to make another call upon the financial resources of their constituent churches. In 1800 the Georgia Association discussed the possibility of engaging in missionary work among the Creek people, and, three years later, eighteen ministries formed the General Committee of Georgia Baptists to promote such work.[82] Similar moves, initiated by the Portsmouth Association in 1804, were also afoot in the Upper South. In 1805 a convention held at Cashie, in Bertie County, North Carolina, agreed to found a Philanthropic Missionary Society that, like its counterpart in Georgia, would focus its attention on the Creeks.[83] During the next few years the Southern Baptists formed a number of other domestic and foreign missions, each of which depended upon the financial donations of individual church members.[84]

Money for missionary work was raised in various ways. Sometimes special collections were taken, perhaps after a sermon or "lecture" on the subject of missions,[85] and sometimes individual churches included the support of missionary work as a fixed item in their annual budgets. Not all congregations contributed or did so regularly, but the donations made by the black Baptist churches are particularly noteworthy. In 1824, for example, eleven churches in the Sunbury Baptist Association gave a total of $77.50 to the Committee for Domestic Missions. Savannah's white Baptist church subscribed 20 percent of this money, and of the remainder, under 12 percent was given by the city's two African churches and the two black congregations at White Bluff and Abercorn. The predominantly black churches at Sunbury, Newport, Great Ogechee, Powers, Salem, and Little Canouchee raised a total of $47, or just over 60 percent of all the money collected.

The following year only $37.90 was donated by the Sunbury Association to the Committee for Domestic Missions, and the proportion given by Savannah's white Baptists had grown to almost one-third. The five dollars given by the city's two black churches and the black congregation at White Bluff, whose combined membership totaled 3,126 people,[86] accounted for 13 percent of all the money raised. On a per capita basis this was an inconsequential sum, except for the fact that it came from the extremely limited financial resources of enslaved church members; it was money that had to be earned and voluntarily sacrificed.

From Andrew Marshall and George Liele in the 1780s and 1790s to the clerk of Richmond's First Baptist Church in the 1820s, commentators insisted that Afro-Baptists and -Methodists were "willing and able" to donate whatever they could to their churches. Indeed, the pastors of some biracial congregations emphasized that the churches concerned depended almost entirely on the money contributed by their enslaved members. They also implied that bondmen and -women were making often enormous financial sacrifices in order to support their churches and, thereby, to maintain their right to public worship.

The disposable incomes that bondpeople in the American South and British Caribbean generated from their quasi-autonomous economic activities and that they might elect to spend on their religious pursuits were variable and never to be entirely depended upon. Although the evidence is fragmentary and the income-generating opportunities for bondpeople varied considerably over time and place, one point is patently clear: Nowhere did their gross annual incomes average much more than three to four dollars per person per week, and often they amounted to considerably less than that.[87] As a general rule bondpeople were forced to spend at least some of these meager earnings on feeding and clothing themselves and their dependents. They could either make do with the often grossly inadequate rations and clothes issued by their owners or use their incomes to enhance their material standard of living. Expenditure on religion, whatever form that religion took, placed an extra strain on individual and family budgets and could entail some hard choices. However, all the evidence indicates that for most black Christians expenditure on their religion assumed a top financial priority.

Some churches, including Richmond's First Baptist Church, held the threat of formal disciplinary action over the heads of those of their members, free or enslaved, who were unwilling or unable to contribute the sums demanded of them.[88] However, there is no evidence that before 1830 any church member, anywhere in the American South, was formally disciplined for either of these reasons. In practice, self-imposed sanctions, especially among enslaved church members, operated most successfully.

On a purely pragmatic level, of course, if Afro-Baptists and -Methodists in the American South, who did not enjoy the financial backing of British missionary societies, wished to continue exercising their right to public worship, then they had little choice but to fund their churches. Moreover, the donation of even the most modest sums, the "penny collections among the negroes," was a way in which they could express their sense of community, their sense of self-worth, and their sense of self-respect. Any larger sums they were able to give, either individually or collectively, might well have been perceived as a way of achieving greater visibility and a higher status within the church.[89] In the mid-1810s, for instance, some of the women members of Savannah's First African Church presented a silver plate to the church. The value of the plate is not recorded, but the gift is indicative of two things: an organized, self-conscious, and probably status-conscious female presence in the church and women who not only earned money but who also enjoyed a considerable say in matters of family expenditure.[90]

If individual and family contributions to evangelical Protestant churches reflected and reinforced very positive values, then precisely the opposite seems to have been true of those enslaved church members who, for whatever reason, found themselves unable to contribute. There is some suggestion that the inability to donate their "mites" produced a sense of embarrassment, humiliation, and inadequacy that might be so intense that those concerned felt that they had no choice but to withdraw from their churches, if only temporarily. Of course, there were other reasons why black Christians might decide to leave their churches, but, as a white Methodist missionary writing from Nevis in 1814 emphasized, "It is a principle on which the Negroes act in general that when they are unable to contribute their mite . . . they must then leave the Society." Many enslaved Methodists in Nevis were leaving their churches, only temporarily, he intimated, because "the scarcity of provisions being great their little spare time (the Lord's day) is employed in planting & raising their ground provisions."[91] The inference was that they would return to church just as soon as their financial situation allowed.

At one time or another black Christians everywhere in the British Caribbean and the American South might have found themselves in exactly the same situation as the Afro-Methodists of Nevis. Even at the best of times their disposable incomes were modest and the material demands made of those incomes could be enormous. At the worst of times enslaved church members might be faced with the choice of contributing their "mite" to the church or feeding their hungry children.

According to contemporary commentators another kind of expenditure over and above "penny collections" came to be universally associated with church membership: an outlay on "Sunday" clothes or the fabrics with which to make them. Expenditure on "Sunday," or "dress," clothes did not necessarily signify church membership, but black Christians "attached a high priority to dressing themselves as well as they could when about the business of their Lord."[92] Throughout the American South and British Caribbean by the turn of the eighteenth century, bondpeople were described as being "clean and neatly dressed . . . and in their best" when they made their way to Sunday services. The "brethren . . . could frequently be seen . . . with their home-made suits, as proud as if dressed in the finest broad-cloth, and the sisters with their slat bonnets and home-spun dresses."[93] Some whites were greatly amused by the "Sabbath toilet" of bondpeople—"the most ludicrous combination of incongruities you can conceive,"[94] wrote Frances Kemble—and signally failed to comprehend the meaning attached to this attire.[95]

The money slaves had to spend on their religiously inspired pursuits was extremely modest, and the financial decisions they were required to make on a regular basis were extremely difficult. Other imperatives adopted by the evangelical Protestant churches served only to further complicate those financial decisions and may well have deterred many enslaved people from becoming, or remaining, church members. These imperatives involved the right they claimed to their own time, but also more specifically to the uses to which that time should be put.

Black Christians were unlikely to be formally disciplined for failing to make financial contributions to their churches, but they could expect to be called upon to explain their nonattendance at Sunday services and week-night classes. Without a satisfactory explanation for their absence they were likely to be publicly admonished by their churches and could even find themselves being excommunicated for their "manifest negligence."[96] The definition of "manifest negligence" varied from congregation to congregation and could be remarkably strict. For example, the convention at Georgia's Bethesda Baptist Church was that any member who missed "two consecutive meetings" would be censured; if any more meetings were missed the member would be "excluded."[97] Not every church was this severe. Many acknowledged that some of their enslaved members might be prevented by their owners and overseers from regularly attending Sunday services and class meetings and took this into account when dealing with absenteeism. But members who were unable to offer this excuse could expect to be disciplined.

Church records indicate that very few Afro-Baptists and -Methodists were excommunicated for chronic absenteeism. During the 1820s, for example, only fourteen black members (ten women and four men) were "expelled" for "neglect of meetings" from Charleston's biracial Trinity

Methodist Episcopal Church, a congregation that at any given time included around 1,500 bondpeople.[98] All the evidence available from the biracial Protestant churches indicates that attendance at Sunday services and weeknight meetings was taken very seriously indeed by bondpeople, not only in Charleston but throughout the American South and British Caribbean. For reasons not always of their own making, they may not have been able to attend their churches every Sunday but managed to do so often enough to avoid being disciplined.

Afro-Baptists and -Methodists were assigned to a specific weeknight class that might meet at the church or, to cater to the needs of believers in remote areas, in the slave quarters of outlying plantations. In the latter event class leaders might "cheerfully" walk "5 or 6 miles once & sometimes twice in the week, after labouring hard all day, in order to instruct in the Classes under their care."[99] But, wherever they were held, attendance at classes and Sunday services was compulsory.

Most church members had a choice of Sunday services to attend, however. In Kingston, for example, George Liele preached "twice on the Lord's Day, in the forenoon and afternoon."[100] Savannah's First African Church held a prayer meeting, the earliest of its Sunday services, "at sunrise." The second and third services, which involved preaching, began at 10 A.M. and at 3 P.M.[101] Until 1792 an additional service was held on Thursday evenings, but this was prohibited by the Georgia government in the aftermath of the San Domingue revolution.[102] Evening services were rarely held, "unless some of the white ministers preached."[103] Sunday services, which could be easily policed by the Savannah authorities, were not prohibited in 1792, but they could be held only between the hours of 10 A.M. and 5 P.M.[104]

In addition to the spiritual comfort and consolation communal worship offered, it also provided black Christians with a context in which bonds of family and friendship could be affirmed and reaffirmed. Moreover, churches were forums that facilitated the dissemination of news over relatively wide areas. They also offered frequent opportunities for the creation of new economic relationships rooted in a shared religious faith, which supplemented those based on common West African origins, family, and kinship networks. Urban churches were a focus for community and magnets for commercial development. Richmond's First Baptist Church, for example, operated a Sunday school, a Female Education Working Society, a Youth's Missionary Society, and various other benevolent societies.[105] On the other hand, whether on Sundays or on weeknights, church attendance entailed a critically important choice concerning one of the bondpeople's most priceless customary rights: the right to their own time. They did not need to be told that the time required of them by their churches, especially on Sundays, was time that could not be put to income-generating pursuits.

Services and classes might last for two or three hours, and it was not uncommon for Methodist love feasts to begin in the early morning and continue for most of the day.[106] For some plantation slaves the round-trip to their church took up as much, if not more, time than the meetings themselves. Sometimes they were able to save time by rowing to their meetinghouses, often in boats and canoes of their own manufacture. This was the way in which many black Baptists got to Sunday services at Savannah's two independent African churches.[107] Many enslaved members of the First Baptist Church in Petersburg, Virginia, walked "three to four miles to Backhurst's Landing on Queen's Creek." From there they paddled roughly eight miles along the James River before turning into the Appomattox River and continuing their journey for another twelve miles to Petersburg.[108]

Some black Christians rode horses and mules to church, and others went in wagons and carts;[109] the majority probably walked there. Slaves are known to have tramped up to fifteen miles to and from the towns of the American South and British Caribbean to market their goods,[110] and they were willing to walk just as far to reach their churches. As one Methodist missionary reported from Jamaica in 1817, some bondmen and -women had to walk so "many miles" to Sunday services that they "begin their journies [sic] on the Saturday evening."[111] One group of "about 80" Jamaican Afro-Baptists were "so earnest in the use of the means of grace that they come from 10 to 16 miles before breakfast on the Sabbath Morning to pray as they term it to the 'great Massa.'"[112]

During the eighteenth century there had been some Baptists who questioned, on biblical grounds, "the divine authenticity of the Christian Sabbath." By 1800, however, all evangelical Protestant congregations recognized Sunday "as a sacred day."[113] Some churches actually inscribed this requirement into their ordinances and rules of procedure,[114] but all insisted that their members strictly observe the Sabbath. Whether or not they chose to devote their entire Sunday to formal worship, Baptists and Methodists were prohibited from engaging in any recreational pursuits or income-generating activities on the only day of the week that bondpeople had to "work in their provision grounds . . . and come to Market."[115]

The choice confronting even the most devout black Christians was well put by George Poole, a Methodist missionary working in St. Vincent in 1813. As he explained, "many of the Bond-servants" who sold their wares in Kingstown on Sundays "would fain keep [Sunday] Holy unto God, yet having this as the day to work for themselves they thus are . . . obliged to sell their articles or in some measure to be in want." Many Afro-Methodists, Poole continued, combined their Sunday marketing with attendance at divine services, but "coming out of Market into Chapel the mind must wether [sic] the person be bond or free, in a very destracted [sic] state, and . . . many of them coming farr [sic], fall asleep."[116]

The disciplinary records of the evangelical Protestant churches suggest that the constant strictures against any form of Sabbath breaking were taken very seriously indeed by black church members. We cannot know how many were informally warned or admonished by their pastors, deacons, or class leaders, but only a minuscule number were formally reprimanded for working or trading on the Sabbath. During the 1820s, for example, only one slave, a man named Tom, was expelled from Charleston's Trinity Methodist Episcopal Church "for persisting to labour on the Sabbath day."[117] Much the same was true in the British Caribbean. Between September 1803 and April 1804, for instance, when Jamaica's Kingston Methodist congregation numbered 520 people, 23 enslaved members were "cut off." But none of these "backsliders" was excommunicated for working or trading on the Sabbath.[118] Neither did these charges appear against any of the names included in the sample of 262 enslaved Southern Baptists who were disciplined by their churches between the 1770s and 1830.[119]

Of course it might have been that some of those who were disciplined for "manifest negligence," or who simply "withdrew" from their church,[120] had concluded that their material needs, and those of their families, must assume a higher priority in their lives than the strict observance of the Sabbath. Unfortunately the records do not lend themselves to a testing of this hypothesis. However, the evidence does suggest that, before 1830, the vast majority of Afro-Baptists and -Methodists in the American South and British Caribbean complied with the demand of their churches that they neither work nor trade on Sundays. Although difficult to document, presumably this meant they had to reorganize their own time on weekdays and, in order to prevent their already miserable material standard of living from plummeting even further, to concentrate their income-generating activities into the hours available to them during the rest of the week.

Evangelical Protestant church leaders, black and white, as well as many ordinary church members, were not always content to order the lives of just their co-religionists. Sometimes they singled out and remonstrated with individuals of other denominations or non-Christians whom they believed were not only guilty of Sabbath breaking themselves but also of encouraging others to do likewise.[121] If successful, such remonstrations were fraught with potentially serious implications for the Sunday activities of every bondperson in the locality, regardless of their religious persuasion.

Some white church leaders, with the full support of their black co-religionists, increasingly became convinced that the total observance of the Sabbath they sought required more than the targeting of individuals, that it could be achieved only by political means, through the agency of secular government. During the first third of the nineteenth century one of their fiercest and most successful campaigns was waged in Savannah. By the 1820s that city's politics had come to be dominated by a single issue: Sunday trading. Success in the bitterly contested city council election of 1829 enabled Savannah's evangelical Protestants to secure the legislation that with very few exceptions forbade any kind of economic or recreational activity on the Sabbath.[122] In practice this legislation proved virtually impossible to enforce. However, it added enormously to the difficulties of all those bondpeople, whatever their religious predilections, whose material standard of living was directly linked to their ability to work or trade in Savannah on Sundays.

As all the evidence indicates, everywhere in the American South and British Caribbean, regardless of the material hardship it entailed for them, black Christians willingly reordered their time and resources in the manner insisted upon by their churches. But enslaved people who chose to remain outside the evangelical Protestant churches, before 1830 the majority in both the South and the British sugar islands, were not immune to the restrictions sought by those churches. For their part, black Christians were faced with choices and decisions, which some must have found easier to make than others, about the exercise of their customary rights to time and to the limited wealth they were able to generate in their own time. Dutchess Simmons, a free black women in late-eighteenth-century Barbados, apparently found it so when she gave up "trafficking" on Sundays to "devote herself to the service of God."[123]

Along with their white co-religionists, black Christians sought to ensure that every enslaved person would have no alternative but to conform to their religiously inspired economic morality. Nevertheless, not only were they never completely successful in this endeavor, but their often strident Sabbatarianism actually may well have deterred many from joining them in their churches. As one unnamed bondwoman explained to Thomas Burchell, a Baptist missionary operating in Jamaica, she would never become a member of his church because that would mean having to give up "buying and selling on Sunday." She was adamant that she "could not subsist" without her Sunday trading.[124] By 1830, the benefits that a growing number of enslaved people perceived in the Baptist, Methodist, and Moravian faiths did not necessarily outweigh what many others still judged to be the material as well as the moral costs of embracing evangelical Protestant Christianity.

AFTERWORD

It would be wrong to assume that with the coming of Christianity all Africans quickly acculturated to this new religious order, or to conclude that religious leadership passed entirely to the new adherents of orthodox Christianity. Many of the early black spiritual leaders were recent arrivals to the New World or direct descendants of African parents already living there.[1] In spreading the gospel, they clearly drew upon native religious traditions, thus threatening a racial indigenization of Christianity. A case in point is the account given by the Baptist minister Edward Baptist, who at age eight or ten, was converted by "a negro in the family" who, Baptist maintained, "kept me looking out for voices, and visions, so that I totally mistook the nature of religion and was disappointed." Baptists' concern that "many early impressions are thus lost for want of proper culture and direction," suggests that this was not an isolated case.[2]

Remnants of traditional leadership roles not only survived but were perpetuated and extended into the structure of evangelical Protestantism itself. The old Welsh Neck Baptist Church of South Carolina professed to be thoroughly Christian, yet African members still partook of traditional practices and leadership roles. The murder of Rachel, an elderly member of the church, by Jim, also a church member, illustrates the point. In his testimony before a special committee of the church Jim confessed that Rachel was a witch and that he had threatened "to draw blood to prevent her from doing him any more mischief." Two other church members, including Jim's wife, Shine, were also implicated in Rachel's murder and, along with Jim, were expelled from the church.

This example of what anthropologists call "ritual regression" exposes the complex dynamic of religious change.[3] The practice of witchcraft, a hereditary trade that represented a direct continuation of an ancient tradition, gave Rachel a kind of social control that depended entirely on psychic power. Through her capacity to excite fear Rachel was able to exercise real power, both as a human and as a woman, power that she refused to abandon even after she embraced Christianity. Jim, and many of his contemporaries, accepted the workings of a witch as an acknowledged part of reality, which suggests that among at least a portion of African Americans, Christianity was merely a glaze over an essentially African culture.[4]

The persistence of traditional female roles inevitably brought black female prophets into competition for power with white male evangelists. For the latter, this entailed the task of discrediting these traditionally powerful women in their religious functions and effectively replacing them as spiritual leaders. An incident recorded by John Travis, the white preacher in the predominantly black Methodist society of Wilmington, North Carolina, suggests how this was accomplished. Travis "made it a point to guard [black members] against fanatical expressions, or wild enthusiastic gestures." On one occasion, however, Travis was obliged to take "a summary process with a certain black women, who, in their love-feast, with many extravagant gestures, cried out that she was 'young King Jesus.'"

From the perspective of the woman, who was known as Aunt Katy, such a prophetic utterance was in keeping with the African tradition of spirits speaking through a prophetess. From the perspective of the white male preacher, Aunt Katy's prophetic version of the androgynous Christ was a challenge not only to male ecclesiastical authority but to the whole notion of the maleness of God upon which it rested. Travis immediately ordered the woman to be seated, and then he "publicly read her out of the membership, stating that we would not have such wild fanatics among us, meantime letting them all know that such expressions were even blasphemous." Aunt Katy "felt it deeply, repented," and was restored to membership. She became "a rational and consistent member of the Church."[5] Through her public admission of defeat, Aunt Katy effectively surrendered final religious authority to the white male missionary.

White church leaders took increasingly aggressive action to root out the vestiges of traditional worship and to guarantee that African converts adhered to orthodox forms of doctrine, worship, and polity, and to ensure that the initiative for religious leadership passed entirely to male adherents of Christianity. In this endeavor they received support from certain black leaders such as Daniel Payne.

If, as indicated in these examples, Christianity in some cases merely touched the surface of lives, its acceptance being more a matter of expedience than of faith, at the same time growing numbers found in Christianity a source of strength that satisfied a deep spiritual or emotional need. The fervent religiosity of these Afro-converts has no better representation than that of Mary Ann Macklin, whose mistress locked her up to prevent her from attending religious services. Mary Ann jumped from a second-floor window and escaped into the woods. For several weeks she subsisted on wild berries and "suffered unspeakable hardships" until she found refuge on a British vessel. On board ship she was "exposed to great temptations but out of them all the Lord delivered her." Befriended by a young sailor, who took her to his mother's home in Northumberland, England, Mary Ann was later freed, and she found work as a domestic. At her request Charles Thompson wrote the details of her ordeal, along with several moralizing sentences, in a letter to Mary Ann's mother, Judith, who remained enslaved in Virginia. Convinced that her mother, being "not a Godly woman," would be "cast into hell," Mary Ann appealed to her to embrace the church and "the God that made the heavens and the Earth and all things" so that mother and daughter might be joined "in blessedness in the world beyond the grave."[6]

The concept of the unity of single creation and the equality among the saved in the afterlife also resonates through a letter written by Hannah, a slave who cooked and washed for Thomas Jefferson at his Poplar Forest estate. Hannah expressed her distress that a recent illness had kept Jefferson from an anticipated visit to Poplar Forest. Her tactful admonition to Jefferson, not a Christian in the theological sense, that "it was god that done it and noother [sic] one we all ought to be thankful for what he has done for us we ought to serve and obey his commandments that you may set to win the prize and after glory run" stands as an implicit reminder that slave and master alike were in the image of God, part of the same gathered world of the saved. Hannah's conspicuous assumption of intellectual inferiority in her description of herself as "a poor ignorant creature" whose "ignorant letter" would offer little solace or encouragement, contrasts sharply with her assumption of religious redemption. Jefferson saved Hannah's letter, an indication perhaps that he fully entered into the spirit of that simple principle of faith, of all-embracing charity, of true Christian morality, and of trust in the ultimate triumph that all formed the core of Hannah's faith.[7] Although Hannah and Mary Ann were content to wait for the realization of God's kingdom in the hereafter, many Afro-Christians found their otherworldly impulses transformed into a desire to bring about the kingdom on earth immediately.

The emergence of black preachers and the black separatist movement coincided with a period of rising social, political, class, and racial tensions marked by the controversy over the Missouri Compromise between 1819 and 1821, the Vesey Revolt of 1822, and the Nat Turner Rebellion of 1831. Within the evangelical community these episodes created a crisis of authority; within the slaveholding community they produced a powerful backlash. Among the manifold effects were new restrictions on black worship, including laws prohibiting slaves from preaching without permission or from attending unsupervised worship. Although a number of large quasi-independent churches survived throughout the antebellum period, the trend was increasingly toward racially stratified biracial churches under white control. The culmination of these developments was the organized mission movement launched by the South Carolina Methodist Conference in 1829 and colonization as an extension of missionary work, both largely white-directed movements whose emergence reflected the view that religious instruction of slaves should serve as an instrument of social control.[8]

The ending of chattel slavery in the British Caribbean in 1838 inaugurated a new chapter in the history of race relations in that region as well as a new phase in its religious transformation. Not surprisingly, though, this momentous event did not mark a complete break with previous racial, social, or religious thought and practice. After 1838 the newly freed people of the British sugar islands found themselves free in name only; everywhere they were forced to contend with the enormous economic, political, legal, and social power retained by an unyielding plantocracy.

Despite the protestations of some metropolitan and local clergymen, the Anglican Church remained a bastion of planter power that attracted comparatively few black converts to its ranks. With one or two notable exceptions, the British Methodist and Baptist missionaries who continued to operate in the sugar islands were accepting of planter power and favored a course of accommodation and amelioration rather than one that sought to further black aspirations. In the years following their emancipation many Afro-Caribbeans continued to reject the missionary churches and the Eurocentric Christianity they represented in favor of their own churches and religious leaders. Despite their often brutal repression, and often against the most appalling odds, black churches and their leaders managed to survive. It would be they who provided Afro-Caribbean peoples with enduring institutional frameworks, with religious ideologies, and with the necessary inspiration and courage to carry forward their struggle to secure the full fruits of their freedom from chattel slavery.[9]

NOTES

INTRODUCTION

1. Peter H. Wood, "'Jesus Christ Has Got Thee at Last,'" 1–7.

2. See, for example, Goodwin, *Colonial Church in Virginia*, Lawrence, "Religious Education of the Negro," Townsend, *South Carolina Baptists*, and Pennington, "Thomas Bray's Associates."

3. See, for example, Simms, *First Colored Baptist Church*, Carrington, "Decoration of Graves," Ames, "African Institutions in America," Hartzel, "Methodism and the Negro," Beckwith, *Black Roadways*, G. G. Johnson, *Social History of the Sea Islands*, Reid, "John Canoe Festival," Botkin, ed., *Lay My Burden Down*, and Frazier, *The Negro in the United States*.

4. Herskovits, *Acculturation*, *The American Negro*, and *Myth of the Negro Past;* "The Negro in the New World."

5. For arguably the most influential, and certainly the most controversial, assertion of this position since World War II see Elkins, *Slavery*. For important exceptions see Goveia, *Slave Society*, Rodney, "Upper Guinea," Mays and Nicholson, *The Negro's Church*, Blassingame, *Slave Community*, Rawick, *From Sundown to Sunup*, Peter H. Wood, *Black Majority*, Levine, *Black Culture*, Raboteau, *Slave Religion*, and Sobel, *Trabelin' On*.

6. Butler, *Awash in a Sea of Faith*, 157 (emphasis in original).

7. See, for example, Mary Turner, *Slaves and Missionaries*, Olwig, *Cultural Adaption*, Stuckey, *Slave Culture*, Creel, *"A Peculiar People,"* Boles, ed., *Religion in the South, Masters and Slaves*, Edward Smith, *Climbing Jacob's Ladder*, Hatch, *Democratization of American Christianity*, Pitts, *Old Ship of Zion*, Paul Johnson, ed., *African American Christianity*, and Kay and Cary, *Slavery in North Carolina*.

8. Genovese, *Roll, Jordan, Roll;* Sobel, *World They Made Together*.

9. Works that have been particularly important in shaping our thinking include Mbiti,

African Religions, Parrinder, *African Traditional Religions,* Ray, *African Religions,* Booth, ed., *African Religions,* and Muzorewa, *Origins and Development.*

10. See especially Horton, "African Conversion," and *Patterns of Thought,* Ranger, ed., *Themes,* Hilton, *Kingdom of Kongo,* Thornton, "Development of an African Catholic Church," and *Africa and Africans,* and Gray, *Black Christians.*

11. Mathews, *Religion in the Old South,* 47–48, 101–24, was among the first to recognize the prominence of women in evangelical churches. Mathews's emphasis was on the numerical majority of white women and on the ideology of white women as "evangelical ideal," which paradoxically allowed women a public life at the same time that it confirmed the evangelical commitment to "women's sphere." The work of Benetta Jules-Rosette has been particularly useful in helping us to appreciate the ritual roles women created for themselves. See especially her "Privilege without Power: Women in African Cults and Churches," in Terborg-Penn, Harley, and Rushing, eds., *Women in Africa.* See also, Hafkin and Bay, eds., *Women in Africa,* Haddad and Findly, eds., *Women, Religion and Social Change,* and Higginbotham, *Righteous Discontent.*

12. See, for example, Mathews, *Religion in the Old South,* 208, Tristano, *Black Religion,* and Mays and Nicholson, *The Negro's Church,* 20–37.

13. Mathews, *Religion in the Old South,* 136–84, details the history of the movement. He also attributes the missionary effort to a desire on the part of Southern evangelicals to create an "orderly and benevolent social system" (137).

14. Mary Turner, *Slaves and Missionaries,* 148–73, 179–91, 195–201.

15. For a recent discussion of these themes see Stewart, *Religion and Society.*

CHAPTER 1

1. For instructive essays on new methods for the study of African religious history see Posnansky, "Archaeology, Ritual and Religion," and Ehret, "Language Evidence and Religious History," in Ranger and Kimambo, eds., *Historical Study,* 29–44, 45–49.

2. Ranger, ed., *Themes,* 4, makes this point.

3. Ibid., 6–8.

4. Horton, *Patterns of Thought,* 162–66.

5. Horton, "African Conversions," 101–4.

6. Horton, *Patterns of Thought,* 174–75.

7. Ranger, ed., *Themes,* 10.

8. Thornton, "On the Trail of Voodoo," 262, 263, 269.

9. Crone, ed. and trans., *Voyages of Cadamosto,* 55. According to Gomes de Zurara, or Azurara, 927 "infidels" were brought to Portugal by 1448, the majority of whom "were turned into the true path of salvation" (Beazley and Prestage, eds. and trans., *Chronicle of the Discovery,* 2:179, 288).

10. Crone, ed. and trans., *Voyages of Cadamosto,* 41.

11. Ibid., 97–98.

12. Ibid., 115.

13. Blake, ed., *Europeans in West Africa,* 1:95, 113.

14. For details see Ryder, *Benin,* 24–76.

15. Thornton, "On the Trail of Voodoo," 263.

16. This is essentially the argument made by Thornton in "Early Kongo-Portuguese Relations," especially 186–88.

17. Hilton, *Kingdom of Kongo*, 49, 50–68, 103.

18. For the importance of literacy in the conversion process see Goody, "Restricted Literacy," in Goody, ed., *Literacy in Traditional Societies*, 199–264; for the role of lay catechists in the spread of literacy see Thornton, "Development of an African Catholic Church," 164–65, and "Demography and History," 513, and Hilton, *Kingdom of Kongo*, 79–83, 205, 217.

19. We are very grateful to John Thornton for loaning us his transcription and translation of Montecuccolo, *Istorica Descrizione*, vol. A, book 2, no. 4, which is the standard source for seventeenth-century Angolan history, upon which the preceding paragraphs are based.

20. For a detailed history of these developments see Law, *Slave Coast*, 156–343, and *The Oyo Empire*, 47–242, and Ryder, *Benin*, 118–19, 168–69, 212–13.

21. Ranger, ed., *Themes*, 5.

22. This is essentially the argument made by Thornton in "Demography and History," 512–13, and "Development of an African Catholic Church," 148, 153.

23. See Hilton, *Kingdom of Kongo*, 91, for a discussion of the BaKongo conception of the supreme being; for figures on the export trade in slaves see Lovejoy, *Transformations*, 52.

24. Horton, *Patterns of Thought*, 174; Nwoga, *The Supreme God*, cited in ibid., 416 n. 52.

25. Law, *Slave Coast*, 111. The Slave Coast (Bight of Benin) accounted for approximately 20 percent of all slaves shipped to the Americas (see Lovejoy, *Transformations*, 54–55).

26. Horton, *Patterns of Thought*, 171.

27. Ibid., 172; Law, *Slave Coast*, 111. See also Booth, "God and the Gods," in Booth, ed. *African Religions*, 159–62.

28. Ikenga-Metuh, "Religious Concepts," 15, 18.

29. Pinkerton, ed., *Voyages*, 16:396, 493–94, 530.

30. Law, *Slave Coast*, 109–11.

31. Although anthropological and historical literature still advances the idea of ancestor worship, Kopytoff, "Ancestors as Elders," 129–41, has argued persuasively against the use of the term and in favor of the more accurate term of ancestor veneration. For a discussion of *kanda* see Hilton, *Kingdom of Kongo*, 10–13, 20–21.

32. Parrinder, *African Traditional Religions*, 101.

33. For the argument that religions that perceive the divine as masculine and subscribe to the doctrine of the Fall tend to deny, on theological grounds, religious leadership to women see Bednarowski, "Outside the Mainstream," 207–31.

34. This paragraph draws heavily on Bay, "Belief, Legitimacy and the *Kpojito*," especially 13–16.

35. Walker, *Ceremonial Spirit Possession*, 8.

36. Bay, "Belief, Legitimacy and the *Kpojito*," 21.

37. Law, *Slave Coast*, 113–55, 332–33.

38. Herskovits, *Myth of the Negro Past*, 215; Walker, *Ceremonial Spirit Possession*, 2–9, 142–45, 150–73. Barber, "How Man Makes God," 724, 734, points out that "devotee and orisa are mutually defining," meaning that the style and personality of the devotee affects the way that the deity is manifested. In that sense, "gods are made by men."

39. See, for example, Adejbite, "The Drum."

40. Law, *Slave Coast,* 113.

41. Bosman, *New and Accurate Description,* 372–74, 384.

42. Astley, ed., *New General Collection of Voyages,* 2:323, 440–41, 540, 666–68, 3:26–27, 85, 99, 282.

43. For details on the early Capuchin missions see Hilton, *Kingdom of Kongo,* 153–54, 157–61, 171–72, 175–76, 182–98, 202–5. For details on the diplomatic role of the Capuchins see Gray, *Black Christians,* 40–41.

44. Pinkerton, ed., *Voyages,* 16:177, 211, 216, 243.

45. Ibid., 159–60.

46. Here we are following Horton, "African Conversions," 101–2, and *Patterns of Thought,* 174–75. For a detailed discussion of these political and social changes see Lovejoy, *Transformations,* 53–54, 74.

47. Thornton, "Development of an African Catholic Church," 152–54.

48. Hilton, *Kingdom of Kongo,* 15, 17, 18, 19.

49. Thornton, "Demography and History," 157–58; Sobel, *World They Made Together,* 15–16.

50. Muzorewa, *Origins and Development,* 10, 12–14, 16; Mbiti, *African Religions,* 213.

51. For a discussion of the relationship between religion and magic and of sacred specialists see Parrinder, *African Traditional Religions,* 20–26, 101–9, 113–27.

52. Pinkerton, ed., *Voyages,* 2:224.

53. Parrinder, *African Traditional Religions,* 82.

54. Pinkerton, ed., *Voyages,* 16:239.

55. Parrinder, *African Traditional Religions,* 79–82. See also, Mbiti, *African Religions,* 179–80.

56. The church at Pinda was built by the Portuguese and dedicated to the Virgin Mary. Pinkerton, ed., *Voyages,* 16:218, 226–27; Astley, ed., *New General Collection of Voyages,* 3:283.

57. Hilton, *Kingdom of Kongo,* 19.

58. Pinkerton, ed., *Voyages,* 16:227, Parrinder, *African Traditional Religions,* 91, and Imasogie, *African Traditional Religion,* 53. Gray, *Black Christians,* 42–43, points to the "ritual significance" of the Capuchins in Sonyo, where by the end of the seventeenth century the chief public rituals were centered around the Christian calender and Christian rituals were an important ritual legitimization for the kings of Kongo.

59. Mbiti, *African Religions,* 134.

60. Pinkerton, ed., *Voyages,* 16:236, 239; Parrinder, *African Traditional Religions,* 91; Imasogie, *African Traditional Religion,* 53; Hilton, *Kingdom of Kongo,* 19.

61. Pinkerton, ed., *Voyages,* 16:388.

62. Parrinder, *African Traditional Religions,* 92–93; Imasogie, *African Traditional Religion,* 54–55.

63. Pinkerton, ed., *Voyages,* 16:423. For an eighteenth-century description of a naming ceremony among the Mandingos see the account by Mungo Park in ibid., 874.

64. Ibid., 595.

65. Hilton, *Kingdom of Kongo,* 98. According to Thornton, "Development of an African Catholic Church," 156 n. 49, salt was still used as part of the ritual of baptism as late as 1798.

66. Pinkerton, ed., *Voyages,* 16:159, 160, 165.

67. Hilton, *Kingdom of Kongo,* 14–18.

68. Ibid., 18, 102, 184–85.

69. Ibid., 102.

70. Pinkerton, ed., *Voyages,* 16:280.

71. For details on the Antonine movement see Hilton, *Kingdom of Kongo,* 26, 92–93, 208–10. For a somewhat different interpretation see Thornton, *Africa and Africans,* 261.

72. Pigafetta, cited in Balandier, *Daily Life,* 255; Pinkerton, ed., *Voyages,* 16:170, 281.

73. Pinkerton, ed., *Voyages,* 16:281.

74. Ibid., 223.

75. Hilton, *Kingdom of Kongo,* 22, 33, 131, 217; Thornton, *Africa and Africans,* 86.

76. Mbiti, *African Religions,* 142–44; Basden, *Among the Ibos,* 97–105.

77. Pinkerton, ed., *Voyages,* 16:168, 238, 255, 259, 260.

78. Ibid., 303–4.

79. Hilton, *Kingdom of Kongo,* 217. Gray, *Black Christians,* 48, maintains that canon law marriage enjoyed as much respect in Sonyo as it did in parts of rural Europe, where, in the eighteenth century, "probably a majority of villagers still lived together without being married according to canon law."

80. Pinkerton, ed., *Voyages,* 16:401.

81. Vlach, *Afro-American Tradition,* 143.

82. Pinkerton, ed., *Voyages,* 16:299.

83. Astley, ed., *New General Collection of Voyages,* 2:439.

84. Pinkerton, ed., *Voyages,* 16:542.

85. Ibid., 877.

86. Astley, ed., *New General Collection of Voyages,* 2:439; Pinkerton, ed., *Voyages,* 16:301. For the practice of mummifying in Loango see "Proyart's History of Loango," in Pinkerton, ed., *Voyages,* 596–97.

87. Pinkerton, ed., *Voyages,* 16:623, 431.

88. Astley, ed., *New General Collection of Voyages,* 2:439.

89. Pinkerton, ed., *Voyages,* 16:301.

90. Astley, ed., *New General Collection of Voyages,* 2:659; Pinkerton, ed., *Voyages,* 16:301, 431, 502.

91. Pinkerton, ed., *Voyages,* 16:623.

92. Ibid., 429; Astley, ed., *New General Collection of Voyages,* 2:439.

93. Pinkerton, ed., *Voyages,* 16:528.

94. Ibid., 300.

95. Ibid., 624.

96. Balandier, *Daily Life,* 170–71.

97. Pinkerton, ed., *Voyages,* 16:300, 245.

98. Cavazzi, *Istorica Descrizione,* book 2, no. 5.

99. Ibid.

100. Gray, *Black Christians,* 9.

101. Groves, *Planting of Christianity,* 1:172–73; Curtin, ed., *Africa Remembered,* 100 n. 3.

102. Bartels, "Jacobus Eliza Johannes Capitein"; Groves, *Planting of Christianity,* 1:151–52.

103. Groves, *Planting of Christianity,* 1:153. After spending five years as a missionary of the SPG for New Jersey, Thompson requested a mission to "Guiney." In November 1751, he sailed from New York for Africa and arrived in Sierra Leone on February 3, 1752. Thomas Thompson, *Two Missionary Voyages,* 24, 26, 30.

104. Thomas Thompson, *Two Missionary Voyages*, 37.

105. Ibid.

106. Ibid., 68, 74.

107. Ibid., 66, 67. Thompson left the Gold Coast in 1756, his school an apparent victim of indifference and of the repercussions on the Gold Coast of the Seven Years' War (see Bartels, "Philip Quaque," 157).

108. Curtin, ed., *Africa Remembered*, 122, 123.

109. Thomas Thompson, *Two Missionary Voyages*, 42; Quaque to the SPG, July 21, 1792, in Curtin, ed., *Africa Remembered*, 137–38 n. 79.

110. Bartels, "Philip Quaque," 158, 159, 161; Curtin, ed., *Africa Remembered*, 109, 110, 118, 121, 135.

111. See Hiskett, *Islam in Africa*, 92–94, 99, Levtzion, *Ancient Ghana and Mali*, 97, 100, 102, 107, and Booth, "Islam in Africa," in Booth, ed., *African Religions*, especially 298–300.

112. Willis, *Cultivators of Islam*, 1:1–31; Curtin, ed., *Africa Remembered*, 23; Gomez, "Muslims in Early America," 678.

113. Astley, ed., *New General Collection of Voyages*, 2:73, 324.

114. Ibid., 323.

115. Thomas Thompson, *Two Missionary Voyages*, 30–31.

116. Levtzion, *Ancient Ghana and Mali*, 186, 196, 200. By the beginning of the nineteenth century 60 percent of the population of Futa Jallon and the Bondu could read and write Arabic script (see J. Suret-Canale and Boubacar Barry, "The Western Atlantic Coast to 1800," in Ajayi and Crowder, eds., *History of West Africa*, 1:490).

117. In the paragraphs below we are following the argument made by Newell Booth for contemporary Africa, in Booth, "Islam in Africa," in Booth, ed., *African Religions*, 328–31. There is no evidence that ordinary African Muslims observed the third pillar, alms, or zakat, or the final pillar, the pilgrimage to Mecca, although rulers might have been bound by it.

118. Jobson, *Golden Trade*, 67.

119. Astley, ed., *New General Collection of Voyages*, 2:295–97.

120. Jobson, *Golden Trade*, 67.

121. Astley, ed., *New General Collection of Voyages*, 2:295–97.

122. Booth, "Islam in Africa," in Booth, ed., *African Religions*, 300.

123. Astley, ed., *A New General Collection of Voyages*, 2:298–99, 300; Levtzion, *Ancient Ghana and Mali*, 189. According to Booth, "Islam in Africa," in Booth, ed., *African Religions*, 337, the use of the Koran for magical purposes persists in modern Africa, especially "in the urban conditions under which many Moslems live."

124. Booth, "Islam in Africa," in Booth, ed., *African Religions*, 315–17.

125. Curtin, ed., *Africa Remembered*, 148 n. 11; Ray, *African Religions*, 175–76.

126. Thornton, "Development of an African Catholic Church," 148, 166–67.

CHAPTER 2

1. Butler, *Awash in a Sea of Faith*, 157.

2. Thornton, *Africa and Africans*, 192–95.

3. Mary Turner, *Slaves and Missionaries*, 51.

4. Gomez, "Muslims in Early America," 671–700.

5. There is an extensive scholarly literature on this subject. See, for example, Walvin, *Black Ivory*, 44–49, and Anstey, *Atlantic Slave Trade*, 28–31. For contemporary accounts see Paul Edwards, ed., *Life of Olaudah Equiano*, and Falconbridge, *An Account of the Slave Trade*.

6. Wish, "American Negro Slave Insurrections"; Martin and Spurrell, eds., *Journal of a Slave Trader*, 22.

7. Robertson and Klein, eds., *Women and Slavery*, 29, 32; Morrissey, *Slave Women in the New World*, 33–39; Inikori, "Export Versus Domestic Demand"; Beckles, *Natural Rebels*, 154–55.

8. Deborah Gray White, *Ar'n't I A Woman?*, 63–64.

9. Mair, "The Arrivals of Black Women," cited in Bush, *Slave Women in Caribbean Society*, 3.

10. Martin and Spurrell, eds., *Journal of a Slave Trader*, 56.

11. Mbiti, *African Religions*, 206, 207–10.

12. *Report of the Lords*, part 2. Evidence submitted by James Arnold.

13. Mbiti, *African Religions*, 37, 206–7.

14. Ray, *African Religions*, 168–71.

15. *Report of the Lords*, part 2. Evidence submitted by James Arnold.

16. Piersen, "White Cannibals, Black Martyrs."

17. Rattray, *Ashanti Law and Constitution*, 235; Ajisafe, *Laws and Customs*, 32.

18. Stanfield, *Observations*, 32–33.

19. Churchill, ed., *A Collection of Voyages and Travels*, 4:187–255.

20. *Boston Weekly News Letter*, Sept. 15, 1737, cited in Wax, "Negro Resistance," 9–10.

21. *Extracts From the Evidence*, [1790, 1791], 11, 25.

22. Snelgrave, *A New Account*, 182–84.

23. Abrahams and Szwed, eds., *After Africa*, 60; Godwyn, *Supplement to the Negroes & Indians Advocate*, 10; Gunkel and Handler, eds., "A Swiss Medical Doctor's Description."

24. Astley, ed., *A New General Collection of Voyages*, 2:244. Captain Thomas Phillips believed that Africans had "a more dreadful apprehension of Barbados than we can have of hell" (Donnan, ed., *Documents*, 2:403).

25. Paul Edwards, ed., *Life of Olaudah Equiano*, 22, 23, 29.

26. Estimates of the volume of the transatlantic slave trade vary. See Curtin, *Atlantic Slave Trade*, Anstey, *Atlantic Slave Trade*, Inikori, "Measuring the Atlantic Slave Trade," Curtin, Anstey, and Inikori, "Discussion," and Lovejoy, "Volume of the Atlantic Slave Trade."

27. Sheridan, *Sugar and Slavery*, 246.

28. Dunn, *Sugar and Slaves*, 313, 321–25.

29. Peter H. Wood, *Black Majority*, 46; Dunn, *Sugar and Slaves*, 229–38.

30. Sheridan, *Sugar and Slavery*, 142.

31. Higman, *Slave Population and Economy*, 75.

32. Kulikoff, *Tobacco and Slaves*, 319–21. See also, Wax, "Black Immigrants," and Berlin, "The Slave Trade," and "Time, Space, and the Evolution of Afro-American Society."

33. Dunn, *Sugar and Slaves*, 312; Sheridan, *Sugar and Slavery*, 150.

34. Peter H. Wood, *Black Majority*, 3–34; Dunn, "English Sugar Islands," in Breen, ed., *Shaping Southern Society*.

35. Peter H. Wood, *Black Majority*, 153.

36. Ibid., 151. For an extended discussion of the slave trade to South Carolina see Littlefield, *Rice and Slaves.*

37. Peter H. Wood, *Black Majority,* 153.

38. Ibid., 88–109.

39. Abrahams and Szwed, eds, *After Africa,* 55.

40. Dunn, *Sugar and Slaves,* 236.

41. Curtin, *Atlantic Slave Trade,* 150.

42. Higman, *Slave Populations of the British Caribbean,* 127.

43. Ibid., 126–27.

44. Higman, *Slave Population and Economy,* 76.

45. Kulikoff, *Tobacco and Slaves,* 321.

46. Peter H. Wood, *Black Majority,* 340–41. The African origins of almost a quarter of those imported through Charleston during these years cannot be determined.

47. Betty Wood, *Slavery in Colonial Georgia,* 103.

48. Higman, *Slave Populations of the British Caribbean,* 128.

49. Peter H. Wood, *Black Majority,* 159–65; Beckles, *History of Barbados,* 23–24, 41–61; Dunn, *Sugar and Slaves,* 46–47, 68–69, 82, 87–89, 91–92, 106–8, 128–29, 141–43, 170–72, 174, 180–82; Kulikoff, *Tobacco and Slaves,* 330–31.

50. Betty Wood, *Slavery in Colonial Georgia,* 104–8; Carroll, ed., *Historical Collections,* 2:20.

51. Kulikoff, *Tobacco and Slaves,* 232.

52. Betty Wood, *Slavery in Colonial Georgia,* 105.

53. Kulikoff, *Tobacco and Slaves,* 331, 334.

54. Paul Edwards, ed., *Life of Olaudah Equiano,* 29.

55. Thornton, *Africa and Africans,* 192–96.

56. Between 1702 and 1721, for example, when Tidewater Virginia was undergoing its transformation from a dependence upon indentured to involuntary servitude, around one-third of newly imported Africans were sold singly and roughly one-fifth were sold in groups of five or more (Kulikoff, *Tobacco and Slaves,* 323–24).

57. Ibid., 196.

58. Ibid., 196–200; Peter H. Wood, *Black Majority,* 178–79.

59. Thornton, *Africa and Africans,* 184–92; Peter H. Wood, *Black Majority,* 178–79.

60. Thornton, *Africa and Africans,* 211–18; Peter H. Wood, *Black Majority,* 170–91; Dunn, *Sugar and Slaves,* 250. See also, Alleyne, *Comparative Afro-American,* and *Language and the Social Construction of Identity,* Cassidy, *Jamaica Talk,* Hancock, *Pidgins and Creoles,* and Holm, *Pidgins and Creoles.*

61. Littleton claimed that in Barbados enslaved Africans "will quarrel and kill one another, upon small occasions" (Littleton, *Groans of the Plantations,* 17).

62. Hughes, *Natural History of Barbados,* 15.

63. Thornton, *Africa and Africans,* 263.

64. Hughes, *Natural History of Barbados,* 15, 16.

65. James Barclay, *Voyages and Travels,* 21.

66. Godwyn, *Negro's & Indians Advocate,* 1, 32, 34, 143 (emphasis in original).

67. Ibid., 32 (emphasis in original).

68. Abrahams and Szwed, eds., *After Africa,* 60.

69. Sloane, *Voyage to the Islands of Barbados*, 1:xlvii.

70. Godwyn, *Negro's & Indians Advocate*, 33 (emphasis in original).

71. Ibid., 32, 143 (emphasis in original); Godwyn, *Supplement to the Negroes & Indians Advocate*, 3, 7 (emphasis in original).

72. Godwyn, *Negro's & Indians Advocate*, 143 (emphasis in original).

73. Godwyn, *Supplement to the Negroes & Indians Advocate*, 7 (emphasis in original).

74. Kulikoff, *Tobacco and Slaves*, 334.

75. Le Jau to the Secretary, SPG, St. James's, Goose Creek, Sept. 15 and Nov. 15, 1708, Oct. 20, 1709, in Klingberg, ed., *Carolina Chronicle*, 42, 48, 60–61.

76. Frey, *Water from the Rock*, 33–35.

77. Gumere, ed., *Journal and Essays*, 194, cited in Frey, *Water from the Rock*, 35.

78. Brickell, *Natural History of North Carolina*, 274 (emphasis in original).

79. James Barclay, *Voyages and Travels*, 29.

80. Gutman, *The Black Family*, 348.

81. Kulikoff, *Tobacco and Slaves*, 348.

82. James Barclay, *Voyages and Travels*, 32.

83. Ibid., 22, 28.

84. Kulikoff, *Tobacco and Slaves*, 348.

85. Frey, *Water from the Rock*, 40–41.

86. Sloane, *Voyage to the Islands of Barbados*, 1:xlvii; Abrahams and Szwed, eds., *After Africa*, 163–64.

87. Ball, *Slavery in the United States*, 264–65.

88. Ann Gilbert to Rev. Richard Pattison, English-Harbor, Antigua, June 1, 1804, Folder 1803–4, Box 111, 1803–13, Methodist Missionary Society Records, West Indies, School of Oriental and African Studies, London (hereafter cited as MMS, West Indies). Ann Gilbert, a Methodist, was recalling the religious life of slaves in the Antigua of the early 1760s.

89. Abrahams and Szwed, eds., *After Africa*, 163–64.

90. Ibid., 171–72.

91. Ibid., 163–64.

92. Ibid., 171–72.

93. Frey, *Water from the Rock*, 40–41, 302–4.

94. *Georgia Gazette*, Dec. 24, 1766.

95. Evangeline Andrews, *Journal of a Lady*, 171.

96. Knight, *Letters from the South*, cited in Tryon, ed., *A Mirror for Americans*, 2:262. Knight intimated that time off work on the day of the second funeral was a gift of owners, but it may have been claimed by slaves as a customary right.

97. "Beliefs and Customs Connected with Death," 19.

98. For examples see the narratives of James Bolton and Willis Cofer in Killion and Waller, eds., *Slavery Time*, 24, 46–47, and the comments of Julia Larkin and Nancy Smith in Rawick, Hillegas, and Lawrence, eds., *The American Slave*, Supp. Ser. 1, vols. 3–4 *(Georgia Narratives)*, 43, 300.

99. Gilman, *Recollections*, 81.

100. Ann Gilbert to Rev. Richard Pattison, English-Harbor, Antigua, June 1, 1804, Folder 1803–4, Box 111, 1803–13, MMS, West Indies.

101. Ibid.

102. For examples see Handler and Lange, *Plantation Slavery in Barbados,* 205, 206, and Hughes, *Natural History of Barbados,* 15.

103. For discussions of the African antecedents of *Jonkonnu* and its functions in the Americas see Ames, "African Institutions in America," Reid, "John Canoe Festival," Victor Turner, ed., *Celebration,* and Barrett, "African Religion," in Booth, ed., *African Religions,* 196.

104. Fenn, "'A Perfect Equality,'" 128–29. See also, Kay and Cary, *Slavery in North Carolina,* 183–86. For a contemporary account of the exploits of John Conny in Axim see Smith, "Voyage to Guinea," [1724], in Astley, ed., *New General Collection of Voyages,* 2: 477.

105. Fenn, "'A Perfect Equality,'" 135–36.

106. For descriptions of *Jonkonnu* in North Carolina and in Suffolk, Virginia, see ibid.

107. Shippen, ed., *Bishop Whipple's Southern Diary,* 51. See also Brathwaite, *Development of Creole Society,* 229–31.

108. Frey, *Water from the Rock,* 36.

109. Dunn, *Sugar and Slaves,* 256–58; Edmund S. Morgan, *American Slavery, American Freedom,* chs. 11–13.

110. Ball, *Slavery in the United States,* 191.

111. James Barclay, *Voyages and Travels,* 21.

112. In the British Caribbean, Obeah was "the general Term to denote those Africans who . . . practice Witchcraft or Sorcery, comprehending also the class that are called Myalmen" *(Report of the Lords,* part 3, Jamaica. Evidence submitted by Mr. Fuller, Agent for Jamaica, Mr. Long and Mr. Chisholm). For the supposed derivation of the word Obeah, or Obi, from the Ashanti see Beckwith, *Black Roadways,* and for the argument that it derives from the Twi word *obeye,* a minor god, see Patterson, *Sociology of Slavery,* 185–86.

113. *Report of the Lords,* part 3, Jamaica. Evidence submitted by Mr. Fuller, Agent for Jamaica, Mr. Long and Mr. Chisholm; Abrahams and Szwed, eds., *After Africa,* 189–90; Bryan Edwards, *History, Civil and Commercial,* 2: 108.

114. In this and succeeding paragraphs we are following the argument of Barrett, "African Religion," in Booth, ed., *African Religions,* 190–94.

115. *Report of the Lords,* part 3. Evidence submitted by Dr. Adair, Messrs. Hutchinson and Burton for Antigua. Testimony of Dr. Adair.

116. *Report of the Lords,* part 3, Jamaica. Evidence submitted by Mr. Fuller, Agent for Jamaica, Mr. Long and Mr. Chisholm; Abrahams and Szwed, eds., *After Africa,* 189–90; Edwards, *History, Civil and Commercial,* 2: 108.

117. Bush, *Slave Women in Caribbean Society,* 159.

118. *Extracts From the Evidence,* 64–65. Evidence of Captain William Littleton.

119. Long, *History of Jamaica,* 2:418, 436.

120. Walvin, *Black Ivory,* 140. For traditional healing in the American South see Tom W. Shick, "Healing and Race in the South Carolina Low Country," in Lovejoy, ed., *Africans in Bondage.*

121. *Report of the Lords,* part 3. Evidence of Mr. Fuller, Agent for Jamaica (emphasis in original).

122. Abrahams and Szwed, eds., *After Africa,* 141–42.

123. Ibid., 142.

124. Long, *History of Jamaica,* 2:416–17. For a brief description of the Azande initia-

tion ceremony see Parrinder, *African Traditional Religions,* 108–9. The principal authority is Evans-Pritchard, *Witchcraft.* For Lewis's description of a Myal-dance see his *Journal of a West India Proprietor,* 58–59.

125. Barrett, "African Religion," in Booth, ed., *African Religions,* 192–93.

126. *South Carolina Gazette,* March 24 to March 31, 1733, May 14, 1750. Caesar's prescription was published in *The South Carolina Gazette,* in *The Massachusetts Magazine* in 1792, and in *Domestic Medicine* in 1799 (Crowder, "Black Physicians," 8).

127. McClure, "Parallel Usage," 291–300.

128. Schwarz, *Twice Condemned,* 103–4.

129. Ibid., 95, 96.

130. Genovese, *Roll, Jordan, Roll,* 616–17.

131. Schwarz, *Twice Condemned,* 103–4.

132. Ibid., 96.

133. Kulikoff, *Tobacco and Slaves,* 334.

134. Lewis, *Journal of a West India Proprietor,* 75, 156–58.

135. For the Virginia legislation of 1748 see Schwarz, *Twice Condemned,* 97–99; for the South Carolina code of 1740 see Cooper and McCord, eds., *Statutes at Large,* 7:397–417; for the Georgia codes of 1765 and 1770 see Candler and Knight, eds., *Colonial Records,* 18:649–88; 19, pt. 1:209–49.

136. Crowder, "Black Physicians."

137. Godwyn, *Negro's & Indians Advocate,* 103 (emphasis in original).

CHAPTER 3

1. Godwyn, *Negro's & Indians Advocate,* 32, 144 (emphasis in original).

2. Tom. II of Baxter's *Christian Directory* consisted of "Directions to those Masters in foreign Plantations who have NEGRO's and other Slaves; being a solution of several cases about them." Baxter anticipated Godwyn's scathing criticism of the way Anglican planters physically maltreated their slaves and neglected their spiritual welfare.

3. In addition to the tracts Godwyn published in 1680 and 1681, see also his *Trade preferr'd before Religion.*

4. Brokesby's main published contribution was a pamphlet entitled *Some Proposals Towards Promoting the Propagation Of The Gospel In Our American Plantations.*

5. For a sketch of Bray's career see Van Horne, ed., *Religious Philanthropy.* For a longer discussion see H. P. Thompson, *Thomas Bray.*

6. For a contemporary account of the founding and early history of the SPG see Humphreys, *An Historical Account.* See also, Pierre, "The Work of the Society."

7. Dunn, *Sugar and Slaves,* 249–60.

8. Butler, *Huguenots in America,* 100–101.

9. See Chapter 4 in this book.

10. For a general study of the Moravians and their activities in the New World prior to the mid-eighteenth century see Hamilton and Hamilton, *History of the Moravian Church,* 13–154.

11. See, for example, Abrahams and Szwed, eds., *After Africa,* 59; Godwyn, *Negro's & Indians Advocate,* 102 (emphasis in original); Le Jau to the Secretary, SPG, St. James's, Goose Creek, Nov. 15, 1708, in Klingberg, ed., *Carolina Chronicle,* 48; and undated Memo-

rial of Samuel Thomas [South Carolina], vol. 17 [microfilm reel 7], 82, 85, 92, 93, The Papers of the Society for the Propagation of the Gospel in Foreign Parts at Lambeth Palace, University of Cambridge Library, London (hereafter cited as SPG, Lambeth Palace).

12. See, for example, Godwyn, *Negro's & Indians Advocate*, 32, 102, 104, and *Supplement to the Negroes & Indians Advocate*, 9, 10 (emphasis in original).

13. Reverend Mr. Taylor, from St. Andrew's Parish, South Carolina, reprinted in *The Gospel Messenger*, April 1828, 114. Taylor did not mention the age, gender, or birthplace of these slaves.

14. Le Jau to the Secretary, SPG, St. James's, Goose Creek, Aug. 5 and Oct. 20, 1709, June 12, 1710, in Klingberg, ed., *Carolina Chronicle*, 57, 60–62, 75.

15. Le Jau to the Secretary, SPG, St. James's, Goose Creek, Dec. 11, 1712 in ibid., 125.

16. James Blair to Bishop Gibson, Williamsburg, Va., July 20, 1730, vol. 12 [microfilm reel 6], 152–53, Fulham Papers at Lambeth Palace, University of Cambridge Library, London (hereafter cited as Fulham Papers).

17. Le Jau to the Secretary, SPG, St. James's, Goose Creek, June 13, 1710, in Klingberg, ed., *Carolina Chronicle*, 76.

18. Le Jau to the Secretary, SPG, St. James's, Goose Creek, Oct. 20, 1709, in ibid., 60–62.

19. Ibid.

20. Ibid., 61–62.

21. Le Jau to the Secretary, SPG, St. James's, Goose Creek, Feb. 1 and 19, 1709/1710, in ibid., 69–70, 74.

22. Ibid., 70.

23. Ibid., 74. There is no evidence that Le Jau taught any of his enslaved catechumens to read. One Anglican missionary in South Carolina who did, as early as 1703/1704, was Samuel Thomas, Le Jau's predecessor at Goose Creek. In that year Thomas claimed that he had taught "abt. 20 Negroes . . . to Read." Writing from St. Paul's, Colleton, in 1707, Reverend William Dunn commented that he had "persuaded some" planters in his parish "to cause the children of their slaves to be taught to read" (Samuel Thomas to Dr. Woodward, Carolina, March 10, 1703/1704, and William Dunn to the Secretary, SPG, Charles Town, April 21, 1707, vol. 16 [microfilm reel 6], 81–82, 151, SPG, Lambeth Palace).

24. Le Jau to the Secretary, SPG, St. James's, Goose Creek, Feb. 1 and 19, 1709/1710, in Klingberg, ed., *Carolina Chronicle*, 69–70, 74, 75–76.

25. Le Jau to the Secretary, SPG, St. James's, Goose Creek, Jan. 22, 1713/1714, in ibid., 136–37.

26. Bolton, *Southern Anglicanism*, 110.

27. Le Jau to the Secretary, SPG, St. James's, Goose Creek, March 22, 1708/1709, Aug. 30, 1712, Feb. 23, 1712/1713, in Klingberg, ed., *Carolina Chronicle*, 54–55, 120–21, 129–30.

28. For the replies from the Southern mainland see vol. 3 [microfilm reel 2] (Maryland); vol. 9 [microfilm reel 5] (South Carolina); and vol. 12 [microfilm reel 6] (Virginia), all in Fulham Papers; for those from the sugar islands see vol. 15 [microfilm reel 8], in ibid.

29. Gibson, *Two Letters*.

30. Ibid., 5–6.

31. Ibid.

32. Ibid., 6.

33. See, for example, Records of the Commissarial Visitations by Jacob Henderson on the Eastern Shore [Maryland], June 24 and July 15, 1730, Records of Visitations on Eastern Shore, June 16, 1731, and Western Shore [Maryland], July 21, 1731, vol. 3 [microfilm reel 2], 151–52, Fulham Papers; and Rev. Mr. Lewis Jones to the SPG, S. Carolina, June 4, 1737, and Reverend Mr. Roe to the SPG, S. Carolina, Dec., 1738, both in vol. 3 [microfilm reel 3], SPG Minutes, 1736–39, SPG, Lambeth Palace.

34. James Blair to Bishop Gibson, Williamsburg, Va., June 28, 1729, vol. 12 [microfilm reel 6], 134–35, Fulham Papers. For a short study of the missionary work of the Anglican clergy in colonial Virginia see Jerome Jones, "The Established Virginia Church."

35. James Blair to Bishop Gibson, Williamsburg, Va., June 28, 1729, May 14, 1731, vol. 12 [microfilm reel 6], 134–35, 152–53, Fulham Papers.

36. James Blair to Bishop Gibson, Williamsburg, Va., May 14, 1731, and Governor Gooch to Bishop Gibson, Williamsburg, Va., May 28, 1731, ibid., 163–64, 169–70.

37. Governor Gooch to Bishop Gibson, Williamsburg, Va., May 28, 1731, ibid., 169–70.

38. James Blair to Bishop Gibson, Williamsburg, Va., June 28, 1729, July 20, 1730, ibid., 134–35, 152–53.

39. Governor Gooch to Bishop Gibson, Williamsburg, Va., May 28, 1731, ibid., 169–70.

40. Answers to the Queries Addressed to the Clergy [1723/1724], vol. 9 [microfilm reel 5], 160, Fulham Papers.

41. For detailed discussions of this abortive rebellion see Gaspar, "The Antigua Slave Conspiracy," and *Bondmen and Rebels*. For reports published in South Carolina see *South Carolina Gazette*, Jan. 29–Feb. 5, 1737, April 16–23, 1737, and July 23–30, 1737.

42. *South Carolina Gazette*, Jan. 29–Feb. 5, July 23–30, 1737.

43. Thornton, "African Dimensions."

44. Kenney, "Alexander Garden and George Whitefield."

45. Whitefield, *A Letter to the Inhabitants*, 37–44.

46. Garden, *Mr. Commissary Garden's Six Letters*, 51–54.

47. For an extended discussion of Whitefield and the Bryan brothers see Chapter 4 in this book. See also, Harvey H. Jackson, "Hugh Bryan," and Gallay, "Origins of Slaveholders' Paternalism," and *Formation of a Planter Elite*.

48. SPG Minutes, Jan. 19, 1740, vol. 4 [microfilm reel 3], 33–34, SPG, Lambeth Palace.

49. SPG Minutes, Jan. 19, 1740, July 16, Dec. 17, 1742, ibid., 34, 143, 165.

50. SPG Minutes, Feb. 14, 1743, ibid., 181–82.

51. See, for example, SPG Minutes, March 5, 1744, ibid., 250, and Sept. 20, 1745, Jan. 15, 1747, vol. 5 [microfilm reel 3], ibid., 37, 116.

52. See, for example, Jones, trans. and ed., "Johann Martin Boltzius' Trip to Charleston," and Bolton, *Southern Anglicanism*, 118.

53. See Chapter 1 in this book.

54. For the origins and activities of this organization prior to the mid-eighteenth century see the introduction to Van Horne, ed., *Religious Philanthropy*.

55. Ibid., 20–25.

56. Ibid., 144–326 passim.

57. Ibid., 275.

58. See, for example, ibid., 237, 249–50, 273–74, 306.

59. The tract is printed in its entirety in ibid., 293–301.

60. We are grateful to Professor Richard Simmons, of Birmingham University, for drawing our attention to this point.

61. Bolton, *Southern Anglicanism*, 96; Bonomi, *Under the Cope of Heaven*, 45–46, 48.

62. Bolton, *Southern Anglicanism*, 124–29; Bonomi, *Under the Cope of Heaven*, 58–59.

63. Reverend Adam Dickie to [Reverend John?] Newman, Drysdale Parish, Virginia, June 27, 1732, vol. 12 [microfilm reel 6], 182–83, Fulham Papers, and Van Horne, ed., *Religious Philanthropy*, 180–83.

64. Bolton, *Southern Anglicanism*, 118 (emphasis added).

65. Knox, *Three Tracts*. The same message was spelled out at greater length by Benjamin Fawcett, who held an Anglican living in Kidderminster, England, in his *Compassionate Address*.

66. Godwyn, *Negro's & Indians Advocate*, 105.

67. April 27, 1773, *Minutes of St. Michael's Church of Charleston*, 108.

68. Roberts and Roberts, trans, and eds., *Moreau de St. Mery's American Journey*, 64.

69. Christ Church, Fairfax Parish, Alexandria, Va., Vestry Book, June 15, 1803, 145, 147, Christ Church, Alexandria.

70. Goodwin, *Colonial Church in Virginia*, 292.

71. Reverend James Maury to [Reverend Dawson], Fredericksville Parish, Oct. 10, 1759, photostat in the Alderman Library, University of Virginia. We are grateful to Professor Constance B. Schulz, of the University of South Carolina, for this citation.

72. Ibid.

73. Ibid.

CHAPTER 4

1. Richard S. Dunn, "Black Society in the Chesapeake," in Berlin and Hoffman, eds., *Slavery and Freedom*, 35.

2. Kulikoff, *Tobacco and Slaves*, 319, 335, 341.

3. Philip D. Morgan, "Black Society in the Lowcountry, 1760–1810," in Berlin and Hoffman, eds., *Slavery and Freedom*, 85. See also, Littlefield, *Rice and Slaves*.

4. Julia Floyd Smith, *Slavery and Rice Culture*, 95; Betty Wood, *Slavery in Colonial Georgia*, 104–8.

5. W. Robert Higgins, "Charleston: Terminus and Entrepôt of the Colonial Slave Trade," in Kilson and Rotberg, eds., *The African Diaspora*, 122–24.

6. Kay and Cary, *Slavery in North Carolina*, 11, 16.

7. Dunn, "Black Society in the Chesapeake," in Berlin and Hoffman, eds., *Slavery and Freedom*, 54.

8. Kulikoff, "Origins of Afro-American Society," 245, 250.

9. Kulikoff, *Tobacco and Slaves*, 335, 341–42.

10. Morgan, "Black Society in the Lowcountry," in Berlin and Hoffman, eds., *Slavery and Freedom*, 85.

11. Julia Floyd Smith, *Slavery and Rice Culture*, 32.

12. The relatively late development of the slave economies of North Carolina is reflected in a higher sex ratio, but even there it was declining (see Kay and Cary, *Slavery in North Carolina*, 25, 161, and Kulikoff, *Tobacco and Slaves*, 357).

13. Higman, *Slave Populations of the British Caribbean*, 43, 53, 54, 93, 116, 121–22.

14. Bossard, ed., *C. G. A. Oldendorp's History*, 270–71. Oldendorp repeatedly refers to Anna as "the original cause of the entire mission" and "the initial cause of the brethren's mission to St. Thomas" (ibid., 353, 387).

15. Conkin, *Uneasy Center*, 73, 75. Moravian institutions borrowed by the Methodists included the society and class system and ritual practices such as the watch night and the love feast, or agape.

16. Thorp, *Moravian Community*, 52–54, 144, and "Chattel with a Soul."

17. Bossard, ed., *C. G. A. Oldendorp's History*, 280, 338–39, 351. In 1738 legal action was taken against the couple on the grounds that their original ceremony was invalid.

18. Ibid., 361.

19. Ibid., 327, 333–34.

20. For the importance of sound in the organization of community see Ong, *Presence of the Word*, 122–31, and Sabean, *Power in the Blood*, 111–12.

21. Bossard, ed., *C. G. A. Oldendorp's History*, 317, 319, 328, 333, 353, 360–61, 375, 394, 418.

22. Ibid., 311, 318, 319, 328, 329.

23. "Moravian Mission in Barbados," 75, 76, 77; James Ramsay, *Essay on the Treatment and Conversion*, 161, 162; Buchner, *Moravians in Jamaica*, 24; Hutton, *History of the Moravian Missions*, 55, 58.

24. Stewart, *Religion and Society*, 10. According to an early Moravian historian, missionaries became "in a measure secularized" by responding to requests by overseers to rebuke troublesome slaves (see Augustus C. Thompson, *Moravian Missions*, 97).

25. James Ramsay, *Essay on the Treatment and Conversion*, 162, 164; Buchner, *Moravians in Jamaica*, 18.

26. Goveia, *Slave Society*, 301, 308. Evidence that Christian slaves rejected the notion of complete submission is clear from the existence of petty marooning and other forms of resistance (see Olwig, *Cultural Adaption*, 25–26).

27. Mary Turner, *Slaves and Missionaries*, 82.

28. Ibid., 20–26.

29. Augustus C. Thompson, *Moravian Missions*, 97, 114.

30. Goveia, *Slave Society*, 272, 280, 281, 283. For the missionary activity of the Moravians in North Carolina see Thorp, *Moravian Community*, 54, 56–57, 140, and Kay and Cary, *Slavery in North Carolina*, 203–5, 370 n. 97.

31. Curnock, ed., *Journal of the Rev. John Wesley*, 1:146–49. See also, Morgan, "John Wesley's Sojourn."

32. Curnock, ed., *Journal of the Rev. John Wesley*, 1:371. For a discussion of Anglicanism in early Georgia see Jackson, "Parson and Squire," in Spalding and Jackson, eds., *Oglethorpe in Perspective*, 44–65.

33. The first was the formation of the Holy Club in Oxford in 1729, the third was the agreement of some forty or fifty persons in London to meet regularly on Wednesdays for prayer and exhortation (Curnock, ed., *Journal of the Rev. John Wesley*, 1:198 n. 1, 219–20 n. 2, 226). In England members of the Holy Club were forming similar societies.

34. Ibid., 274 n. 1.

35. Ibid., 255.

36. Harvey H. Jackson, "Hugh Bryan," 605 n. 25.

37. Harvey H. Jackson and Allan Gallay both give Whitefield credit for persuading the

planters to offer religious instruction to their bondpeople (ibid., 594–614, and Gallay, *Formation of a Planter Elite*, 33–45).

38. Curnock, ed., *Journal of the Rev. John Wesley*, 1:350–51.

39. Ibid., 352.

40. Ibid., 352–53.

41. To George Whitefield and his Friends at Oxford, quoted in Telford, ed., *Letters of Rev. John Wesley*, 1:204. Mr. Delamotte was Charles Delamotte, who went with Wesley to Georgia and remained there for some time after Wesley returned to England.

42. Curnock, ed., *Journal of the Rev. John Wesley*, 1:421.

43. Ibid., 435.

44. Wale, ed., *Whitefield's Journals*, 151.

45. Ibid., 386–87.

46. Ibid., 408.

47. Ibid., 377, 383, 384.

48. Ibid., 444, 446.

49. Ibid., 377, 384.

50. Ibid., 451.

51. Cited in Gallay, *Formation of a Planter Elite*, 38–39.

52. Ibid., 49–51.

53. Ibid., 33.

54. Ibid., 40–41.

55. For details see ibid., 42–47.

56. Cited in ibid., 45.

57. *South Carolina Gazette*, April 17–24, 1742.

58. Cited in Howe, *History of the Presbyterian Church*, 1:247.

59. Jones, trans. and ed., *Detailed Reports*, 8:512.

60. Jones, trans. and ed., "Johann Martin Boltzius' Trip to Charleston," 106–7.

61. Bryan, *Living Christianity Delineated*, 70.

62. For details of Davies's conflict with the authorities see Isaac, *Transformation of Virginia*, 151–54.

63. Samuel Davies, *Letters*, 10. See also, Pilcher, "Samuel Davies."

64. Foote, *Sketches of Virginia*, 293.

65. Kulikoff, *Tobacco and Slaves*, 143–45.

66. Foote, *Sketches of Virginia*, 284.

67. Harris, *History of Louisa County*, 178–83.

68. Foote, *Sketches of Virginia*, 45, 50, 53–55.

69. Samuel Davies, *Letters*, 10.

70. Foote, *Sketches of Virginia*, 50–51, 55.

71. For a powerful analysis of Davies's spiritual relationship with the black converts see Calhoon, *Evangelicals and Conservatives*, 14–20.

72. Samuel Davies, *Letters*, 10.

73. Ibid.

74. Ibid.

75. Ibid., 37.

76. Ibid., 28–31.

77. Sobel, *Trabelin' On*, 84–85.

78. For a brief biography of Marshall see Marshall, "Biography of the Late Rev. Daniel Marshall."

79. Semple, *History of the Rise and Progress of Baptists in Virginia*, 15.

80. Cited in Taylor, "Elder Shubal Stearns," 102–3.

81. Greene, ed., *Writings of John Leland*, 105.

82. Isaac, *Transformation of Virginia*, 63.

83. Hooker, ed., *Carolina Backcountry*, 101.

84. For a discussion of the Baptist worldview see Sobel, *Trabelin' On*, 79–98.

85. Sieber and Walker, *African Art*, 46–51.

86. The Regular, or Particular, Baptists preached a limited or partial atonement. In 1787 the Separate and Regular Baptists were joined as the United Baptist Churches of Christ in Virginia (Sobel, *Trabelin' On*, 83). See also, Beeman and Isaac, "Cultural Conflict," for an analysis of the correlation between wealth and religion in Lunenburg County.

87. Greene, ed., *Writings of John Leland*, 120; Semple, *History of the Rise and Progress of Baptists in Virginia*, 16.

88. Mathews, *Religion in the Old South*, 25–26.

89. Semple, *History of the Rise and Progress of Baptists in Virginia*, 291–92.

90. Benedict, *General History*, 650.

91. Ibid., 706, 724.

92. Strickland, "Across Space and Time," 192–93.

93. Winchester, *Universal Restoration*, ix, x, xi. See also the Welsh Neck Baptist Church Minutes, June 27–Aug. 29, 1779, South Carolina Baptist Historical Society. For the most complete discussion of the "inherently millennial black interpretation of Christianity" see Strickland, "Across Space and Time," 192.

94. Welsh Neck Baptist Church Minutes, Aug. 19, 24, Sept. 5, Oct., 1779, Jan. 1, 1797, April 21, 1798, South Carolina Baptist Historical Society.

95. Ann Gilbert to the Rev. Richard Pattison, English-Harbor, Antigua, June 1, 1804, Folder 1803–4, Box 111, 1803–13, MMS, West Indies.

96. Curnock, ed., *Journal of the Rev. John Wesley*, 4:247–48, 292.

97. Coke, *History of the West Indies*, 2:427.

98. Ann Gilbert to the Rev. Richard Pattison, English-Harbor, Antigua, June 1, 1804, Folder, 1803–4, Box 111, 1803–13, and Elizabeth Montague to the Methodist Conference, Antigua, April 26, 1814, Folder 1814, Box 112, 1814–15, both in MMS, West Indies.

99. When he arrived in Antigua in 1763, Francis Gilbert reported to Wesley that "I have directed my discourse to the whites; being at a great loss how to speak to the blacks, so as to be understood" (Francis Gilbert to Rev. Mr. Wesley, May 16, 1763, in *Methodist Magazine*, Sept. 1797, 425).

100. Eleanor Montague to the Methodist Conference, Antigua, April 26, 1814, Folder 1814, Box 112, 1814–15, MMS, West Indies.

101. Ann Gilbert to the Rev. Richard Pattison, English-Harbor, Antigua, June 1, 1804, Folder 1803–4, Box 111, 1803–13, and Eleanor Montague to the Methodist Conference, Antigua, April 24, 1814, Folder 1814, Box 112, 1814–15, both in MMS, West Indies.

102. Unsigned letter to Mr. Joseph Benson, Antigua, June 12, 1804, Folder 1803–4, Box 111, 1803–13, MMS, West Indies.

103. Coke, *History of the West Indies*, 2:429, 430, 431, 439, 441, 443.

104. Edwin Schell, "Beginnings," in Baker, ed., *Those Incredible Methodists*, 5, 17, main-

tains that the first Maryland society predated that of Philip Embury in New York, often considered the oldest in America. According to Rev. Schell, Embury began to preach in New York in the fall of 1766. The John Street Church was not opened until Oct. 30, 1768.

105. Ibid., 13.

106. Journal and Autobiography of Littlejohn, United Methodist Historical Society, Baltimore, 4.

107. *Minutes of the Annual Conferences of the Methodist Episcopal Church,* 1:7.

108. Bennett, *Memorials of Methodism,* 47.

109. Journal and Autobiography of Littlejohn, United Methodist Historical Society, Baltimore, 4.

110. Mason and Maag, eds., *Journal of Joseph Pilmore,* 149.

111. Simpson, ed., *American Methodist Pioneer,* 95.

112. Umphrey, *Historic Background,* especially 25, 30, 35–36.

113. There is a vast body of literature on the subject of spirit possession, much of which deals with theories of causality. For representative discussions of mediumship see Beattie and Middleton, *Spirit Possession;* Jules-Rosette, "Privilege without Power," in TerborgPenn, Harley, and Rushing, eds., *Women in Africa;* and the essays in Jules-Rosette, ed., *New Religions.*

114. Wale, ed., *Whitefield's Journals,* 417–18.

115. Whitefield, *Continuation of Mr. Whitefield's Journal,* 29.

116. Jones, trans. and ed., *Detailed Reports,* 8:512.

117. "Experiences and Travels of Mr. Garrettson," in *The Arminian Magazine* 17 (1794): 116.

118. We are following the argument of Richey, "From Quarterly to Camp Meetings."

119. Jesse Lee, *Short History of the Methodists,* 42.

120. "Memoirs of Thomas Rankin," in Sandford, comp., *Memoirs of Mr. Wesley's Missionaries,* 231, 235.

121. Ibid., 235. See also Piersen, *Black Yankees,* 10, which raises the question: Did "black emotional responses encourage white evangelical preachers to adjust their style of preaching" or did the black "participatory religious aesthetic of possession . . . merely reinforce white emotional religion"?

122. Cited in Bennett, *Memorials of Methodism,* 130.

123. Mason and Maag, eds., *Journal of Joseph Pilmore,* 137.

124. Clark, Potts, and Payton, eds., *Journal and Letters of Francis Asbury,* 1:190.

125. Journal and Autobiography of Littlejohn, United Methodist Historical Society, Baltimore, 4.

126. Freeborn Garrettson, who shortly after his conversion in 1775 announced during family prayers that "it is not right to keep our fellow-creatures in bondage," is believed by some scholars to have been the first Methodist in America to denounce slavery. See Baker, ed., *Those Incredible Methodists,* 193.

127. Sandford, comp., *Memoirs of Mr. Wesley's Missionaries,* 233. Rankin's sermon was preached on July 20, 1775.

128. O'Connell, "George Whitefield and Bethesda Orphan-House."

129. Robert Keen to the Countess of Huntingdon, Sept. 15, 1774, A1/12/4, Countess of Huntingdon Papers, Westminster College, Cambridge (hereafter cited as Huntingdon Papers).

130. William Piercy to the Countess of Huntingdon, Bethesda, Jan. 24, 1775, A4/2.13, Huntingdon Papers.

131. Ibid.

132. William Piercy to the Countess of Huntingdon, Bethesda, n.d. [1775?], A4/2.16 (leaf C), Huntingdon Papers.

133. Ibid.

134. William Piercy to the Countess of Huntingdon, Bethesda, n.d. [1775?], A4/2.16 (leaf B), Huntingdon Papers.

135. William Piercy to the Countess of Huntingdon, n.d. [1775?], A4/2.16 (leaf C), Huntingdon Papers.

136. During his short stay in Charleston David Margate preached on at least three occasions (John Edwards to William Piercy, Charles Town, Jan. 1, 1775, A3/6.9, and Robert Keen to the Countess of Huntingdon, July 1, 1775, A1/12.33, both in Huntingdon Papers).

137. Richard Piercy to the Countess of Huntingdon, June 16, 1775, A1/13.10, Huntingdon Papers.

138. William Piercy to the Countess of Huntingdon, n.d. [1775?], June 13, 1775, A4/2.16 (leaf C), A4/1.20, Huntingdon Papers. For James Habersham's account of Margate's preaching (which was based on reports he received from William Piercy) and his part in securing the black missionary's escape from Savannah on the *Georgia Planter* see James Habersham to Robert Keen in London, Savannah, May 11, 1775, in Georgia Historical Society, *Collections,* 6:243–44.

139. At the fourth Methodist conference in Baltimore, Maryland and Virginia reported 3,615 members out of a total of 4,921 Methodists in British North America *(Minutes of the Annual Conferences of the Methodist Episcopal Church,* 1:7).

140. Journal and Autobiography of Littlejohn, United Methodist Historical Society, Baltimore, 14.

141. Clark, Potts, and Payton, eds., *Journal and Letters of Francis Asbury,* 1:229 n. 4, 235, 249.

142. Schell, "Prelude," in Baker, ed., *Those Incredible Methodists,* 49; Bennett, *Memorials of Methodism,* 96.

143. McLean, ed., *Sketch of the Rev. Philip Gatch,* 44–46.

144. *Virginia Gazette,* March 26, Oct. 1, 1767, July 11, 1771, Feb. 27, 1772, Sept. 5, 1775, May 9, 26, 1777, April 8, June 19, 1778, May 29, 1779; *Maryland Gazette,* Aug. 11, 1777; and *South Carolina Gazette,* Nov. 8, 1751.

145. Semple, *History of the Rise and Progress of Baptists in Virginia,* 148.

146. The preceding paragraphs are based on Liele's own account of his conversion and on data gathered by Morgan Edwards, a Welsh minister appointed evangelist by the Philadelphia Baptist Association who spent parts of 1771 and 1772 in the South. See also "Letters Showing the Rise and Progress of the Early Negro Churches," 69–70, and Robert G. Gardner, "Primary Sources," 103.

147. "An Account of the Life of Mr. David George," in Asplund, *Annual Register of the Baptist Denominations, in North America,* 474–75. See also Brooks, "Priority of the Silver Bluff Church."

CHAPTER 5

1. Parts of this chapter have appeared in a different form in Frey, "'Shaking the Dry Bones,'" in Ownby, ed., *Black and White*, 23–44, and are reprinted here with permission. We would like to thank Mary Turner for her insightful comments on an earlier draft of this chapter. Any remaining errors of fact or interpretation are our responsibility.

2. Mary Turner, *Slaves and Missionaries*, 67.

3. Clark, Potts, and Payton, eds., *Journal and Letters of Francis Asbury*, 2:360.

4. Sweet, *The Methodists*, 4:8, 11.

5. Benedict, *General History*, 366.

6. Journal and Autobiography of Littlejohn, United Methodist Historical Society, Baltimore, 127.

7. Extract of a Letter from John Hagerty to Bishop Asbury, Annapolis, Feb. 17, 1789, in *The Arminian Magazine*, 2:355–57.

8. We are grateful to Cora Presley for helping us to appreciate this distinction.

9. Extract of a Letter from Philip Bruce, Elder of the Methodist Episcopal Church, to Bishop Coke, Portsmouth, Va., March 25, 1788, in *The Arminian Magazine*, 2:563–64.

10. Journal and Autobiography of Littlejohn, United Methodist Historical Society, Baltimore, 33.

11. George Wells Journal, Sept. 11, 1791, United Methodist Historical Society, Baltimore.

12. Abrahams and Szwed, eds., "Diary of Joshua Nichols Glenn," 151.

13. Ong, *Presence of the Word*, 111–12, 123–24.

14. Clark, Potts, and Payton, eds., *Journal and Letters of Francis Asbury*, 3:218.

15. Coke, *Extracts of the Journals*, 110–12.

16. Clark, Potts, and Payton, eds., *Journal and Letters of Francis Asbury*, 1:403; Coke, *Extracts of the Journals*, 16, 18; Simpson, ed., *American Methodist Pioneer*, 237, 238, 269, 270.

17. "Eighteenth-Century Slaves As Advertised By Their Masters," 202–5.

18. John S. Moore, ed., "Richard Dozier's Historical Notes," 1414, 1417, 1439.

19. James Meacham Journal, May 10, 1789, and William Ormond Journal, 3:51, both in Manuscript Division, Perkins Library, Duke University.

20. Asplund, *Annual Register of the Baptist Denominations, in North America*, 68.

21. Upper King and Queen Baptist Church Minutes, June 19, 1790, Virginia Baptist Historical Society. Judging by the absence of surnames the majority of these self-proclaimed preachers were slaves.

22. Berryville (Buck Marsh) Baptist Church Minutes, Aug. 1791, March 31, 1792, Oct. 6, 1804, Virginia Baptist Historical Society.

23. Goshen Baptist Association Minutes, 5, Virginia Baptist Historical Society.

24. Wallers Baptist Church Minutes, Aug. 2, 1800, Virginia Baptist Historical Society.

25. Lumpkin, "The Role of Women," 164–65.

26. There were several women who preached for the Christian connection in the early nineteenth century, all of them northern born. At least one, Nancy Gove Cram, preached in Charleston (see Hatch, *Democratization of American Christianity*, 78–80).

27. Barbara Leslie Epstein, *Politics of Domesticity*, 36–37, maintains that the question of relations between the sexes was not an issue in the New England revivals of the late eigh-

teenth century, which she attributes to the fact that "male domination was not widely experienced by women as an issue in their lives."

28. Journal and Autobiography of Littlejohn, United Methodist Historical Society, Baltimore, 59.

29. For this argument see Lyerly, "Enthusiasm, Possession, and Madness."

30. Cited in ibid., 5.

31. Ranck, "'The Travelling Church,'" 6, 7, 13, 22, 22 n.

32. Kulikoff, "Uprooted Peoples," in Berlin and Hoffman, eds., *Slavery and Freedom,* 143–71.

33. Ranck, "'The Travelling Church,'" 22; Benedict, *General History,* 813.

34. Kulikoff, "Uprooted Peoples," in Berlin and Hoffman, eds., *Slavery and Freedom,* 143–71.

35. Clark, Potts, and Payton, eds., *Journal and Letters of Francis Asbury,* 2:567.

36. Bucke et al., eds., *History of American Methodism,* 1:371.

37. David Ramsay, *History of South-Carolina,* 2:18, 19.

38. Coke, *History of the West Indies,* 1:406, 409.

39. Craton, "Reluctant Creoles," in Bailyn and Morgan, eds., *Strangers within the Realm,* 356.

40. Figures derived from Berlin, *Slaves without Masters,* 46, 396–98.

41. Ibid., 46; Mary Turner, *Slaves and Missionaries,* 12.

42. Mary Turner, *Slaves and Missionaries,* 39.

43. Goveia, *Slave Society,* 245. For a recent discussion of African cultural survival in the Low Country see Creel, *"A Peculiar People."*

44. Asplund, ed., *Universal Annual Register of the Baptist Denomination,* 87.

45. For details see Frey, *Water from the Rock,* 202–3.

46. Mary Turner, *Slaves and Missionaries,* 7, 8; Conkin, *Uneasy Center,* 142; Cox, *History of the Baptist Missionary Society,* 2:21. The person appointed by the Society was John Rowe, who arrived in Montego Bay on Feb. 23, 1814.

47. Cox, *History of the Baptist Missionary Society,* 2:14–17.

48. Ibid., 14, 15.

49. Mary Turner, *Slaves and Missionaries,* 58–59.

50. For more detail see ibid., 148–73, 179–91, 195–201.

51. Goveia, *Slave Society,* 280–81.

52. For details of Anglican mission efforts see ibid., 264–69.

53. James Ramsay, *Essay on the Treatment and Conversion,* 138–40, 157–59.

54. Goveia, *Slave Society,* 287.

55. W. Stanford to Bishop Porteus, Westmoreland, Jamaica, July 22, 1788, vol. 18 [microfilm reel 9], 65–70, Fulham Papers.

56. Frey, *Water from the Rock,* 204.

57. Coke, *History of the West Indies,* 3:17. The linkages could be extended. In Nassau in the Bahamas there were three congregations of black Methodists from America, each led by a black preacher (see William Gordon to Bishop Porteus, Sept. 7, 1792, vol. 15 [microfilm reel 8], 87–93, Fulham Papers).

58. Goveia, *Slave Society,* 291.

59. Duncan, *Narrative of the Wesleyan Missions,* 9–14.

60. Coke, *History of the West Indies*, 1:415, 420, 424. In the early 1790s Hammett, "who had been completely worn down by intermittent fevers, as well as by his laborious efforts to extend the gospel," left Jamaica for the American South, where he founded the Primitive Methodist Church, a movement that was particularly strong in Charleston, South Carolina, and Wilmington, North Carolina. Hammett's Charleston congregation "erected for him a large and spacious chapel," but eventually his following there "dwindled away [and he] purchased slaves, settled on a plantation, and became a man of the world" (Duncan, *Narrative of the Wesleyan Missions*, 24; Bucke et al., eds., *History of American Methodism*, 1:617–22).

61. Duncan, *Narrative of the Wesleyan Missions*, 18–19.

62. Ibid., 28–29, 32–35. Constant, who also served as a class leader in Hammett's congregation, died in 1797.

63. Coke, *History of the West Indies*, 1:431, 438, 439, 442, 443.

64. Ibid., 421.

65. Ibid., 422, 442; William Fish to Mr. Joseph Butterworth, March 9, 1804, Folder 1803–4, Box 111, 1803–13, MMS, West Indies.

66. Mary Turner, *Slaves and Missionaries*, 13, 34 n. 60; Goveia, *Slave Society*, 13.

67. We would like to thank Mary Turner for drawing our attention to the fact that the chapel established by Liele on the Windward Road in Kingston continued to be known as "Lyles Chapel" through the 1820s *(St. Jago de la Vega Gazette*, Aug. 15–22, 1829). However, as she points out, there is no firm evidence to support Brathwaite's claim that Liele himself "continued to work as an itinerant preacher [between 1807] and his death in 1820 or thereabouts" (Brathwaite, *Development of Creole Society*, 253).

68. Coke, *History of the West Indies*, 1:452.

69. Mary Turner, *Slaves and Missionaries*, 16–17.

70. Coke, *History of the West Indies*, 1:447–48.

71. Excerpt of a Letter from John Wiggins, Kingston, June 17, 1808, *Methodist Magazine* (London) 32 (1809): 139; Wiggins to Missionary Committee, Kingston, April 4, 1813, and John Davies to Rev. Mr. Benson, April 29, 1814, *Methodist Magazine* (London) 37 (1814): 46; Mr. Burgar to Mr. Buckley, Morant Bay, Dec. 22, 1815, *Methodist Magazine* (London) 39 (1816): 379.

72. Coke, *History of the West Indies*, 2:145, 147, 149.

73. Charges Against the Methodist Missionaries in Jamaica by the Common Council and Assembly, Feb. 10, 1811, Folder 1809–11, Box 111, 1803–11, MMS, West Indies.

74. Extract of a Letter from Mr. Morgan to Mr. Slugg, Dec. 21, 1814, *Methodist Magazine* 38 (1815): 479; Extract of a Letter from Mr. Shipman to the late Mr. Rodda, Oct. 5, 1815, *Methodist Magazine* 39 (1816): 234.

75. Extract of a Letter from Mr. Bradnock to Mr. Lomas, July 12, 1806, ibid., 29 (1806): 568; Extract of a Letter Lately Received from Jamaica, Oct. 15, 1814, ibid., 35 (1812): 427; Extract of a Letter from Mr. Wiggins to the Mission Committee, April 21, 1815, ibid., 38 (1815): 568.

76. Mary Turner, *Slaves and Missionaries*, 18.

77. For details of these developments see ibid., 16–19.

78. Goveia, *Slave Society*, 253, 259, 297.

79. S. P. Woolley to Mr. Buckley, May 3, 1816, Folder Jan.–June 1816, Box 113, 1816–18, MMS, West Indies.

80. S. P. Woolley to Mr. Buckley, May 2, 1816, *Methodist Magazine* 39 (1816): 564.

81. John Wiggins to [Methodist Missionary Society Committee], Morant Bay, Jamaica, Jan. 1, 1817, Folder Jan.–April 1817, Box 113, 1816–18, MMS, West Indies.

82. Mary Turner, *Slaves and Missionaries,* 120.

83. Duncan, *Narrative of the Wesleyan Missions,* 98; Mary Turner, *Slaves and Missionaries,* 17.

84. Some historians reject the notion of a Second Great Awakening. See, for example, Butler, *Awash in a Sea of Faith,* 165, which denies its existence. Other recent works accept the idea of a Second Awakening but emphasize its eclectic character (see Hatch, *Democratization of American Christianity,* 35, and Conkin, *Uneasy Center,* 124–29).

85. For descriptions of campgrounds see Henry Smith to Benjamin Lakin, Nov. 11, 1806, in Henry Smith, *Recollections and Reflections,* 184, and Carter, Van Horne, and Formwalt, eds., *Journals of Benjamin Henry Latrobe,* 3:109. For a detailed discussion of the camp meeting layout see Frey, "'Shaking the Dry Bones,'" in Ownby, ed., *Black and White,* 40–41.

86. Davidson, *History of the Presbyterian Church,* 134–37.

87. John McGee to Rev. Thomas L. Douglass, June 23, 1820, *Methodist Magazine* 4 (1821): 189–91.

88. M'Nemar, *The Kentucky Revival,* 63.

89. Carter, Van Horne, and Formwalt, eds., *Journals of Benjamin Henry Latrobe,* 3:111–13.

90. For a comparison of the physical manifestations see Tyerman, *Life and Times of the Reverend John Wesley,* 1:139–40, 162; 2:25, 26, 35, 36, 38. For American revival behavior see Foote, *Sketches of North Carolina,* 412–13, Davidson, *History of the Presbyterian Church,* 145–53, MacLean, "The Kentucky Revival," 247–50, Cartwright, *Autobiography,* 48–51, and Howe, *History of the Presbyterian Church,* 1:113.

91. See, for example, Levine, *Black Culture,* 19–31.

92. For problems with sources and a discussion of the difficulties in analyzing the process of cultural exchange see Malone, "Blacks and Whites," in Ownby, ed., *Black and White,* 151–52, 157.

93. Leland, *Virginia Chronicle,* 36.

94. Jesse Lee, *Short History of the Methodists,* 134.

95. Watson, *Methodist Error,* 30, 122. For a discussion of the origins of black and white spirituals see Levine, *Black Culture,* 19–31, and Southern, *Music of Black Americans,* 12, 16, 96.

96. Watson, *Methodist Error,* 28.

97. For a general discussion of musical behaviors see Standifer, "Musical Behaviors of Black People," 61–62. Soon after the turn of the century the Reverend Ralph Williston "proclaimed war against shouting" in the predominantly black Annapolis society. Williston found support from "some of the most influential members" of the society (see Henry Smith, *Recollections and Reflections,* 257).

98. Most recent research follows Herskovits's argument that "shouting" and the religious dance known as the ring shout are African influenced. See Raboteau, *Slave Religion,* 68–73, Emery, *Black Dance,* 121–29, Southern, *Music of Black Americans,* 99, and Stuckey, *Slave Culture,* 11, 25. For a discussion of white forms of song and dance see Patterson, "Word, Song, and Motion," in Victor Turner, ed., *Celebration,* 220–30.

99. Sobel, *Trabelin' On,* 141.

100. For a contemporary description of the Myal-dance see Lewis, *Journal of a West India Proprietor*, 158–59.

101. Robert Simpson, "The Shout and Shouting," 35, makes a distinction between shouting as an individual act and the shout as a collective act. Emery, *Black Dance*, 121, differentiates between two forms based on the locale of the performance: the ring shout found in Georgia and South Carolina, and the solo shout found in North Carolina and Virginia.

102. Carter, Van Horne, and Formwalt, eds., *Journals of Benjamin Henry Latrobe*, 3:204.

103. Watson, *Methodist Error*, 30–31. Southern, *Music of Black Americans*, 98–99, cites Watson's 1819 description as the earliest account; Epstein, in *Sinful Tunes and Spirituals*, 233, puts it even later, citing Charles Lyell's 1849 description.

104. Carter, Van Horne, and Formwalt, eds., *Journals of Benjamin Henry Latrobe*, 3:204.

105. John Pierpoint Journal, Pierpoint Morgan Library, New York.

106. See, for example, the essays in Ottenburg, ed., *African Religious Groups*; see also Courlander, *The Drum and the Hoe*, 126–35, and Yvonne Daniel, "The Potency of Dance."

107. Cited in Frey, "'Shaking the Dry Bones,'" in Ownby, ed., *Black and White*, 43. For additional examples of African dancing witnessed by white observers in the nineteenth century see Stuckey, *Slave Culture*, 60–61, and Emery, *Black Dance*, 121–28.

CHAPTER 6

1. For statistics on denominational growth see Conkin, *Uneasy Center*, 130, 312, and Hatch, *Democratization of American Christianity*, 3.

2. There is sharp disagreement among historians over the conversion rate of African Americans. Sobel, *Trabelin' On*, 98–102, 219–356 passim, offers a more optimistic assessment of the effects of Christianization during the colonial period. Raboteau, *Slave Religion*, 128–32, 147–49, 152, and Kay and Cary, *Slavery in North Carolina*, 214–16, maintain that relatively few blacks were converted before 1800. The statistics quoted here are from Hatch, *Democratization of American Christianity*, 102–3.

3. John Wiggins to Secretary of the Mission Committee, December 15, 1815, *Methodist Magazine* 35 (1815): 377–79.

4. Mary Turner, *Slaves and Missionaries*, 21.

5. Goveia, *Slave Society*, 307, 324.

6. Conkin, *Uneasy Center*, 130.

7. Cited in Harrison, *Gospel among the Slaves*, 65.

8. In Calvert County there were 1,553 Methodists in a black population of 3,937. Both Calvert and Prince George's Counties had black majorities (see Dunn, "Black Society," in Berlin and Hoffman, eds., *Slavery and Freedom*, 68, 81).

9. *Minutes of the Annual Conferences of the Methodist Episcopal Church*, 1:182, 346.

10. Ibid., 2:59.

11. Ibid., 1:92–93.

12. In New Bern black Methodists outnumbered whites by two to one (ibid.).

13. Asplund, *Universal Annual Register of the Baptist Denomination*, 68, 82. Asplund estimated that there were 20,443 Baptists in Virginia in 1790, approximately 8,000 of whom were black.

14. See Dover Baptist Association Minutes, 1810, 2–4, and Portsmouth Association Minutes, 1809, 3, both in Virginia Baptist Historical Society, and Semple, *History of the*

Rise and Progress of Baptists in Virginia, 387. The estimate is from Harrison, *Gospel among the Slaves,* 65. The Virginia Conference reported 5,739 black Methodists in 1809 (*Minutes of the Annual Conferences of the Methodist Episcopal Church,* 1:171).

15. Antioch Baptist Church (Boar Swamp) Minutes, 1787, 1791–1828; Upper King and Queen County Baptist Church Minutes, 1774–1816; and Morattico Baptist Church Minutes, 1778–87, 1792–1844; Records of Wicomico Baptist Church, 1807–47; and Nomini Baptist Church Minutes, 1824–43, all in Virginia Baptist Historical Society.

16. Portsmouth Association Minutes, 1801, 2–3, 1830, 3, Virginia Baptist Historical Society. There are no membership totals for the intervening years.

17. Dunn, "Black Society," in Berlin and Hoffman, eds., *Slavery and Freedom,* 63 n.24, 65.

18. Benedict, *General History,* 662.

19. Semple, *History of the Rise and Progress of Baptists in Virginia,* 145, 163, 169. Dover Baptist Association Minutes, 1827, 5, 7, Virginia Baptist Historical Society, reveal that a committee was appointed to "inquire into the state" of the African church in Charles City County "claiming privileges of being a Baptist church." The committee was discharged in 1828, indicating perhaps that the church was disbanded.

20. Dover Baptist Association Minutes, 1800, 4–5, 1830, 1–3, Virginia Baptist Historical Society.

21. Semple, *History of the Rise and Progress of Baptists in Virginia,* 456, 457; Portsmouth Association Minutes, 1800, 2–3, Virginia Baptist Historical Society.

22. Portsmouth Association Minutes, 1826, 4, 1827, 5, 1830, 3, Virginia Baptist Historical Society.

23. Benedict, *General History,* 663 n. 2.

24. This trend is visible in membership rolls of individual churches in which whites almost always outnumbered blacks. In Meherrin Church in Lunenburg County the white-black ratio was roughly five to one (Meherrin Baptist Church Minute Book, 1771–1844, Virginia Baptist Historical Society). In Burruss' in Carolina County in north central Virginia, whites outnumbered blacks by slightly over one and a half to one (Burruss' Baptist Church Minute Book, 1779–1819, Virginia Baptist Historical Society). In Sandy Creek (County Line) Church in Pittsylvania County, southwestern Virginia, abutting North Carolina, there was a white majority of better than two to one (Sandy Creek Church Minute Book, 1790–1814, 1814–32). The church was known as Sandy Creek until 1788. We are grateful to Michael Plunkett of the Manuscript Division of the Alderman Library, Charlottesville, for calling this church book to our attention. In churches in western Virginia, such as Mill Creek in Culpepper County, there were seven white members for every black member (Mill Creek Baptist Church Minute Book, 1757–1928, Virginia Baptist Historical Society).

25. William S. White, *African Preacher,* 8, 10, 14, 35, 'Rusticus,' "The Pious African," 22–25.

26. Strickland, "Across Space and Time," 219–20, Table IV.2, 252–54.

27. *Minutes of the Annual Conferences of the Methodist Episcopal Church,* 1:182.

28. Charleston City included St. Michael's, St. Philip's in the city, and St. Philip's out of the city; Charleston District included Charleston City, plus St. Stephen's, St. James' Santee, St. John's, Berkeley, St. Thomas, Christ Church, St. James', Goose Creek, St. Andrew's, and St. John's Colleton parishes (*Second Census 1800, Return of the Whole Number of persons,* n.p.).

29. Annie Hughes Mallard, "Religious Work of South Carolina Baptists," 82–83. Mallard's estimate is based on an analysis of sixteen church books for the period between 1810 and 1830. From 1800 to 1815 black conversions represented about 43 percent of the whole and from 1813 to 1830 about 45 percent.

30. Benedict, *General History*, 711.

31. According to Benedict, ibid., 710 n. 10, the black membership of the Charleston Association remained nearly double that of the white as late as 1846.

32. Ibid., 86–87.

33. Morgan, "Black Society in the Lowcountry," in Berlin and Hoffman, eds., *Slavery and Freedom*, 84–85, Table 1.

34. *Minutes of the Charleston Baptist Association*, 1826, 18–19; *Minutes of the Charleston Baptist Association*, 1827.

35. Julia Floyd Smith, "Marching to Zion," 49, 50.

36. *Minutes of the Sunbury Baptist Association*, 1818, 6, 1821, 6, 1823, 8, 1824, 5, 1825, 5, 1826, 5, 1827, 3; *Minutes of the Georgia [Baptist] Association*, 1788, 1815, 1824; *Minutes of the Savannah River Baptist Association*, 1812, 1814, 1830, 1831.

37. Julia Floyd Smith, *Slavery and Rice Culture*, 217; Betty Wood, *Women's Work, Men's Work*, 164–65.

38. Julia Floyd Smith, *Slavery and Rice Culture*, 157.

39. George G. Smith Jr., *History of Methodism*, 416, 418, 427.

40. *Minutes of the Annual Conference of the Methodist Episcopal Church*, 2:91.

41. Extract from *Life of William Capers* in Joseph F. Waring Papers, Georgia Historical Society.

42. Roper, *A Narrative*, 9, 51, 52.

43. Luther P. Jackson. "Religious Development of the Negro," 183.

44. Kulikoff, "Uprooted Peoples," in Berlin and Hoffman, eds., *Slavery and Freedom*, 151. From 1815 to 1820, the Virginia Conference reported a net loss of 1,405. When black gains of 274 are taken into account, the actual decline amounted to 1,679 white Methodists (*Minutes of the Annual Conferences of the Methodist Episcopal Church*, 1:258, 344).

45. Between 1812 and 1836, the Baptist population of Kentucky doubled, from 17,000 to 35,000 (see Benedict, *General History*, 811–12). The number of Methodists grew from 1,626 to 26,958 between 1800 and 1830 (*Minutes of the Annual Conferences of the Methodist Episcopal Church*, 2:74).

46. Between 1810 and 1820, Mississippi and Alabama received an estimated 51,000 slaves (Kulikoff, "Uprooted Peoples," in Berlin and Hoffman, eds., *Slavery and Freedom*, 151, 152, Table 2).

47. Sellers, *Slavery in Alabama*, 295; Stanley, *Journal of a Tour*, n.p.; Hosea Holcombe, *History of the Rise and Progress of the Baptists*, 45.

48. Bailey, *Shadow on the Church*, 117–18.

49. Sparks, *On Jordan's Stormy Banks*, 291–330.

50. Ibid., 88.

51. James Williams, *Narrative*, 36, 70.

52. Hosea Holcombe, *History of the Rise and Progress of the Baptists*, 110–11.

53. Henson, *Father Henson's Story*, 56–58.

54. Abdy, *Journal of a Residence*, 2:70–71.

55. Ibid., 2:346–47.

56. Hosea Holcombe, *History of the Rise and Progress of the Baptists,* 110–11.

57. Contract, Roberts Family Papers, Library of Congress.

58. Thomas Mann Journal, vol. 1, July 21, 1805, May 18, 1806, June 8, 1808, and vol. 2, April 19, 1810, Oct. 16, 1812, Jan. 16, 1813, Manuscript Division, Perkins Library, Duke University.

59. Harrison, *Gospel among the Slaves,* 178–80.

60. Hodgson, *Remarks During a Journey,* 59.

61. Sherwood, *Memoir,* 113.

62. Wade Barclay, *Early American Methodism,* vol. 1 of *History of Methodist Missions,* 149.

63. Historians have noted that the preponderance of women was a national and biracial phenomenon (see Mathews, *Religion in the Old South,* 47–48, and Sparks, *On Jordan's Stormy Banks,* 44, 214 n. 6).

64. Robert W. Gardner, *Baptists of Early America,* 102.

65. Antioch (Boar Swamp) in Henrico County, Broad Run in Loudoun County, Goose Creek in Fauquier County, Burruss' in Caroline County, Mossingford in Charlotte County, Sandy Creek in Pittsylvania County, Wicomico in Northumberland County, Mount Edd Baptist Church in Batesville near Charlottesville, Mill Creek in Berkeley County, Morattico in Lancaster County, Upper King and Queen in Rappahannock, South Quay in Southampton County, and Tussekiah in Lunenburg County. Only four Baptist churches, Frying Pan in Loudoun County, Meherrin in Lunenburg County, Antioch (Raccoon Swamp) in Sussex County, and Hartwood in Shenandoah County showed a small male majority (Broad Run Baptist Church Minutes, 1762–1859, and Goose Creek Baptist Church Records, 1750–95, both in Virginia State Library; Mount Edd Baptist Church Minute Book, 1823–44, and Sandy Creek Church Minute Book, 1790–1814, 1814–32, both in Alderman Library, University of Virginia; Records of Wicomico Baptist Church, 1804–47, Mossingford Baptist Church Minute Book, 1823–69, Burruss' Baptist Church Minute Book, 1779–1819, Mill Creek Baptist Church Minute Book, 1757–1928, Meherrin Baptist Church Minute Book, 1771–1844, Frying Pan Baptist Church Records, 1791, 1828–79, Hartwood Baptist Church Minutes, 1775–1825, 1835–41, Morattico Baptist Church Minute Book, 1778–87, 1792–1844, Antioch Baptist Church (Raccoon Swamp) Minutes, 1772–1837, Tussekiah Baptist Church Minutes, 1784–1826, Upper King and Queen Baptist Church Minute Book, 1774–1816, South Quay Baptist Church Minutes, 1775–1827, all in Virginia Baptist Historical Society).

66. Strickland, "Across Space and Time," 283–84, 286.

67. Trinity United Methodist Church Register, 1801–7, Lloyd House Library; and Sharp Street Methodist Episcopal Church, White and Colored Classes, United Methodist Historical Society, Baltimore.

68. Records of the Trinity Methodist Episcopal Church, Charleston, Book C, Roll of Colored Members, South Carolina Historical Society.

69. Pinckney, ed., *Register of St. Philip's Church.*

70. Lewis, *Journal of a West India Proprietor,* 121.

71. James Meacham Journal, July 3–Sept. 14, 1790, Manuscript Division, Perkins Library, Duke University.

72. Booth, "Some Aspects of Zulu Religion," in Booth, ed., *African Religions,* 22–23.

73. Sandy Creek Church Minute Book, 142, 230, 234, Alderman Library, University of Virginia.

74. Clarke's Station Baptist Church, Church Minutes, June 6, Sept. 5, 1830, Manuscript Division, Perkins Library, Duke University.

75. Gillfield Baptist Church Records, June 30, 1827, Alderman Library, University of Virginia.

76. James Meacham Journal, Feb. 15–May 29, 1790, Manuscript Division, Perkins Library, Duke University.

77. Baltimore Circuit, Methodist Episcopal Church, Quarterly Conference Reports, 1794–1815, United Methodist Historical Society, Baltimore, 154–55 (emphasis in original).

78. Harrison, *Gospel among the Slaves*, 91.

79. Berryville Baptist Church Minutes, Jan. 5, Nov. 2, June 4, 1805, Feb. 4, 1809, Virginia Baptist Historical Society.

80. First Baptist Church of the City of Richmond Minutes, July 11, 1826, Virginia Baptist Historical Society, 12.

81. Wallers Baptist Church Minutes, Aug. 1808, Aug. 1811, South Quay Baptist Church Minutes, June 4, 1813, and Carmel Baptist Church Minutes, Sept. 1818, all in Virginia Baptist Historical Society.

82. Robert W. Gardner, *History of the Georgia Baptist Association*, 18, 33.

83. Lower Fork of Lynches Creek Baptist Church Minutes, Jan. 1827, South Carolina Baptist Historical Society.

84. Black Creek Baptist Church, Dovesville, Records, Sept. 6, 1829, South Carolina Baptist Historical Society.

85. Minutes of Big Creek [Baptist Church], Aug. 1, 1809, April 6, 1811, June 2, 1821, Oct. 4, 1823, Dec. 4, 1824, May 6, 1828, South Carolina Baptist Historical Society.

86. "Eighteenth-Century Slaves As Advertised By Their Masters," 202–5.

87. Wade Barclay, *Early American Methodism*, vol. 2 of *History of Methodist Missions*, 56; Clark, Potts, and Payton, eds., *Journal and Letters of Francis Asbury*, 2:432 n. 25, 3:366.

88. General Conference Journals, 1:44, cited in Wade Barclay, *Early American Methodism*, vol. 1 of *History of Methodist Missions*, 268n.

89. List of Black Speakers, April 20, 1800, vol. 1, Sharp Street Methodist Episcopal Church, Records, United Methodist Historical Society, Baltimore.

90. Colored Members of the Quarterly Conference in Baltimore, March 1815, vol. 3, Sharp Street Methodist Episcopal Church, Records, United Methodist Historical Society, Baltimore.

91. John Fortie Notebook, Marshall Collection of Jacob Forty, Maryland State Archives.

92. The Steward's Book for Calvert Circuit, United Methodist Historical Society, Baltimore.

93. Journal of the Baltimore Annual Conference, 1:109, 244, 171, 177, 190, 196, 210, 227, 235, 237, 187, 211, 235, United Methodist Historical Society, Baltimore. The Baltimore Conference extended from the Susquehanna River in the north to the Rappahannock River in the south, and from Chesapeake Bay in the east to the Ohio River in the west.

94. Minutes of the Quarterly Conference, Dec. 1816, Dec. 1817, Stephen B. Weeks Papers, vol. 2, no. 8, Minutes, 1815–17, Southern Historical Collection, University of North Carolina.

95. Bennett, *Memorials of Methodism*, 705.

96. Methodist Episcopal Church, Virginia and North Carolina Conferences, Newbern

and Neuse Districts, New River, Newport, and Trent Circuits, Quarterly Conference Minutes, Manuscript Division, Perkins Library, Duke University.

97. Strickland, "Across Space and Time," 288.

98. Minutes of the Quarterly Conference of the Georgetown Society, 1818–32, Georgetown Methodist Church Records, South Carolina Historical Society.

99. Knight, "Notes on John Chavis," in Wills and Newman, eds., *Black Apostles,* 21–41.

100. "Elizabeth," in Loewenberg and Bogin, eds., *Black Women,* 130, 133; "Memoirs of . . . Mrs. Zilpha Elaw," in William L. Andrews, ed., *Sisters of the Spirit,* 67, 73–74, 77, 82. See also, Jarena Lee, *Religious Experiences and Journal,* 10.

101. Mott, comp., *Biographical Sketches,* 50–53.

102. Ibid., 52, and Henry Holcombe, *First Fruits,* 59.

103. Jarena Lee, *Religious Experiences and Journal,* 11. Gilkes, "Dual-Sex Political Systems," in Paul Johnson, ed., *African American Christianity,* 99, traces the origins of black biblical feminism to Allen's refusal to license Lee as a preacher. According to Evelyn Brooks Higginbotham, the institutional basis for black feminism emerged at the end of the nineteenth century (see *Religious Discontent,* 2:121–49, 150–84).

104. "Elizabeth," in Loewenberg and Bogin, eds., *Black Women,* 131–32.

105. Jarena Lee, *Religious Experiences and Journal,* 11, 17.

106. "Memoirs of . . . Mrs. Zilpha Elaw," in Loewenberg and Bogin, eds., *Black Women,* 92, 97, 99, 101; Jarena Lee, *Religious Experiences and Journal,* 16, 61, 78.

107. Higginbotham, *Religious Discontent,* 2. Mathews, *Religion in the Old South,* 102–3, and Sparks, *On Jordan's Stormy Banks,* 41–59, both emphasize the important role played by white women. The older work by Mathews stresses women's roles as helpmeets to male missionaries and as evangelical ideals. Sparks underscores white women's liturgical roles in worship service.

108. From Thomas Richardson, Feb. 1, 1803, in Coke, *History of the West Indies,* 2:361.

109. Ibid., 1:442.

110. [Fragment of a letter, author unknown], to Revs. Marsden and Watson, Kingston, Jamaica, Jan. 25, 1817, Folder Jan.–June 1817, Box 113, 1816–18, MMS, West Indies.

111. W. Watcliffe to Rev. Thos. Wood, Kingston, Jamaica, April 18, 1817, Folder Jan.–June 1817, Box 113, 1816–18, MMS, West Indies.

112. Wightman, *Life of William Capers,* 396.

113. Chreitzberg, *Early Methodism,* 259.

114. Georgetown Methodist Church Records, 1817–19, South Carolina Historical Society.

115. Baker, ed., *Those Incredible Methodists,* 392.

116. Gillfield Baptist Church Records, June 17, Sept. 2, 16, 1827, Alderman Library, University of Virginia.

117. Goveia, *Slave Society,* 324.

118. Peter H. Wood, *Black Majority,* 181–86, was one of the first scholars to employ naming practices to study slave culture. More recent works include Inscoe, "Carolina Slave Names," and Cody, "There was No 'Absalom.'"

119. Cody, "'There was No 'Absalom,'" 583, 585, 589, 591, 595; Inscoe, "Carolina Slave Names," 534, 538, 541, 544–45.

120. Ball, *Slavery in the United States,* 168–69.

121. Ibid., 170.

122. Ibid. The notion of hell as a place of torment was rare in African cosmologies (see Kay and Cary, *Slavery in North Carolina*, 210).

123. For a discussion of the evolution of the concept of evil in Africa see Gray, *Black Christians*, 5–6, 96–117, which also informs our understanding of the process of assimilation and resistance.

124. Frey, *Water from the Rock*, 304–10, contains a more detailed discussion of the distinctive theology created by African American Christians.

125. Lewis, *Journal of a West India Proprietor*, 152.

126. For a discussion of the African side see Gray, *Black Christians*, 96–97.

127. For the demand of men and women for literacy see Rev. Raby to Mr. Benson, Oct. 16, 1816, St. Kitts, Folder July–Dec. 1816, Box 113, 1816–18, MMS, West Indies; and Thomas Morgan to James Buckley, Aug. 10, 1815, St. John's, Antigua, *Methodist Magazine* 39 (1816): 234.

128. Lewis, *Journal of a West India Proprietor*, 169.

129. Frey, *Water from the Rock*, 309–10.

130. Richard Beck to Samuel Thomas [Tailor, Liverpool], July 21, 1814, Barbados, Folder 1814, Box 112, 1814–15, MMS, West Indies.

131. Chreitzberg, *Early Methodism*, 159–60.

132. Janson, *Stranger in America*, 100.

133. Abdy, *Journal of a Residence*, 2:189–90; Issac Robins to Henry Slicer, Aug. 2, 1832, Slicer Collection, United Methodist Historical Society, Baltimore; Goose Creek Baptist Church, Fauquier County, Va., Register of Members, April 3, 1826, Virginia Baptist Historical Society; and John H. Moore, ed., "The Abiel Abbot Journals," 70. Bailey, *Shadow on the Church*, 92–93, reports a similar trend toward physical separation of the races in the Southwest after 1820.

134. Coan Baptist Church Minute Book, Aug. 2, 1812, April 24, 1813, June, 1813, 86, 89, 90, Virginia State Library, Richmond.

135. *The Maryland Journal and Baltimore Advertiser*, June 14, 1793.

136. Sweet, *Religion on the American Frontier*, 330.

137. See [?] to James Fort, ca. Summer, 1821, Neill Brown Papers. We are grateful to Linda McCurdy of the Manuscript Reading Room, Special Collections Department of the Perkins Library, Duke University, for bringing this document to our attention and to Robert C. Calhoon for providing us with an accurate reading of the text.

138. For details of the separation see Thomas, *History of the Sharp Street Memorial Methodist Episcopal Church*, and Winch, *Philadelphia's Black Elite*, 4, 5, 10.

139. Clark, Potts, and Payton, eds., *Journal and Letters of Francis Asbury*, 2:51, 65, 128, 129; Henry Smith, *Recollections and Reflections*, 252.

140. Edward Smith, *Climbing Jacob's Ladder*, 78.

141. William Henry Williams, *Garden of American Methodism*, 115–16.

142. Cited in Macoll and Stansfield, eds., *Alexandria*, 126–27.

143. Cromwell, "First Negro Churches," 65; Edward Smith, *Climbing Jacob's Ladder*, 80.

144. Chreitzberg, *Early Methodism*, 159–60.

145. Sobel, "'They Can Never Prosper Together,'" 299.

146. Semple, *History of the Rise and Progress of Baptists in Virginia*, 361; Gillfield Baptist Church Records, History, Alderman Library, University of Virginia; Dover Baptist

Association Minutes, 1813, 5, Virginia Baptist Historical Society; *Organization and Development of the Elam Baptist Church*, 10–13.

147. Dover Baptist Association Minutes, 1821, 6, Virginia Baptist Historical Society; George Drumgoole to Rev. Ed. Drumgoole Sr., Richmond, Dec. 24, 1823, Drumgoole Papers, Box 1, Folder 23 (1823), Southern Historical Collection, University of North Carolina Library.

148. Bonomi, *Under the Cope of Heaven*, 157, 159.

149. See, for example, William S. White, *African Preacher*, 33, 61, Lyell, *Second Visit*, 1:14–15, and Sherwood, *Memoir*, 113.

150. Jenkins, *Experiences*, 50; Faux, *Memorable Days*, 420.

151. See, for example, Circular Letter, Oct. 1809, Dover Baptist Association Minutes, 10, Virginia Baptist Historical Society, and Tydings, *A Refutation*, 313, Sherwood, *Memoir*, 140, Lambert, *Travels*, 175, and Ebenezer Davies, *American Scenes*, 199.

152. Faux, *Memorable Days*, 108–9; Harrison, *Gospel among the Slaves*, 275; James L. Smith, *Autobiography*, 27.

CHAPTER 7

1. W. Harrison Daniel, "Virginia Baptists and the Negro," 65.

2. In 1802, for example, the Goshen Baptist Church in Lincoln County, Georgia, drafted as its Seventh Rule the requirement that any of its black members who wished to marry "shall first make it known to their master, mistress or overseer" (Lincoln County, Georgia, Goshen Baptist Church Records, Minutes and Miscellaneous Records, vii–viii, Hargrett Rare Book and Manuscript Library, University of Georgia).

3. Between 1799 and 1801, for example, four members of Baltimore's Methodist Episcopal Church (three whites and one black) were "excluded" or "excommunicated" for marrying an "unawakened" person (Sharp Street Methodist Episcopal Church [Baltimore City Station], White and Colored Classes, United Methodist Historical Society, Baltimore).

4. Queries by Euhaw Church to the Charleston Association of Baptist Churches, *Minutes of the Charleston Association* (1788), 2.

5. W. Harrison Daniel, "Virginia Baptists and the Negro," 65.

6. Buchner, *Moravians in Jamaica*, 44–45.

7. Ibid. South Carolina's Big Stephen Creek Baptist Church (Edgefield District) took a similar position. In 1819 it agreed that any black church member whose spouse had been forcibly removed "to a distant place" should be "at liberty to take another" (Big Stephen Creek Baptist Church, Records, Oct. 1819, South Carolina Baptist Historical Society).

8. Records of the Wicomico Baptist Church, 1807, and Dover Baptist Association Minutes, 1793, both in Virginia Baptist Historical Society.

9. Query from the Damascus Church to the Georgia Association, *Minutes of the Georgia Association* (1824), 34. In 1809 the Georgia Association had advised its constituent churches that it was not "consistent with gospel discipline, to retain members in the Church who have lived together as man and wife for a considerable time, then *parting without any constraint and taking others* in the lifetime of the former: they being slaves" (*Minutes of the Georgia Association* [1809], 2 [emphasis in original]).

10. *Minutes of the Charleston Baptist Association*, 1818, 2.

11. Berryville Baptist Church Minutes, 1804, Virginia Baptist Historical Society.

12. Lower Fork of Lynches Creek Baptist Church Minutes, Oct. 17, 1828, South Carolina Baptist Historical Society.

13. Welsh Neck Baptist Church Minutes, Feb. 18, 1820, South Carolina Baptist Historical Society.

14. Black Creek Baptist Church, Dovesville, Records, Sept. 6, 1829, South Carolina Baptist Historical Society.

15. Proceedings of the Dover Baptist Association Meeting (1802), cited in Semple, *History of the Rise and Progress of Baptists in Virginia*, 130.

16. See, for example, the Rules of the Emmaus (New Kent) Baptist Church that were drawn up in 1792 in Emmaus Baptist Church Minutes, Virginia Baptist Historical Society.

17. Dover Baptist Association Minutes, 1801, Virginia Baptist Historical Society.

18. Black Creek Baptist Church, Southampton County, Va., Minute Book, April 30, 1803, Virginia Baptist Historical Society.

19. Smith's Creek, Lyville's Creek Baptist Church, Augusta County, Va., Minute Book, March 8, 1807, Virginia Baptist Historical Society.

20. The churches in the sample are as follows: In *Georgia*, Goshen (Lincoln County), 1802–30, and Little Ogechee, 1829; in *North Carolina*, Little River, 1794; in *South Carolina*, Big Creek, 1803, 1811, 1821, Big Stephen Creek, 1805, 1810, 1812–13, 1815, 1825, Society Hill (formerly Welsh Neck), 1815–16, 1820–21, 1823–24, Turkey Creek, [Abbeville County] 1805, 1807, 1827; and in *Virginia*, Albemarle, 1777, 1803–4, 1809, Antioch (Boar Swamp), 1791, 1793, 1804–5, 1812–13, 1818, 1822, Berryville, 1803–4, 1808, 1817, Black Creek, 1789–90, 1792–94, 1798, 1800–1802, 1804–5, 1807–14, 1816, 1818, 1822–23, 1827–28, Broad Run, 1774, 1782–83, 1805, 1820, Buck Marsh, 1792, Burruss', 1804–5, 1807–8, 1810–16, 1829, Carmel, 1804, 1806, 1808, 1811, 1813–14, Emmaus, 1812–13, Hartwood, 1774, 1776, 1792, Lyville's Creek, 1805, 1813, Meherrin, 1772–73, 1776, 1794, 1797, Millfield, 1827, Mill Swamp, 1794, 1799, Morattico, 1780, 1783, 1786, 1792, 1810, 1813, Mossingford, 1827, Nomini, 1824–25, 1828, Smith's Creek, 1794, 1814, South Quay, 1779–82, 1805, 1810–11, 1813–14, Tussekiah, 1822, and Upper King and Queen, 1815.

21. Only 1.7 percent of the men compared with 5.6 percent of the women in the sample faced these charges.

22. Records of the Trinity Methodist Episcopal Church, Charleston, Book C, Roll of Colored Members, South Carolina Historical Society.

23. During the 1820s two other black class leaders, Polladore Mazyck and Abram Owen, were also expelled from the church. Mazyck was found guilty of drunkenness; the reason for Owen's excommunication was not recorded.

24. There is no record of why 33 bondmen (38.8 percent of those excommunicated) and 40 bondwomen (35.7 percent of those excommunicated) were expelled from the church. It is possible that the reasons may have included fornication and other sexual transgressions.

25. The churches in the sample are as follows: In *Georgia*, Goshen (Lincoln County), 1802–30; and in *South Carolina*, Big Creek, 1803, 1811, 1821, 1823, Big Stephen Creek, 1805, 1810, 1812–13, 1815, 1825, Brushy Creek, 1795–1821, Lynches Creek (Gum Branch), 1796–1825, Mountain Creek, 1799–1807, and Skull Shoals (Pacolet, Cherokee County), 1788–1802.

26. These improprieties included adultery, living apart from their husbands, fornication, "whoredom," and giving birth to an illegitimate child.

27. There is a growing corpus of scholarship on the quasi-independent economic ac-

tivities of slaves in the American South and British West Indies. For pertinent examples see Mintz and Hall, "Origins of the Jamaican Internal Marketing System," Peter H. Wood, *Black Majority,* 195–217, Philip D. Morgan, "Work and Culture," "Black Life in Eighteenth-Century Charleston," and "Black Society in the Lowcountry, 1700–1810," in Berlin and Hoffman, eds., *Slavery and Freedom,* 83–141, and Morgan and Berlin, eds., *The Slaves' Economy,* and *Cultivation and Culture,* and Betty Wood, *Women's Work, Men's Work.*

28. Jabez Marshall, *Memoirs of the Late Rev. Abraham Marshall,* 129–30. In 1791 James Meacham was similarly moved when some "poor blacks" to whom he preached in Cumberland, Virginia, "bestowed" on him "their presents of pears and apples" (Meacham, *Journal and Travels,* Series 10, 91.

29. See Chapter 2 in this book.

30. Gilbert claimed that "Obeah men and women [are] very rich people, possessed of large sums of money, being kept in constant pay, by those that could afford it" (Ann Gilbert to Rev. Richard Pattison, English-Harbor, Antigua, June 1, 1804, Folder 1803–4, Box 111, 1803–13, MMS, West Indies). For similar comments from late-eighteenth-century Jamaica see *Reports of the Lords,* part 3, Jamaica. Evidence of Mr. Fuller, Agent for Jamaica, Mr. Long and Mr. Chisholm.

31. See Chapter 4 in this book.

32. Goveia, *Slave Society,* 282, 292.

33. "Letters Showing the Rise and Progress of the Early Negro Churches," 71–74, 84 (emphasis in original). Two years later Liele commented that he had "purchased a piece of land in Spanish-Town, for a burying ground, with a house upon it, which serves for a Meeting-house" (ibid., 84).

34. In the 1760s, for example, the Baptist congregation at Stono, South Carolina, received significant gifts of land and money from two of its members, Joseph and William Elliott. A female member, Mrs. Elizabeth Williamson, donated £200 in Carolina currency to the church (King, *History of the South Carolina Baptists,* 36). King's study is an updated version of Townsend, *South Carolina Baptists.*

35. Simms, *First Colored Baptist Church,* 23–24, and Robert G. Gardner, "Primary Sources," 106.

36. Bryan secured his freedom from his co-religionist owner, Jonathan Bryan for a nominal sum in the early 1790s (Simms, *First Colored Baptist Church,* 30).

37. Ibid., 31.

38. David Ramsay, *History of South-Carolina,* 2:19.

39. Semple, *History of the Rise and Progress of Baptists in Virginia,* cited in Tupper, int., *First Century,* 119–20.

40. Clark, Potts, and Payton, eds., *Journal and Letters of Francis Asbury,* 2:423–24 (emphasis in original).

41. "History of Little Briar Creek Baptist Church," 2, Hargrett Rare Book and Manuscript Library, University of Georgia.

42. Jenkins, *Experiences,* 120–21. In 1792 James Meacham recorded that he had preached to a black congregation in Cumberland, Virginia, "who hath built there a good meeting-house" (Meacham, *Journal and Travels,* Series 10, 91).

43. Christopher Teal, a white member of the congregation, gave "1 acre of land for the church" (King, *History of the South Carolina Baptists,* 54).

44. Semple, *History of the Rise and Progress of Baptists in Virginia,* 160–61.

45. Simms, *First Colored Baptist Church*, 34.

46. King, *History of South Carolina Baptists*, 150.

47. In 1797, for example, the biracial Baptist congregation at the Lower Fork of Lynches Creek, South Carolina, asked two of its white members "to conclude a plan for the building the Meeting House on Gum Branch." They "Brought in their report to hire in a man" (ibid., 58–59).

48. Ibid., 54.

49. For the occupations of bondwomen see Shammas, "Black Women's Work"; Jacqueline Jones, "Race, Sex, and Self-Evident Truths," in Hoffman and Albert, eds., *Women in the Age of the American Revolution;* Jacqueline Jones, *Labor of Love, Labor of Sorrow*, 11–29; and Deborah Gray White, *Ar'n't I a Woman?*, 112–30, 142–60. For those in the British West Indies see Beckles, *Natural Rebels*, 24–71, Bush, *Slave Women in Caribbean Society*, 33–50, and Morrissey, *Slave Women in the New World*, 62–90.

50. Ann Gilbert to Rev. Richard Pattison, English-Harbor, Antigua, June 1, 1804, Folder 1803–4, Box 111, 1803–13, MMS, West Indies.

51. Simms, *First Colored Baptist Church*, 35.

52. Mary Turner, *Slaves and Missionaries*, 80.

53. In 1826, for example, the Bethesda Baptist Church in Greene County, Georgia, reported that "The Sweeping & keeping of the meeting house was let to the lowest bidder for eleven months To Philip H. Greene at Eight Dollars." Six years earlier the same congregation paid one of its members, John Mercer, "2 Dollars it being the Balance due as Door-keeper for the past year" (Cates, trans., *Conference Minutes of Bethesda Baptist Church*, 9, 13).

54. In 1790, for example, the Baptist congregation at Welsh Neck paid around £120 sterling for repairs to its church that included "new sills and the House raised on pillars of brick; and a new Pulpit. To have the Stairs of the Gallery removed, and a shed the length of the House . . . for the use of the Negroes and a good board and post fence round the burying ground" (King, *History of South Carolina Baptists*, 45–46).

55. In 1789, for example, a subscription was "solicited" to move the Baptist church at Welsh Neck to a new location at Society Hill. The church built at Society Hill was "a plain substantial building without a porch in front, but with a large addition on one side the whole length of the building for the use of the Negroes." There is no record of how much the church cost to build (ibid., 46–47).

56. For some indication of this expenditure see Coke, *An Account of the Rise, Progress, and Present State of the Methodist Missions*.

57. Mary Turner, *Slaves and Missionaries*, 85; Goveia, *Slave Society*, 292.

58. The breakdown of this sum was as follows: one shilling and six-pence per quarter for the admission ticket; the same amount monthly for class meetings; and one and a half pence for the weekly collection. Whites were expected to pay an additional sixteen shillings and six-pence a year for their seats in the chapel (Goveia, *Slave Society*, 292).

59. Ryland, *Baptists of Virginia*, 148.

60. King, *History of South Carolina Baptists*, 36, 45–46, 52, 121.

61. Ibid., 141.

62. Simms, *First Colored Baptist Church*, 50, 75. Simms derived his information from "An Account of the Negro Church at Savannah, and of two Negro Ministers" (Jonathan Clarke, Savannah, Dec. 22, 1792, in Rippon, *Baptist Annual Register*, 540, 541). Henry Holcombe claimed that Bryan's estate "is worth upwards of five thousand dollars" (*Georgia*

Analytical Repository, vol. 1, no. 4, 185). For the estimate of $3,000 see Benedict, *General History,* 192.

63. Clerk of Council, Savannah, Register of Free Persons of Color, Georgia Historical Society, unpaginated entries for 1817, 1823, 1824, 1825.

64. Middle District [Virginia] Association, Letter, 1791, cited in Ryland, *Baptists of Virginia,* 149.

65. Roanoke Association, Article 19, Abstract of Principles (1790), cited in ibid. See also, Middle District Association, Circular Letter (1791), Dover Baptist Association, Circular Letter (1795), and Portsmouth Baptist Association, Circular Letter (1796), all in ibid., 149–50.

66. Ibid., 150.

67. David Ramsay, *History of South-Carolina,* 2:19.

68. Ibid.

69. Shipp, *History of Methodism,* 416 (emphasis added), and Washington, D.C.: Ebenezer Stewards, Leaders and Quarterly Conference Records, May 3, 1824–Sept. 11, 1826, United Methodist Historical Society, Baltimore. Cartwright's stipend was a quarter of that received by white preachers in the Conference.

70. Portsmouth Baptist Association, Circular Letter (1796), cited in Ryland, *Baptists of Virginia,* 150.

71. Dover Baptist Association, Circular Letter (1799), cited in Alley, *History of the Baptists,* 134.

72. Morattico Baptist Church Minute Book, May 1781, Virginia Baptist Historical Society, 13.

73. Upper King and Queen County Baptist Church Minute Book, Sept. 18, 1785, Virginia Baptist Historical Society.

74. Semple, *Baptists in Virginia,* 131–32, 392.

75. Goshen [Virginia] Association Minutes, 1802, in ibid., 193–94.

76. July 22, 1839, Nomini Baptist Church, Constitution, Articles 4 and 5, Nomini Baptist Church Minute Book, Virginia State Library.

77. Tupper, int., *First Century,* 119–20.

78. Ibid., 120.

79. First Baptist Church of the City of Richmond Minutes, Jan. 17, 1825, April 7, Dec. 11, 1827, Virginia Baptist Historical Society, 1, 19, 30.

80. King, *History of South Carolina Baptists,* 45–46.

81. Congregations did not always itemize the contributions they made to their Associations and Conferences. The estimate of around five dollars is derived from the records of some of the churches that did record their contributions. See, for example, Lincoln County, Georgia, Goshen Baptist Church Minutes, 1802–69, Cates, trans., *Conference Minutes of Bethesda Baptist Church,* 3, 5–6, and *Minutes of the Georgia Association* (1824), 2.

82. Mallory, *Memoirs of Elder Jesse Mercer,* 153–54.

83. Ryland, *Baptists of Virginia,* 179–80.

84. Ibid., 169–90.

85. In 1814, for example, Luther Rice preached in Petersburg and Fredericksburg specifically to raise money for missionary work. A collection taken after his sermon in Petersburg's courthouse raised just over forty-four dollars for the Richmond Baptist Missionary Society (ibid., 181). In the late 1810s the predominantly black congregation of Richmond's

First Baptist Church "collected near one hundred dollars per annum" to help support missionary work in Africa (Tupper, int., *First Century*, 221–23).

86. *Minutes of the Sunbury Baptist Association* (1824, 1825).

87. For recent discussions of the income-generating activities of bondpeople see the works listed in note 27 (above).

88. In the case of the Richmond church, defaulters were "dealt with as members out of order" (First Baptist Church of the City of Richmond Minutes, April 7, 1827, Virginia Baptist Historical Society, 19).

89. Mary Turner, *Slaves and Missionaries*, 47.

90. This plate can still be seen at the First African Church.

91. T. Morgan to Rev. Robert Smith, Nevis, Jan. 20. 1814, Folder 1814, Box 112, 1814–15, MMS, West Indies.

92. Betty Wood, *Women's Work, Men's Work*, 173.

93. R. Q. Mallard, *Plantation Life*, 83; *Organization of Elam Baptist Church*, 10; Stephen Swinyard to Rev. Marsden, Parham, Antigua, April 12, 1817, Folder Jan.–June 1817, Box 113, 1816–18, MMS, West Indies; Roberts and Roberts, trans. and eds., *Moreau de Saint-Mery's American Journey*, 60.

94. Kemble, *Journal of a Residence*, 68–69.

95. Genovese, *Roll, Jordan, Roll*, 556.

96. William Fish to Mr. Benson, Kingston, Jamaica, April 26, 1804, Folder 1803–4, Box 111, 1803–13, MMS, West Indies. Fish noted that during the previous six months twenty-three, or just under 4.5 percent, of his congregation had been disciplined. Over one-half of these "Backsliders" had been expelled because of their "manifest negligence." Fish did not comment on their race or sex; nor did he suggest that their "manifest negligence" might have been because of their inability to contribute financially to the church.

97. Cates, ed., *Conference Minutes of Bethesda Baptist Church*, 2.

98. Records of the Trinity Methodist Episcopal Church, Charleston, Book C, Roll of Colored Members, South Carolina Historical Society.

99. William Lill to Rev. James Buckley, Grenada, April 18, 1816, Folder Jan.–June 1816, Box 113, 1816–18, MMS, West Indies.

100. "Letters Showing the Rise and Progress of the Early Negro Churches," 71, 88–89. Writing from Kingston in 1804 William Fish commented that "we used to have 6 [prayer meetings] in the Week" (William Fish to Mr. Benson, Kingston, Jamaica, April 26, 1804, Folder 1803–4, Box 111, 1803–13, MMS, West Indies.

101. Betty Wood, *Women's Work, Men's Work*, 164.

102. For the law in question see Cobb, comp., *A Digest of the Statute Laws*, 920–21.

103. Simms, *First Colored Baptist Church*, 63.

104. *Georgia Republican and Savannah Ledger*, Dec. 15, 1804.

105. Dover Baptist Association Minutes, 1832, 15, Virginia Baptist Historical Society.

106. John Taylor to Jos. Benson, St. Vincent, April 7, 1804, Folder 1803–4, Box 111, 1803–13, MMS, West Indies. Writing from Antigua, Stephen Swinyard described a divine service followed by a love-feast that began at 10 A.M. and continued until 4 P.M. Some people walked "8 or 9 miles" in order to be there (Stephen Swinyard to Rev. Marsden, Parham, Antigua, April 12, 1817, Folder Jan.–June 1817, Box 113, 1816–18, MMS, West Indies.

107. Simms, *First Colored Baptist Church*, 19.

108. *Organization of Elam Baptist Church*, 10.

109. Betty Wood, *Women's Work, Men's Work,* 163; R. Q. Mallard, *Plantation Life,* 83.

110. Betty Wood, *Women's Work, Men's Work,* 90.

111. W. Ratcliffe to Rev. Marsden, Kingston, Jamaica, Oct. 20, 1817, Folder Sept.–Dec. 1817, Box 113, 1816–18, MMS, West Indies.

112. Anon to Revs. Marsden and Watson, Kingston, Jamaica, June 25, 1817, Folder Jan.–June 1817, Box 113, 1816–18, MMS, West Indies.

113. Semple, *History of the Rise and Progress of Baptists in Virginia,* 307.

114. In 1802, for example, Georgia's Goshen Baptist Church adopted as its "Sixth Rule" that "members of this church be required to observe the Lord's day by forsaking their temporal interest & consecrating that day holy to the Lord with the exception of particular acts of necessity & mercy" (Lincoln County Georgia, Goshen Baptist Church Records, Rules, 1802, vii–viii).

115. John Taylor to Jos. Benson, St. Vincent, April 7, 1804, Folder 1803–4, Box 111, 1803–13, MMS, West Indies.

116. George Poole to Rev. Robert Smith, St. Vincent, Jan. 16, 1813, Folder 1812–13, Box 111, 1803–13, MMS, West Indies.

117. Records of the Trinity Methodist Episcopal Church, Charleston, Book C, Roll of Colored Members, South Carolina Historical Society.

118. William Fish to Mr. Benson, Kingston, Jamaica, April 26, 1804, Folder 1803–4, Box 111, 1803–13, MMS, West Indies.

119. For the churches in this sample see note 25, above.

120. The church records do not always distinguish between those who voluntarily "withdrew" and those who were forced to leave because they had been sold away by their owners. Sometimes, as in the case of Charleston's Trinity Methodist Episcopal Church, the word "removed" was also used to indicate a change of class. It seems that comparatively few enslaved people voluntarily "withdrew" from this church. Only seventeen names (nine men and eight women) were listed as having "withdrawn," "dropped off," or "Gone." They included two women who had "Joined the Baptists," another woman who had "gone to [the] Presbyterians," and one man who had "Joined the Romans" (Records of the Trinity Methodist Episcopal Church, Charleston, Book C, Roll of Colored Members, South Carolina Historical Society.

121. See, for example, the exchange between a white exhorter named Frith and an unnamed black woman in Nevis, in John Taylor to Rev. Coke, Nevis, May 7, 1803, Folder 1803–4, Box 113, 1816–18, MMS, West Indies.

122. For an extended discussion of this political battle and its outcome see Betty Wood, *Women's Work, Men's Work,* 140–59, and "'Never on a Sunday?,'" in Mary Turner, ed., *From Chattel Slaves to Wage Slaves.*

123. Dutchess Simmons was about seventy-three years old in 1790 when she was converted by Samuel Painter, a free black Antiguan (*Methodist Magazine,* 1805, 302–3).

124. Burchell, *Memoir of Thomas Burchell,* 59. We are most grateful to Helen Plant for drawing our attention to this reference.

AFTERWORD

1. Frey, "'The Year of Jubilee Is Come,'" in Hoffman and Albert, eds., *Religion in a Revolutionary Age,* 111.

2. Edward Baptist Diary, 1790–1861, Virginia State Historical Society.

3. Barrett, "African Religion," in Booth, ed., *African Religions*, 194.

4. Welsh Neck Church Minutes, May 21, June 3, 1826, South Carolina Baptist Historical Society. The tensions and festering conflicts generated by this episode lasted for four years (see ibid., Jan. 2, Jan. 17, Feb. 6, March 6, March 21, June 5, 1830).

5. Deems, ed., *Annals of Southern Methodism for 1855*, 260.

6. Charles Thompson [of North Shields, Northumberland, England] to Judith [a Negro slave belonging to George Garrett of Urbanna, Middlesex County, Va.], Temple Family Papers, Virginia Historical Society.

7. Reprinted in Chambers, *Poplar Forest*, 119.

8. For these developments see Frey, *Water from the Rock*, 323–35, Sparks, *On Jordan's Stormy Banks*, 134–45, Bailey, *Shadow on the Church*, 206–7, 223–26, and Hall, "Black and White Christians in Florida," and Touchstone, "Planters and Slave Religion," in Boles, ed., *Masters and Slaves*.

9. For more detail see Stewart, *Religion and Society*, Heuman, *"The Killing Time,"* and Green, "Was British Emancipation a Success?," in Richardson, ed., *Abolition and Its Aftermath*.

SELECTED BIBLIOGRAPHY

Primary Sources: Unpublished

GREAT BRITAIN

School of Oriental and African Studies, London
  Methodist Missionary Society Records, West Indies, 1803–57 (Boxes 111–39).
University of Cambridge Library
  The Fulham Papers at Lambeth Palace (American Colonial Section), 1624–1824. 36
    vols. Microfilm.
  The Papers of the Society for the Propagation of the Gospel in Foreign Parts at
    Lambeth Palace. 17 vols. Microfilm.
Westminster College, Cambridge
  Countess of Huntingdon Papers, Cheshunt Foundation.

UNITED STATES OF AMERICA

Georgia
Georgia Historical Society, Savannah
  Clerk of Council, Savannah, Register of Free Persons of Color, 1817–29.
  Joseph F. Waring Papers. Box 22, Churches—Methodist, MSS 1275.
Hargrett Rare Book and Manuscript Library, University of Georgia
  "History of Little Briar Creek Church [Georgia] Constituted in 1777." ed. Mamie R.
    Mathews. Typescript, 1967.
  Lincoln County, Georgia. Goshen Baptist Church Records. Minutes, 1802–69, and
    Miscellaneous Records to 1911. Indexed. Typescript.

Stetson Memorial Library, Mercer University
  Records of the Little Ogechee Baptist Church, Screven County, Georgia, 1797–1905. Microfilm.

Maryland
Maryland State Archives, Annapolis
  Annapolis Station Methodist Episcopal Church Quarterly Conference Records, 1826–46.
  John Fortie Notebook, Marshall Collection of Jacob Forty, Special Collection, 1383.
  Methodist Conferences, Baltimore, City Station, Marriages, 1799–1838.
United Methodist Historical Society of the Baltimore Annual Conference Library and Museum, Lovely Lane, Baltimore
  Baltimore Circuit, Methodist Episcopal Church, Quarterly Conference Reports, 1794–1815 (are called Steward's Book).
  William Colbert Journal, 1805.
  Journal and Autobiography of John Littlejohn. (Original in Louisville Conference Historical Society, Nashville, Tenn.). Typescript.
  Sharp Street Methodist Episcopal Church (Baltimore City Station), White and Colored Classes, 1799–1812, Records.
  Henry Slicer Journal [1801–74], 1828–72.
  The Steward's Book for Calvert Circuit, A.D. 1827 to 1838.
  Washington, D.C.: Ebenezer (later 4th Street, then Trinity, now Capitol Hill) Stewards, Leaders and Quarterly Conference Records, May 3, 1824–September 11, 1826.
  George Wells Journal, 1791–92. Abstracted typescript.

New York
The Pierpoint Morgan Library, New York
  John Pierpoint Journal, 1805.

North Carolina
Manuscript Division, Perkins Library, Duke University
  Neill Brown Papers.
  Clarke's Station Baptist Church, Church Minutes, 1812–32.
  Thomas Mann Journal, 1805–30. 7 vols.
  James Meacham Journal, 1788–97.
  Methodist Episcopal Church, Virginia and North Carolina Conferences. Newbern and Neuse Districts, New River, Newport, and Trent Circuits. Quarterly Conference Minutes, 1805–44.
  William Ormond Journal, 1791–1803. 5 vols. Typescript.
Southern Historical Collection, University of North Carolina Library, Chapel Hill
  Edward Drumgoole (1751–1815) Papers (no. 230), 1766–1871.
  Stephen B. Weeks (1865–1918) Papers, 1746–1913.

South Carolina
South Carolina Baptist Historical Society, Furman University Library, Greenville.
  Big Stephen Creek Baptist Church, Edgefield District, Records, 1803–1901.

Black Creek Baptist Church, Dovesville, Records, 1798–1896.

Brushy Creek Baptist Church, Greenville County, and Association, Records, 1795–1927.

Lower Fork of Lynches Creek Baptist Church (Gum Branch) Minutes, 1796–1887.

Minutes of Big Creek (Baptist Church), Williamston, South Carolina, 1801–50, 1801–1936. Typescript.

Mountain Creek Baptist Church, Anderson, Minutes and Historical Sketch, 1798–1956. Typescript.

Skull Shoals (Pacolet) Baptist Church, Cherokee County, Minutes, 1787–1805. Microfilm.

Turkey Creek Baptist Church, Abbeville County, Minutes, 1785–1869. Microfilm.

Welsh Neck Baptist Church (Society Hill) Minutes, 1737–1841.

South Carolina Historical Society, Charleston

Georgetown Methodist Church Records, 1811–97. Microfilm.

Records of the Trinity Methodist Episcopal Church, Charleston, S.C., Book C, Roll of Colored Members, 1821–66. Microfilm.

Virginia

Alderman Library, University of Virginia, Charlottesville

Gillfield Baptist Church (Petersburg, Va.) Records, 1827–39.

Mount Edd (Batesville, Va.) Baptist Church, Minute Book, 1823–44 (photostat).

Sandy Creek (County Line) Church, Minute Book, 1790–1814, 1814–32.

Christ Church, Alexandria

Christ Church, Fairfax Parish, Alexandria, Va., Vestry Book, 1765–1842.

Lloyd House Library, Alexandria

Trinity United Methodist Church (Alexandria, Va.) Register, 1801–7. Microfilm.

Virginia Baptist Historical Society, Richmond

Antioch Baptist Church (Boar Swamp) Minutes, 1787–1827.

Antioch Baptist Church (Raccoon Swamp) Minutes, 1772–1837.

Berryville (Buck Marsh) Baptist Church Minutes, 1785–1803, 1785–1841.

Black Creek Baptist Church, Southampton County, Va., Minute Book, 1774–1804.

Burruss' Baptist Church (Caroline Co.) Minute Book, 1779–1819.

Carmel Baptist Church Minutes, 1799–1819.

Dover Baptist Association (Virginia) Minutes, 1801–40.

Emmaus Baptist Church Minutes, 1792–1841.

Frying Pan Baptist Church, Loudoun County, Va., Records, 1791, 1828–79 (photocopy).

Goose Creek Baptist Church, Bedford County, Va., Minutes, 1787–1821 (photocopy).

Goose Creek Baptist Church (now Upperville), Fauquier County, Va., Register of Members, 1775–1860 (photostat).

Goshen Baptist Association Minutes.

Hartwood Baptist Church, Shenandoah County, Va., Minutes, 1775–1825, 1835–41.

Meherrin (South Side) Baptist Church, Lunenburg County, Va., Minute Book, 1771–1844.

Mill Creek Baptist Church, Berkeley County, Va., Minute Book, 1757–1928 (photocopy).

Mill Swamp Baptist Church Minutes, 1774–90.

Morattico Baptist Church, Lancaster County, Va., Minute Book, 1778–87, 1792–1844 (photocopy).

Mossingford Baptist Church, Appomattox County, Va., Minute Book, 1823–69.

Portsmouth (Virginia) Association Minutes, 1791–1800, 1801–40.

The Records of the Wicomico Baptist Church of Christ (Northumberland Co.), 1804–47.

Richmond. First Baptist Church of the City of Richmond Minutes, 1825–30. Typescript.

Smith's Creek (1756–74), Lyville's Creek Baptist Church (1775–77, 1787–1818), Augusta County, Va., Minute Book. Typescript.

Smith's Creek Baptist Church, Shenandoah County, Va., Minute Book, 1779–1805 (photocopy).

South Quay Baptist Church Minutes, 1775–1827.

Tussekiah Baptist Church Minutes, 1794–1826.

Upper King and Queen Baptist Church Minute Book, 1774–1816.

Wallers (Goshen) Baptist Church Minutes, 1799–1818.

Virginia Historical Society, Richmond

Edward Baptist Diary, 1790–1861, Xerox copy of a copy in possession of James W. Baptist.

Temple Family Papers, 1675–1901.

Virginia State Library, Richmond

Broad Run Baptist Church, Fauquier County, Va., Minutes, 1757–1859.

Coan Baptist Church, Northumberland County, Va., Minute Book, 1804–51 (photostat).

Goose Creek Baptist Church Records, 1750–95.

Nomini Baptist Church, Westmoreland County, Va., Minute Book, 1824–43 (photostat).

Washington, D. C.
Library of Congress
Roberts Family Papers, 1734–1944.

Public Documents

GREAT BRITAIN

Extracts From the Evidence Delivered Before A Select Committee Of The House of Commons, In The Years 1790 and 1791: On the Parts of the Petitioners For The Abolition Of The Slave Trade. London, 1791.

Report of the Lords of the Committee of Council Appointed for the Consideration of all Matters Relating to Trade and Foreign Plantation. The Evidence and Information they have collected in consequence of his Majesty's Order in Council, date the 11th of February 1788, concerning the present State of the Trade to Africa, and particularly the Trade in Slaves; and Concerning the Effects and Consequences of this Trade, as well in Africa, and the West Indies, as to the general Commerce of this Kingdom. London, 1789.

UNITED STATES OF AMERICA

Second Census 1800. Return of the Whole Number of persons Within the Several Districts of the United States. Washington, D.C. Printed by Order of the House of Representatives, 1801.

Georgia

Candler, Allen D., and Lucian L. Knight, eds. *The Colonial Records of the State of Georgia.* 26 vols. Atlanta: Franklin Printing and Publishing Co., 1904–16.

Cobb, Thomas R. R., comp. *A Digest of the Statute Laws of the State of Georgia, IN Force Prior TO The Session Of The General Assembly of 1851.* Athens, Ga.: Christy, Kelsea & Burke, 1851.

South Carolina

Cooper, Thomas, and David J. McCord, eds., *The Statutes at Large of South Carolina.* 10 vols. Columbia, S.C.: A. S.Johnston, 1836–41.

Printed Primay Sources

CHURCH RECORDS

Georgia

Minutes of the Georgia [Baptist] Association (1788). Augusta, Ga., n.d.

Minutes of the Georgia Association, which was at Tirzoh, Putnam County, on the 7th, 8th, 9th and 10th of October, 1809. N.p., 1809.

Minutes of the Georgia Association, Assembled at Long Creek, Warren County, The 7th, 8th, 9th & 10th days of October, 1815. Augusta, Ga., 1815.

Minutes of the Georgia Association, Held at Centre, Oglethorpe County, October the 9th, 10th and 11th, 1824. N.p., 1824.

Minutes of the Sunbury Baptist Association, Held Sunbury, Liberty County, Georgia, Commencing November 7th, 1818. N.p., 1818.

Minutes of the Sunbury Baptist Association, Held At The Baptist Meeting House, Savannah, Georgia, Commencing on Saturday, the Sixth of January 1820. Savannah, Ga., 1820.

Minutes of the Sunbury Baptist Association, Held At The Baptist Meeting House, Upper Black Creek, Effingham County, Georgia, Commencing on Saturday The Twelfth of November, 1821. Savannah, Ga., 1821.

Minutes of the Sunbury Baptist Association, Convened at the Power's Church, Effingham County, Georgia, On the 7th and 8th Days of November 1823. Savannah, Ga., 1823.

Minutes of the Sunbury Baptist Association, Convened in Sunbury, Liberty County, Georgia, On The 12th and 13th Days of November 1824. Savannah, Ga., 1824.

Minutes of the Sunbury Baptist Association, Convened at New Providence Meeting House, Effingham County, Georgia, On The 11th & 12th Days of November 1825. Savannah, Ga., 1825.

Minutes of the Sunbury Baptist Association, Convened at Salem Meeting House, Chatham County, Georgia, on the 4th and 6th Days of November, 1826. Savannah, Ga., 1826.

Minutes of the Sunbury Baptist Association, Convened at New-Hope Meeting House, Montgomery County, Georgia, On the 10th and 12th Days of Nov. 1827. Savannah, Ga., 1827.

Minutes of the Sunbury Baptist Association, Convened at the Newington Church, Screven County, Georgia, The 7th, 8th and 9th days of November 1829. Savannah, Ga., 1829.
Minutes of the Sunbury Baptist Association, Held at Power's Meeting House, Effingham County, Friday and Saturday, Nov. 12th & 13th 1830. Savannah, Ga., 1830.

Georgia/South Carolina
Minutes of the Savannah River Baptist Association. Convened at Sunbury, Georgia, 21st November 1812. N.p., 1812.
Minutes of the Savannah River Baptist Association, Convened at the Euhaw Church, Beaufort District, South-Carolina, 26th November 1814. N.p., 1814.
Minutes of the Savannah River Baptist Association At Their Twenty Eighth Anniversary Held At Little Saltcatcher Church November 27th, 28th, 29th, and 30th 1830. Charleston, S.C., 1831.

South Carolina
The Minutes of St. Michael's Church of Charleston, S.C., From 1758–1779. N.p., n.d.
Minutes of the Charleston Association, Charleston, October 17 1788. Charleston, S.C., n.d.
Minutes of the Charleston Baptist Association, Convened at the High Hills of Santee, on Saturday the 31st of October 1818. Charleston, S.C., 1818.
Minutes of the Charleston Baptist Association, Convened at the High Hills Church, November 4, 1826. Charleston, S.C., 1826.
Minutes of the Charleston Baptist Association, Convened at Gapway Church, Marion District, November 3rd, and continued to November 7th, 1827. Charleston, S.C., 1827.

Other
Minutes of the Methodist Conferences, Annually Held in America, From 1773 to 1794, Inclusive. Philadelphia, Pa.: Henry Thickness, 1795.
Minutes Taken at the Seventh Annual Conference of the Methodist Episcopal Church for the Year 1825. New York: Nathan Bangs and J. Emory, 1825.
Minutes of the Annual Conferences of the Methodist Episcopal Church for the Years 1773–1828, 1829–1839. 2 vols. New York: T. Mason and G. Lane, 1846.

NEWSPAPERS AND MAGAZINES

The Arminian Magazine. Consisting of Extracts and Original Treatises on General Redemption. 20 vols. London: J. Fry, 1778–97.
Georgia Analytical Repository. ed. Henry Holcombe. 6 vols. 2d. ed. Savannah, Ga.: Seymour, Woolhopter, and Stebbins, 1802–3.
The Georgia Gazette, 1763–75.
The Gospel Messenger and Southern Christian Register. By a Society of Gentlemen, Members of the Protestant Episcopal Church. Charleston, S.C.: C. C. Sebring, 1824–
The Maryland Gazette, 1745–90.
The Maryland Journal and Baltimore Advertiser, 1773–90.
The Massachusetts Magazine, 1790.
The Methodist Magazine. New York: J. Saule and T. Mason for the Methodist Episcopal Church in the United States, 1818–28.

The South Carolina Gazette, 1732–75.
The Virginia Gazette, 1736–80.

BOOKS AND ARTICLES

Abdy, Edward S. *Journal of a Residence and a Tour in the United States, from April, 1833, to October, 1834.* London: J. Murray, 1835.

Abrahams, Roger D., and John F. Szwed, eds. *After Africa: Extracts from British Travel Accounts and Journals of the Seventeenth, Eighteenth and Nineteenth Centuries Concerning the Slaves, their Manners and Customs in the British West Indies.* New Haven, Conn.: Yale University Press, 1983.

———. "A Diary of Joshua Nichols Glenn, St. Augustine in 1823." *Florida Historical Quarterly* 24 (1945): 121–61.

Andrews, Evangeline Walker, ed. *Journal of a Lady of Quality. Being the Narrative of a Journey from Scotland to the West Indies, North Carolina, and Portugal in the Years 1774 to 1776.* New Haven, Conn.: Yale University Press, 1921.

Andrews, William L., ed. *Sisters of the Spirit: Three Black Women's Autobiographies of the Eighteenth Century.* Bloomington: Indiana University Press, 1986.

Asbury, Francis. *An Extract of the Journal of Francis Asbury, Bishop of the Methodist Episcopal Church in America, from Aug. 7, 1771, to Dec. 29, 1778.* 3 vols. Philadelphia, Pa.: Jos. Crukshank, 1792.

Asplund, John. *The Annual Register of the Baptist Denominations, in North America: To the First of November, 1790. Containing an Account of the Churches and Their Constitutions, Ministers, Members, Associations, their Plans and Sentiments, Rule and Order, Proceedings and Correspondence. Also Remarks Upon Practical Religion.* Richmond, Va.: Dixon, Nicholson and Davis, 1792.

———, ed. *The Universal Annual Register of the Baptist Denomination, in North-America, For the Years 1794 and 1795.* Hanover, N.H.: Dunham and True, 1796.

Astley, Thomas, ed. *A New General Collection of Voyages and Travels: Consisting Of the most Esteemed RELATIONS, which have been hitherto published in any LANGUAGE.* 5 vols. London: Printed for Thomas Astley, [1743]–47.

Ball, Charles. *Slavery in the United States: A Narrative of the Life and Adventures of Charles Ball, a Black Man.* New York: Negro Universities Press, 1969.

Barclay, James. *The Voyages and Travels of James Barclay, Containing Many Surprising Adventures, and Interesting Narratives.* London: For the Author, 1777.

Baxter, Richard. *A Christian Directory.* London: Robert White for Nevil Simmons, 1673.

Beazley, Charles R., and Edgar Prestage, eds. and trans. *The Chronicle of the Conquest and Discovery of Guinea. Written by Gomes Ennes De Azurara.* 2 vols. N.p.: Hakluyt Society, 1896. Reprint, New York, 1899.

Benedict, David. *A General History of the Baptist Denomination in America, and Other Parts of the World.* New York: Lewis Colby and Co., 1848. Reprint, Freeport, N.Y.: Books for Libraries Press, 1971.

Bennett, William A. *Memorials of Methodism in Virginia, From Its Introduction into the State in the Year 1772, to the Year 1829.* Richmond, Va.: Published by the Author, 1871.

Blake, John William, ed. *Europeans in West Africa, 1450–1560.* 2 vols. London, 1942.

Bosman, William. *A New and Accurate Description of the Coast of Guinea. Divided into the Gold, the Slave, and the Ivory Coasts.* London: New edition, 1967.

Bossard, Johann Jakob, ed. *C. G. A. Oldendorp's History of the Evangelical Brethren on the Caribbean Islands of St. Thomas, St. Croix, and St. John.* Ann Arbor, Mich.: Karoma Publishers, 1987.

Brickell, John. *The Natural History of North Carolina. With an Account of the Trade, Manners and Customs of the Christian and Negro Inhabitants.* Dublin, Ireland, 1737. Reprint, New York: Johnson Reprint, 1969.

Brokesby, Francis. *Some Proposals Towards Promoting the Propagation Of The Gospel In Our American Plantations. Humbly Offered in a Letter to Mr. Nelson. A Worthy Member of the Society for Propagating the Gospel in Foreign Parts. To which is added a Postscript.* London: G. Sawbridge, 1708.

Bryan, Hugh. *Living Christianity Delineated, in the Diaries and Letters of Two Eminently Pious Persons Lately Deceased, viz. Mr. Hugh Bryan, and Mrs. Mary Hutson, Both of South-Carolina.* London: Printed for J. Buckland, 1750.

Burchell, W. P. *Memoir of Thomas Burchell.* London: Benjamin L. Green, 1845.

Carroll, Bartholomew R., ed. *Historical Collections of South Carolina; Embracing many Rare and Valuable Pamphlets, and other Documents, Relating to the History of that State From its First Discovery to its Independence, in the Year 1776.* 2 vols. New York: Harper and Brothers, 1836.

Carter, Edward C., II, John C. Van Horne, and Lee W. Formwalt, eds., *The Journals of Benjamin Henry Latrobe, 1770–1820. From Philadelphia to New Orleans.* 3 vols. New Haven, Conn.: Yale University Press, 1980.

Cartwright, Peter. *Autobiography of Peter Cartwright, The Backwoods Preacher.* New York: Carlton and Porter, 1856.

Cates, Vivian Toole, trans. *Conference Minutes of Bethesda Baptist Church Union Point (Greene County), August 1817 To December 1865.* Tyler, Tex.: E. Texas Genealogical Society, 1991.

Churchill, John, ed. *A Collection of Voyages and Travels: some now first printed from original manuscripts, others now first published in English . . . With a general preface, giving an account of navigation, from its first beginning.* 6 vols. London: J. Walthoe etc by assignment from Messrs. Churchill, 1732. Reprint, London, 1746.

Clark, Elmer T., J. Manning Potts, and Jacob S. Payton, eds. *The Journal and Letters of Francis Asbury.* 3 vols. London: Epworth Press, 1958.

Coke, Thomas. *An Account of the Rise, Progress and Present State of the Methodist Missions in the West-Indies, And The British Dominions in America, In Ireland, And In North-Wales, With A Statement Of The Receipts and Disbursements.* London: Conference Office, 1805.

———. *Extracts of the Journals of the Late Rev. Tho. Coke, L.L.D.* Dublin, Ireland: R. Napper, 1816.

———. *Extracts of the Journals of the Rev. Dr. Coke's Five Visits to America.* London: G. Paramore, 1793.

———. *A History of the West Indies, Containing the Natural, Civil, and Ecclesiastical History of Each Island; With an Account of the Missions Instituted in those Islands, from the Commencement of their Civilization, but More Especially of the Missions which have been*

Established in the Archipelago by the Society late in Connexion with the Rev. John Wesley. 3 vols. Liverpool, England: Nuttall, Fisher, and Dixon, 1808.

Cox, F. A. *History of the Baptist Missionary Society From 1792 to 1842. To Which Is Added A Sketch Of The General Baptist Mission.* 2 vols. London: T. Ward & Co., 1842.

Crone, G. R., ed. and trans. *The Voyages of Cadamosto and Other Documents on Western Africa in the Second Half of the Fifteenth Century.* N.p.: Nendeln/Liechtenstein, 1967.

Curnock, Nehemiah, ed. *The Journal of the Rev. John Wesley, A.M.: Sometime Fellow of Lincoln College.* 9 vols. London: Epworth Press, 1938.

Curtin, Philip D., ed. *Africa Remembered. Narratives by West Africans from the Era of the Slave Trade.* Madison: University of Wisconsin Press, 1967.

da Montecuccolo, Giovanni Antonio Cavazzi. *Istorica Descrizione de'tre regni Congo, Matamba ed Angola.* Bologna, 1687.

Davidson, Robert. *History of the Presbyterian Church in the State of Kentucky; With a Preliminary Sketch of the Churches in the Valley of Virginia.* New York: Robert Carter, 1847.

Davies, Ebenezer. *American Scenes and Christian Slavery. A Recent Tour of 4,000 Miles in the United States.* London: John Snow, 1849.

Davies, Samuel. *Letters From the Reverend Samuel Davies, Shewing the State of Religion in Virginia, Particularly Among the Negroes.* London: J. Oliver, 1757.

Davies, William V., ed. *George Whitefield's Journals* (1737–41). Gainesville, Fla.: Scholars Facsimiles and Reprints, 1969.

Deems, Charles Force, ed. *Annals of Southern Methodism for 1855.* Nashville, Tenn.: Stevenson and Owen, 1856.

Donnan, Elizabeth, ed. *Documents Illustrative of the History of the Slave Trade to America.* 4 vols. Washington, D.C.: Carnegie Institution of Washington, 1930–35.

Duncan, Peter. *A Narrative of the Wesleyan Missions to Jamaica. With Occasional Remarks On The State Of Society In That Colony.* London: Partridge and Oakey, 1849.

Edwards, Bryan. *The History, Civil and Commercial, of the British West Indies.* 4 vols. Philadelphia, Pa.: James Humphreys, 1806.

Edwards, Paul, ed., *The Life of Olaudah Equiano, or Gustavus Vassa, the African. Written by Himself.* London: n.p., 1789. Reprint, London: Longman, 1992.

"Eighteenth-Century Slaves as Advertised By Their Masters." *Journal of Negro History* 1 (1916): 163–216.

Falconbridge, Alexander. *An Account of the Slave Trade on the Coast of Africa.* London: J. Phillips, 1788. Reprint, London: Frank Cass & Co. Ltd., 1969.

Faux, William. *Memorable Days in America: Being a Journal of a Tour to the United States.* London: W. Simpkin and R. Marshall, 1823.

Fawcett, Benjamin. *A Compassionate Address to the Christian Negroes in Virginia.* Salop, England: J. Eddowes and J. Cotton, 1756.

Garden, Alexander. *Mr. Commissary Garden's Six Letters To The Rev. Mr. Whitefield.* 2d. ed., Boston, Mass., 1740.

Gardner, Robert G. "Primary Sources in the Study of Eighteenth-Century Georgia Baptist History." *Viewpoints. Georgia Baptist History* 7 (1980): 59–118.

Georgia Historical Society. *Collections.* Savannah, Ga.: Georgia Historical Society, 1840–19–.

Gibson, Edmund. *Two Letters of the Lord Bishop of London: The FIRST, to the Masters and Mistresses of Families in the English PLANTATIONS abroad; Exhorting them to Encourage and Promote the Instruction of their NEGROES in the Christian Faith. The SECOND, To the MISSIONARIES there: Directing them to distribute the said Letter, and Exhorting them to give their Assistance towards the Instruction of the Negroes within their Several Parishes, to both of which is prefix'd An Address to Serious Christians among Our Selves to assist the Society for Propagating the Gospel in carrying on this work.* London: J. Downing, 1727.

Gilman, Caroline H. *Recollections of a Southern Matron.* New York: Harper & Brothers, 1838.

Godwyn, Morgan. *The Negro's & Indians Advocate, Suing for their Admission into the Church or, A Persuasive to the Instructing and Baptizing of the Negro's and Indians in our Plantations, Shewing, that as the Compliance therewith can prejudice no Man's just Interest; So the wilful Neglecting and Opposing of it, is no less than a Manifest Apostacy from the Christian Faith. To which is added, A Brief Account of Religion in Virginia.* London: Printed for the Author by J. D., 1680.

———. *A Supplement To The Negro's & Indians Advocate; Or, Some further CONSIDERATIONS and PROPOSALS for the effectual and speedy carrying of the Negro's Christianity in our Plantations (Notwithstanding the late pretended IMPOSSIBILITIES) without any prejudice to their Owners.* London: J. D., 1681.

———. *Trade preferr'd before Religion, and Christ made to give place to Mammon; represented in a sermon relating to the plantations, first preached at Westminster Abbey and afterwards in diverse churches in London.* London: B. Took & I. Cleaver, 1685.

Greene, L. F., ed. *The Writings of John Leland.* New York: Arno Press, 1969.

Gunkel, Alexander, and Jerome S. Handler, eds. "A Swiss Medical Doctor's Description of Barbados in 1661: The Account of Felix Christian Spoeri." *Journal of the Barbados Museum and Historical Society* 33 (1969): 3–13.

Henson, Josiah. *Father Henson's Story of His Own Life.* Boston, Mass.: John P. Jewett and Co., 1858.

Hodges, Graham Russell, ed. *Black Itinerants of the Gospel. The Narratives of John Jea and George White.* Madison: University of Wisconsin Press, 1993.

Hodgson, Adam. *Remarks During a Journey Through North-America in the Years 1819, 1820, and 1821. In a Series of Letters.* Westport, Conn.: Negro Universities Press, 1970.

Holcombe, Henry. *The First Fruits. In A Series of Letters.* Philadelphia, Pa.: Author, 1812.

Holcombe, Hosea. *A History of the Rise and Progress of the Baptists in Alabama.* Philadelphia, Pa.: King and Baird, 1840.

Hooker, Richard J., ed. *The Carolina Backcountry on the Eve of the Revolution. The Journal and Other Writings of Charles Woodmason, Anglican Itinerant.* Chapel Hill: The University of North Carolina Press, 1953.

Hughes, Griffith. *The Natural History of Barbados In Ten Books.* London: Printed for the Author, 1750.

Humphreys, David. *An Historical Account of the Incorporated Society for the Propagation of the Gospel in Foreign Parts. Containing their Foundation, Proceedings and the Success of their Missions to the British Colonies, to the Year 1728.* London: Joseph Downing, 1730.

Janson, Charles William. *The Stranger in America: Containing Observations Made During a Long Residence in That Country.* London: Albion Press, 1807.

Jenkins, James. *Experiences, Labours And Sufferings of Rev. James Jenkins, Of The South Carolina Conference.* N.p.: privately printed, 1842.

Jobson, Richard. *The Golden Trade: Or, A Discovery of the River Gambra.* London: Nicholas Okes, 1623. Reprint, New York: Da Capo Press, 1968.

Jones, George Fenwick, trans. and ed. *Detailed Reports on the Salzburger Emigrants Who Settled in America . . . Edited by Samuel Urlsperger.* 15 vols. to date. Athens: University of Georgia Press, 1968–90.

———. "Johann Martin Bolzius' Trip to Charleston, 1742." *South Carolina Historical Magazine* 82, no. 2 (1981): 87–110.

Kemble, Frances Anne. *Journal of a Residence on a Georgia Plantation in 1838–1839.* New York: Harper & Brothers, 1863.

Killion, Ronald, and Charles Waller, eds. *Slavery Time. When I Was Chillun Down on Marster's Plantation.* Savannah, Ga.: The Beehive Press, 1973.

Klingberg, Frank J., ed. *The Carolina Chronicle of Dr. Francis Le Jau, 1706–1717.* Berkeley: University of California Press, 1956.

Knox, William. *Three Tracts Respecting the Conversion and Instruction of Free Indians and Negro Slaves in the Colonies. Addressed to the Venerable Society for the Propagation of the Gospel.* London: J. Debret, 1789.

Lambert, John. *Travels Through Canada and the United States of North America in the Years 1806, 1807, and 1808.* 2 vols. 2d. ed. London: Printed for C. Craddock and W. Joy, 1814.

Lee, Jarena. *Religious Experience and Journal of Mrs. Jarena Lee: Giving an Account of Her Call to Preach the Gospel.* Philadelphia, Pa.: J. Lee, 1849.

Lee, Jesse. *A Short History of the Methodists in the United States of America; Beginning in 1766, and Continued till 1809: To Which is Prefixed, A Brief Account of their Rise in England, in the Year 1729.* Baltimore, Md.: Magill and Clime, 1810.

Leland, John. *The Virginia Chronicle: With Judicious and Critical Remarks, under XXIV Heads.* Fredericksburg, Va.: T. Green, 1790.

"Letters of the Honorable James Habersham, 1756–1775." Georgia Historical Society, *Collections,* Savannah, Ga.: Georgia Historical Society, 1840–19–, 6 (1904): 9–245.

"Letters Showing the Rise and Progress of the Early Negro Churches of Georgia and the West Indies." *Journal of Negro History* 1 (1916): 69–92.

Lewis, Matthew Gregory. *Journal of a West India Proprietor, Kept During a Residence in the Island of Jamaica.* London: J. Murray, 1845.

Littleton, Edward. *The Groans of the Plantations: OR, A True Account Of Their Grievances and Extreme Sufferings By the Heavy IMPOSITIONS upon SUGAR, AND OTHER HARDSHIPS, relating more particularly to the ISLAND OF BARBADOS.* London: M. Clark, 1689.

Loewenberg, Bert James, and Ruth Bogin, eds. *Black Women in Nineteenth-Century American Life.* University Park: The Pennsylvania State University Press, 1976.

Long, Edward. *The History of Jamaica: Or, General Survey of the Antient and Modern State of the Island: With Reflections on its Situation, Settlements, Inhabitants, Climate, Produce, Commerce, Laws, and Government.* 3 vols. London: T. Lowndes, 1774. Rev. ed. London: Frank Cass & Co. Ltd., 1970.

Lyell, Charles. *A Second Visit to the United States of America.* 2 vols. London: J. Murray, 1849.

McLean, John, ed. *Sketch of the Rev. Philip Gatch.* Cincinnati, Ohio: Swormstedt and Poe for the Methodist Episcopal Church, 1854.

Mallard, R. Q. *Plantation Life before Emancipation.* Richmond, Va.: Whittet & Shepperson, 1892.

Mallory, Charles D. *Memoirs of Elder Jesse Mercer.* New York: John Gray, 1844.

Marshall, Jabez P. *Memoirs of the Late Rev. Abraham Marshall: Containing A Journal Of The Most Interesting Parts Of His Life.* Mount Zion, Hancock County, Ga.: Printed for the Author, 1824.

Martin, B., and M. Spurrell, eds., *Journal of a Slave Trader [John Newton].* London: Epworth Press, 1962.

Mason, Frederick E., and Howard T. Maag, eds. *The Journal of Joseph Pilmore, Methodist Itinerant, for the Years August 1, 1769 to January 2, 1774.* Philadelphia, Pa.: Messenger Publishing for the Historical Society of the Philadelphia Annual Conference of the United Methodist Church, Philadelphia, Pa., 1969.

Meacham, James. *A Journal And Travels of James Meacham.* Durham, N.C.: The Trinity College Historical Society and The North Carolina Conference Historical Society, Series 9, 1912, 66–95; Series 10, 87–102.

M'Nemar, Richard. *The Kentucky Revival; or, A Short History of the Late Extraordinary Outpouring of the Spirit of God in the Western States of America.* Albany, N.Y.: E. and W. Hosford, 1807; reprinted by Edward D. Jenkins, 1846.

Moore, John H., ed. "The Abiel Abbot Journals. A Yankee Preacher in Charleston, South Carolina, 1818–1827." *South Carolina Historical Magazine* 68, no. 2 (1967): 51–73.

Moore, John S., ed. "Richard Dozier's Historical Notes, 1771–1818." *The Virginia Baptist Register* 28 (1989): 1391–442.

"The Moravian Mission in Barbados." *The Journal of the Barbados Museum and Historical Society* 31 (1965): 73–78.

Mott, Abigail, comp. *Biographical Sketches and Interesting Anecdotes of Persons of Color.* 2d. ed. New York: M. Day, 1837.

Pilmore, Joseph. *The Journal of Joseph Pilmore, Methodist Itinerant, for the Years August 1, 1769 to January 2, 1774.* Philadelphia, Pa.: Printed by Message Pub. Co. for the Historical Society of the Philadelphia Conference of the United Methodist Church, 1969.

Pinckney, Elise, ed. *Register of St. Philip's Church, Charleston, South Carolina 1810 through 1822.* N.p.: The National Society of the Colonial Dames of America in the State of South Carolina, 1973.

Pinkerton, John, ed. *A General Collection of the Best and Most Interesting Voyages and Travels in all Parts of the World: Many of Which are now First Translated into English. Digested on a New Plan.* 17 vols. London: Longman, Hurst, Rees, and Orme, 1808–14.

Ramsay, David. *Ramsay's History of South-Carolina: From Its First Settlement In 1670 To The Year 1808.* First published in 2 vols. Charleston, S.C.: David Longworth, 1808. Reprint, complete in one volume, Newberry, S.C., 1858.

Ramsay, James. *An Essay on the Treatment and Conversion of African Slaves in the British Sugar Colonies.* London: J. Phillips, 1784.

Rawick, George P., Jan Hillegas, and Ken Lawrence, eds. *The American Slave. A Composite Autobiography.* Supplement, Series 1, 12 vols. Westport, Conn.: Greenwood

Publishing Co., 1977; Supplement, Series 2, 10 vols. Westport, Conn.: Greenwood Publishing Co., 1979.

Rippon, John. *The Baptist Annual Register.* 4 vols. London: n.p., 1793–1802.

Roberts, K., and A. M. Roberts, trans. and eds. *Moreau de St. Mery's American Journey [1793–98].* Garden City, N.J.: Doubleday & Company, 1947.

Roper, Moses. *A Narrative of the Adventures and Escape of Moses Roper from American Slavery.* Philadelphia, Pa., 1838. 2d. ed. Reprint, New York: Negro Universities Press, 1970.

'Rusticus.' "The Pious African." *The Literary and Evangelical Magazine* 10 (Richmond, Va., 1827): 22–25.

Sandford, Rev. Peter P., comp. *Memoirs of Mr. Wesley's Missionaries in America. Compiled from Authentic Sources.* New York: G. Lane & P. P. Sandford for the Methodist Episcopal Church, 1843.

Semple, Robert A. *A History of the Rise and Progress of the Baptists in Virginia.* Richmond, Va.: John O'Lynch, 1810. Rev. and Ext. ed. by Rev. G. W. Beale, Richmond, Va.: Pitt and Dickinson, 1894.

Sherwood, Adiel. *Memoir of Adiel Sherwood, D.D.* Philadelphia, Pa.: Grant and Faires, 1884.

Shippen, Lester B., ed. *Bishop Whipple's Southern Diary, 1843–1844.* New York: Da Capo Press, 1968.

Sloane, Sir Hans. *A Voyage to the Islands of Barbados, Nieves, St. Christophers, and Jamaica.* 2 vols. London: Printed by B. M. for the Author, 1707–25.

Smith, Henry. *Recollections and Reflections of an Old Itinerant. A Series of Letters Originally Published in the Christian Advocate.* New York: Lane & Tippett for the Methodist Episcopal Church, 1848.

Smith, James L. *Autobiography of James L. Smith: including, also, Reminiscences of Slave Life, Recollections of the War, Education of Freedmen, Causes of the Exodus, etc.* Norwich, Conn.: Press of the Bulletin Co., 1881.

Snelgrave, William. *A New Account of Guinea and the Slave Trade.* London: n.p., 1754. Reprint, London: Frank Cass & Co. Ltd., 1971.

Stanfield, James Field. *Observations on a Guinea Voyage in a Series of Letters Addressed To The Rev. Thomas Clarkson.* London: Printed by J. Phillips, 1788.

Stanley, Edward George Geoffrey Smith. *Journal of a Tour in America, 1824–1825.* N.p.: privately printed, 1930.

Sweet, William W., ed. *Religion on the American Frontier. The Baptists 1783–1830. A Collection of Source Materials.* Chicago, Ill.: Henry Holt & Co., 1931.

Telford, John, ed. *The Letters of Rev. John Wesley.* 8 vols. London: Epworth Press, 1931.

Thompson, Thomas. *An Account of Two Missionary Voyages. By the Appointment of the Society for the Propagation of the Gospel in Foreign Parts. The One to New Jersey in North America, the Other from America to the Coast of Guinea.* London: Printed for Benjamin Dodd, 1758. Reprint, London: Society for the Propagation of the Gospel in Foreign Parts for the SPCK, 1937.

Thorp, Daniel B. "Chattel with a Soul: The Autobiography of a Moravian Slave." *Pennsylvania Magazine of History and Biography* 112 (1988): 433–51.

Tryon, W. S., ed. *A Mirror for Americans. Life and Manners in the United States, 1790–1870 as Recorded by American Travelers.* 3 vols. Chicago, Ill.: University of Chicago Press, 1952.

Tydings, Richard. *A Refutation of the doctrine of uninterrupted apostolic succession, with a correction of errors concerning Rev. John Wesley & Dr. Coke.* Jeffersonville, Iowa.: A. J. Tilden, 1844.

Tyerman, Luke. *The Life and Times of the Reverend John Wesley, M.A., Founder of the Methodists.* 3 vols. New York: Harper and Brothers, 1872.

Van Horne, John C., ed. *Religious Philanthropy and Colonial Slavery. The American Correspondence of the Associates of Dr. Bray, 1717–1777.* Urbana: University of Illinois Press, 1985.

Wale, William, ed. *Whitefield's Journals. To Which Is Prefixed His "Short Account" and "Further Account."* London: Henry J. Drane, n.d.

Watson, John E. *Methodist Error: or Friendly Christian Advice to those Methodists, Who indulge in extravagant emotions and bodily exercises.* Trenton, N.J.: D. and E. Fenton, 1819.

White, William S. *The African Preacher. An Authentic Narrative.* Freeport, N.Y.: Books for Libraries Press, 1972.

Whitefield, George. *A Continuation of Mr. Whitefield's Journey From His Leaving Stanford in New-England, October 29, 1740, to His Arrival at Falmouth in England, March 11, 1741.* Boston, Mass.: S. Kneeland and T. Green, 1741.

———. *A Letter to the Inhabitants of Maryland, Virginia, North and South-Carolina, Concerning their Negroes.* Savannah, Ga.: n.p., 1740.

Wightman, William May, ed. *Life of William Capers, D.D.* Nashville, Tenn.: Southern Methodist Publishing House, 1859.

Williams, James. *Narrative of James Williams. An American Slave.* New York: American Antislavery Society, 1838; Afro-American Series Collection 2: Slave Narratives, Wilmington, Del., n.d.

Winchester, Elhanan. *The Universal Restoration. Exhibited in Four Dialogues Between a Minister and His Friend.* Philadelphia, Pa.: T. Dobson, 1792.

Secondary Sources

Adejbite, Ademola. "The Drum and Its Role in Yoruba Religion." *Journal of Religion in Africa* 18 (1988): 15–26.

Ajayi, J. F. A., and Michael Crowder, eds., *History of West Africa.* 2 vols. New York: Columbia University Press, 1976.

Ajisafe, A. J. *The Laws and Customs of the Yoruba People.* London: G. Routledge, 1924.

Alley, Reuben E. *A History of the Baptists in Virginia.* Richmond, Va.: Virginia Baptist General Board, 1973.

Alleyne, Mervyn C. *Comparative Afro-American: An Historical Comparative Study of English-Based Afro-American Dialects of the New World.* Ann Arbor, Mich.: Karoma Publishers, 1980.

———. *Language and the Social Construction of Identity in Creole Situations.* Los Angeles: Center for Afro-American Studies, University of California, Los Angeles, 1994.

Ames, Hubert H. S. "African Institutions in America." *Journal of American Folk-Lore* 18 (1905): 15–32.

Anstey, Roger. *The Atlantic Slave Trade and British Abolition, 1760–1810.* Atlantic Highlands, N.J.: Humanities Press, 1975.

Bailey, David T. *Shadow on the Church: Southwestern Evangelical Religion and the Issue of Slavery.* Ithaca, N.Y.: Cornell University Press, 1985.

Bailyn, Bernard, and Philip D. Morgan, eds. *Strangers within the Realm: Cultural Margins of the First British Empire.* Chapel Hill: The University of North Carolina Press, 1991.

Baker, Gordon Pratt, ed. *Those Incredible Methodists.* Baltimore, Md.: Commission on Archives and History, The Baltimore Conference, 1972.

Balandier, Georges. *Daily Life in the Kingdom of the Kongo from the Sixteenth to the Eighteenth Century.* Translated by Helen Weaver. New York: Pantheon Books, 1968.

Barber, Karin. "How Man Makes God in West Africa: Yoruba Attitudes Towards the *orisa.*" *Africa* 51 (1981): 724–45.

Barclay, Wade C. *History of Methodist Missions.* 6 vols. New York: Board of Missions and Church Extension of the Methodist Church, 1949–.

Bartels, F. L. "Jacobus Eliza Johannes Capitein, 1717–1747." *Transactions of the Historical Society of Ghana* 4 (1959): 3–13.

———. "Philip Quaque, 1741–1816." *Transactions of the Gold Coast and Togoland Historical Society* 1 (1955): 153–77.

Basden, George. *Among the Ibos of Nigeria.* London: Seeley, Service & Co. Ltd., 1921. Reprint, London: Frank Cass & Co. Ltd., 1966.

Bay, Edna G. "Belief, Legitimacy and the *Kpojito:* An Institutional History of the 'Queen Mother' in Precolonial Dahomey." *Journal of African History* 36 (1995): 1–27.

Beattie, John, and John Middleton. *Spirit Mediumship and Society in Africa.* New York: Africana Publishing Corporation, 1969.

Beckles, Hilary McD. *A History of Barbados. From Amerindian Settlement to Nation-State.* Cambridge, England: Cambridge University Press, 1990.

———. *Natural Rebels. A Social History of Enslaved Black Women in Barbados.* London: Zed Books, 1989.

Beckwith, Martha W. *Black Roadways: A Study of Jamaican Folk Life.* Chapel Hill: The University of North Carolina Press, 1929. Reprint, New York: Negro Universities Press, 1969.

Bednarowski, Mary Farrell. "Outside the Mainstream: Women's Religious Leaders in Nineteenth-Century America." *Journal of the American Academy of Religion* 48 (1980): 202–31.

Beeman, Richard, and Rhys Isaac. "Cultural Conflict in the Revolutionary South." *Journal of Southern History* 46 (1980): 525–50.

"Beliefs and Customs Connected With Death and Burial." *The Southern Workman* 26, no. 1 (Jan. 1897): 19.

Berlin, Ira. *Slaves without Masters. The Free Negro in the Antebellum South.* New York: Pantheon Books, 1974.

———. "The Slave Trade and the Development of Afro-American Society in English Mainland North America, 1619–1775." *Southern Studies* 20 (1981): 112–36.

———. "Time, Space, and the Evolution of Afro-American Society in British Mainland North America." *American Historical Review* 85 (1980): 44–78.

Berlin, Ira, and Ronald Hoffman, eds. *Slavery and Freedom in the Age of the American Revolution.* Charlottesville: University Press of Virginia, 1983.

Blassingame, John W. *The Slave Community: Plantation Life in the Antebellum South.* New York: Oxford University Press, 1972.

Boles, John B., ed. *Masters and Slaves In The House Of The Lord. Race and Religion In The American South, 1740–1870.* Lexington: University Press of Kentucky, 1988.

———. *Religion in the South: Essays.* Jackson: University Press of Mississippi, 1985.

Bolton, S. Charles. *Southern Anglicanism. The Church of England in Colonial South Carolina.* Westport, Conn.: Greenwood Press, 1982.

Bonomi, Patricia U. *Under the Cope of Heaven. Religion, Society and Politics in Colonial America.* New York: Oxford University Press, 1986.

Booth, Newell S., ed. *African Religions.* London and Lagos: NOK Publishers International, 1977.

Botkin, B. A., ed. *Lay My Burden Down.* Chicago, Ill.: University of Chicago Press, 1945.

Brathwaite, Edward. *The Development of Creole Society in Jamaica, 1770–1820.* Oxford, England: The Clarendon Press, 1971.

Breen, T. H., ed. *Shaping Southern Society. The Colonial Experience.* New York: Oxford University Press, 1976.

Brooks, Walter H. "Priority of the Silver Bluff Church and Its Promoters." *Journal of Negro History* 7 (1922): 172–96.

Buchner, J. H. *The Moravians in Jamaica. History of the Mission of the United Brethren's Church to the Negroes in the Island of Jamaica, From the Year 1754 to 1854.* London: Longman, Brown & Co., 1854.

Bucke, Emory Stevens, et al., eds. *The History of American Methodism.* 3 vols. New York and Nashville, Tenn.: Abingdon Press, 1964.

Bush, Barbara. *Slave Women in Caribbean Society 1650–1838.* Bloomington and Indianapolis: Indiana University Press, 1989.

Butler, Jon. *Awash in a Sea of Faith: Christianizing the American People.* Cambridge, Mass.: Harvard University Press, 1990.

———. *The Huguenots in America: A Refugee People in New World Society.* Cambridge, Mass.: Harvard University Press, 1983.

Calhoon, Robert M. *Evangelicals and Conservatives in the Early South, 1740–1861.* Columbia: University of South Carolina Press, 1988.

Carrington, H. Bolton. "Decoration of Graves of Negroes in South Carolina." *Journal of American Folk-Lore* 44 (1891): 241.

Cassidy, Frederic. *Jamaica Talk: Three Hundred Years of the English Language in Jamaica.* London: Macmillan, 1961.

Chambers, S. Allen. *Poplar Forest and Thomas Jefferson.* Forest, Va.: n.p., 1993.

Chreitzberg, Abel McKee. *Early Methodism in the Carolinas.* Nashville, Tenn.: Publishing House of the Methodist Episcopal Church, South, 1897. Reprint, Spartanburg, S.C.: Reprint Co., 1972.

Cody, Cheryl Ann. "There was No 'Absalom' on the Ball Plantations: Slave-Naming Practices in the South Carolina Low Country, 1720–1865." *American Historical Review* 92 (1987): 563–96.

Conkin, Paul K. *The Uneasy Center: Reformed Christianity in Antebellum America.* Chapel Hill: The University of North Carolina Press, 1995.

Courlander, Harold. *The Drum and the Hoe: Life and Lore of the Haitian People.* Berkeley: University of California Press, 1960.

Creel, Margaret Washington. *"A Peculiar People": Slave Religion and Community-Culture Among the Gullahs.* New York: New York University Press, 1988.

Cromwell, John. "First Negro Churches in the District of Columbia." *Journal of Negro History* 7 (1922): 64–106.

Crowder, Ralph L. "Black Physicians and the African Contribution to Medicine." *The Western Journal of Black Studies* 4 (1980).

Curtin, Philip D. *The Atlantic Slave Trade: A Census.* Madison: University of Wisconsin Press, 1969.

Curtin, Philip D., Roger Anstey, and J. E. Inikori. "Discussion: Measuring the Atlantic Slave Trade." *Journal of African History* 17 (1976): 595–627.

Daniel, W. Harrison. "Southern Presbyterians and the Negro in the Early National Period." *Journal of Negro History* 58, no. 3 (1973): 291–312.

———. "Virginia Baptists and the Negro in the Early Republic." *Virginia Magazine of History and Biography* 80 (1972): 60–69.

Daniel, Yvonne. "The Potency of Dance: A Haitian Examination." *Black Scholar 11* (1980): 61–73.

Davidson, Rev. Robert. *History of the Presbyterian Church in the State of Kentucky; With a Preliminary Sketch of the Churches in the Valley of Virginia.* New York and Pittsburgh, Pa.: R. Carter, 1847.

Dunn, Richard S. *Sugar and Slaves: The Rise of the Planter Class in the English West Indies, 1642–1713.* Chapel Hill: The University of North Carolina Press, 1972.

Elkins, Stanley M. *Slavery: A Problem in American Institutional and Intellectual Life.* Chicago, Ill.: University of Chicago Press, 1959.

Emery, Lynne Fauley. *Black Dance in the United States from 1619 to 1970.* Palo Alto, Calif.: National Press Books, 1972.

Epstein, Barbara Leslie. *The Politics of Domesticity. Women, Evangelism and Temperance in Nineteenth-Century America.* Middletown, Conn.: Wesleyan University Press, 1981.

Epstein, Dena J. *Sinful Tunes and Spirituals: Black Folk Music to the Civil War.* Urbana: University of Illinois Press, 1977.

Evans-Pritchard, E. E. *Witchcraft, Oracles and Magic Among the Azande.* Oxford, England: The Clarendon Press, 1937.

Fenn, Elizabeth A. "'A Perfect Equality Seemed to Reign': Slave Society and Jonkonnu." *The North Carolina Historical Review* 65, no. 2 (1988): 127–53.

Foote, William Henry. *Sketches of North Carolina; Historical and Biographical, Illustrative of the Principles of Her Early Settlers.* New York: R. Carter, 1846.

———. *Sketches of Virginia, Historical and Biographical.* 2d. Ser., 2d. rev. ed., Philadelphia, Pa.: J. B. Lippincott and Co., 1856.

Frazier, E. Franklin. *The Negro in the United States.* New York: The Macmillan Company, 1949.

Frey, Sylvia R. *Water from the Rock: Black Resistance in a Revolutionary Age.* Princeton, N.J.: Princeton University Press, 1991.

Gallay, Allan. *The Formation of a Planter Elite. Jonathan Bryan and the Southern Colonial Frontier.* Athens: University of Georgia Press, 1989.

———. "The Origins of Slaveholders' Paternalism: George Whitefield, the Bryan Family, and the Great Awakening in the South." *Journal of Southern History* 53 (1987): 369–94.

Gardner, Robert W. *Baptists of Early America: A Statistical History, 1639–1790.* Atlanta, Ga.: Georgia Baptist Historical Society, 1983.

———. *A History of the Georgia Baptist Association, 1784–1984.* Atlanta, Ga.: Georgia Baptist Historical Society, ca. 1988.

Gaspar, David Barry. "The Antigua Slave Conspiracy of 1736: A Case Study of the Origins of Collective Resistance." *William and Mary Quarterly,* 3d. ser., 35 (1978): 308–23.

———. *Bondmen and Rebels: A Study of Master-Slave Relations in Antigua, With Implications for Colonial British America.* Baltimore, Md.: Johns Hopkins University Press, 1985.

Genovese, Eugene D. *Roll, Jordan, Roll: The World the Slaves Made.* New York: Pantheon Books, 1974.

Gomez, Michael A. "Muslims in Early America." *Journal of Southern History* 60 (1994): 671–700.

Goodwin, Edward Lewis. *The Colonial Church in Virginia.* Milwaukee: Morehouse Publishing Co., 1927.

Goody, Jack, ed. *Literacy in Traditional Societies.* Cambridge, England: Cambridge University Press, 1968.

Goveia, Elsa V. *Slave Society in the British Leeward Islands at the End of the Eighteenth Century.* New Haven, Conn.: Yale University Press, 1965.

Gray, Richard. *Black Christians and White Missionaries.* New Haven, Conn.: Yale University Press, 1990.

Groves, Charles P. *The Planting of Christianity in Africa.* 3 vols. London: Lutterworth Press, 1948–58.

Gutman, Herbert G. *The Black Family in Slavery and Freedom, 1750–1925.* New York: Pantheon Books, 1976.

Haddad, Yvonne Yazbeck, and Ellison Banks Findly, eds. *Women, Religion and Social Change.* Albany: State University of New York Press, 1985.

Hafkin, Nancy J., and Edna G. Bay. *Women in Africa. Studies in Social and Economic Change.* Stanford, Calif.: Stanford University Press, 1976.

Hamilton, J. T., and K. G. Hamilton. *History of the Moravian Church. The Renewed Unitas Fratrum, 1722–1957.* Bethlehem, Pa.: n.p., 1967.

Hancock, Ian F. *Pidgins and Creoles: Current Trends and Prospects.* Washington D.C.: Georgetown University Press, 1974.

Handler, Jerome S., and Frederick W. Lange. *Plantation Slavery in Barbados. An Archaeological and Historical Investigation.* Cambridge, Mass.: Harvard University Press, 1979.

Harris, Malcom H. *History of Louisa County, Virginia.* Richmond, Va.: The Dietz Press, 1936.

Harrison, William P. *The Gospel among the Slaves: A Short Account of Missionary Operations among the African Slaves of the Southern States.* Nashville, Tenn.: Publishing House of the Methodist Episcopal Church, South, 1893. Reprint, New York.: AMS Press, 1973.

Hartzel, Joseph C. "Methodism and the Negro in the United States." *Journal of Negro History* 8 (1923): 301–15.

Hatch, Nathan O. *The Democratization of American Christianity*. New Haven, Conn.: Yale University Press, 1989.

Herskovits, Melville J. *Acculturation: The Study of Cultural Contact*. New York: J. J. Augustin, 1938.

———. *The American Negro: A Study in Racial Crossing*. New York: A. A. Knopf, 1928.

———. *The Myth of the Negro Past*. New York: Harper and Brothers, 1941.

———. "The Negro in the New World: The Statement of a Problem." *American Anthropologist* 32 (1930): 145–55.

Heuman, Gad. *'The Killing Time': The Morant Bay Rebellion in Jamaica*. London: The Macmillan Press Ltd., 1994.

Higginbotham, Evelyn Brooks. *Righteous Discontent: The Women's Movement and the Black Baptist Church, 1880–1920*. Cambridge, Mass.: Harvard University Press, 1993.

Higman, B. W. *Slave Population and Economy in Jamaica*. Cambridge, England: Cambridge University Press, 1976.

———. *Slave Populations of the British Caribbean, 1807–1834*. Baltimore, Md.: Johns Hopkins University Press, 1984.

Hilton, Anne. *The Kingdom of Kongo*. Oxford, England: Clarendon Press, 1985.

Hiskett, Mervyn. *The Course of Islam in Africa*. Edinburgh: University of Edinburgh Press, 1994.

Hoffman, Ronald, and Peter J. Albert, eds. *Religion in a Revolutionary Age*. Charlottesville: University Press of Virginia, 1994.

———. *Women in the Age of the American Revolution*. Charlottesville: The University Press of Virginia, 1989.

Holm, John. *Pidgins and Creoles*. 2 vols. Cambridge, England: Cambridge University Press, 1988–89.

Horton, Robin. "African Conversions." *Africa* 41 (1971): 95–107.

———. *Patterns of Thought in Africa and the West: Essays on Magic, Religion, and Science*. Cambridge, England: Cambridge University Press, 1993.

Howe, George. *History of the Presbyterian Church in South Carolina*. 2 vols. Columbia, S.C.: Duffie and Chapman, 1870.

Hutton, J. E. *A History of the Moravian Missions*. London: Moravian Mission Office, 1922.

Ikenga-Metuh, Emefie. "Religious Concepts in West African Cosmologies." *Journal of Religion in Africa* 13 (1982).

Imasogie, Osadolor. *African Traditional Religion*. Ibadan, Nigeria: University Press, 1985.

Inikori, J. E. "Export Versus Domestic Demand: The Determinants of Sex Ratios in the Transatlantic Slave Trade." *Research in Economic History* 14 (1992): 117–66.

———. "Measuring the Atlantic Slave Trade: An Assessment of Curtin and Anstey." *Journal of African History* 17 (1976): 197–223.

Inscoe, John C. "Carolina Slave Names: An Index to Acculturation." *Journal of Southern History* 49 (1983): 526–54.

Isaac, Rhys. *The Transformation of Virginia, 1740–1790*. Chapel Hill: The University of North Carolina Press, 1982.

Jackson, Harvey H. "Hugh Bryan and the Evangelical Movement in Colonial South Carolina." *William and Mary Quarterly*, 3d. ser., 43 (1986): 594–614.

Jackson, Luther P. "Religious Development of the Negro in Virginia from 1760 to 1860." *Journal of Negro History* 16 (1931): 168–239.

Johnson, G. G. *A Social History of the Sea Islands. With Special Reference to St. Helena Island, South Carolina.* Chapel Hill: The University of North Carolina Press, 1930.

Johnson, Paul E., ed. *African American Christianity: Essays in History.* Berkeley: University of California Press, 1994.

Jones, Jacqueline. *Labor of Love, Labor of Sorrow: Black Women, Work and the Family from Slavery to the Present.* New York: Basic Books, 1985.

Jones, Jerome W. "The Established Virginia Church and the Conversion of Negroes and Indians." *Journal of Negro History* 46 (1961): 12–23.

Jules-Rosette, Bennetta, ed. *The New Religions of Africa.* Norwood, N.J.: Ablex Publishing Corporation, 1979.

Kay, Marvin L. Michael, and Lorin Lee Cary. *Slavery in North Carolina, 1748–1775.* Chapel Hill: The University of North Carolina Press, 1995.

Kenney, William H., III. "Alexander Garden and George Whitefield: The Significance of Revivalism in South Carolina, 1738–1741." *South Carolina Historical Magazine* 71 (1970): 1–16.

Kilson, Martin L., and Robert I. Rotberg, eds. *The African Diaspora: Interpretative Essays.* Cambridge, Mass.: Harvard University Press, 1976.

King, Joe E. *A History of the South Carolina Baptists.* Columbia, S.C.: General Board of the South Carolina Baptist Convention, 1964.

Kopytoff, Igor. "Ancestors as Elders in Africa." *Africa* 41 (1971): 129–41.

Kulikoff, Allan. "The Origins of Afro-American Society in Tidewater Maryland and Virginia, 1700–1790." *William and Mary Quarterly,* 3d. ser., 35 (1978): 226–59.

———. *Tobacco and Slaves. The Development of Southern Cultures in the Chesapeake, 1680–1800.* Chapel Hill: The University of North Carolina Press, 1986.

Law, Robin. *The Oyo Empire c.1600–c.1836: A West African Imperialism in the Era of the Atlantic Slave Trade.* Oxford, England: Oxford University Press, 1977.

———. *The Slave Coast of West Africa, 1550–1750: The Impact of the Atlantic Slave Trade on an African Society.* Oxford, England: The Clarendon Press, 1991.

Lawrence, James B. "Religious Education of the Negro in the Colony of Georgia." *The Georgia Historical Quarterly* 14 (1930): 41–57.

Levine, Lawrence W. *Black Culture and Black Consciousness: Afro-American Folk Thought from Slavery to Freedom.* New York: Oxford University Press, 1977.

Levtzion, Nehemia. *Ancient Ghana and Mali.* London, 1973. Reprint, New York: Africana Pub. Co., 1980.

Littlefield, Daniel C. *Rice and Slaves: Ethnicity and the Slave Trade in Colonial South Carolina.* Baton Rouge: Louisiana State University Press, 1981.

Lovejoy, Paul E. *Transformations in Slavery: A History of Slavery in Africa.* Cambridge, England: Cambridge University Press, 1983.

———. "The Volume of the Atlantic Slave Trade: A Synthesis." *Journal of African History* 23 (1982): 473–501.

———, ed. *Africans in Bondage: Studies in Slavery and the Slave Trade: Essays in Honor of Philip D. Curtin on the Occasion of the Twenty-Fifth Anniversary of African Studies at the University of Wisconsin.* Madison: University of Wisconsin Press, 1986.

Lumpkin, William L. "The Role of Women in Eighteenth-Century Virginia Baptist Life." *Baptist History and Heritage* 8 (1973): 158–67.

Lyerly, Cynthia Lynn. "Enthusiasm, Possession, and Madness: Gender and Opposition to Methodism in the South, 1770–1810," unpublished paper presented at the triennial meeting of the Southern Association for Women Historians, Houston, Tex., June, 1994.

Maclean, J. P. "The Kentucky Revival and Its Influence on the Miami Valley." *Ohio Archaeological and Historical Quarterly* 12 (1903): 24–50.

McClure, Susan A. "Parallel Usage of Medicinal Plants by Africans and their Caribbean Descendants." *The Western Journal of Black Studies* 4 (1982): 291–301.

McCulloch, S. C. "The Foundation and Early Work of the Society for Promoting Christian Knowledge." *Historical Magazine of the Protestant Episcopal Church* 18 (1949): 3–22.

Macoll, John D., and George J. Stansfield, eds. *Alexandria: A Towne In Transition, 1800–1900.* Alexandria, Va.: Alexandria Bicentennial Commission, Alexandria Historical Society, 1977.

Mallard, Annie Hughes. "Religious Work of South Carolina Baptists among the Slaves from 1781 to 1830." M.A. thesis, University of South Carolina, 1946.

Mathews, Donald G. *Religion in the Old South.* Chicago, Ill.: University of Chicago Press, 1977.

Mays, Benjamin, and Joseph Nicholson. *The Negro's Church.* New York: Russell and Russell, 1969.

Mbiti, John S. *African Religions and Philosophy.* New York: Frederick Praeger, 1969.

Mintz, Sidney W., and Douglass G. Hall. "The Origins of the Jamaican Internal Marketing System." *Yale University Publications in Anthropology* 57 (1960).

Morgan, David T. "John Wesley's Sojourn in Georgia Revisited." *The Georgia Historical Quarterly* 64 (1980): 253–63.

Morgan, Edmund S. *American Slavery, American Freedom: The Ordeal of Colonial Virginia.* New York: Norton, 1975.

Morgan, Philip D. "Black Life in Eighteenth-Century Charleston." *Perspectives in American History,* n.s., 1 (1984): 187–232.

———. "Work and Culture: The Task System and the Work of Lowcountry Blacks, 1700–1800." *William and Mary Quarterly,* 3d. ser., 4 (1982): 563–99.

Morgan, Philip, and Ira Berlin, eds. *Cultivation and Culture: Labor and the Shaping of Slave Life in the Americas.* Charlottesville: The University Press of Virginia, 1993.

———. *The Slaves' Economy: Independent Production by Slaves in the Americas.* London: Frank Cass & Co. Ltd., 1991.

Morrissey, Marietta. *Slave Women in the New World. Gender Stratification in the Caribbean.* Lawrence: University of Kansas Press, 1989.

Muzorewa, Gwinyai H. *The Origins and Development of African Theology.* Maryknoll, N.Y.: Orbis Books, 1985.

O'Connell, Neil J. "George Whitefield and Bethesda Orphan-House." *The Georgia Historical Quarterly* 55 (1970): 41–62.

Olwig, Karen Fog. *Cultural Adaption and Resistance on St. John: Three Centuries of Afro-Caribbean Life.* Gainesville: University of Florida Press, 1985.

————. *Global Culture, Island Identity: Continuity and Change in the Afro-Caribbean Community of Nevis.* Philadelphia, Pa.: Harwood Academic Publishers, 1993.

Ong, Walter J. *The Presence of the Word: Some Prolegomena for Cultural and Religious History.* New Haven, Conn.: Yale University Press, 1967.

Organization and Development of Elam Baptist Church, Virginia. Ruthville, Va.: n.p., 1976.

Ottenburg, Simon, ed. *African Religious Groups and Practices: Papers in Honor of William R. Bascom.* Meerut, India: Published by Archana Publications for Folklore Institute, 1982.

Ownby, Ted, ed. *Black and White. Cultural Interaction in the Antebellum South.* Jackson: University Press of Mississippi, 1993.

Parrinder, E. Geoffrey. *African Traditional Religions.* 3d. ed. London: Sheldon Press, 1974.

Patterson, Orlando. *The Sociology of Slavery: An Analysis of the Origins, Development and Structure of Negro Slave Society in Jamaica.* 1st. ed. Rutherford, N.J.: Fairleigh University Press, 1969.

Pennington, Edgar L. "Thomas Bray's Associates And Their Work Among Negroes." *American Antiquarian Society Proceedings,* n.s., 48 (1938): 311–403.

Pierre, C. E. "The Work of the Society for the Propagation of the Gospel in Foreign Parts among the Negroes in the Colonies." *Journal of Negro History* 1 (1916): 349–60.

Piersen, William D. *Black Yankees: The Development of an Afro-American Subculture in Eighteenth-Century New England.* Amherst: University of Massachusetts Press, 1988.

————. "White Cannibals, Black Martyrs: Fear, Depression, and Religious Faith as Causes of Suicide among New Slaves." *Journal of Negro History* 62 (1977): 147–59.

Pilcher, G. W. "Samuel Davies and the Instruction of Negroes in Virginia." *Virginia Magazine of History and Biography* 64 (1966): 293–300.

Pitts, Walter F. *Old Ship of Zion: The Afro-Baptist Ritual in the African Diaspora.* New York: Oxford University Press, 1993.

Raboteau, Albert J. *Slave Religion: The "Invisible Institution" in the Antebellum South.* New York: Oxford University Press, 1978.

Ranck, George W. "'The Travelling Church': An Account of the Baptist Exodus from Virginia to Kentucky in 1781 Under the Leadership of the Rev. Lewis Craig and Captain William Ellis." N.p., 1910.

Ranger, T. O. *Themes in the Christian History of Central Africa.* Berkeley: University of California Press, 1975.

Ranger, T. O., and I. N. Kimambo, eds. *The Historical Study of African Religions.* Berkeley: University of California Press, 1972.

Rattray, Robert S. *Ashanti Law and Constitution.* Oxford, England: Clarendon Press, 1929. Reprint, New York: Negro Universities Press, 1969.

Rawick, George P. *From Sundown to Sunup: The Making of the Black Community.* Westport, Conn.: Greenwood Publishing Co., 1972.

Ray, Benjamin C. *African Religions: Symbol, Ritual, and Community.* Englewood Cliffs, N.J.: Prentice-Hall, Inc., 1976.

Reid, Ira De A. "The John Canoe Festival: A New World Africanism." *Phylon* 3, no. 4 (1942): 349–70.

Richardson, David, ed. *Abolition and Its Aftermath. The Historical Context, 1790–1816.* London: Frank Cass & Co. Ltd., 1985.

Richey, Russell E. "From Quarterly to Camp Meetings: A Reconsideration of Early American Methodism." *Methodist History* 23 (1985): 199–213.

Robertson, Claire, and Martin Klein, eds. *Women and Slavery in Africa*. Madison: University of Wisconsin Press, 1983.

Rodney, Walter. "Upper Guinea and the Significance of the Origins of Africans Enslaved in the New World." *Journal of Negro History* 54, no. 4 (1969): 327–45.

Ruether, Rosemary R., and Rosemary S. Keller, eds. *Women and Religion in America: The Colonial and Revolutionary Periods*. 2 vols. San Francisco: Harper and Row, 1981.

Ryder, A. F. C. *Benin and the Europeans, 1485–1897*. New York: Humanities Press, 1969.

Ryland, Garnett. *The Baptists of Virginia, 1699–1926*. Richmond, Va.: n.p., 1955.

Sabean, David Warren. *Power in the Blood: Popular Culture and Village Discourse in Early Modern Germany*. Cambridge, England: Cambridge University Press, 1984.

Schwarz, Philip J. *Twice Condemned: Slaves and the Criminal Laws of Virginia, 1705–1865*. Baton Rouge: Louisiana State University Press, 1988.

Sellers, James Benson. *Slavery in Alabama*. Tuscaloosa: University of Alabama Press, 1950.

Shammas, Carole. "Black Women's Work and the Evolution of Plantation Society in Virginia." *Labor History* 26 (1985): 5–28.

Sheridan, R. B. *Sugar and Slavery: An Economic History of the British West Indies, 1623–1775*. Eagle Hall, Barbados: Caribbean Universities Press, 1974.

Shipp, Albert M. *The History of Methodism in South Carolina*. Nashville, Tenn.: Southern Methodist Publishing, 1883. Reprint, Spartanburg, S.C.: Reprint Co., 1972.

Sieber, Roy, and Rosalyn A. Walker. *African Art and the Cycle of Life*. Washington, D.C.: Smithsonian Institution Press, 1987.

Simms, Joseph M. *The First Colored Baptist Church in America Constituted at Savannah January 20, 1788*. Philadelphia, Pa.: J. B. Lippincott, 1888.

Simpson, Robert. "The Shout and Shouting in the Slave Religion of the United States." *The Southern Quarterly* 23, no. 3 (1985): 34–47.

Simpson, Robert Drew, ed. *American Methodist Pioneer: The Life and Journals of the Reverend Francis Asbury, 1752–1827*. Rutland, Vt.: Academy Books, 1984.

Smith, Edward D. *Climbing Jacob's Ladder: The Rise of Black Churches in Eastern American Cities, 1740–1877*. Washington, D.C.: Smithsonian Institution Press, 1988.

Smith, George G., Jr. *The History of Methodism in Georgia and Florida: From 1785 to 1865*. Macon, Ga.: J. W. Burke & Co., 1877.

Smith, Julia Floyd. "Marching to Zion: The Religion of Black Baptists in Coastal Georgia Prior to 1865." *Georgia Baptist History* 6 (1978): 47–54.

———. *Slavery and Rice Culture in Low Country Georgia, 1750–1860*. Knoxville: University of Tennessee Press, 1985.

Sobel, Mechal. "'They Can Never Prosper Together': Black and White Baptists in Nashville, Tennessee." *Tennessee Historical Quarterly* 38 (1979): 296–307.

———. *Trabelin' On: The Slave Journey to an Afro-Baptist Faith*. Westport, Conn.: Greenwood Press, 1979.

———. *The World They Made Together: Black and White Values in Eighteenth-Century Virginia*. Princeton, N.J.: Princeton University Press, 1987.

Southern, Eileen. *The Music of Black Americans: A History*. New York: W. W. Norton, 1971.

Spalding, Phinizy, and Harvey H. Jackson, eds. *Oglethorpe in Perspective: Georgia's Founder after Two Hundred Years*. Tuscaloosa: University of Alabama Press, 1989.

Sparks, Randy J. *On Jordan's Stormy Banks: Evangelism in Mississippi, 1773–1876*. Athens: The University of Georgia Press, 1994.

Standifer, James. "Musical Behaviors of Black People in American Society." *Journal of Black Music Research* 1 (1980), 51–62.

Stanley, Geoffrey Smith. *Journal of a Tour in America, 1824–1825*. N.p.: privately printed, 1930.

Stewart, Robert J. *Religion and Society in Post-Emancipation Jamaica*. Knoxville: University of Tennessee Press, 1992.

Strickland, John Scott. "Across Space and Time: Conversion, Community and Cultural Change Among South Carolina Slaves." Ph.D. diss., The University of North Carolina, 1985.

Stuckey, Sterling. *Slave Culture: Nationalist Theory and the Foundations of Black America*. New York: Oxford University Press, 1987.

Sweet, William Warren. *The Methodists*. Vol. 4 of *Religion and the American Frontier, 1783–1840*. Chicago, Ill.: University of Chicago Press, 1946.

Taylor, C. E. "Elder Shubal Stearns." *North Carolina Baptist Historical Papers* 2 (1897): 99–105.

Terborg-Penn, Rosalyn, Sharon Harley, and Andrea Benton Rushing, eds. *Women in Africa and the African Diaspora*. Washington, D.C.: Howard University Press, 1987.

Thomas, Bettye C. *History of the Sharp Street Memorial Methodist Episcopal Church, 1787–1820*. Baltimore, Md.: n.p, 1977.

Thompson, Augustus C. *Moravian Missions. Twelve Lectures*. London: Hodder and Stoughton, 1883.

Thompson, H. P. *Thomas Bray*. London: S.P.C.K., 1954.

Thornton, John K. *Africa and Africans in the Making of the Atlantic World, 1400–1680*. Cambridge, England: Cambridge University Press, 1992.

———. "African Dimensions of the Stono Rebellion." *The American Historical Review* 96 (1991): 1101–13.

———. "Demography and History in the Kingdom of Kongo, 1550–1750." *Journal of African History* 18 (1977): 507–30.

———. "The Development of an African Catholic Church in the Kingdom of Kongo, 1491–1750." *Journal of African History* 25 (1984): 147–67.

———. "Early Kongo-Portuguese Relations: A New Interpretation." *History in Africa* 8 (1981): 183–98.

———. "On the Trail of Voodoo: African Christianity in Africa and the Americas." *The Americas* 44 (1988): 261–78.

Thorp, Daniel B. *The Moravian Community in Colonial North Carolina: Pluralism on the Southern Frontier*. Knoxville: University of Tennessee Press, 1989.

Townsend, Leah. *South Carolina Baptists, 1670–1805*. Florence, S.C.: Florence Printing, 1935.

Tristano, Richard. *Black Religion in the Evangelical South*. Atlanta, Ga.: Glenmary Research Center, 1986.

Tupper, H. A. *The First Century of the First Baptist Church of Richmond, Virginia, 1780–1880*. N.p., n.d.

Turner, Mary. *Slaves and Missionaries: The Disintegration of Jamaican Slave Society, 1787–1834*. Urbana: University of Illinois Press, 1982.

———, ed. *From Chattel Slaves to Wage Slaves. The Dynamics of Labour Bargaining in the Americas*. Bloomington and Indianapolis: Indiana University Press, 1995.

Turner, Victor, ed. *Celebration: Studies in Festivity and Ritual*. Washington, D.C.: Smithsonian Institution Press, 1982.

Umphrey, Lee. *The Historic Background of Early Methodist Enthusiasm*. New York: AMS, 1967.

Vlach, John M. *The Afro-American Tradition in Decorative Arts*. Cleveland, Ohio: Cleveland Museum of Art, 1978.

Walker, Sheila S. *Ceremonial Spirit Possession in Africa and Afro-America: Forms, Meanings, and Functional Significance for Individuals and Social Groups*. Leiden: E. J. Brill, 1972.

Walvin, James. *Black Ivory: A History of British Slavery*. London: Harper Collins, 1992.

Wax, Darold D. "Black Immigrants: The Slave Trade in Colonial Maryland." *Maryland Historical Magazine* 73 (1978): 30–45.

———. "Negro Resistance to the Early American Slave Trade." *Journal of Negro History* 51, no. 1 (1966): 1–15.

White, Deborah Gray. *Ar'n't I A Woman? Female Slaves in the Plantation South*. New York: Norton, 1985.

Williams, William Henry. *The Garden of American Methodism: The Delmarva Peninsula, 1769–1820*. Wilmington, Del.: Scholarly Resources for The Peninsula Conference of the United Methodist Church, 1984.

Willis, John Ralph. *The Cultivators of Islam*. Studies in West African Islamic History. 3 vols. London: Cass & Co. Ltd., 1979.

Wills, David W., and Richard Newman, eds. *Black Apostles at Home and Abroad: Afro-Christians and the Christian Mission from the Revolution to Reconstruction*. Boston, Mass.: G. K. Hall & Co., 1982.

Winch, Julie. *Philadelphia's Black Elite: Activism, Accommodation, and the Struggle for Autonomy*. Philadelphia, Pa.: Temple University Press, 1988.

Wish, H. "American Negro Slave Insurrections Before 1861." *Journal of Negro History* 22, no. 3 (1936): 299–320.

Wood, Betty. *Slavery in Colonial Georgia, 1730–1775*. Athens: University of Georgia Press, 1984.

———. *Women's Work, Men's Work. The Informal Slave Economies of Lowcountry Georgia, 1750–1830*. Athens: University of Georgia Press, 1995.

Wood, Peter H. *Black Majority: Negroes in Colonial South Carolina from 1670 through the Stono Rebellion*. New York: Knopf, 1974.

———. "'Jesus Christ Has Got Thee at Last': Afro-American Conversion as a Forgotten Chapter in Eighteenth-Century Southern Intellectual History." *The Bulletin of the Center for the Study of Southern Culture and Religion* 3, no. 3 (1979): 1–7.

INDEX

Augusta (Ga.), 102, 117, 160, 166
"Aunt Katy" (a slave), 210

Bacon, Rev. Thomas, 50, 51
Bacon's Rebellion, 55
Bahamas, 131, 235 (n. 57). *See also*
  British Caribbean
Baker, Moses, 131, 136
Ball, Charles, 51–52, 56, 173–74
Baltimore (Md.), 82, 152, 164, 167,
  168, 170, 179
Baptists: associations, 115, 126, 128,
  153, 154, 156, 158, 160, 161, 180,
  184, 185, 187, 197, 198, 200, 233 (n.
  146), 240 (n. 31), 245 (n. 9); biracial
  churches, 103–4, 126, 154–55, 158–
  60, 161, 180–81, 184, 185, 186, 194,
  195, 200, 201; black churches, 114–15,
  116, 128, 131–32, 154–55, 192–94,
  195–56, 200; discipline, 186–90;
  growth and expansion after the American Revolution, 121, 128, 132, 150–56,
  157–59; support of churches and
  pastors, 191–99, 201–2, 203; support
  of missionary work, 200–201
Barbados, xiii, 39–40, 42–44, 46, 47–49,
  51, 55, 64–65, 82, 86–87, 89, 129,
  134, 137–38, 175, 207, 221 (n. 24).
  See also British Caribbean
Barclay, James, 46–47, 50, 56
Baxter, John, 105, 106, 138
Baxter, Rev. Richard, 63
Beaufort (S.C.), 158, 170
Bellinger, William, 89, 90, 91
Benedict, David, 150, 156
Ben-Solomon, Job, 39
Berry, Mary Ann, 172
Bolzius, Pastor Johann Martin, 94
Bosman, William, 13, 22, 27
Botsford, Rev. Edmund, 104, 159
Bray, Rev. Dr. Thomas, 63
Bremer, Frederika, 147
Brickell, John, 50
Bridgetown (Barbados), 137
British Caribbean, xi, xii, 9, 40, 42, 52, 57,
  58, 64, 68, 79, 81, 82, 83. *See also* Antigua;
  Bahamas; Barbados; Jamaica; Nevis

Brokesby, Francis, 63
Brown, Abraham, 180
Bruce, Rev. Phillip, 122–23
Bryan, Rev. Andrew, 159, 181, 190,
  192–93, 195–96, 248 (n. 62)
Bryan, Hugh, 72, 89, 91, 92–95, 109–10
Bryan, James, 167
Bryan, Jonathan, 72, 92–94, 109
Bryan, Mary, 95
Bryan, William, 192
Bull, Col. Stephen, 89, 91, 93
Bunn, Seely, 142
Burchell, Rev. Thomas, 207
Byrd, William, 99, 102

Caboceer, Cudjo, 28, 29, 30
Caesar (a slave), 60, 225 (n. 126)
Calendric rites, 9, 14, 22, 26, 30, 54–55,
  146–47, 218 (n. 58). *See also* Ancestors:
  veneration of
Ca'Mosto, Alvise da, 3, 4, 10
Campbell, Sophia, 104–5, 171, 191. *See
  also* Women: and exercise of religious
  authority
Camp meetings, 140–45, 162, 237 (n. 85)
Cannibalism, 8, 39
Cape Coast Castle, 28–29, 73
Capers, Bishop William, 157, 160, 172,
  197
Capitein, Jacobus Elisa Johannes, 27–28
Capuchins, 6, 8, 14–16 18–22, 25. *See
  also* Africa, West and West Central;
  Missionaries
Carlbin, James, 167
Carli, Father Dennis, 19
Cartwright, Joseph, 168, 197, 249 (n. 69)
Cavazzi, Father Giovanni, 9, 26
Chalmers, Rev. John, 165–66
Charity (a slave), 166
Charleston (S.C.), 44, 70, 72, 73, 77, 89,
  92, 93, 113, 116, 129, 147, 157, 164,
  168, 172, 179, 203, 296, 233 (n. 136),
  234 (n. 26), 236 (n. 60), 239 (n. 28), 251
  (n. 120)
Chatham County (Ga.), 82, 159, 160
Chavis, John, 169
Chesapeake, 42, 49, 51, 55, 73, 82, 106, 111,

150. *See also* Maryland; North Carolina; Virginia

Childbirth, 17–19. *See also* Communal rites

Church attendance: African American, 203–6

Church of England, 62, 63, 87, 88, 91, 94. *See also* Anglicans

Church of the Brethren. *See* Moravians

Clarinda (a slave), 170

Clay, Margaret Meuse, 126

Clean, Joseph, 167

Coates, Jonathan, 125

Coates, Nanny, 172

Codrington Estate (Barbados), 129

Coke, Rev. Dr. Thomas, 91, 106, 124, 134, 136, 192

Coker, Daniel, 179

Cole, James, 167

Communal rites, 14, 16, 19, 22–26, 47–18, 51–56. *See also* Calendric rites

Company of Merchants Trading to Africa, 28, 30

Constant, John H., 135–36

Corbin, Jane, 53

Cosson, John, 112–13

Courtney, Elder, 198–99

Craig, Rev. Joseph, 128

Craig, Rev. Lewis, 128

Cults, 11, 13, 59

Cunningham, Rev. Henry, 159

D'Ajaccio, Friar Angelo Maria, 22

Dancing. *See* Calendric rites; Communal rites; Festivals

Danish West Indies, 64, 86, 87. *See also* St. Thomas

Da Sorrento, Father Jerom Merolla, 14, 19–20, 22, 24, 25

Davies, Rev. Samuel, 95–97, 143

Death and burial. *See* Communal rites

Delaware, 95, 119, 167, 179

Deluce (a slave), 165

Dennis, Rev. Benjamin, 76

Di Firenze, Friar Bonaventura, 22

Dober, Johann Leonhard, 83

Dominica, 106, 134

Dover Baptist Association, 115, 153, 154, 180, 187, 197. *See also* Baptists: associations

Dozier, Richard, 125

Edwards, Rev. Morgan, 100, 233 (n. 146)

Elaw, Zilpha, 170. *See also* Women: and exercise of religious authority

Elizabeth (a slave), 169–70. *See also* Women: and exercise of religious authority

Ellis, Capt. William, 128

England, 104, 113, 142, 211

Equiano, Olaudah, 45

Evans, Henry, 157, 181

Evil: concepts of, 15–16, 19, 173–74

Fayetteville (N.C.), 157, 193

Festivals, 9, 30, 54–55. *See also* Calendric rites; Communal rites

First African Church (Savannah, Ga.), 116, 131, 159, 194, 196, 200, 202

First Baptist Church (Norfolk, Va.), 155, 180, 250 (n. 85)

First Baptist Church (Richmond, Va.), 154, 166, 180, 198–99, 201, 204

Florida, 55, 71, 123

Fort, Rev. John, 177–78

Fortie, Jacob, 167

Forty (a slave), 165

French Revolution, 136

Freundlich, Matthaus, 84

Funeral rites. *See* Communal rites

Galphin, George, 116

Galphin, Jesse, 116–17

Galphin, Venture, 163

Garden, Rev. Alexander, 70, 72–73, 79, 89

Garrettson, Freeborn, 91, 108, 110, 124, 232 (n. 126)

Gatch, Philip, 114

George (a slave), 94, 95

George, David, 116–17

Georgetown (S.C.), 142, 145, 157, 164, 168, 172, 193

Georgia, 42–45, 53–54, 81–83, 87–88, 99,

Literacy, 8, 67, 85–86, 220 (n. 116), 226 (n. 23)
Littlejohn, Rev. John, 107, 111, 114, 121, 123, 127
Littleton, Edward, 46, 47
London (England), 29, 46, 66, 73
Long, Edward, 54, 58, 59
Louisiana, 149
Low Country, 42–43, 49, 50, 55, 60, 64, 71–72, 73, 82, 89, 92, 95, 112–13, 117, 130, 151, 156, 158, 160, 164. *See also* Georgia; South Carolina
Lunenburg County (Va.), 97, 102, 239 (n. 24)
Lutherans, 83, 160
Lydia (a slave), 52

McGee, John, 141
Macklin, Mary Ann, 211, 212
Margate, David, 112–14, 116, 233 (nn. 136, 137)
Marriage, 21–22, 48–51, 65–66, 84, 183–86, 219 (n. 79). *See also* Communal rites
Marsden, Rev., 171
Marshall, Rev. Abraham, 190
Marshall, Rev. Andrew, 196, 201
Marshall, Rev. Daniel, 99, 100, 102
Maryland, 42, 50, 81, 82, 119, 130, 151, 169, 177, 179. *See also* Chesapeake
Maury, Rev. James, 77–78
Maxwell, John, 128
Maynard, John, 106
Meacham, Rev. James, 125, 164, 165, 247 (nn. 28, 42)
Mead, Stith, 160
Meredith, William, 157
Methodist Episcopal Church, 121, 122, 152, 167
Methodist Episcopal Church (South), 172
Methodists: biracial churches, 105–6, 121, 123, 124, 128–29, 134–35, 137–38, 157, 160, 161, 164, 193; black churches, 134, 136, 157, 163, 179–80, 192; circuits, 106, 110, 123, 125, 129, 153, 163, 168; conferences, 152–53, 154, 160, 168, 240 (n. 44), 242

(n. 93); discipline, 186–87; growth and expansion after the American Revolution, 119–20, 121–22, 124–25, 128–29, 131, 134–39, 149–52, 156–57; opposition to slavery, 111–12; support of churches and pastors, 191–99. *See also* Wesley, Rev. John; Whitefield, Rev. George
Millennialism, 69, 93, 101, 103
Mingo, John, 167, 168
Missionaries, xiii–xiv, 1–34, 62–80, 82, 83–99, 104–17
Mississippi, 149, 161
Montague, Elizabeth, 105
Montego Bay (Jamaica), 131, 235 (n. 46)
Mood, Rev. F. A., 172
Moore, Rev. John, 29
Moore, Matthew, 115–16
Morattico Baptist Church (Va.), 154, 197, 198
Moravians, xiii, 27, 64, 83–87, 129, 131–33, 138, 184–86, 191, 195
Morris, Samuel, 95
Moses (a slave), 114
Mulkey, Philip, 102
Murphy, William, 102
Music. *See* Calendric rites; Communal rites; Festivals

Nanny (a slave), 89, 90
Native Americans, 87, 88, 116, 162
Nevis, 42, 134, 202, 252 (n. 121). *See also* British Caribbean
New Orleans (La.), 146, 147
Nitschmann, David, 83
Nomini Baptist Church (Va.), 154, 198
Norfolk (Va.), 73–75, 106–7, 153, 155, 180
North Carolina, 49, 53, 55, 73, 81, 92, 96, 99, 108, 119, 150, 151, 153, 161, 163, 164, 210. *See also* Chesapeake

Oaths, 22, 37–38, 65–66, 71
Obeah, 46, 56–58, 59. *See also* Sacred specialists
Ohio, 149, 162
Owings, Deborah Lynch, 127